The Best of
GOOD HOUSEKEEPING

The Best of
GOOD
HOUSEKEEPING

Compiled by

GOOD HOUSEKEEPING
INSTITUTE

Ebury Press

First published in Great Britain 1973
by Ebury Press
Chestergate House, Vauxhall Bridge Road
London SW1V 1HF

Second impression 1974
Third impression 1975

ISBN 0 85223 041 9

Line drawings by Chris Evans

Filmset in Great Britain by
Typesetting Services Ltd, Glasgow
and printed and bound in Italy by
Interlitho, s.p.a., Milan

Contents

List of Plates

Foreword

There are many times when the most useful cookery book is the one which gives basic advice about buying meat, fish and vegetables, and has straightforward information on roasting, cake making, etc., as well as the right kind of recipes. For this book, we have selected the cookery and marketing information we are most often asked for and over 800 recipes, many of them illustrated, which will give you a good repertoire for everyday cooking and party fare. All the recipes are tried and tested favourites from Good Housekeeping Institute's famous kitchens.

If you have any queries about the recipes in this book write to us at Good Housekeeping Institute, Chestergate House, Vauxhall Bridge Road, London SW1V 1HF.

CAROL MACARTNEY
Director

METRIC CONVERSION SCALE

Capacity	Mass	Temperature
¼ pint = 142 ml	1 oz = 28.35 g	32°F = 0°Celsius
½ pint = 284 ml	2 oz = 56.7 g	212°F = 100°C
1 pint = 568 ml	4 oz = 113.4 g	225°F = 107°C
½ litre = 0.88 pints	8 oz = 226.8 g	250°F = 121°C
1 litre = 1.76 pints	12 oz = 340.2 g	275°F = 135°C
	16 oz = 453.6 g	300°F = 149°C
Length	1 kilogramme = 2.2 lb	325°F = 163°C
1 inch = 2.54 cm		350°F = 177°C
6 inches = 15.2 cm		375°F = 190°C
100 cm = 1 metre		400°F = 204°C
= 39.37 inches		425°F = 218°C
		450°F = 232°C

Note: ml = millilitre(s); cm = centimetre(s); g = gramme(s).

Note: To convert the recipes in this book to metric measures we have found that it is more practical to use a 25-g unit in place of the oz, a 5-ml spoon in place of the teaspoon, a 15-ml spoon in place of the tablespoon, and to reckon 500 ml to the pint. Recipes converted in this manner will yield slightly less than the original.

The above is based on information agreed by the UK Federation for Education in Home Economics, 1970.

OVEN TEMPERATURE SCALES

As the metrication programme advances, electric cookers will be introduced with the oven thermostat dial marked in °Celsius instead of °Fahrenheit. If you have one of these new cookers, or use metric recipes where oven temperatures are given in °C, follow the table of equivalents below.

°Celsius Scale	Electric Scale °F	Gas Oven Marks
110°C	225°F	¼
130	250	½
140	275	1
150	300	2
170	325	3
180	350	4
190	375	5
200	400	6
220	425	7
230	450	8
240	475	9

First Courses

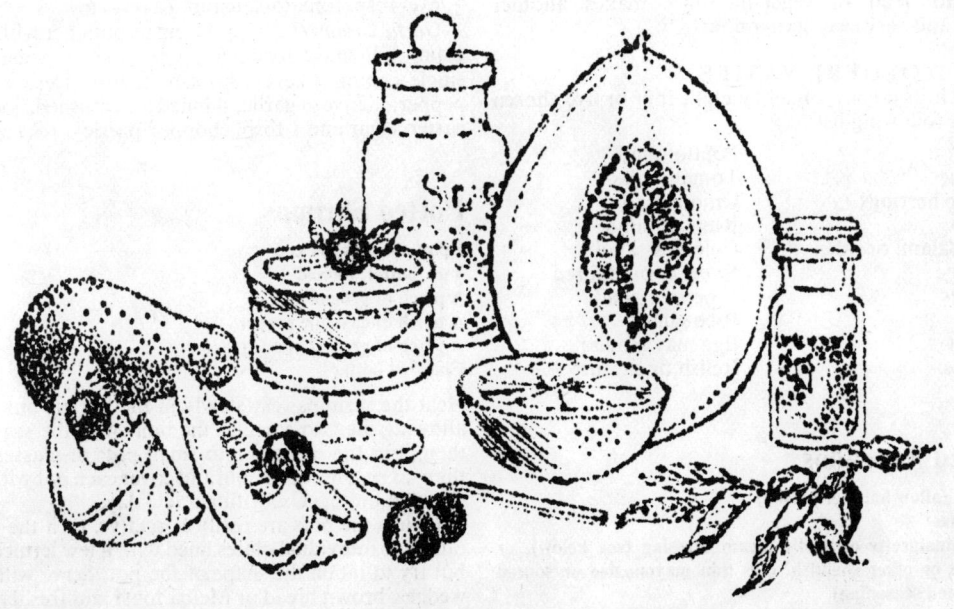

These can be a single ingredient, simply served (for example, sliced Continental sausage, oysters, tomato juice) or a selection, set out either on individual plates or on a large platter or a trolley. If you are serving *hors d'oeuvre variés*, choose ingredients that are well contrasted to each other in appearance, flavour and texture. It is usual to include some meat, some fish and some vegetables and/or salad, with perhaps rice, pasta or a pulse vegetable; often a pickle, relish or chutney is added to give a piquant note. The hors d'oeuvre should contrast with, not echo, the other courses, and the portions should be small (except when you are serving mixed hors d'oeuvre as the main course in an informal lunch or supper).

Tomato, fruit or vegetable juice makes another popular and very easy starter course.

HORS D'OEUVRE VARIÉS
A mixed hors d'oeuvre might include four or five chosen from the following list:

Sardines	Potato salad
Anchovies	Tomato salad
Rollmop herrings	Onion salad
Shrimps	Russian salad
Garlic, salami or other	Coleslaw salad
sausage	Sweet corn and red
Gherkins	pepper salad
Olives	Rice salad
Beetroot	Egg mayonnaise
Radishes	Relish or chutney

Dressed Avocados

Avocados (allow half per person)
Lemon juice
Tomato vinaigrette or garlic cream dressing (see below), or shrimps or other shellfish, plus thin mayonnaise or soured cream and seasoning)
Lettuce leaves (optional)

Cut open the avocados, using a stainless knife, and making a deep cut through the flesh, up to the stone and entirely encircling the fruit. Separate the halves by gently rotating them in opposite directions and discard the stone. Brush the cut surfaces with lemon juice.

Serve with one of the following dressings, spooned into the hollow of each avocado-half, or fill the hollow with shelled shrimps, prawns, flaked crab or lobster meat, moistened with thin mayonnaise or well-seasoned soured cream. If you wish, serve the pears on lettuce leaves.

Tomato Vinaigrette: Using a container with a tight-fitting lid, shake together $\frac{1}{4}$ pint salad oil, $\frac{1}{8}$ pint red wine vinegar, $\frac{1}{4}$ level tsp. salt, a little freshly ground pepper, $\frac{1}{4}$ level tsp. dry mustard, $\frac{1}{2}$ level tsp. caster sugar and $\frac{1}{2}$ level tbsp. tomato ketchup. *(Serves 6.)*

Garlic Cream Dressing: Using a container with a tight-fitting lid, shake together $\frac{1}{8}$ pint garlic vinegar, $\frac{1}{4}$ pint single cream, $\frac{1}{2}$ level tsp. salt, a little freshly ground pepper, 1 clove of garlic, skinned and crushed, $\frac{1}{4}$ level tsp. caster sugar and 1 tbsp. chopped parsley. *(Serves 6.)*

Potted Shrimps

1 pint shrimps, picked
4 oz. butter, melted
A pinch of ground mace
A pinch of cayenne pepper
A pinch of ground nutmeg
Clarified butter

Heat the shrimps very slowly in the butter, but without allowing them to come to the boil. Add the seasonings, then pour the shrimps into small pots or glasses. Leave them to become quite cold and cover each pot with a little clarified butter. Use within a few days.

Unless the pots are really attractive, turn the shrimps out on to individual plates lined with a few lettuce leaves, but try to retain the shape of the pot. Serve with lemon wedges, brown bread or Melba toast and freshly ground pepper.

Oysters

Oysters should be served in their shells and if possible on a bed of chopped ice. Thin brown bread and butter, slices of lemon and cayenne pepper are the correct accompaniments. Tabasco sauce may also be served with them.

SMOKED (CANNED) OYSTERS: Remove from the can and drain. Serve with thin brown bread and butter, lemon wedges and freshly ground black pepper.

Caviare

This is served ice-cold, with freshly made toast and butter. Lemon juice may be sprinkled over it if you wish. Alternatively, spread the caviare on croûtes of fried bread or toast and sprinkle with a few grains of cayenne pepper.

Taramasalata *(Using an Electric Blender)*

A thin slice of white bread
An 8-oz. can of pressed cod's roe
A small boiled potato
1 clove of garlic, skinned
A few sprigs of parsley
Juice of ½ a lemon
1 tsp. cooking oil
Salt and pepper
Parsley or olives for garnish

Using a powerful electric blender, make breadcrumbs from the bread. Add the cod's roe to the breadcrumbs in the goblet; switch to 'high' and blend until smooth. Add the potato, garlic and parsley and blend for a few more seconds. Add the lemon juice, oil and seasoning and again blend until smooth. Turn the mixture into a shallow dish, spreading it evenly, and mark with a fork into lines. Garnish with parsley or olives. *(Serves 4–6.)*

Snails à la Bourguignonne

1 can of snails
½ pint dry white wine
1 onion stuck with cloves
2 cloves of garlic, skinned and crushed
¼ pint brandy
A bouquet garni
Salt and butter

For the Snail Butter
4 oz. softened butter
½ a shallot, skinned and finely chopped
1 clove of garlic, skinned and crushed
1–2 tsps. chopped parsley
A good pinch of mixed spice
Salt and pepper

Oven temperature: very hot (450°F., mark 8)

Remove the snails from the can and place in a pan with the rest of the ingredients. Simmer gently for 1 hour, remove from the heat and allow to cool in the liquor. Meanwhile, mix the ingredients for the snail butter, blending well. Put a snail into each shell, fill up with snail butter and put the shells in an ovenproof dish. Bake them for 10 minutes and serve hot.

Note: If shells are not provided with the can of snails, simmer the snails as before, put them into an ovenproof dish, place the butter over and round them and bake as above.

Chicken Liver Pâté

2 oz. butter
2 bay leaves
A pinch of dried thyme
1 small onion, skinned and chopped
1 lb. chicken livers
Salt and pepper
Stuffed olives and celery sprigs to garnish

Melt the butter in a pan, add the bay leaves, thyme and onion, and cook gently for 2–3 minutes. Prepare the chicken livers, cut each into 2–3 pieces, add to the pan, and simmer gently for 5–7 minutes until the liver is cooked. Remove the bay leaves and mince the liver once or twice, using a fine grinder (the second mincing gives a smoother pâté). Season well and place in a lined loaf tin. Weigh down carefully and chill well. Serve garnished with stuffed olives and celery. *(Serves 6–8)*

(See colour picture facing page 32)

French-style Pâté Maison

¼ lb. bacon rashers, rinded
1½ lb. calf's or lamb's liver
½ lb. chicken livers
1 clove of garlic, skinned and crushed
1 egg, beaten
2 tbsps. double cream
2 tsps. brandy
Salt and pepper

Oven temperature: warm (325°F., mark 3)

Line a 2-lb. loaf or pâté tin with the strips of bacon. Mince the two kinds of liver and add the garlic, egg, cream, brandy and seasoning to taste. Mix well, place in the tin and cover with foil. Stand the tin in a shallow dish of water and bake just below the centre of the oven for about 2 hours. Allow to cool, cover with a plate, put a weight on top to press the pâté and chill overnight. Turn it out of the mould just before serving, garnish as desired and slice thinly.

French Style Pâté Maison

Fresh Salmon Pâté

2 oz. butter
2 oz. flour
¾ pint milk
1 bay leaf
Salt and pepper
¼ level tsp. ground nutmeg
½ lb. fresh haddock fillet, skinned
1 lb. fresh salmon, skinned and boned
Grated rind and juice of 1 lemon
1 tbsp. chopped parsley
2 eggs, beaten
Melted butter
Parsley sprigs and lemon for garnish

Oven temperature: Cool (300°F., marks 1–2)

Melt the butter in a pan, remove from the heat and stir in the flour; cook for 2–3 minutes. Slowly add the milk, beating after each addition. Add the bay leaf, salt, pepper and nutmeg, and boil gently for 2–3 minutes. Discard the bay leaf. Finely chop or mince the haddock and 12 oz. of the salmon. Add to the sauce. Stir in the lemon rind and juice, parsley and eggs. Butter 6–8 individual soufflé dishes (3 fl. oz. capacity) and divide the mixture between them. Brush the tops with melted butter. Slice the remainder of the salmon and decorate the tops. Place the dishes in a large roasting tin or similar tin and pour in enough water to come halfway up the dish. Cook for about 40 minutes. Chill in the refrigerator. Garnish with parsley and lemon, and serve Melba toast separately. *(Serves 6–8.)*

Soups

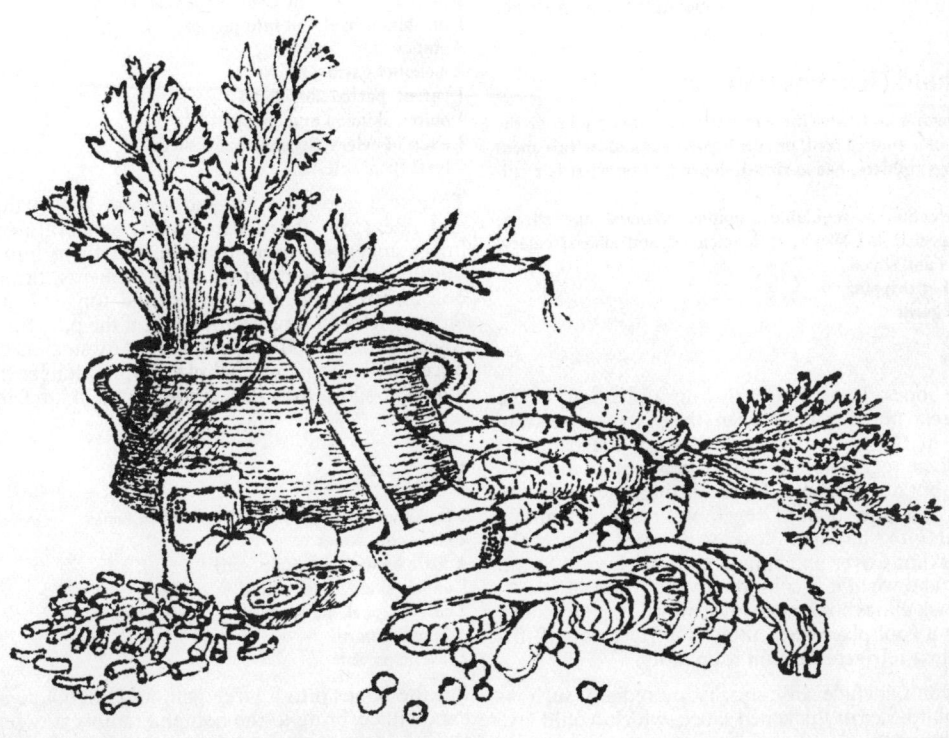

Soup may be thin and clear, thickened, or so crammed with meat, vegetables, pasta or rice that it almost qualifies as solid food and makes a really filling meal. We mostly think of soup as being savoury, but there are fruit soups. Soup can be a luxury dish or it may have an economical basis of vegetable trimmings and bone stock.

The main ingredient of soup is generally a stock made from meat, poultry, vegetables or fish, plus whatever ingredient is needed to give the characteristic flavour. Egg yolks, cream, grated cheese, croûtons and chopped parsley are among the many suitable garnishes, while toast, bread or rolls can be served with soup to add bulk.

Stock

There are numerous ready-made stock preparations – the most popular probably being bouillon cubes or powders – which save much time and trouble, but we include several recipes for home-made stocks. First of all we give a general recipe for a stock that you can make from the bones of a roast joint or a bird. This 'household' stock is suitable for most soups, as it is fairly light-coloured; you can put in a little browning if you wish to make it darker. Otherwise, brown stock is used for dark soups and chicken or white stock for light-coloured ones. Consommé requires a really well-flavoured brown stock.

Household (Kitchen) Stock

A 2-lb. selection of bones (the bones from a cooked joint or the carcase of a cooked bird, or raw bones; cooked or raw meat trimmings; giblets; bacon rinds), depending on what is available
A 1-lb. selection of vegetables: onions, skinned and sliced; carrot, peeled and sliced; leek, cleaned and sliced; celery, scrubbed and sliced
1½ oz. lard or dripping
A bouquet garni
Salt
Cold water

Chop the bones. To give extra flavour and colour to the soup, you can put them in the oven (the exact temperature does not matter) to brown slightly and you can also lightly fry the vegetables in the fat for about 10 minutes, until soft but not coloured, but both these steps may be omitted. Put the bones, vegetables and remaining ingredients into a large pan, cover with water, bring to the boil and skim. Cover and simmer for 3–4 hours. Strain the stock and when it is cold, remove all trace of fat.

Any stock that is not used at once may be kept for a day or two in a cool place, preferably a refrigerator. If it is not kept in a refrigerator, boil it up daily.

Notes: Don't include any starchy ingredient such as bread, potato, rice or thickened sauce, which would give a cloudy stock.

Strongly flavoured vegetables such as turnips and cabbage, should not be used, as they tend to give a bitter taste.

Chicken, Turkey or Game Stock

A carcase of chicken, turkey or game bird
Cleaned feet of the bird
Giblets
½ level tbsp. salt
Cold water to cover
1 onion, skinned and sliced
1 carrot, peeled and sliced
Outside sticks of celery, scrubbed and sliced
A bouquet garni

Place all the ingredients in a large pan, bring to the boil, skim, cover and simmer for 3–4 hours. Strain and when cold remove all trace of fat. Store in a cool place; if not in a refrigerator, boil up daily as above.

Brown Stock

1 lb. marrow bone or knuckle of veal, chopped
1 lb. shin of beef, cut into pieces
3 pints water
A bouquet garni
1 carrot, peeled and sliced
1 onion, skinned and chopped
1 stick of celery, scrubbed and sliced
½ level tbsp. salt

To give a good flavour and colour, brown the bones and meat in the oven (exact temperature of no importance) before using them. Put them into a large saucepan with the rest of the ingredients, bring to the boil and remove any fat from the top with a spoon. Simmer for 4–5 hours with a lid on the pan. Strain, and when cold, skim off any more fat. Any stock not used at once may be kept in a cool place for not longer than 2 or 3 days; boil up each day, if not stored in a refrigerator.

White Stock

2 lb. knuckle of veal or veal or mutton bones
4 pints cold water
A little lemon juice (optional)
1 onion, skinned and sliced
2 carrots, peeled and sliced
A bouquet garni
2 level tsps. salt

Put the bones into a large pan, add the cold water and lemon juice, bring to the boil and remove any scum that rises. Add the vegetables, bouquet garni and salt, re-boil,

16

cover with a lid and simmer for 4 hours. Strain and when cold remove any fat. Keep as for brown stock.

Fish Stock

1 cod's head or fish bones and trimmings
Cold water
Salt
A bouquet garni
1 onion, skinned and sliced

Clean the cod's head or wash the fish trimmings. Put in a saucepan, cover with water, add some salt, bring to the boil and skim. Reduce the heat and add the bouquet garni and onion. Cover, simmer for 40 minutes and strain. Use on the same day, or store in the refrigerator for not more than 2 days.

Bouquet Garni

A bay leaf	**tied in a**
A sprig of parsley	**small piece**
A sprig of thyme	**of leek**
A few peppercorns	**leaf**

(Using dried herbs)
A small bay leaf
A pinch of mixed herbs
6 peppercorns
1 clove
A pinch of dried parsley

Most soups are improved by the addition of a small bunch of herbs, called a 'faggot' or 'bouquet garni'. The herbs can be made into a small bunch or (if dried) tied up in muslin, so that they are easily removed before the soup is served.

The combination of herbs is very much a matter of choice. At its simplest, a bouquet garni can be a sprig of thyme, some stalks of parsley and a bay leaf. For long, slow meat stews, more aromatic bouquets are often used, with mixtures like chervil, basil, tarragon, rosemary and dried celery seed. We give two examples.

Tie the herbs together in a small square of muslin with string or cotton, leaving a long end free to tie the bouquet garni to the handle of the pan.

Classic Consommé

2 pints brown stock (cold)
¼ lb. lean beefsteak, e.g., rump
¼ pint cold water
1 carrot, peeled and quartered
1 small onion, skinned and quartered
A bouquet garni
1 egg white
Salt
2 tsps. sherry (optional)

A completely clear, well-flavoured broth, made from good brown stock. Both the stock and the utensils must be quite free from any trace of grease, to prevent droplets of fat forming on the surface of the soup.

Remove any fat from the stock. Shred the meat finely and soak it in the ¼ pint water for 15 minutes. Put the meat and water, vegetables, stock and bouquet garni into a deep saucepan; lastly add the egg white. Heat gently and whisk continuously until a thick froth starts to form. Stop whisking and bring to the boil. Reduce the heat immediately and simmer gently for 2 hours. If the liquid boils too rapidly, the froth will break and cloud the consommé.

Scald a clean cloth or jelly bag, wring it out, tie it to the four legs of an upturned stool and place a bowl underneath. Pour the soup through, keeping the froth back at first with a spoon, then let it slide out on to the cloth. Again pour the soup through the cloth and through the filter of egg white.

The consommé should now be clear and sparkling. Re-heat it, add salt if necessary and if liked a little sherry to improve the flavour, but add nothing that would make the liquid cloudy.

Consommé may be served hot or cold, plain or varied by the addition of one of the following garnishes – in which case the consommé takes its name from the garnish.

To prevent the soup becoming cloudy, rinse the garnish in water and add it to the hot consommé just before it is served.

Consommé Julienne

Cut small quantities of vegetables such as carrot, turnip and celery into thin strips and boil separately; rinse and add as above.

Consommé à la Royale

The garnish consists of steamed savoury egg custard cut into tiny fancy shapes. Make the custard by mixing 1 egg yolk, 1 tbsp. stock, milk or cream and salt and pepper to taste; strain it into a small greased basin, cover with foil or greaseproof paper and stand the basin in a saucepan containing enough hot water to come half-way up its sides. Steam the custard slowly until it is firm; turn it out, cut into thin slices and from these cut the fancy shapes. Add as above.

Consommé à la Jardinière

Prepare a mixture of vegetables such as carrots and turnips, cut into pea shapes or finely diced, tiny sprigs of cauliflower, green peas and so on. Cook in boiling salted water and add as above.

Consommé au Riz

Cook long-grain rice (allow ½ oz. per pint of comsommé) in boiling salted water for 15 minutes; rinse and add to the consommé as above.

Consommé a l'Italienne

Cook some Italian soup pasta (tiny letters, shells, stars or wheels) in boiling salted water until tender. Rinse, drain and add as above.

Consommé Princesse

Add asparagus tips, cooked and drained.

Quick Consommé

3 stock cubes
2 pints hot water
6 oz. lean beefsteak, e.g., rump
1 carrot, peeled and quartered
1 onion, skinned and quartered
1 egg white
2 tsps. sherry

The day before, make the stock from the cubes and water, cool, then refrigerate or leave in a cool place. The next day skim off any fat from the top of the stock and continue as for Classic Consommé.

CREAM SOUPS

Cream soups have a smooth, creamy texture, achieved by adding cream or egg yolks or more frequently by thickening them with flour, cornflour or some similar cereal. They can be made with any kind of stock or with milk and may contain vegetables, meat, poultry or fish.

Using Cream
To prevent curdling, put the cream in a basin, add a little of the hot soup, then stir into the saucepan of soup. Re-heat but don't boil.

Using Flour or Other Fine Cereal
Blend it in the usual way with a little cold milk or other liquid, add a little of the hot soup, then stir into the saucepan of soup, bring back to the boil and boil for a few minutes, until thickened.

Using Egg Yolks
Mix the egg yolks with a little milk or cream. Slowly add a little of the soup, mixing well. Strain the mixture back into the soup, away from the heat. Don't re-heat or you may curdle the egg. (It won't matter if the soup already contains flour, as it will be less likely to curdle.)

Adjusting the Consistency
If the soup is too stiff after the thickening has been added, stir in more stock or milk. If it is too thin, boil the soup until it is sufficiently reduced (provided it does not contain egg yolks – see above).

Cream of Artichoke

2–3 bacon rinds
1½ lb. Jerusalem artichokes, peeled and sliced
1 stalk of celery, scrubbed and chopped
1 small onion, skinned and sliced
½ oz. butter, if needed
2 pints chicken stock
Salt and pepper
3 level tbsps. flour or cornflour
¼ pint milk
Chopped parsley
1 tbsp. cream

Fry the bacon rinds lightly to extract the fat. Cook the artichokes, celery and onion in the fat for about 5 minutes, until soft but not coloured; add the butter if necessary. Add the stock and seasonings, bring to the boil, cover and simmer for about 30 minutes until the vegetables are soft. Sieve (or put in an electric blender) and return the soup to the saucepan. Blend the flour and milk to a smooth cream, stir in a little of the hot soup and return the mixture to the pan. Bring to the boil, stirring until it thickens, and cook for a further 2–3 minutes. Re-season if necessary and add the finely chopped parsley and the cream just before serving the soup.

Cream of Asparagus

1 large bundle of asparagus
½ an onion, skinned and sliced
1 pint white stock
2 oz. butter
3 level tbsps. flour
Salt and pepper
½ pint milk
2–3 tbsps. cream

Wash and trim the asparagus, discarding the woody part of the stem, and cut the remainder into short lengths, keeping a few tips for garnish. Cook the tips for about 5–10 minutes in boiling salted water. Put the rest of the asparagus, the onion, ¼ pint of the stock and the butter in a saucepan, cover and simmer for about 20 minutes until the asparagus is soft. Blend the flour and the remaining stock to a smooth cream. Stir in a little of the hot soup and return this mixture to the pan; bring to the boil, stirring until it thickens. Cook for a further 2–3 minutes. Season to taste and sieve the soup or put it in an electric blender. Stir in the remaining milk and the cream, re-heat and garnish with the asparagus tips.

Cream of Cucumber

1 large or 2 medium-sized cucumbers
1 oz. butter
1 blade of mace
1 pint white stock
1 pint milk
2 egg yolks
2–3 tbsps. cream
Salt and pepper

Consommé Julienne

Peel and slice the cucumber, discarding the stalk end (which might give a bitter flavour). Scald in boiling water and strain. Melt the butter and add the scalded cucumber, the mace and stock, bring to the boil and simmer for about 20 minutes, until soft. Sieve the soup or put in an electric blender and return it to the pan. Add the milk to the purée and bring to the boil Mix the egg yolks and cream together, stir in a little of the hot liquid and stir into the soup. Season to taste and re-heat, without boiling.

Cream of Carrot

1 lb. carrots, peeled and chopped
A stick of celery, scrubbed and chopped
$\frac{1}{4}$ of a small turnip, peeled and chopped
$\frac{1}{4}$ of an onion, skinned and sliced
1 oz. bacon, chopped
1 oz. butter
1$\frac{1}{2}$ pints white stock
A bouquet garni
Salt and pepper
3 level tbsps. flour
$\frac{1}{4}$ pint milk
1–2 tbsps. cream
Chopped parsley (optional)

Lightly fry the vegetables and bacon in the butter for about 5–7 minutes, until soft but not coloured. Add the stock, bouquet garni, salt and pepper. Cover and allow to simmer gently for about 1 hour, or until the vegetables are soft. Remove the bouquet garni and sieve the soup or put in an electric blender and return to the pan. Blend the flour and milk to a smooth cream. Stir in a little of the hot liquid and return the mixture to the pan. Bring to the boil, stirring until it thickens, and cook for 2–3 minutes; re-season if necessary and add the cream just before serving – also the parsley, if used.

Cream of Celery

1 large head of celery, scrubbed and sliced
1 medium-sized onion, skinned and sliced
1 oz. butter
2 pints white stock or milk and stock mixed
Salt and pepper
A bouquet garni
3 level tbsps. flour
$\frac{1}{4}$ pint milk
2–3 tbsps. cream
Chopped parsley

Lightly fry the celery and onion in the butter for 5–7

minutes, until soft but not coloured. Add the stock or milk and stock, seasoning and bouquet garni, bring to the boil and simmer for about 1 hour, until the vegetables are quite soft. Remove the bouquet garni. Sieve the soup or put in an electric blender and return to the pan. Blend the flour and milk to a smooth cream. Stir in a little of the hot soup and return the mixture to the pan. Bring to the boil, stirring until it thickens. Cook for 2–3 minutes, re-season if necessary and add the cream and freshly chopped parsley just before serving.

Cream of Chicken

3 tbsps. flour
¼ pint milk
2 pints chicken stock
4 oz. cooked chicken meat, diced
Salt and pepper
1 tsp. lemon juice
Grated nutmeg
2 tbsps. cream

Blend the flour with a little of the milk to a smooth cream. Boil the stock and pour it on to the blended mixture, stirring well. Return it to the pan and simmer gently for about 20 minutes. Stir in the chicken meat, seasoning, lemon juice and a little nutmeg. Mix the rest of the milk with the cream and stir into the soup; re-heat without boiling.

The stock can be made from the carcase of a roast chicken and the meat can be the trimmings from it. *(See Stocks.)* Alternatively, chicken bouillon cubes and ready-cooked chicken can be used.

Cream of Leek and Potato

4 medium-sized leeks, thoroughly cleaned and sliced
1 small onion, skinned and sliced
3 medium-sized potatoes, peeled and sliced
1 oz. butter
2 pints white stock
Salt and pepper
2–3 tbsps. cream

Lightly fry the vegetables in the butter for about 5 minutes, until soft but not coloured. Add the stock, cover and simmer for about 45 minutes until the vegetables are cooked. Sieve the soup or put in an electric blender and return it to the pan. Re-heat, re-season if necessary and stir in the cream just before serving.

Crème Dubarry

1 firm white cauliflower
1½ oz. butter
3 level tbsps. flour
1½ pints white stock
Salt, pepper and nutmeg
¼ pint cream

Divide the cauliflower into sprigs, discarding the green leaves, and wash in salted water. Melt the butter, stir in the flour and cook for 2–3 minutes. Remove the pan from the heat and gradually stir in the stock, bring to the boil and continue to stir until it thickens. Add the cauliflower (reserving a dozen well-shaped pieces) and seasonings, cover and simmer for about 30 minutes. Meanwhile, cook the remaining cauliflower in salted water for 10–15 minutes, until soft but not broken. Sieve the soup or put in an electric blender, re-season if necessary and add a pinch of grated nutmeg. Reheat the soup, stir in the cream and serve garnished with the cauliflower sprigs.

Cream of Mushroom

½ lb. mushrooms, sliced
1 small onion, skinned and sliced
½ pint white stock
1 oz. butter
3 level tbsps. flour
¾ pint milk
Salt and pepper
2–3 tbsps. cream

Cook the mushrooms and onion in the stock for about ½ hour, until soft; sieve or put in an electric blender. Melt the butter, stir in the flour and cook for 2–3 minutes. Remove the pan from the heat and gradually stir in the milk; bring to the boil and continue to stir until it thickens. Add the mushroom purée and seasoning and simmer for 15 minutes. Allow to cool slightly and stir in the cream. Re-heat without boiling and if liked serve with a garnish of lightly fried sliced mushrooms.

Cream of Onion

1½ lb. onions, skinned and sliced
1 oz. butter or margarine
1½ pints white stock
A bouquet garni
3 level tbsps. flour
¼ pint milk
Salt and pepper
3–4 tbsps. cream

Lightly fry the onions in the butter for about 5 minutes, until soft but not coloured. Add the stock and bouquet garni, cover, bring to the boil and simmer for about 45 minutes, until the onions are cooked. Remove the bouquet garni. Sieve the soup or put in an electric blender, return it to the saucepan and re-heat. Blend the flour and milk to a smooth cream, stir in a little of the hot soup and return the mixture to the pan; season, bring to the boil, stirring until it thickens, and cook for a further 2–3 minutes. Stir in the cream just before serving.

Note: For brown onion soup, use brown (beef) stock and brown the onions very slowly in the fat for about 20 minutes before adding the stock.

Cream of Green Pea

1 small onion, skinned and chopped
1 oz. butter
¾ pint white stock
2 lb. peas, shelled (or 1 large and 1 small pkt. frozen peas)
1 pint Béchamel sauce (pouring consistency)
2 tbsps. cream
A pinch of sugar; salt and pepper

Lightly fry the onion in the butter for about 5 minutes, until soft but not coloured. Add the stock, bring to the boil, add the peas (saving a few for garnish) and cook until soft – 20–30 minutes for shelled peas, 8 minutes for frozen. Sieve or put in an electric blender, add to the Béchamel sauce and heat through. Stir in the cream and sugar and re-season if necessary. Serve garnished with the remaining peas.

A sprig of mint can be added to the peas while they are cooking or a little freshly chopped mint can be used as a garnish.

Cream of Tomato

1 stick of celery, scrubbed and chopped
1 carrot, peeled and sliced
1 small onion, skinned and chopped
1½ oz. bacon, chopped
1 oz. butter
2 level tbsps. flour
1½ lb. tomatoes, quartered
1 pint white or brown stock
A bouquet garni
Salt, pepper and a pinch of sugar
2 tbsps. cream
Chopped chervil, basil or parsley to garnish

Lightly fry the celery, carrot, onion and bacon in the butter for 5 minutes, until soft but not coloured. Sprinkle in the flour and stir. Add the quartered tomatoes, stock and bouquet garni, cover and cook gently for about 30 minutes, until soft. Remove the bouquet garni and sieve the soup or put it in an electric blender. Return it to the pan with the seasonings, add the cream and re-heat, but don't let it boil. Garnish with freshly chopped chervil or basil, when in season – otherwise use chopped parsley.

If the tomatoes lack flavour, add a little tomato paste. Canned tomatoes can be used to replace the fresh ones; drain off the liquor and make it up to 1 pint with stock. When fresh celery is not available, use a few flakes of dehydrated celery.

Cream of Watercress

2 bunches of watercress (about ½ lb.)
½ oz. butter
1¼ pints white stock
Salt and pepper
2 level tbsps. flour or cornflour
¼ pint milk
2–3 tbsps. cream

Wash the watercress and remove the coarse stalks. Reserve a few sprigs for the garnish. Lightly cook the rest of the watercress in the butter for 2–3 minutes, add the stock, salt and pepper, cover and simmer gently for about 20 minutes, until soft. Sieve or put in an electric blender and return it to the saucepan. Blend the flour and milk to a smooth cream. Stir in a little of the hot purée and return the mixture to the pan. Bring to the boil, stirring until it thickens, cook for a further 2–3 minutes, re-season if necessary and just before serving stir in the cream. Garnish with the sprigs of watercress.

MEAT SOUPS

Oxtail Soup

1 oxtail, jointed
1 oz. butter
2 onions, skinned and chopped
1 carrot, peeled and sliced
2 sticks of celery, scrubbed and sliced
3–4 pints brown stock
1 oz. lean ham or bacon, chopped
A bouquet garni
Salt and pepper
3 level tbsps. flour
A little port wine (optional)
A squeeze of lemon juice

Wash and dry the oxtail and trim off any excess fat. Fry the pieces of oxtail in the butter with the vegetables for 5 minutes. Add a squeeze of lemon juice and seasoning stock and bring to the boil. Add the chopped ham or bacon, bouquet garni and seasoning. Cover the saucepan and simmer gently for about 3–4 hours, or until the tail meat is tender. As oxtail is very fatty, it is necessary to skim the soup occasionally with a metal spoon. Strain the soup, remove the meat from the bones and cut it up neatly. Return the meat and strained liquor to the pan and re-heat. Blend the flour and a little water (or port wine, if used) to a smooth cream. Stir in a little of the hot liquid and return the mixture to the pan. Bring to the boil, stirring until it thickens, and cook for about

5 minutes. Add a squeeze of lemon juice and seasoning to taste before serving.

This 'hearty' soup can be made into a meal in itself by adding some small dumplings (*see recipe at end of chapter*), putting them in 20 minutes before the end of the cooking time.

Hare or Rabbit Soup

½ a hare or rabbit
2 oz. butter or dripping
1 onion, skinned and sliced
2 oz. lean ham or bacon, diced
A stick of celery, scrubbed and sliced
Carrot and turnip, peeled and chopped
A bouquet garni
Salt and pepper
3 pints beef stock
3 level tbsps. flour
1 glass port
  tsps. redcurrant jelly
A squeeze of lemon juice
Forcemeat balls (optional) – see *Stuffings chapter*

The tougher parts of a hare or rabbit (legs, head) may be used for making soup. Cut them into pieces and break or chop the bones. Fry the meat and bones in the fat with the onion and the ham or bacon for 5–10 minutes, until well browned. Add the other vegetables, bouquet garni, seasoning and stock, mix well, cover and simmer gently for 3–4 hours. When the meat and vegetables are soft, strain off the liquid through a sieve and rub some of the meat through. Allow the soup to become cold, skim off any fatty layer and return it to a saucepan to re-heat. Blend the flour with the wine to a smooth cream. Stir in a little of the hot soup and return the mixture to the pan with the redcurrant jelly. Bring to the boil, stirring until the soup thickens, then cook for a further 5 minutes and add the lemon juice and more seasoning if necessary. If the blood from the hare has been kept, stir it into the soup, but don't boil again, or the soup will curdle.

A garnish of forcemeat balls can be served with this soup.

Kidney Soup with Dumplings

½ lb. ox kidney
Seasoned flour
1 onion, skinned and finely chopped
1½ oz. dripping
2 pints brown stock
A small bouquet garni
2 level tbsps. flour
Gravy browning (if liked)
Herb dumplings *(see end of chapter)*

Skin the kidney, wiping if it necessary. Cut it into small pieces, discarding the fatty core, and toss in seasoned flour. Fry the prepared kidney and onion in the dripping

for 5 minutes, or until lightly browned. Pour in the stock gradually, stirring well. Add the bouquet garni and simmer for 1½ hours, skimming and stirring occasionally. When the kidney is tender, blend the flour to a smooth cream with a little water. Stir in a little of the hot soup and return the mixture to the pan. Colour if desired with a little gravy browning. Re-boil, stirring, until the soup thickens. Add the dumplings and cook for a further 15–20 minutes, until the dumplings are cooked.

Minestrone

½ a leek, cleaned and shredded
1 onion, skinned and finely chopped
1 clove of garlic, skinned and crushed
1 oz. butter
2 pints white stock
1 carrot, peeled and cut in thin strips
1 turnip, peeled and cut in thin strips
1 stick of celery, scrubbed and thinly sliced
1 oz. macaroni
¼ of a cabbage, washed and finely shredded
3 runner beans, thinly sliced
1 oz. peas, shelled
1 level tsp. tomato paste or 4 tomatoes, skinned and diced
1–2 rashers of bacon, chopped and fried
Salt and pepper
Grated Parmesan cheese

Lightly fry the leek, onion and garlic in the melted butter for 5–10 minutes, until soft. Add the stock, bring to the boil, add the carrot, turnip, celery and macaroni and simmer for 20–30 minutes. Add the cabbage, beans and peas and simmer for a further 20 minutes. Stir in the tomato paste or tomatoes, bacon and seasoning to taste. Serve the grated Parmesan cheese in a separate dish.

Pot-au-Feu

1½ pints well-flavoured stock
½ lb. chuck steak, cut into cubes
4 carrots, diced
2 bay leaves
A sprig of rosemary
2 tbsps. long-grain rice
3 leeks, sliced
A small cauliflower, broken into florets
4 oz. peas
2 tomatoes, skinned and diced
Salt and pepper
A pinch of cayenne

Put the stock in a saucepan, add the steak and carrots, with the bay leaves and rosemary. Bring to the boil and simmer gently for 1–1½ hours. Add the rice, leeks, cauliflower and peas and simmer for 15–20 minutes. Remove the bay leaves. Finally, add the tomatoes and seasonings. Serve piping hot. (*Serves 4–6*)

(*See colour picture facing page 64*)

Minestrone

Cock-a-Leekie

1 boiling fowl – about 2½ lb.
2 pints stock or water
4 leeks, cleaned and sliced
Salt and pepper
6 prunes (optional)

Cover the fowl with stock or water and add the leeks and seasoning. Bring to the boil and simmer gently for 3½ hours, until tender. Remove the chicken from the stock, carve off the meat and cut into fairly large pieces. Serve the soup with the chicken pieces in it, or serve the soup on its own, with the chicken as a main course.

If prunes are used, soak them overnight in cold water, halve and stone them and add to the stock 30 minutes before the end of the cooking.

French Onion Soup

½ lb. onions, skinned and sliced
1½ oz. butter
1½ level tbsps. flour
1½ pints brown stock
Salt and pepper
A bay leaf
Slices of French bread
Grated cheese

Fry the onions in the butter for 5–10 minutes, until browned. Stir in the flour, mixing well. Pour in the stock gradually, season, add the bay leaf, bring to the boil and simmer in a covered pan for 30 minutes. Remove the bay leaf. Put a slice of bread into each individual soup bowl, pour on the soup and top with cheese. Alternatively, put all the soup into a fireproof casserole, float the slices of bread on it, cover with grated cheese and put under the grill or in a hot oven until the cheese is melted and bubbling.

Mushroom Bouillon

2 carrots
2 leeks
2 sprigs of parsley
1 bay leaf
¼ level tsp. dried thyme
1½ pints beef stock
1 level tsp. salt
Pepper
½ lb. fresh mushrooms
Chopped parsley to garnish

Prepare the vegetables and place all the ingredients except the mushrooms in a pan, bring to the boil and simmer until the vegetables are soft; strain. Slice the

mushrooms very thinly and add to the strained liquor. Cover and simmer for 30 minutes. Season to taste and sprinkle with parsley.
(See colour picture facing page 65)

Scotch Broth

1½ lb. neck of mutton or shin of beef
4 pints water
Salt and pepper
1 carrot and 1 turnip, peeled and chopped
1 onion, skinned and chopped or diced
2 leeks, cleaned and chopped
1½ oz. pearl barley
1 tbsp. finely chopped parsley

Cut up the meat and remove any fat, put in a pan, cover with the water, add some salt and pepper, bring slowly to boiling point and simmer gently for 1½ hours. Add the vegetables and the barley. Simmer for about 1 hour, until the vegetables and barley are soft. Remove any fat on the surface with a spoon or with kitchen paper and serve the soup garnished with parsley.

Traditionally, the meat is served with a little of the broth and the remaining broth is served separately.

Mulligatawny Soup

1 onion, skinned and finely chopped
1 carrot, peeled and finely chopped
½ lb. tomatoes, skinned and chopped
½ a green pepper, seeded and chopped
2 sticks of celery, scrubbed and finely chopped
1 apple, peeled and finely chopped
1 oz. butter
1¾ pints brown stock
1–2 tbsps. curry powder
2 cloves
1 tbsp. chopped parsley
Sugar, salt and pepper
3 level tbsps. flour or cornflour
¼ pint milk
Leftovers of cold cooked chicken or meat, cut small
1 oz. rice (already cooked)

Cook the vegetables and apple in the butter for 5 minutes. Add the stock, flavourings and seasonings, cover and simmer for 2–2½ hours. Sieve the soup, return it to the pan and re-heat. Blend the flour and milk to a smooth cream, stir in a little of the hot soup and return the mixture to the pan. Add the chicken and the rice, bring to the boil, stirring until the soup thickens, and cook for a further 2–3 minutes. Re-season if necessary before serving.

Mock Turtle Soup

½ a calf's head
2 carrots, peeled and chopped
2 onions, skinned and chopped
1 stick of celery, scrubbed and chopped
A small turnip, peeled and chopped
½ lb. knuckle of veal, cut into rough pieces
½ lb. shin of beef, cut into rough pieces
1 oz. dripping
3 pints water
A bouquet garni
Salt and pepper
2–3 tbsps. sherry

Soak the calf's head in water for 1 hour. Cut the meat from the bones of the head, omitting the ear. Trim the meat and tie it in a roll. Fry the vegetables and all the meat in the dripping for about 5 minutes, until well browned. Remove the pan from the heat and add the water, bouquet garni and seasoning. Bring to the boil and skim if necessary with a metal spoon. Add the head and bones, return to the boil and skim again; cover and simmer for 2–3 hours. Take out the head meat and press it between 2 plates. Strain the rest of the soup through a fine cloth or strainer and leave until cold, when it should have formed a thick jelly. Remove any fat from the surface and re-heat the soup, adding some of the pressed meat, cut in small squares. Re-season if necessary and add sherry to taste.

FISH SOUPS AND CHOWDERS

Bouillabaisse

2 lb. mixed fish: John Dory, red mullet, whiting, mackerel, rock salmon, gurnet, bass, crawfish or lobster, crab, prawns, eel or conger eel
2–3 onions, skinned and sliced
1 stick of celery, scrubbed and chopped
¼ pint olive oil
½ lb. tomatoes, skinned and sliced
2 cloves of garlic, crushed
1 bay leaf
A pinch of dried thyme and fennel (if available)
A few sprigs of parsley
Finely shredded rind of ½ an orange
Salt and pepper
A pinch of saffron (if available)
French bread

This is a traditional dish from the South of France. The authentic version is made from at least 8 different types of fish, many of which are available only along the Mediterranean coasts. However, any variety of white and shell fish can be used to give quite a good imitation. The French themselves differ about the traditional recipe and indeed get quite heated about it!

Have the fish cleaned, skinned and cut in fairly thick pieces; have the shell fish removed from the shells. Lightly fry the onions and celery in the oil for about 5 minutes, until soft but not coloured. Stir in the tomatoes, garlic, herbs, orange rind and seasoning. Put all the firmer-fleshed fish in a layer over the vegetables, just cover with water (in which the saffron has been dissolved, if used), bring to the boil and boil for about 8 minutes. Add the softer-fleshed fish and continue cooking for a further 5–8 minutes, until all the ingredients are cooked but still in shape.

The bouillabaisse can be served as a complete dish, or the cooking liquid can be strained off and served in individual bowls containing a slice of French bread – the fish is then served separately.

In some areas sliced potatoes are included in the bed of vegetables; the cooking liquid is sometimes enriched with 2 egg yolks and 3–4 tbsps. cream, blended together and added just before serving.

Lobster Bisque

1 cooked hen lobster
2 pints fish stock or water
A small carrot, peeled and sliced
A small onion, skinned and sliced
1 bay leaf
A sprig of parsley
Salt and pepper
1 oz. butter
3 level tbsps. flour
A squeeze of lemon juice
A little cream
¼ glass white wine
Lobster butter

Remove the lobster meat from the shell and cut it into neat pieces, reserving the coral. Break up the shell and cook it with the stock, vegetables, herbs and seasoning for ¾–1 hour, then strain off the liquid. Melt the butter, stir in the flour and cook for 2–3 minutes. Remove the pan from the heat and gradually stir in the lobster stock, bring to the boil and continue to stir until it thickens; cook for a further 3 minutes. Re-season if necessary and add the lemon juice, cream and wine. Add the pieces of lobster meat and whisk in the lobster butter.

LOBSTER BUTTER: Pound ½ oz. lobster coral with 1 oz. butter and sieve the mixture.

Fish Chowder

1 onion, skinned and sliced
2 rashers of bacon, chopped
½ oz. butter
3 potatoes, peeled and sliced
1 lb. fresh haddock, skinned and cubed
A 15-oz. can of tomatoes
1 pint fish stock
Salt and pepper
1 bay leaf and 2 cloves
Chopped parsley to garnish

Lightly fry the onion and bacon in the butter for about 5 minutes, until soft but not coloured. Add the potatoes and the fish. Beat the tomatoes to a thick purée, add to the fish stock, combine with the fish mixture and add the seasoning and flavourings. Simmer for about ½ hour, until all the fish is soft but still in shape. Remove the bay leaf and cloves and sprinkle with parsley before serving.

CHILLED SOUPS

Crème Vichyssoise

4 leeks, cleaned and sliced
1 onion, skinned and sliced
2 oz. butter
Salt and pepper
2 pints white stock
2 potatoes, peeled and thinly sliced
⅓ pint cream
Chopped chives to garnish

Lightly fry the leeks and onion in the butter for about 10 minutes, until soft but not coloured. Add the seasoning, stock and potatoes, cover and cook until the vegetables are soft. Sieve the soup or put it in an electric blender, stir in the cream, with more seasoning if necessary, and chill. Sprinkle with chives before serving.

Gazpacho *(Cold Uncooked Soup from Spain)*

½ lb. tomatoes, skinned and sliced
2 oz. bread, cubed
3 tbsps. olive oil
1 clove of garlic
1 pint water
3 tbsps. vinegar
Salt, pepper and sugar
For the Garnish
1 tomato, skinned and diced
½ a green pepper, seeded and diced
¼ of a cucumber, peeled and diced
1 thick slice of bread, diced and fried

Mix the tomatoes and bread with the oil, crushed garlic and some of the water until creamy. Sieve the mixture into a bowl, then add the remaining water and the vinegar. Season to taste with salt, pepper and sugar.
  Either add the garnishes to the soup, or serve them in separate bowls.

Chilled Cucumber Soup

1 small onion, skinned and sliced
1½ pints white stock
1 large cucumber, peeled and finely chopped
A sprig of mint
1 level tbsp. cornflour
2–3 tbsps. cream
Seasoning
Green colouring

Simmer the onion for 15 minutes in a pan with the stock. Add the cucumber (saving a little for garnish), with the mint; simmer for about 20 minutes, or until the cucumber is cooked. Sieve the soup or put it in an electric blender, return it to the pan and re-heat. Blend the cornflour with a little cold water to a smooth cream. Stir in a little of the hot soup, return the mixture to the pan and bring to the boil, stirring until it thickens. Cook for a further 2–3 minutes. Stir in the cream and re-season if necessary. Tint the soup delicately with green colouring, pour it into a large bowl, cover and chill. Serve sprinkled with small cucumber dice or shredded mint.

Chilled Asparagus Soup

Follow the recipe given earlier under Cream Soups, but after sieving the cooked soup, pour it into a large bowl, cover and chill. Before serving, stir in the remaining milk and the cream and garnish with the asparagus tips.

Jellied Consommé

Jellied consommé is a good soup for summer days. Use the 'classic' recipe given earlier and leave the soup to cool and set. Serve it broken up, in individual dishes. It can also be made from the quick recipe if 1 level tbsp. gelatine is dissolved in a little water and added to each 2 pints of the soup before it is chilled. Alternatively use a well chilled canned consommé.

Here are some variations of cold consommé:
1. Add 2–3 tbsps. chopped herbs (chives, parsley and tarragon) to 2 pints consommé. Garnish with whipped cream which has been flavoured with curry powder or

sprinkled with toasted almonds.
2. Add 2–3 tbsps. chopped mint leaves to 2 pints consommé. Garnish with whipped cream mixed with chopped mint.

CANNED AND PACKET SOUP VARIATIONS

An interesting soup can be quickly made by combining two cans or packets of soup or adding other ingredients.

Oxtail and Tomato
Use a can of each and add lemon juice or sherry to taste; serve with grated cheese or toast.

Pea and Tomato
Use a can of each. Grill 4 bacon rashers till crisp, chop them (alternatively, mince 2 oz. cooked ham), and sprinkle over the soup before serving.

Pea and Asparagus
Use a can of each soup and serve sprinkled with 1 oz. chopped shelled shrimps.

Celery and Mushroom
Use a can of each soup. Serve garnished with sour cream and sprinkled with chopped chives or with about

1 oz. sliced and lightly fried mushrooms.

Quick Minestrone
Mix a can of vegetable beef broth with one of tomato soup. Add 1 oz. short-cut macaroni and simmer for about 15 minutes, until it is cooked. Serve sprinkled with grated Parmesan cheese.

Quick Mulligatawny
Make up a packet of French onion soup and simmer for 5 minutes. Add a can of oxtail soup with a bay leaf or a pinch of dried mixed herbs and 2 level tsps. curry powder; simmer for a further 10 minutes.

Chicken and Almond
Fry 1 tbsp. each of finely chopped onion, parsley and blanched almonds in ½ oz. butter for 5 minutes. Add a can of cream of chicken soup and simmer for 10 minutes.

SOUP ACCOMPANIMENTS AND GARNISHES

Certain soups have a recognised accompaniment or garnish, but with the others you can ring the changes on a variety of simple and more elaborate finishing touches. Some of them, like dumplings, also give more 'body' turning the soup into a main course.

MUSHROOMS: Slice thinly and lightly fry in a little butter for 3–5 minutes, until soft but not coloured.

ONIONS: Fried onion rings give a good flavour. Cut them thinly, dip in egg white or milk and flour and fry until golden-brown and crisp in a little dripping, bacon fat or butter; add to the soup just before serving.

LEEK: Fried chopped leek adds flavour to potato soup.

CUCUMBER: Slice very finely and serve with soup of any flavour, but especially with chicken.

BACON: Rind some lean rashers, cut into small strips or dice and fry lightly. These are most suitable for thick soups. Alternatively, grill the bacon until just crisp, crumble roughly and sprinkle over the soup.

SAUSAGES AND SAUSAGE-MEAT: Left-over cooked sausages go well with vegetable soups such as spinach. Cut in rounds and heat in the soup. Make sausage-meat into small balls and cook in the soup for 20 minutes.

MELBA TOAST: Traditionally this is made by toasting ¼-inch slices of bread, splitting them through the middle and toasting the uncooked surfaces.

Alternatively, cut stale bread into very thin slices, lay them on baking sheets and dry off in the bottom of a very slow oven until they are crisp and curled. Before serving, brown them slightly under a very slow grill.

CROÛTONS – *fried*: Cut bread into ¼- to ½-inch cubes and fry quickly in lard or oil until crisp and golden; *Toasted*: Cut slices of toast into ¼- to ½-inch dice. Serve croûtons separately or sprinkle them over the soup.

RICE: Left-over dry boiled rice may be added to soup shortly before it is served, together with freshly chopped parsley or chives. Rice may also be cooked in the actual soup or broth; give it about ¼ hour's cooking.

MACARONI, TAGLIATELLE AND SPAGHETTI: These are good with minestrone and any thin soup. Break them into short lengths, cook separately for about 15 minutes, drain and add to the soup. Italian soup pasta in the shape of letters, shells, stars and wheels can also be used – add about 10–15 minutes before the soup is served. Allow 1–1½ oz. pasta to 2 pints of soup.

NOODLES: Cook them in the soup or separately in boiling water for about 15 minutes.

CELERY: Pick the leaves from the ends of the centre stems and wash well; serve one or two sprigs in each bowl of soup.

LEMON: Thin slices are delicious with many of the clear soups and with tomato soups.

CHEESE: Freshly grated hard cheese is a pleasant accompaniment to almost any vegetable soup. Grated cheese is usually served separately, but may also be sprinkled on the soup just before it is served. A little of some chopped fresh herb, e.g. parsley, can be mixed with the cheese for added colour.

DUMPLINGS: Either plain or herb-flavoured dumplings may be added to almost any meat or vegetable soup, to make it more substantial. To make herb dumplings, mix 4 oz. self-raising flour, 2 oz. shredded or chopped suet, $\frac{1}{2}$ a small onion, skinned and finely grated, $\frac{1}{2}$ level tsp. mixed dried herbs, salt and pepper, with sufficient cold water to make an elastic dough. Divide into about 16 portions, roll into small balls, using a little flour, add to the soup and simmer for about 15–20 minutes. For plain dumplings, omit the onion and herbs.

Fish Cookery

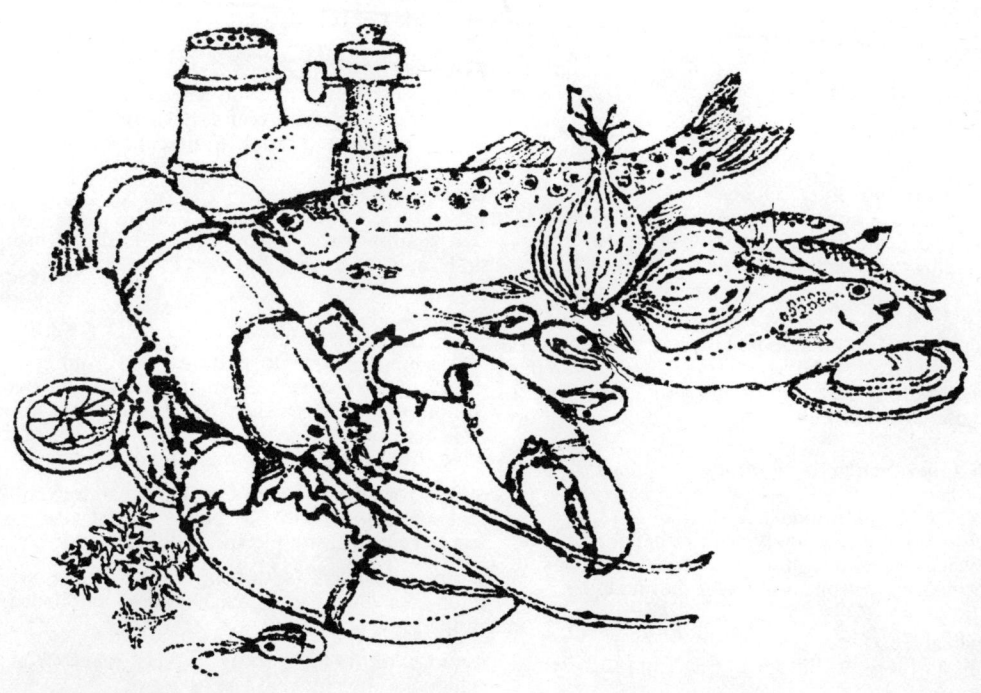

A common way of grouping fish is into sea and fresh-water types. Another classification, which cuts across these two groups, is into white and oily fish. White fish have a low fat content and characteristic white flesh; familiar examples are cod, haddock, hake, sole, plaice and turbot. Oily fish have quite a high fat content and their flesh is usually darker; the best-known are herring, mackerel, sprat, eel and salmon.

Shellfish – lobster, scampi, shrimps and so on – make a separate group.

Fish is a good source of protein and the oily fish also supply vitamins A and D.

A DICTIONARY OF FISH

The entries are arranged alphabetically under the headings 'Sea Fish', 'Fresh-water Fish' and 'Shellfish'.

SEA FISH

Anchovies
Small fish, which are filleted and cured, and packed in either bottles or cans, in brine or olive oil. They are used – in small amounts only, for they are very salty – in appetisers and cocktail nibblers, as a pizza topping and in Salade Niçoise. They also make anchovy butter, for use in savouries and sandwiches and as a spread for toast.

Bass
In season May to August.
    Bass is not unlike salmon in shape, but the flesh is very white. Large bass, which have a good flavour, are usually poached or baked; small ones can be grilled or fried.

Bloater: *See Herring*

Bream (Sea)
At its best from June to December.
    A round-bodied, coarse-skinned fish with white flesh and a rather delicate flavour. Bream is often stuffed and baked, but may also be poached, fried or grilled.

Brill
In season all the year, but at its best from April to August.
    A flat fish with a good flavour and texture resembling those of turbot. It may be poached, served cold with mayonnaise, or cooked like turbot.

Coalfish, Coley, Saithe *(occasionally also called Rock Salmon)*
Available all the year round.
    A member of the cod family, with rather coarse flesh, greyish when raw, although it turns white when cooked. It can be used in the same ways as cod or haddock.

Cod, Codling
In season all the year, but at its best from October to May.

A large round-bodied fish with close, white flesh, somewhat lacking in flavour, but improved if cooked with herbs, vegetables or a stuffing. Cod can be grilled, baked or fried in batter and may also be used in made-up dishes such as fish pie.

SMOKED COD FILLETS: Cook as for smoked haddock fillets, which they resemble, though the flavour is not so good.

SMOKED COD'S ROE: On sale at delicatessen shops, is sliced and served on lettuce, with lemon wedges and fingers of toast, as an appetiser.

Dab
Small, white-fleshed fish of the plaice family – excellent either fried or baked.

Flounder
In season from February to September.
    Flounders resemble plaice, but have not such a good texture and flavour; cook in the same ways.

Gurnet, Gurnard
In season from July to April.
    A small fish with a large, bony head and firm white flesh, of good flavour. Cook as for haddock.

Haddock
At its best from September to February.
    A round-bodied fish, distinguished from cod by the dark streak which runs down the back and the two black 'thumb marks' above the gills. Haddock has firm white flesh and may be cooked by any method suitable for white fish; it is useful for made-up dishes.

SMOKED OR FINNAN HADDOCK: Whole haddock, split open and smoked. Usually poached or grilled; also good for use in kedgeree, fish pie and haddock soufflé.

GOLDEN CUTLETS (SOMETIMES CALLED FILLETS): Small haddocks, similar to Finnan haddocks, but boned. Cook in the same ways.

SMOKED HADDOCK FILLETS: Fillets taken from large haddocks and smoked. Use as above.

Hake

In season all the year, but at its best from June to January.

Hake is somewhat like cod in shape, but has a closer white flesh and a better flavour; it is cooked like cod.

Halibut

In season all the year, but best from August to April.

Halibut is a very large flat fish with an excellent flavour, and like turbot is regarded as one of the 'good-class' fish. It is usually baked or grilled, but may also be cooked by any recipe suitable for turbot or cod.

Herring

In season all the year, but best from June to December.

Fairly small, round-bodied, oily fish with creamy-coloured flesh of distinctive flavour. They are usually grilled, fried or sautéed. Though they are generally sold whole, the fishmonger will fillet them for you on request. Herrings are also sold prepared in various special ways, the chief ones being as follows:

KIPPERS: Herrings that have been split open, soaked in brine, then smoked over wood chips and sawdust to give them their unique smoky flavour. Some of them are now dyed. They are usually poached or grilled.

BLOATERS: Herrings that have been soaked in brine, smoked and cured; unlike kippers, they are cured whole and for a shorter period.

SALT HERRINGS: The fish are gutted and preserved between layers of salt in barrels.

ROLLMOPS: The herrings are filleted, packed in barrels with brine and vinegar, then later rolled up and packed in jars with spices, onions or other flavourings, according to the manufacturer's particular recipe.

BISMARCK HERRINGS: These are pickled and spiced like roll-mops, but left whole.

BUCKLING: Herrings smoked whole, at a higher temperature and for a longer time than kippers, so that they are lightly cooked during the curing. Very delicate in flavour.

John Dory

In season from October to December.

An ugly fish, with very large jaws and a body that is nearly oval in shape; it has firm white flesh with a good flavour. After the head and fins have been removed the fish can be poached or baked whole, but it is more usually filleted and cooked according to any recipe for sole.

Kipper: *See Herring*

Mackerel

In season from October to July, but at its best during April, May and June.

A fairly small, round-bodied, oily fish, rather bigger than a herring, with characteristic blue-black markings on the back, creamy-coloured flesh and a distinctive flavour. It can be left whole or filleted and cooked by any method suitable for herrings. Mackerel must be eaten very fresh.

Mullet *(Red and Grey)*

At its best from April to October.

Red mullet is a round-bodied fish, similar in size to a herring and with firm white flesh, which may be baked, grilled or fried. Grey mullet is larger and coarser; cook it in any way suitable for white fish.

Plaice

In season all the year round, but best towards the end of May.

Plaice has soft white flesh and a very delicate flavour. You can cook it whole or filleted, by most methods, including steaming, frying, grilling and baking.

Rock Salmon *(sometimes called Huss)*

A name given by fishmongers to several kinds of fish such as the common catfish, rock eel or nurse (dog fish). The fish is sold skinned and has firm, pinkish-tinged flesh. Considerable quantities are bought for the fried fish trade and it can also be used in fish stews and so on.

Salmon Trout

In season from March to August.

This resembles salmon, but when cooked has slightly pinker flesh; it has not quite such a good flavour, so is cheaper. Salmon trout is cooked whole and is usually poached or baked; it may be served hot or cold.

Sardine

Sardines are strictly speaking young pilchards, but the name is also applied to the young of other fish (e.g. sprats and herrings) which are canned in olive oil or tomato sauce. Fresh sardines can be grilled or fried as for sprats.

Skate

In season from September to April.

Only the 'wings' or side parts of this large white fish are eaten. Cook by poaching or frying.

Smelt

In season from September to April.

A small, round-bodied, silvery fish with a delicate flavour. To prepare smelts, make a small cut with scissors just below the gills and gently press out the entrails, then wash the fish well. Smelts are usually fried, but larger ones may be baked.

Sole

In season all the year round.

One of the finest flat fish. Its flesh is firm and delicate, with a delicious flavour.

The true or 'Dover' sole is easily distinguished by its dark brownish-grey back skin from the lemon, witch and Torbay soles, which are not considered to have quite such a fine flavour.

Sole can be cooked by most methods, especially grilling, frying, baking and steaming, and is the basis of many classic fish dishes.

Sprat

In season from November to March.

A fairly small, round-bodied fish of the same family as

the herring. To prepare sprats, wash them and draw them through the gills, as for smelts. Fry or grill.

Sturgeon
In season from August to March, although not usually available in this country.

The hard roe of various members of the sturgeon family is known as caviare when it is salted.

Turbot
In season all the year, but at its best from March to August.

Turbot has creamy-white flesh with a very delicious flavour and is considered to be the finest of the flat fish. It is usually cut in steaks and grilled or baked – very often with wine.

Whitebait
At their best in May, June and July.

Very small silvery fish (the fry of various kinds, chiefly herring and sprat). They are fried whole and served as the first course of a meal.

Whiting
In season all the year, but at its best from December to March.

A round-bodied fish with a delicate flavour. Cook it whole or in fillets, by any of the usual methods.

FRESH-WATER FISH

Carp
In season October to February.

A round-bodied fish. If small, it may be grilled or fried, but when larger, it is better stuffed and baked.

To counteract the somewhat muddy flavour which the flesh tends to have, soak the fish in salted water for 3–4 hours and rinse well before cooking.

Eel *(Fresh-water)*
Best during the autumn and winter.

Eels can be baked, stewed or jellied and are also sold smoked.

Perch
In season from the beginning of June to the end of February.

Perch, though seldom on sale in a fishmonger's shop, are one of the commonest fresh-water fish. They are very difficult to scale, but the job is easier if you first plunge the fish into boiling water for 2 minutes. The fish is scored on both sides and either grilled or fried.

Pike
No special season.

A large fish, which tends to have dry, rather coarse flesh and a lot of sharp bones. Soak it in salted water, as for carp. Pike is best stuffed and baked.

Salmon
In season here February to August, but imported the year round. Also available as canned and smoked salmon.

A round-bodied fish, highly regarded and expensive. The flesh is bright red, turning pink on cooking, and very close in texture, with a delicate and distinctive flavour.

Salmon is best poached, baked or grilled. It is equally good served hot or cold.

Trout *(River)*
In season from February to early September, but at its best from April to August.

Trout are much prized for their excellent though delicate flavour, which is best appreciated if they are cooked very simply; they are usually grilled or egg-and-crumbed and fried.

SHELLFISH

Crab
At its best from May to August. Can also be bought canned.

Crabs are usually sold ready boiled and many fishmongers will also prepare and dress them.

The edible portion of the crab consists of two parts – the white flesh of the claws and the 'brown' meat or liver, a soft, rich, yellow substance which nearly fills the interior of the shell.

Crawfish
Often called the spiny lobster, it resembles a lobster without the big claws, and is prepared and cooked like that fish. Also obtainable canned.

Crayfish
In season from September to April.

Crayfish resemble miniature lobsters. They have a delicate flavour and the smaller ones can be used for soups and garnishes, while the larger ones can be served hot in a cream sauce or cold with salad and brown bread and butter.

To prepare crayfish, wash them well and remove the intestinal tube under the tail, using a pointed knife. Place the fish in salted water and cook for about 10 minutes after the liquid has reached boiling point.

Dublin Bay Prawns
These large prawns can be substituted for scampi, which they closely resemble – in fact, most of the so-called scampi sold in this country are really Dublin Bay prawns. They can be served fried (after egg-and-crumbing or coating with batter), au gratin, in risottos or in any way suitable for prawns.

Lobster
In season all the year round, but at their best in the summer months; lobsters are sometimes difficult to obtain from December to April. Lobster meat may be bought ready prepared in cans.

Like crabs, lobsters are usually sold ready boiled.

They can be served hot, grilled or in such classic dishes

Chicken Liver Pâté, *page 13;* Grilled Salmon, *page 41;* Strawberry Yog, *page 166*

Vegetables form the basis of many a good soup

as Lobster Newburg or Thermidor. The remains can be curried, scalloped or served up in the form of patties or omelettes, but there is really nothing to equal plainly dressed lobster, or Lobster Mayonnaise.

Mussels
In season from September to March.
They must be alive when bought – discard any with gaping shells, as the fish inside will be dead.
Mussels are usually served as Moules Marinière – mussel soup.

Oysters
In season from September to April.
When oysters are bought, the shells should be firmly closed.
Oysters can be served raw 'on the shell' or cooked in various ways – in patties, as oysters au gratin, or added to steak and kidney pudding.

Prawns
Obtainable all the year round, but at their best from February to October. Also sold canned, bottled and frozen.
Fresh prawns are usually sold ready boiled – in the shell or picked. They can be served hot or cold in fish cocktails, salads and moulds, curried and in rice dishes.

Scallops
In season from October to March and at their best in January and February. Frozen scallops are obtainable at any time of the year.
The roe of scallops should be a bright orange colour and the flesh white. They are delicious fried with bacon or served in a cheese sauce.

Scampi
Strictly speaking, these giant prawns are found only in the Mediterranean and Adriatic. In this country they are usually replaced by Dublin Bay prawns – see separate entry.

Shrimps
Fresh shrimps are available all the year round; they may also be bought frozen, potted in butter and canned. The fresh ones are usually sold ready boiled.
Shrimps may be served in the same ways as prawns, but being cheaper, they are also used in fish sauces, chowders and casseroles. Potted shrimps are served as a 'starter' and can be used in sandwiches.

BUYING FISH

Fresh Fish
Buy fish when it is in season and at its best. Some kinds can be bought all the year round, others have a close season (usually covering the spawning period).
Buy fish the day you intend to use it. Look for firm flesh, silvery scales and clear marking, red gills and bright eyes and reject any that does not have a fresh smell.

Frozen Fish
Most frozen fish is of high quality, there is no waste and it is quick to cook. The freezing does not affect the flavour or the food value. Frozen fish can be bought in a variety of ways – whole, filleted, in cutlets, or as fingers or cakes. Shellfish are also available.
Use it like fresh fish; but follow the manufacturers' individual instructions concerning the storage, thawing and cooking.

CLEANING FISH

Whole Fish
Remove any scales, using a knife and scraping from tail to head, with frequent rinsing.
To remove the entrails from round-bodied fish such as herrings or trout, make a slit along the abdomen from the gills half-way to the tail, draw out the insides and clean away any blood. Rub with a little salt to remove the black skin.
With flat fish, such as sole and plaice, open the cavity which lies in the upper part of the body under the gills and clean out the entrails in the same way.
Cut off the fins and gills, if the fish is to be served whole. The head and tail may be cut off if you prefer, but if the head is left on, take out the eyes. Rinse the fish in cold water.

Fillets and Cutlets
Wash and wipe with a paper towel.

SKINNING FISH

Whole Flat Fish *(e.g. Sole)*
Wash the fish and cut off the fins. Make an incision across the tail, slip the thumb between the skin and the flesh and loosen the dark skin round the sides of the fish. Hold the fish down firmly with one hand and with the other take hold of the skin and draw it off quickly, upwards

towards the head. The white skin can be removed in the same way, but unless the fish is particularly large, it is generally left on.

Fillets of Flat Fish

Lay the fillet on a board, skin side down, salt the fingers and hold the tail end of the skin firmly with the fingers. They separate the flesh from the skin by sawing with a sharp knife from side to side, pressing the flat of the blade against the flesh. Keep the edge of the blade close to the skin while cutting, but don't press it down at too

sharp an angle or the skin will be cut.

Round Fish

These are more usually cooked with the skin on, but if you want them skinned, start from the head.

Cut off a narrow strip of skin along the spine and cut across the skin just below the head; loosen the skin under the head with the point of a sharp knife, dip the fingers in salt and gently pull the skin down towards the tail, working carefully to avoid breaking the flesh. Skin the other side of the fish in the same way.

FILLETING FISH

Flat Fish *(e.g. Plaice)*

Four fillets are taken from the fish, two from each side. Using a small, sharp, pointed knife, make an incision straight down the back of the fish, following the line of the bone. Insert the knife under the flesh and carefully remove it with long, clean strokes. Take the first fillet from the left-hand side of the fish, working from head to tail, then turn the fish round and cut off the second fillet from tail to head. Fillet the other side of the fish in the same way. When you have finished, no flesh should be left on the bone.

Round Fish *(e.g. Haddock)*

Cut along the centre of the back to the bone, using a sharp knife, and cut along the abdomen of the fish. Remove the flesh cleanly from the bones, working from the head down, pressing the knife against the bones and working

with short, sharp strokes. Remove the fillet from the other side in the same way. If the fish is large, cut the fillets into serving-size pieces. Skin the fillets or not, as preferred.

Herring and Mackerel

Cut off the head, tail and fins. Split the fish open along the underside, remove the entrails and rub off the black inner skin, using a little salt on the fingers. Put the fish on a board, cut side down, and press lightly with the fingers down the middle of the back to loosen the bone. Turn the fish over and ease the backbone up with the fingers, removing with it as many of the small bones as possible. If the fish contains roes, remove these before filleting it (to cook and serve with the fish or separately, as you prefer).

METHODS OF COOKING

POACHED FISH

Suitable for:

Fillets, steaks or small whole fish – halibut, turbot, brill, haddock, flounder, salmon, salmon trout, smoked haddock, kippers.

Although we sometimes speak of 'boiling' fish, true boiling spoils it and it should actually be poached – that is, simmered in the liquid. The cooking may be done either in a saucepan on top of the stove or in a shallow covered casserole in a moderate oven (350°F., mark 4).

Whole fish and large pieces are usually cooked on top of the stove, completely covered with the liquid. This may be salted water, flavoured with some of the following: parsley sprigs, a small piece of onion and/or carrot, a few mushroom stalks, a squeeze of lemon juice, ½ a bay leaf or some peppercorns. For the more classic dishes you can cook whole fish such as trout and large pieces such as salmon or turbot in Court-Bouillon. *(See the recipe given on the opposite page.)*

Heat the liquid until it is simmering, put in the fish, cover and simmer very gently until tender, allowing 10–15 minutes per lb., according to the thickness of the cut,

or about 20 minutes in all for a small piece. Drain the fish, place on a hot dish and serve with a sauce made from the cooking liquid (see Sauces chapter). Alternatively, serve the poached fish cold, in aspic or with a mayonnaise dressing. *(See recipes for Salmon and Trout in Aspic later in this chapter.)* Fish fillets are often cooked in the oven and they need only be half-covered with cold liquid – whether seasoned milk and water, cider or dry white wine – which is then used as basis for a sauce to accompany the cooked fish.

Court-Bouillon for Poached Fish

1 quart water (or dry white wine and water mixed)
1 small carrot, peeled and sliced
1 small onion, skinned and sliced
1 small stalk of celery, scrubbed and chopped (optional)
1 tbsp. vinegar or lemon juice
A few sprigs of parsley
½ a bay leaf
3–4 peppercorns
2 level tsps. salt

Place all the ingredients in a pan and simmer for about ½ hour. Allow to cool and if preferred, strain the liquid before using it.

STEAMED FISH
Suitable for:
Thin fillets of sole, plaice.

Wash and wipe the fish and lay it on a greased plate; dot with a few pieces of butter, add 1 tbsp. milk and a little salt and pepper, cover with another plate and place over a pan of boiling water. Cook for 10–15 minutes. The liquid round the fish plus a little milk can be made into a sauce – for instance, parsley, shrimp, egg or cheese. *(See Sauces chapter.)*

GRILLED FISH
Suitable for:
Small fish, thin fillets and thicker cuts – sole, plaice, halibut, turbot, hake, brill, cod, haddock, flounder, salmon, salmon trout, trout, herring, mackerel, smoked haddock, kippers.

Wash the fish. If it is whole, remove the scales and fins. When it is too plump to allow the heat to penetrate easily (e.g. herring, mackerel) make 3–4 diagonal cuts in the body on each side.
  White fish such as plaice, halibut, sole, cod and haddock should be brushed with oil or melted butter to prevent drying, but oily ones like herrings, mackerel and salmon do not need it.
  Thin fillets or steaks can be cooked by grilling on one side only, but thicker pieces or whole fish should be turned once (use a fish slice or palette knife) to ensure thorough cooking on both sides.
  Cook under a moderate heat, allowing 4–5 minutes for thin fillets, 10–15 minutes for thicker fillets, steaks and small whole fish; adjust the times as necessary according to the size and thickness of the fish.
  Serve with maître d'hôtel or melted butter, lemon wedges and parsley.

FRIED FISH
Most fish can be fried and the method is especially good for those kinds that have little natural flavour or colour. Both shallow and deep-fat frying are used. Wash and dry the fish and coat it well with one of the following:

SEASONED FLOUR *See Cooking Terms*
EGG AND CRUMBS *See Cooking Terms*
COATING BATTER *See under Deep-Fried Fish*

  Chipped potatoes are a very popular accompaniment for most kinds of fried fish. Any sauce should be served separately.

SHALLOW-FRIED FISH
Suitable for:
Fillets, steaks and small whole fish – sole, plaice, dabs, bass, bream, cod, haddock, mackerel, herring, trout, perch, pike – also for fish cakes, etc.

Coat the fish with seasoned flour or with egg and bread-crumbs. Heat some shallow fat gently until it is fairly hot – if you let it smoke it is too hot. Lard or oil is usually used, but for fish cooked *à la meunière (see below)*, butter is essential. Put in the piece of fish so that the side which you wish to be uppermost when it is served goes down first into the fat or oil. Cook gently and when the first side is browned, turn the fish and cook the other side. Allow about 10 minutes in all, according to thickness. Use a slice or palette knife to turn fish and to lift it out of the pan. Drain well on crumpled kitchen paper and serve with lemon and parsley or maître d'hôtel butter.

FISH À LA MEUNIERE
Suitable for:
Fillets or whole fish – sole, plaice, trout, pike, perch.

Shallow-fry the fish in butter. When it is cooked, transfer it to a hot dish. Lightly brown a little extra butter in the frying pan, add a squeeze of lemon juice and pour it over the fish. Garnish with chopped parsley.

DEEP-FRIED FISH
Suitable for:
Fillets coated with batter or egg and breadcrumbs, small whole fish – cod, haddock, hake, whiting, coley, gurnet, skate, sprats, smelts, fresh sardines, whitebait; also fish cakes, etc.

You need a deep pan with a wire basket (except for batter-coated fish), and enough fat (2–3 lb.) or oil to come about three-quarters up the pan. Clarified dripping, lard and cooking oil are suitable. The fat must be pure and free from moisture.
  Heat the fat to 350–370°F. A simple way to test it is to put in a 1-inch cube of bread, which should brown in 60 seconds. If the fat is too cool, the fish will be soggy; if it is too hot, the outside will brown before the inside is cooked. While the fat is heating coat the fish with egg and breadcrumbs or with batter *(see below)*.
  Lower the fish gently into the fat, using the basket for egg-and-crumbed pieces; cook only a little at a time, to avoid lowering the temperature. As soon as the fish is golden-brown – 5–10 minutes – lift it out and drain it really well on crumpled kitchen paper before serving. The fat may be strained into a clean basin and kept for future use.

Coating Batter – 1

4 oz. flour
A pinch of salt
1 egg
¼ pint milk or milk and water (approx.)

Mix the flour, salt, egg and sufficient liquid to give a stiff batter which will coat the back of the spoon; beat well until smooth. Dip the fish into the batter, holding the pieces on a skewer or fork, and drain slightly before putting into the hot fat.

Coating Batter – 2

4 oz. flour
A pinch of salt
1 tbsp. oil
1 egg, separated
2–3 tbsps. water or milk and water

Mix the flour, salt, oil and egg yolk with sufficient water to give a stiff batter which will coat the back of the spoon; beat until smooth. Just before using, whisk the egg white stiffly and fold it into the batter. Dip the fish pieces into seasoned flour before coating them as above.

This method gives a lighter, crisper batter than the first recipe.

BAKED FISH

Suitable for:
Fillets, steaks, cuts from large fish and small whole fish – cod, haddock, hake, whiting, sole, plaice, turbot, halibut, salmon.

Unless otherwise directed in the particular recipe, use a moderate oven (350 F., mark 4)

Wash and wipe the fish and prepare according to type. Put in a stuffing if you wish and place the fish in an oven-proof dish. Add 3–4 tbsps. milk or white or red wine and a bouquet garni (or a small piece of onion and $\frac{1}{2}$ a bay leaf). Cover with a lid or foil and bake in the centre of the oven until tender – allow 10–20 minutes for fillets, 20 minutes for steaks, 25–30 minutes for small whole fish.

Alternatively, wrap the prepared fish in buttered foil and add a squeeze of lemon juice and a sprinkling of salt and pepper. Wrap loosely and put on a baking tray. Bake in the centre of the oven, allowing about 20 minutes for steak and 6–10 minutes per lb. plus 6–10 minutes over for large pieces, according to size. This method is particularly suitable for thicker cuts and whole fish.

SEA FISH RECIPES

Haddock with Cheese Sauce

$1\frac{1}{2}$ lb. haddock fillets or any white fish
Salt and pepper
$\frac{1}{4}$ pint milk
1 oz. butter or margarine
3 level tbsps. flour
6 oz. cheese, grated

Wash and wipe the fish, cut it into 4 even-sized pieces, place in a saucepan, just covered with cold water and add a little salt. Cover the pan, bring slowly to the boil, turn off the heat and leave covered for 5 minutes. Drain off the liquid, retaining $\frac{1}{4}$ pint, and mix it with the milk. Remove the skin from the fish, keeping the pieces as whole as possible, put in a shallow ovenproof dish and keep warm. Melt the fat, stir in the flour and cook for 2–3 minutes. Remove from the heat and gradually stir in the milk and fish stock. Bring to the boil and stir until the sauce thickens. Remove from the heat, stir in 4 oz. cheese and season to taste; pour over the fish and sprinkle with the remaining cheese. Place under a hot grill until golden and bubbling.

Haddock Baked in Cream

$1\frac{1}{2}$ lb. fresh haddock fillet
1 onion, skinned and finely chopped
Juice of $\frac{1}{2}$ a lemon
1 tsp. Worcestershire sauce
Salt and pepper
$\frac{1}{4}$ pint single cream

Wash and wipe the fish, place it in a greased oven-proof dish and sprinkle with the onion. Mix the lemon juice, Worcestershire sauce, seasoning and cream and pour over the fish. Cover with a lid or foil and bake in the centre of the oven for 20–30 minutes, or until the fish and onions are cooked. (Don't worry if the cream curdles.)

Stuffed Cod Steaks

4 cod steaks (or cutlets)
$\frac{1}{2}$ an onion, skinned and finely chopped
4 oz. streaky bacon, chopped
$\frac{1}{2}$ oz. butter
2 tomatoes, skinned and chopped
2 oz. fresh white breadcrumbs
Salt and pepper
$\frac{1}{4}$ pint milk (approx.)

Oven temperature: moderate (350 F., mark 4)

Wash and wipe the fish, trim off the fins and remove the central bone with a sharp-pointed knife; place the fish in a greased ovenproof dish. Fry the onion and bacon gently in the butter for about 5 minutes, until soft; stir in the tomatoes and crumbs. Season well and add enough milk to bind the mixture. Fill the centre of each steak with this stuffing, pour 2–3 tbsps. milk round the fish, cover with a lid or foil and bake in the centre of the oven for about 20 minutes.

As an alternative filling use veal forcemeat made with 2 oz. breadcrumbs (*see Stuffings chapter*) or the following mixture.

Sole Bonne Femme

Fried Whiting

Clean, wash and skin the whiting, removing the eyes but not the head of the fish; dry well in a cloth. A few minutes before the whiting are to be fried, remove them from the cloth and put the tail of each fish into its mouth. Brush the fish over with beaten egg, roll them in breadcrumbs and, shake off any loose crumbs. Heat some deep fat until it will brown a 1-inch cube of bread in 1 minute; fry the whiting for 5–10 minutes, handling them carefully, as they break easily. Drain well on crumpled kitchen paper, garnish with fried parsley and serve with anchovy or other suitable sauce.

Stuffed Rolled Plaice

2 hard-boiled eggs, shelled and chopped
2 oz. cheese, grated
1 tbsp. parsley, chopped
3 oz. fresh white breadcrumbs
2 oz. butter, melted
Salt and pepper
2 plaice, filleted and skinned

Oven temperature: moderate (350°F., mark 4)

Mix the eggs with the cheese, parsley and 2 oz. of the breadcrumbs. Bind with the butter and add seasoning.

Spread this mixture over the skinned side of the fillets and roll them up, starting from the tail end; secure them if necessary with a wooden cocktail stick. Place in a buttered shallow ovenproof dish, sprinkle with the remaining breadcrumbs and bake in the centre of the oven for about 20 minutes, until the fish is tender and the breadcrumbs crisp on top. The liquid that comes from the fish as it cooks can be strained off and used with milk to make a white or parsley sauce to serve with the fish. *(See Sauces chapter.)*

Sole Bonne Femme

2 soles, filleted
2 shallots (or 2–3 slices of onion), skinned and finely chopped
4 oz. button mushrooms
3 tbsps. dry white wine (e.g. Graves, Chablis)
1 tbsp. water
Salt and pepper
1 bay leaf
1½ oz. butter
2 level tbsps. flour
¼ pint milk (approx.)
2–3 tbsps. cream

Oven temperature: moderate (350°F., mark 4)

Trim off the fins, wash and wipe the fillets and fold each

in three. Put the shallot or onion in the bottom of an ovenproof dish, with the stalks from the mushrooms, finely chopped. Cover with the fish fillets, pour round them the wine and water, sprinkle with salt and pepper and add the bay leaf. Cover with foil or a lid and bake in the centre of the oven for about 15 minutes, until tender. Strain off the cooking liquid and keep the fish warm.

Fry the mushroom caps lightly in half the butter. Melt the remaining butter, stir in the flour and cook for 2–3 minutes. Remove the pan from the heat and gradually stir in the cooking liquid from the fish, made up to $\frac{1}{2}$ pint with milk. Bring to the boil and continue to stir until the sauce thickens, remove from the heat and stir in the cream. Pour the sauce over the fish and serve garnished with the mushroom caps.

Note: The classic Sole Bonne Femme may next be coated with Hollandaise sauce and is browned under a hot grill before being served, but the recipe given here is the one more usually followed.

Plaice and other white fish can also be cooked in this way.

Sole Véronique

2 sole, filleted
2 shallots (or 2–3 slices of onion) skinned and chopped
2–3 button mushrooms, sliced
A few sprigs of parsley
$\frac{1}{2}$ a bay leaf
Salt and pepper
$\frac{1}{4}$ pint dry white wine, e.g. Graves, Chablis
$\frac{1}{4}$ pint water
4 oz. white grapes
$\frac{3}{4}$ oz. butter
2 level tbsps. flour
$\frac{1}{4}$ pint milk, approx.
A squeeze of lemon juice
1–2 tbsps. single cream

Oven temperature: moderate (350°F., mark 4)

Trim off the fins, wash and wipe the fillets and lay them in a shallow ovenproof dish with the shallots, mushrooms, herbs, salt and pepper, wine and water. Cover with foil or a lid and bake in the centre of the oven for about 15 minutes or until tender. Simmer the grapes for a few minutes in a little water or extra white wine, peel them and remove the pips.

Meanwhile, strain the liquid from the fish and reduce it slightly by boiling rapidly; keep the fish warm. Melt the butter, stir in the flour and cook for 2–3 minutes. Remove the pan from the heat and gradually stir in the reduced fish liquor, made up to $\frac{1}{2}$ pint with milk. Bring to the boil and continue to stir until the sauce thickens. Remove from the heat and stir in most of the grapes, the lemon juice and the cream. Pour over the fish and serve decorated with the remaining grapes.

Note: You can cook plaice fillets in the same way.

Fillets of Sole Dugléré

2 sole, filleted, or 8 fillets of plaice
1–2 shallots, chopped
$\frac{1}{2}$ a bay leaf
A few sprigs of parsley
$\frac{1}{4}$ pint white wine
$\frac{1}{4}$ pint water
Salt and pepper
1 oz. butter
3 level tbsps. flour
3 tbsps. single cream
2 tomatoes, skinned and diced, with seeds removed
2 tsps. chopped parsley

Oven temperature: moderate (350°F., mark 4)

Wash and wipe the fish and put in an ovenproof dish with the shallots, herbs, wine, water, salt and pepper. Cover with foil or a lid and bake in the centre of the oven for about 15 minutes, or until tender. Strain off the cooking liquid and keep the fish warm. Melt the butter, stir in the flour and cook for 2–3 minutes. Remove the pan from the heat and gradually stir in the cooking liquid from the fish. Bring to the boil and continue to stir until the sauce thickens. Remove from the heat and stir in the cream, tomatoes and parsley. Adjust the seasoning if necessary and pour over the fish.

Note: You can cook most white fish in Dugléré style.

Sole with Orange

4 sole, skinned
Seasoned flour
2 oz. butter
1 small orange, skinned and sliced
1 tbsp. sherry
$\frac{1}{2}$ tbsp. tarragon vinegar
Chopped parsley

Cut off the fins and wash and wipe the fish. Coat them with seasoned flour and fry gently, one at a time, in $1\frac{1}{2}$ oz. of the butter, turning them once to brown and cook the second side; keep them warm. Meanwhile combine the orange slices and any juice, the sherry and vinegar and heat very gently. When all the fish are cooked, arrange them on a heated serving dish and keep hot. Clean out the pan and brown the remaining butter lightly. Place the orange slices in a line down the centre of the fish, add the liquid in which they were heated to the browned butter in the pan and pour over the fish. Serve at once, garnished with chopped parsley.

Note: Plaice may be cooked in the same way.

Grilled Halibut or Turbot

Allow 6 oz. fish per person. Wash and trim the fish, wipe and place on a greased grill grid. Brush with melted butter and sprinkle with salt and pepper. Grill gently for about 15 minutes altogether, turning the pieces once, brushing the second side with butter and sprinkling with

Herring Calaisienne

salt and pepper. Serve with grilled mushrooms and a tomato or other well-flavoured sauce.

Mackerel or Herring Calaisienne

4 mackerel or herrings, cleaned and boned

For the Stuffing

$\frac{1}{2}$ **an onion, skinned and chopped**
1 hard-boiled egg, shelled and chopped
1 tbsp. chopped parsley
2 oz. fresh white breadcrumbs
Grated rind of $\frac{1}{2}$ a lemon (optional)
Salt and pepper
Milk to mix

Oven temperature: moderate (350°F., mark 4)

Trim off the heads, tails and fins from the fish. Mix the rest of the ingredients to make a stuffing and fill the fish with it; place in an ovenproof dish with 2–3 tbsps. water, cover and bake in the centre of the oven for 20–30 minutes. Serve with a tomato sauce.

If the fish have soft roes, these can be chopped and mixed with the stuffing.

Herrings in Oatmeal (Fried)

Have the herrings boned and the heads and tails removed. Clean the flesh by rubbing with a little salt, rinse and dry well. Sprinkle with salt and pepper and coat with fine oatmeal, pressing it well into the fish on both sides. Fry in a small amount of lard or butter in a frying pan, turning the fish once, until brown on both sides. Drain well on kitchen paper and serve with lemon and parsley.

Skate with Black Butter

1$\frac{1}{2}$–2 lb. skate
2 oz. butter
1 tbsp. vinegar
2 tsps. capers
2 tsps. chopped parsley

Simmer the fish in salted water or Court-Bouillon until tender, drain and keep warm. Heat the butter until lightly browned. Add the vinegar and capers, cook for a further 2–3 minutes and pour over the fish. Sprinkle with the parsley and serve at once.

Kedgeree

12 oz. smoked haddock
6 oz. long-grain rice
2 hard-boiled eggs
3 oz. butter or margarine
Salt and cayenne pepper
Chopped parsley

Cook and flake the fish. Cook the rice in the usual way and drain if necessary. Shell the eggs, chop one and slice the other into rings. Melt the butter or margarine in a saucepan, add the fish, rice, chopped egg, salt and pepper and stir over a moderate heat for about 5 minutes, until hot. Pile on a hot dish and garnish with lines of chopped parsley and the sliced egg.

Kippers

If you suspect that they are very salty, trim, place in a tall jug, pour boiling water over and leave for 3 minutes; drain and finish by one of these methods:

GRILLING: Dot with butter, sprinkle with salt and pepper and grill gently for 4–5 minutes on each side.

BAKING: Place in a greased ovenproof dish, season and dot with butter. Cover with foil and bake in a fairly hot oven (400°F., mark 6) for 10–15 minutes.

POACHING: Place in a frying pan, cover with water and simmer until tender – about 5 minutes.
   Serve with a knob of butter on each kipper.

Fish Pie

1 lb. cod fillet or any other white fish
1½–2 lb. potatoes
1½ oz. butter
¼ pint milk, plus 2–3 tbsps.
3 level tbsps. flour
2 tbsps. chopped parsley
Salt and pepper
2–4 oz. cheese, grated

Oven temperature: fairly hot (400° F., mark 6)

Cook and flake the fish, retaining ¼ pint of the cooking liquid. Boil and mash the potatoes in the usual way, add ½ oz. butter and 2–3 tbsps. milk and beat with a wooden spoon until creamy. Melt the remaining butter, stir in the flour and cook for 2–3 minutes. Remove the pan from the heat and gradually stir in the fish liquid and ¼ pint milk; bring to the boil. When the sauce has thickened, remove it from the heat and stir in the flaked fish, the parsley and seasoning to taste. Pour into an ovenproof dish and cover with the creamed potatoes, sprinkle with the cheese and bake near the top of the oven for about 30 minutes, until the pie is well heated through and the cheese golden.
   The parsley sauce can be replaced by a white sauce to which one of the following has been added:

4 oz. mushrooms, chopped and lightly fried
4 oz. peeled shrimps
2–4 oz. grated cheese

FRESH-WATER FISH RECIPES

Salmon

1. A 2–2½-lb. Piece of Salmon

FOIL-BAKED METHOD: Pre-heat the oven to cool (300°F., mark 1–2). Wipe the fish, removing the fins, etc. Butter well a large piece of foil. Place the fish in the centre and season lightly with salt and pepper. Package the foil loosely and place on a baking sheet. Bake for about 1 hour, depending on the thickness of the fish. Cool in the foil, unwrap and remove the skin. Carefully lift the flesh from the bones. *(Serves 4–6.)*

SLOW-COOKING METHOD: Prepare the fish. Fill a fish kettle or large saucepan with sufficient water almost to cover the salmon. Add ¼ pint white wine, a bay leaf, a sprig of parsley, salt and 2–3 peppercorns. Bring this to the boil and simmer for 10 minutes. Lower in the salmon, and boil gently for 3 minutes. Take the fish kettle from the heat, remove the lid and leave on one side until cold. Lift out the fish, remove the skin and, if wished, lift the flesh from the bones.

2. Salmon Steaks, Cutlets

These should be cut about ¾ inch thick. If very large, serve one between two people rather than asking for the steaks to be cut thinly. Wipe, and remove any blood from the backbone area. Close the flaps, and to keep the pieces a good shape, secure with a cocktail stick. When individual portions of cold salmon are required for coating with mayonnaise, etc., and especially for small numbers, it is sometimes easier to cook cutlets. After cooking, carefully ease away the bones, remove the skins and portion the fish as desired.

TO POACH: Place in a deep frying-pan (preferably not a saucepan, as a shallow utensil makes removal of the fish much easier), with Court-Bouillon to cover. Cover the pan with a lid and simmer gently for 5–10 minutes. Serve hot or cold.

TO BAKE: Line a baking sheet with a larger piece of foil, and butter the surface. Place the prepared salmon on the foil. Dot each steak with butter and season with salt, pepper and lemon juice. Package loosely and cook in the centre of a warm oven (325°F., mark 3) for 20–40

Baked Salmon Steaks

minutes, according to its thickness. Serve with maître d'hôtel butter or Hollandaise sauce or garnish as photograph, with poached diced cucumber, sliced lemon and parsley sprigs. If it is to be eaten cold, leave to cool, still wrapped in the foil.

TO GRILL: Season the prepared fish with salt and pepper and brush well with melted butter. Cook on a greased grill grid under a medium heat. When the top side is cooked, and tinged light brown, brush with more butter and continue to cook for about 10–20 minutes altogether. Serve hot; traditional accompaniments are poached diced cucumber, new potatoes and asparagus or peas.

Whole Salmon Trout or Grilse

COOKED ON TOP OF THE STOVE: For this you need a fish kettle or similar large utensil. Prepare a Court-Bouillon as for Poached Salmon Steaks; lower in the cleaned fish and reduce the heat. The stock should only just show signs of movement – the bubbles should not be allowed to break. Allow 10 minutes per lb. for the first 6 lb., plus 8 minutes per lb. for the next 6 lb. Leave the fish in the liquor for 10 minutes, then if it is to be served hot, lift it out (most fish kettles have a rack which makes this easy). If the fish is to be served cold (see Salmon in Aspic), leave it in the liquor until lukewarm.

Note: If the fish kettle does not have a rack, wrap the fish in muslin or buttered greaseproof paper to avoid spoiling it when it is lifted.

OVEN-POACHED: Clean the fish, leaving on the head and tail, but removing the eyes. Curl the fish round to fit a large roasting tin. Pour over it a mixture of 1 part dry white wine and 1 part water, with slices of onion, peppercorns, a bay leaf and a slice of lemon. The liquid should come halfway up the fish. Cover the dish with buttered foil, but don't let the foil touch the fish. Cook in a warm oven (325°F., mark 3) for about 10 minutes per lb.; a fish weighing $3\frac{1}{2}$–$4\frac{1}{2}$ lb. will take 45–60 minutes. Baste occasionally. Leave to cool in the liquor, basting occasionally, and glaze as in Salmon in Aspic.

Salmon in Aspic

Have the fish cleaned but left whole. Poach or bake it in the usual way (*see separate recipes*). Remove the skin from the body, leaving on the head and tail. Make up the aspic according to the makers' instructions and when it is just beginning to thicken, coat the fish thinly. Decorate the fish, using thin rings of radish, strips of cucumber skin or thin cucumber slices, diamonds or strips of tomato skin, rings of olive, sprigs of parsley, picked shrimps, etc. Cover with further layers of aspic until the decoration is held in place. Serve with a mixed salad and mayonnaise.

Notes: For a really professional finish and to ease carving, the salmon bones should be removed before the fish is glazed. Loosen the flesh along the ridge of the backbone and use scissors to cut the bone through just below the head and above the tail. Gently pull and ease out the bone. (To lift the fish, easing it on to the flat part of the arm is the simplest method.)

Probably the easiest way to carry out the glazing is on a cooling tray, with a large plate underneath to catch the drips of aspic as they fall through. When the aspic has set, transfer the fish carefully to a large dish. Leave any remaining aspic to set, chop it on damp greaseproof paper and use as a garnish.

Truite au Bleu

Suitable only for freshly killed fish. Clean immediately, leaving the fish whole and the head on; put in a saucepan with 1–2 tbsps. boiling vinegar and cover with boiling Court-Bouillon (*see beginning of chapter*). The fish will curl round, which is quite usual. Reduce the heat and simmer for about 15 minutes, or until tender. Serve with melted butter to which lemon juice has been added.

Trout and Almonds

4 trout (about 4–5 oz. each)
Seasoned flour
6 oz. butter
2 oz. blanched almonds, cut in slivers
Juice of ½ a lemon

Clean the fish, but leave the heads on. Wash and wipe them and coat with seasoned flour. Melt 4 oz. butter in a large frying pan and fry the fish in it two at a time, turning them once, until they are tender and golden on both sides – 12–15 minutes. Drain and keep warm on a serving dish. Clean out the pan and melt the remaining butter: add the almonds and heat until lightly browned,

add a squeeze of lemon juice and pour over the fish. Serve at once, with lemon.

Trout in Cream

4 trout
Juice of 1 lemon
1 tbsp. chopped chives
1 tbsp. chopped parsley
⅛–¼ pint single cream
2 tbsps. white breadcrumbs
A little melted butter

Oven temperature: moderate (350°F., mark 4)

Have the fish cleaned (the heads can be left on or removed). Wash and wipe the fish, lay in a greased shallow ovenproof dish and sprinkle with the lemon juice, herbs and about 1 tbsp. water. Cover with foil and bake in the centre of the oven for 10–15 minutes, or until tender. Heat the cream gently and pour over the fish, sprinkle with the breadcrumbs and melted butter and brown under a hot grill. Serve at once.

Trout in Aspic

Prepare like Salmon in Aspic. This is a good fish for a formal buffet.

SHELLFISH RECIPES

Crab, simply dressed

A crab is usually sold ready cooked; in fact, many fishmongers will prepare and dress it as well. If it is bought alive, cook it as follows: wash it, place in cold salted water, bring slowly to boiling point and boil fairly quickly for 10–20 minutes, according to size – don't overcook it, or the flesh will become hard and thready. Allow to cool in the water. To give extra flavour, you can add a few parsley stalks, a bay leaf, a few peppercorns and a very little lemon juice or vinegar to the cooking water.

Lay the cooked crab on its back, hold the shell firmly with one hand and the body (to which the claws are attached) in the other hand and pull apart.

Take the shell part and use a spoon to remove the stomach bag (which lies just below the head); discard this. Carefully scrape all the meat from the shell into a basin and reserve it – this is called the soft or dark meat. Wash and if necessary scrub the shell; dry it and rub with a little oil to give a gloss. Knock away the edge of the shell up as far as the dark line round the rim.

Add 1–2 tbsps. fresh breadcrumbs to the brown meat, season with salt, pepper and lemon juice and add a little chopped parsley; pack the mixture into the sides of the

prepared shell, leaving a space in the middle for the white meat.

Take the body section and remove from it all the greyish-white frond-like pieces (called the 'dead men's fingers'), which are inedible. Crack the claws (except the very tiny ones) with a weight and take out all the flesh or white meat from both claws and body. Use the handle of a teaspoon or a skewer to reach into the crevices and take care not to get splinters of shell amongst the meat. Season the flesh with salt, pepper, cayenne and vinegar and pile it into the centre of the shell.

Decorate the crab with a little paprika and chopped parsley and lay it on a bed of lettuce, garnished with the small claws.

Lobster, simply served

Connoisseurs consider that lobster is best served quite simply with an oil and vinegar dressing or mayonnaise.

A lobster is generally sold ready boiled, but if it has been cought alive. cook it as for crab, allowing 15–25 minutes according to size and taking care not to overcook it, as the flesh tends to become hard and thready.

First twist off the large claws and crack them without

injuring the flesh. Remove the smaller claws, which are only used for garnishing. Cut off the head. Split the lobster right down the middle of the body from head to tail, using a strong pointed knife. Remove the intestine (which looks like a small vein running through the centre of the tail), the stomach, which lies near the head, and the spongy-looking gills, which are not edible.

Stand the head upright on a dish, arrange the cracked claws and split tail round it and garnish with parsley or salad. Serve the oil and vinegar dressing or mayonnaise separately.

Lobster Newburg

2 small cooked lobsters, weighing ½ lb. each
1 oz. butter
White, cayenne and paprika pepper
Salt
4 tbsps. Madeira or sherry
2 egg yolks
¼ pint single cream
Buttered toast or boiled rice
Chopped parsley to garnish

Cut the lobsters in half, carefully detach the tail meat in one piece and cut it into fairly thin slices. Crack the claws and remove the meat as unbroken as possible. Melt the butter in a frying pan, lay the lobster in the pan, season well and heat very gently for about 5 minutes, without colouring. Pour the Madeira or sherry over and continue to cook a little more quickly until the liquid is reduced by half. Beat the egg yolks with a little seasoning and add the cream. Take the lobster off the heat, pour the cream mixture over and mix gently over a slow heat till the sauce reaches the consistency of cream. Adjust the seasoning, pour at once on to hot buttered toast or boiled rice and sprinkle with parsley.

Lobster Thermidor

2 small cooked lobsters (½ lb. each)
2 oz. butter
1 tbsp. chopped shallot
2 tsps. chopped parsley
1–2 tsps. chopped tarragon
4 tbsps. white wine
½ pint Béchamel sauce
3 level tbsps. grated Parmesan cheese
Mustard, salt and paprika pepper

Remove the lobster meat from the shells, chop the claw and head meat roughly and cut the tail meat into thick slices. Melt 1 oz. butter in a saucepan and add the shallot, parsley and tarragon. After a few minutes add the wine and simmer for 5 minutes. Add the Béchamel sauce and simmer until reduced to a creamy consistency. Add the lobster meat to the sauce, with 2 tbsps. of the cheese, the remaining butter, in small pieces, and mustard, salt and paprika to taste. Arrange the mixture in the shells, sprinkle with the remaining cheese and put under the grill to brown the top quickly. Serve at once.

Moules Marinière

1 quart fresh mussels
1 pint water
1 onion, skinned and chopped
1 stick of celery, scrubbed and chopped
1 carrot, scraped and chopped
1 clove of garlic, skinned and chopped
A bouquet garni
Salt and pepper
1 oz. butter
3 level tbsps. flour
Chopped parsley to garnish

Wash the mussels, thoroughly scrubbing each shell and scraping the joint to remove the filament; lift the shells out of the water with the hands, leaving behind the sediment and filaments. Put them into a large pan with the 1 pint fresh water, the vegetables, garlic, herbs, salt and pepper. Cover, bring to the boil and cook gently for a few minutes, shaking the pan over the heat. As the shells open, remove the mussels, keeping them on the half-shell; place in a dish and keep covered to prevent them from drying. Reduce the liquid a little by boiling and remove from the heat. Work together the butter and flour and stir in the liquid. Return the mixture to the pan, stirring well until it thickens. Pour the sauce over the mussels and sprinkle with parsley.

Scampi Provençale

1 onion, skinned and finely chopped
1 clove of garlic, skinned and finely chopped
1 oz. butter or 2–3 tbsps. cooking oil
¾–1 lb. tomatoes, peeled and chopped (or a 15-oz. can of tomatoes, drained)
4 tbsps. dry white wine
Salt and pepper
A pinch of sugar
1 tbsp. chopped parsley
8 oz. frozen scampi, thawed

Fry the onion and garlic gently in the butter or oil for about 5 minutes, until soft but not coloured. Add the tomatoes, wine, seasoning, sugar and parsley, stir well and simmer gently for about 10 minutes. Drain the scampi well, add to the sauce and continue simmering for about 5 minutes, or until they are just heated through. Serve with crusty French bread or boiled rice.

Fried Scampi

8 oz. scampi or Dublin Bay prawns
Seasoned flour
4 oz. plain flour
A pinch of salt
1 tbsp. oil
1 egg, separated
2–3 tbsps. water or milk and water
Fat for deep frying

Scallops au Gratin

If fresh scampi or prawns are used, discard their heads, remove the flesh from the shells and remove the dark veins; if frozen, allow to defrost, then drain well. Dip the prawns in the seasoned flour. Mix the plain flour, salt, oil and egg yolk with sufficient liquid to give a stiff batter which will coat the back of the spoon; beat until smooth. Just before cooking, whisk the egg white stiffly and fold it into the batter. Dip the scampi in the batter. Heat the fat until a cube of bread dropped into it takes 20–30 seconds to brown. Fry the scampi a few at a time until they are golden-brown, drain and serve with Tartare or tomato sauce.

Alternatively, the scampi can simply be coated with beaten egg and fresh breadcrumbs and fried until golden-brown.

Cockles, Winkles and Whelks

These small shellfish must be washed free of sand and then soaked for 2–3 hours before they are cooked. The most usual way of serving is to eat them cold, sprinkled with vinegar.

Cockles are cooked in a pan with a little water; heat gently, shaking the pan to prevent burning, for about 5 minutes, until the shells open.

Winkles and Whelks can be simmered in boiling salted water until tender.

Scallops au Gratin

8 scallops, prepared
$\frac{3}{4}$ pint milk
$1\frac{1}{2}$ oz. butter
$1\frac{1}{2}$ oz. flour
4 oz. cheese, grated
Salt and pepper
Browned crumbs

Grease 4 individual dishes or deep scallop shells. Cut each scallop into 2–3 pieces and simmer in a little of the milk until tender – about 10 minutes. Drain, reserving the milk, and make this up to $\frac{3}{4}$ pint.

Melt the butter in the pan, stir in the flour and cook for 2–3 minutes. Remove the pan from the heat and gradually stir in the milk. Bring to the boil and continue to stir until it thickens. Add 3 oz. of the cheese and some salt and pepper. Divide the fish between the dishes or shells and pour the sauce over. Mix the crumbs with the rest of the cheese and sprinkle over the top; brown under a hot grill.

Meat Cookery

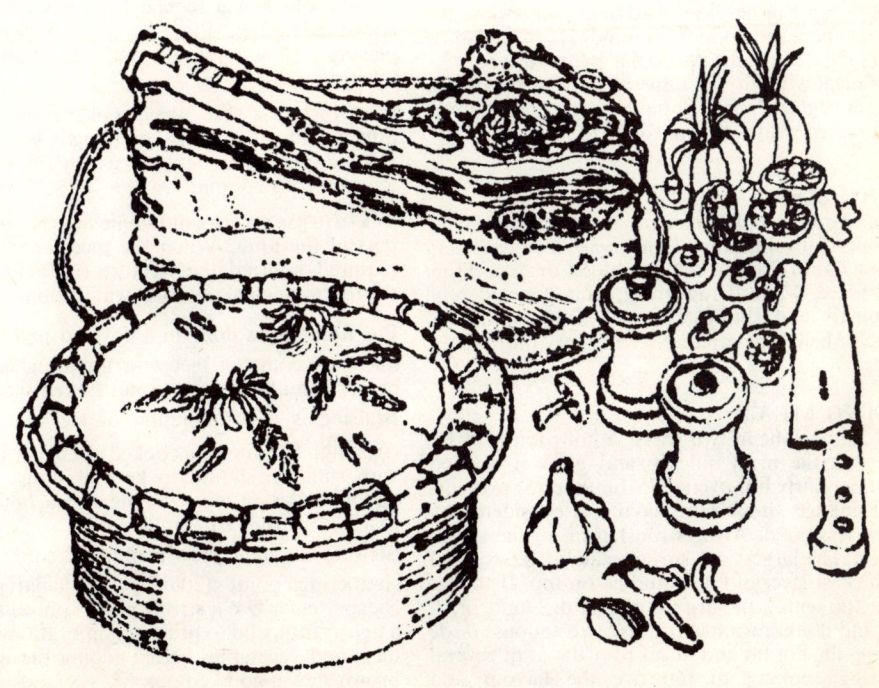

Meat supplies protein, some of the B vitamins and iron; the fat, which helps to give the meat some of its characteristic flavour, is of high energy value. The price varies according to cut – the most expensive cuts usually being the most tender; cheaper cuts need slower methods of cooking but have as much flavour and nutritional value as more expensive ones.

CHOICE OF MEAT
Find a reliable butcher who keeps a wide range of meat in prime condition. Never hesitate to ask his advice; he is an expert and will be pleased to help you choose the right cut for the dish you have in mind. He may also be willing to prepare or bone particular joints for you.

Choose meat without an undue amount of fat (which should never be discoloured or flabby); lean meat should be finely grained with a fine marbling of fat.

STORING MEAT
Unwrap and put on a plate or wrap in polythene leaving the ends open for ventilation. Don't wash it; if necessary wipe with a damp cloth to remove blood or dust. Store in a cool place. Minced raw meat, sausages and offal perish quickly and should be used within a day of purchase. Re-heat stews and casseroles very thoroughly.

ROASTING MEAT
Roasting can be done in two ways; a hot oven (425°F., mark 7) seals the meat quickly and gives it a good flavour, and a fairly hot oven (375°F., mark 5) prevents a lot of shrinkage, though the flavour is considered by some to be less good. Always roast meat in the centre of the oven. The largest cut surface should be exposed and the thickest layer of fat should be on top. If the fat is meagre, top with 2 oz. dripping or lard. Don't prick the meat, and if you turn or lift it use two spoons. *Baste* by spooning the hot fat and juices over the joint several times during cooking to improve the flavour and

juiciness of the meat. *Searing* gives the joint a browned outside. Fry on all sides in hot fat before roasting. Sprinkle with flour and salt $\frac{1}{4}$ hour before the meat is ready; this is called *Frothing* and gives a crisp outside.

ROASTING ON A GRID: the finished result will be less fatty.

ROASTING IN FOIL: the meat will not shrink so much and will be moist and tender. The foil should be opened for the last $\frac{1}{2}$ hour for the joint to crisp and brown.

ROASTING BAGS: as with foil the meat will not shrink, when cooked in a special plastic bag. These have the added advantage that the meat browns through the plastic. Follow manufacturer's directions for temperature and time.

ROASTING ON A SPIT: some cookers have a spit roasting attachment, or one can be bought separately. A joint roasted on an open spit has a much better flavour than an oven-roasted joint.

MEAT THERMOMETERS should be inserted into the thickest part of the joint. When the thermometer registers the required internal temperature (normally indicated on the thermometer) the meat will be done.

Pot Roasting is done in a covered pan and is suitable for small compact pieces or for 'tougher' cuts such as breast of mutton, topside and stuffed sheep's heart.

Braising is a combination of stewing, steaming and roasting. The meat is cooked over a bed of vegetables with sufficient liquid to keep it moist. For a 'roast' flavour bake or roast the meat in a hot oven (425°F., mark 7) for the last $\frac{1}{2}$ hour.

Stewing is a long, slow method of cooking in liquid at simmering point (205°F.), particularly suitable for cheaper cuts. Use a strong pan to prevent burning, with a tightly fitting lid to prevent evaporation. Lightly brown meat and vegetables before adding the liquid to give a brown stew a good colour.

Boiling: meat is simmered at 205°F., usually with root vegetables for flavour. Barely cover the meat with water and bring slowly to simmering point; the vessels should have a tightly fitting lid.

Grilling is suitable only for best-quality meat – tender chops, steak, liver, kidneys, gammon and back rashers. Season with salt and pepper and brush with melted fat or oil before cooking in a ready-heated grill.

Frying: use meats of the same quality as for grilling and cook in hot fat or oil.

PICKLING MEAT

Silverside or brisket of beef, leg or belly of pork, ox tongue and pig's head are particularly suited to pickling or salting. The only equipment required is a large earthenware crock, bowl or basin or a polythene bowl or pail, with a board or lid to keep out the dust.

Home pickling is best done in cold weather. Trim and wash the meat, then rub it over with salt to remove all traces of blood.

Of the two methods given below, the first is the easier, but the second gives a more interesting flavour to the meat.

Wet Pickle

Put 1 gallon water, $1\frac{1}{2}$ lb. bay or common salt, 1 oz. saltpetre and 6 oz. brown sugar in a large pan, bring to the boil and boil for 15–20 minutes, skimming carefully. Strain the liquid into the container you are using, allow to cool, put in the meat and cover.

Dry Pickle

Pound $\frac{1}{2}$ lb. bay salt, mix with $\frac{1}{2}$ lb. common salt, $\frac{1}{2}$ lb. brown sugar, 1 oz. saltpetre, $\frac{1}{2}$ oz. black pepper and 1 level tsp. allspice. Rub the meat daily with this mixture, leaving it meantime in the covered container.

Pickling Time

A thick cut of beef needs about 10 days, whereas a thinner cut, or a pig's head split in half, may be sufficiently salted in 4–5 days.

Cooking Pickled Meat

Remove the meat from the pickle and wash it thoroughly in cold water. If you wish, soak it for 1 hour in cold water before cooking. Tie the meat up neatly if necessary, put it into a pan of cold water, bring slowly to the boil and skim. Add some sliced carrot, turnip and onion, a few peppercorns and a bouquet garni and let the water simmer very gently until the meat is tender; allow 1 hour per lb. for joints up to 3 lb., a total of 3–4 hours for joints weighing 4–5 lb. (The liquid may be used for making soups.)

CARVING

When meat is well carved it looks attractive and goes further. Given a sharp knife, it is an art most people can easily master. Use a steel or patent sharpener to keep the knife in trim. A sharp two-pronged fork will hold the meat steady and must have a guard to protect your hand if the knife slips. A meat dish with prongs is a great help, and the meat should be put on the dish while the gravy is served separately. Meat is usually best cut across the grain (though the undercut is carved with the grain). Learn where the bone is and how the meat and fat are distributed. Carved meat should be served on very hot plates as it cools surprisingly quickly. Beef and veal (except fillet) are carved very thinly, pork and lamb in slices about $\frac{1}{4}$ inch thick. If the joint has a bone, take the knife right up to it so that the bone is left clean.

Sirloin of Beef

Stand the joint on its back with the fillet uppermost; remove the strings. Carve the fillet, loosening each slice from the bone with the knife-tip; turn the joint over and carve in long slices right up to the bone.

Rib of Beef

Stand the joint on edge on the bone. Slice downwards along the full length of the joint, cutting each slice down to the bone and slanting a little away from the cut edge, so that the bone is left clean. Support the slices with the fork to prevent their breaking.

Boneless Joints of Beef

Carve across the grain, usually horizontally. In the case of a long piece of roast fillet, however, you will need to carve downwards.

Stuffed Breast of Lamb or Veal

Cut downwards in fairly thick slices, right through the joint.

Fillet of Veal

The bone is usually removed and replaced by stuffing. Cut across the grain (i.e., horizontally) into medium-thick slices, right across the joint.

If the bone has been left in, cut the meat down to it on one side, then turn the joint over and do the same on the underside.

Leg of Lamb

Begin by cutting a wedge-shaped slice from the centre of the meatier side of the joint. Carve slices from each side of the cut, gradually turning the knife to get larger slices and ending parallel to the bone. Turn the joint over and carve in long slices.

Shoulder of Lamb

Cut a thick wedge-shaped slice from the centre of the meatiest side of the joint. Carve small slices from each side down to the shank and the shoulder-bone. Turn the joint over and carve in long slices.

Best End of Neck of Lamb

Cut the joint right through, downwards, into cutlets. (This is easier if it has previously been chined.)

Saddle of Lamb

First carve the meat from the top of the joint in long slices, cutting downwards to and parallel with the backbone. Do this at each side of the bone, taking about 4 slices. Then carve diagonal slices from either side of the saddle.

Loin of Pork

Sever the chined bone from the chop bones and put to one side. Divide into chops by cutting between the bones and the scored crackling.

Boned and Rolled Pork

Remove the string from each part of the joint as it is carved. Cut through the crackling where it was scored half-way along the joint. Lift off the crackling and cut into pieces. Carve the meat into slices.

Leg of Pork

Use the point of the knife to cut through the crackling; it is usually easier to remove it and then divide it into portions. Carve as for leg of lamb, but medium-thick.

Spare Rib of Pork

Cut between the score marks into moderately thick slices.

BEEF

CHOICE

1. The lean should be bright red, the fat a creamy-yellow.
2. There should be small flecks of fat through the lean; this fat (called 'marbling') helps to keep the lean moist and tender when the meat is cooking.
3. Avoid meat with a line of gristle between lean and fat, which usually suggests it has come from an old animal.
4. The quantities to allow refer to the weight of meat as bought.

CUTS AND METHOD OF COOKING

SIRLOIN: a large joint from the ribs and including the undercut; usually sold on the bone, but can also be boned and rolled. It is always roasted.

With bone, allow 8–12 oz. per person.

Without bone, allow 6–8 oz. per person.

RIBS: a fairly large joint, next to the sirloin and without the undercut. It can be bought on the bone or boned and rolled, and is roasted.

Quantities as for sirloin.

TOPSIDE: a lean joint, containing no bone and therefore economical. It is usually roasted, but can also be braised or pot roasted and is more tender when cooked in these two ways.

Allow 6–8 oz. per person.

BRISKET: can be sold on or off the bone and is often salted. It is rather a fatty joint but has a good flavour. Brisket can be slow-roasted or braised; when salted, it should be boiled.

With bone, allow 8–12 oz. per person.

Without bone, allow 6–8 oz. per person.

SILVERSIDE: a boneless joint. Needs long, slow cooking, such as boiling or braising. Often salted.

Allow 8–12 oz. per person.

AITCH-BONE: a cheaper joint, but has a large bone and tends to be rather fatty on the top of the joint. Usually roasted, but also boiled or braised. Sometimes salted and then boiled.

Allow 12 oz. per person.

FLANK: a cheaper cut, known as thick or thin flank, that comes from the belly of the animal and tends to be coarse. Needs slow, moist cooking, such as stewing, braising or pot roasting.

Allow 6–8 oz. per person.

LEG AND SHIN: cheap cuts containing a lot of bone, but quite lean and with a good flavour. Long, slow cooking is needed, such as stewing. They can be used for curries, goulash, stews, meat pies and puddings.

Allow 6–8 oz. per person.

FILLET AND RUMP STEAK ENTRECOTE, etc.: *see Steaks, later.*

CHUCK OR BLADE STEAK: a cheaper cut, without bone, taken from the shoulder. Fairly lean and suitable for stewing, casseroles, pies and so on.

Allow 6–8 oz. per person.

STEWING STEAK: this is a general term that covers chuck, blade, leg, clod and sticking piece, buttock steak, shin and flank, and as it could be any of these cuts, it is often slightly cheaper than a specific cut such as chuck.

Accompaniments for Beef

With a roast joint, serve Yorkshire pudding and horse-radish sauce or mustard.

Suitable accompaniments for steaks are suggested in the separate section which follows overleaf.

Roast Beef

Oven temperature: hot (425°F., mark 7)

Wipe the meat, trim if necessary, then weigh it and calculate the cooking time, allowing 20 minutes per lb. plus 20 minutes if the meat is on the bone; 25 minutes per lb. plus 25 minutes if rolled. Put the meat in a roasting tin so that the thickest layer of fat is uppermost and the cut sides are exposed to the heat. Add about 2 oz. dripping if the meat is lean. Put the joint in the middle of the oven and cook uncovered for the calculated time, basting from time to time with the juices from the tin. Serve slightly rare, accompanied by Yorkshire Pudding, horseradish sauce, thin brown gravy and vegetables as desired.

To roast meat in a moderate oven (350°F., mark 4), which tends to give a moister joint, prepare and cook as above, but allow 27 minutes per lb. plus 27 minutes for joints on the bone; 33 minutes per lb. plus 33 minutes for rolled joints.

SUITABLE JOINTS: sirloin, ribs, rump, topside, aitch-bone.

Pot Roast of Beef

4 lb. topside or brisket, in a piece
Salt and pepper
1 oz. fat or oil
2–3 cloves
1 onion, skinned
½ pint water

Use a heavy-based pan on top of the stove or an iron or heavy enamelled casserole with a well-fitting lid in the oven.

Season the meat on all sides and fry it in the hot fat or oil in the pan or casserole until lightly browned all over. Stick the cloves into the onion, add it to the meat, with the water, cover and cook over a gentle heat for about 3 hours, or until the meat is tender, turning it occasionally. Alternatively, cook the meat in a cool oven (300°F., mark 2). If liked a few thickly sliced vegetables such as onions, carrots, parsnips or turnips can be added about 1 hour before cooking is complete. Remove the meat, lay the vegetables in the bottom of the casserole or pan, then replace the meat on top of the vegetables, cover and continue cooking. Serve the meat hot, surrounded by any vegetables which were added.

To make a gravy, pour off any excess fat, add ½ pint stock or vegetable water to the casserole and stir round to mix in any browned residue sticking to the bottom. Bring to the boil, season well and serve. Clear gravy is the more usual choice, but it can be thickened by the addition of 3–4 level tsps. flour or cornflour, blended with the stock or water.

Braised Beef

4 lb. topside, silverside or rolled ribs of beef in a piece
Salt and pepper
½ oz. fat or oil
3–4 onions, skinned and sliced
3–4 carrots, peeled and left whole or sliced
1 small turnip, peeled and quartered
1–2 sticks of celery, sliced
1 parsnip, peeled and quartered
2–3 bacon rinds
1 bay leaf
A few parsley stalks
3–4 peppercorns

Meat can be braised on top of the cooker in a solid-based pan or in a casserole in a warm oven (325°F., mark 3). The container must have a tightly-fitting lid. Season the meat well on all sides and fry in the hot fat or oil until lightly browned all over. Remove it and fry the vegetables and bacon rinds in the same fat or oil until lightly browned. Pour off the excess fat. Add the bay leaf, parsley stalks and peppercorns, more seasoning and water to come about three-quarters up the vegetables. Put the meat on to the bed of vegetables, cover with a lid and simmer until it is tender. Allow about 2 hours for meat up to 3 lb. and 25 minutes per lb. plus 25 minutes for larger pieces. Baste 2 or 3 times during the cooking. Remove the lid and finish in a hot oven (425°F., mark 7) for ½ hour, until brown. Serve sliced, with a gravy made from the cooking liquid – left clear or thickened with a little blended flour or cornflour (2 level tsps. to ½ pint of liquid).

Stewing steak can be sliced and braised as above for about 2 hours.

Boiled Beef with Vegetables and Herb Dumplings

A 4-lb. piece of fresh brisket or silverside
Water to cover
Salt (2 level tsps. per lb. of meat)
A bouquet garni
3–4 onions, skinned and left whole
4–6 small carrots, peeled and left whole or sliced
2–3 leeks, cleaned and cut in 2-inch lengths, or
 1–2 sticks of celery
1 small turnip, peeled and quartered

For the Dumplings
4 oz. self-raising flour
Salt
½ tsp. mixed herbs
2 oz. shredded suet

Weigh the meat and calculate the cooking time, allowing 30 minutes per lb. and 30 minutes over for meat up to 3 lb.; 45 minutes per lb. for joints any larger than this – i.e. 3 hours for a 4-lb. piece. Put it in a large pan with the salt and enough water to cover, bring slowly to the boil, skim off any scum that rises, add the bouquet garni, cover with a lid, reduce the heat and leave to simmer. Three-quarters of an hour before the cooking is complete, add the vegetables and continue cooking.

To make the dumplings, combine all the ingredients and bind with water to give an elastic dough; divide into 12 small pieces and roll into balls. Add to the pan about ¼ hour before cooking is complete, cover and simmer for 15–20 minutes, or until the dumplings swell and rise to the top of the pan. If the pan is rather full, pour off some of the cooking liquid into a separate pan, bring this to the boil, drop in the dumplings and cook as above.

Remove the bouquet garni and serve the meat hot,

surrounded by the vegetables and dumplings. Any meat left over is excellent used cold for sandwiches or served with salad.

Salted brisket, silverside or belly of pork can also be cooked in this way. If very salty, soak for 3–4 hours before cooking, rinse, then cover with fresh water and proceed as for unsalted meat, but allow 1 hour per lb. for joints up to 3 lb. and 3–4 hours for joints weighing 4–5 lb.

Spiced Silverside

A 4-lb. piece of salted silverside
1 onion, skinned and sliced
2 carrots, peeled and sliced
1 small turnip, peeled and sliced
1–2 sticks of celery, chopped
8 cloves
4 oz. soft brown sugar
½ level tsp. dry mustard
1 level tsp. ground cinnamon
Juice of 1 orange

Oven temperature: moderate (350°F., mark 4)

Soak the meat for several hours or overnight, then rinse it, put in a large pan with the vegetables, cover with water and bring slowly to the boil. Remove any scum, cover with a lid and simmer until tender, allowing about 1 hour for 1 lb., 2–3 hours for 2–3 lb. and 3–4 hours for 4–5 lb. Allow to cool in the liquid. Drain, put into a roasting tin and stick the cloves into the fat. Mix together the remaining ingredients and spread over the meat. Bake in the centre of the oven for ¾–1 hour, basting from time to time. Serve hot or cold.

If you wish, you can press the meat after cooking it until tender. Fit it snugly into a casserole or foil-lined tin, spoon a few tbsps. of the liquor over and place a board or plate on top, with a heavy weight. Leave in a cold place.

STEAKS

RUMP
The joint next to the sirloin and one of the commonest cuts used for grilling or frying. The 'point' is considered the best part for tenderness and flavour.

FILLET
The undercut of the sirloin, probably one of the best-known and the most expensive of the cuts used for grilling and frying. Very tender, although it usually has less flavour than rump. The 'centre' or 'eye' of the fillet is considered the best part. The fillet is often cut and shaped into small rounds, known as Tournedos, weighing about 5 oz. each.

A Filet Mignon is a small round steak, weighing about 3 oz., cut from the end of the fillet.

CHATEAUBRIAND
A thick slice taken from the middle of the fillet, generally regarded as the most superb cut of all. It can weigh about 12 oz. Grill and serve with maître d'hotel butter.

SIRLOIN (OR CONTRE-FILET)
Cut into two parts. Porterhouse steak is cut from the thick end of the sirloin, giving a large juicy piece that can weigh 30 oz.; when it is cooked on the bone it is called T-bone steak in the United States. Minute steak

is a very thin steak from the upper part of the sirloin, weighing 5–6 oz., without any trimmings of fat.

ENTRECÔTE
By definition this is the part of the meat between the ribs of beef, but a slice cut from the sirloin or rump is often served under this name.

Preparation of Steaks
Very little need be done. Trim the steak to a good shape if necessary and wipe it well. Salt and pepper or 'seasoned' salt and 'seasoned' pepper can be sprinkled over the meat before cooking; if there is doubt as to its tenderness the steak can be beaten with a rolling pin or steak hammer.

Cooking Steaks
TO GRILL: brush with melted butter or oil and put under a pre-heated grill. Cook under a medium heat, turning them regularly and using a blunt tool so as not to pierce the meat and allow juices to escape.

TO FRY: if the steak is large, brown it quickly on both sides in shallow oil or melted butter, then reduce the heat and cook gently for the remaining time. With small steaks, fry over medium heat for half the cooking time on one side, then turn them and cook for remaining time.

Cooking Times for Steaks (in minutes)

Thickness	Rare	Medium Rare	Well-done
$\frac{3}{4}$ in.	5	9–10	12–15
1 in.	6–7	10	15
1$\frac{1}{2}$ ins.	10	12–14	18–20

TO SERVE: a piece of maître d'hôtel butter, placed on each steak before it is served, is the traditional but not invariable accompaniment. Other accompaniments are matchstick or chipped potatoes, grilled tomatoes and mushrooms.

Steak Diane

4 pieces of fillet steak, $\frac{1}{4}$ inch thick
1 oz. butter
2 tbsps. oil
2 tbsps. Worcestershire sauce
1 tbsp. lemon juice
1 tbsp. grated onion
2 tsps. chopped parsley

Fry the steaks in the butter and oil for 1–2 minutes on each side. Remove them (keeping them hot) and add the Worcestershire sauce and lemon juice to the juices in the pan. Stir well and warm through; add the onion and parsley and cook gently for 1 minute. Serve the sauce spooned over the steaks.

Fondue Bourguignonne

6–8 oz. fillet or rump steak per person
Oil for frying
Finely chopped onion or shallot
Finely chopped parsley
Chutney (optional)
Roughly chopped pineapple (optional)
Dips *(see below)*

Cut the steak into 1-inch cubes with a sharp knife; arrange on plates. Place a metal container of oil over a spirit stove to heat to around 375°F.

Give each guest a long-handled wooden skewer or two-pronged fondue fork for spearing the meat cubes, which they cook in the hot oil and then cool a little, or transfer to a second fork. The cooked cube of meat is then dipped in one of the sauces given below, then in a mixture of chopped onion and parsley. Chopped chutney and pineapple also make a good mixture for this purpose. Have crusty bread as an accompaniment, and if you wish, offer two or more of the following as side dishes: chopped banana, sliced gherkins, sliced olives, chopped parsley, chopped chives.

Horseradish Dip: Whisk together 6 tbsps. whipped cream, 3 tbsps. horseradish sauce and some freshly ground black pepper.
Curry Dip: Mix together 3 tbsps. home-made mayonnaise, 3 tbsps. whipped cream, 1 level tsp. curry powder and 1 tsp. chutney sauce.

Paprika Dip: Beat 3 oz. cream cheese until soft, combine with 4 tbsps. home-made mayonnaise, 1 level tsp. paprika and 3 gherkins, finely chopped.
Tomato Dip: Mix together 3 tbsps. home-made mayonnaise, 3 tbsps. whipped cream, 2 tbsps. tomato ketchup, 2 tsps. condensed tomato purée and a good dash of Worcestershire sauce.
Mustard Dip: Blend 1$\frac{1}{2}$ level tsps. dry mustard with 2 tsps. port. Add 3 tbsps. home-made mayonnaise and 4–6 tbsps. whipped cream.
Hollandaise or Tartare Sauce (see Sauces chapter) may also be used.

Beef Olives

8 thin slices of topside
Seasoned flour
1 oz. fat or oil
$\frac{3}{4}$ pint stock or water
2 onions, sliced

For the Stuffing
2 oz. shredded suet
2 oz. ham or bacon, chopped
4 oz. fresh breadcrumbs
2 tsps. chopped parsley
$\frac{1}{4}$ level tsp. mixed herbs
Grated rind of $\frac{1}{2}$ a lemon
Salt and pepper
Beaten egg to mix

Oven temperature: moderate (350°F., mark 4)

Combine the ingredients for the stuffing and bind with the egg. Spread each slice of meat with stuffing, roll up, secure with fine string and toss in seasoned flour. Heat the fat or oil in a frying pan and brown the beef olives lightly, remove and place in a casserole. Add 2 level tbsps. of the seasoned flour to the frying pan, brown well, gradually add the stock and bring it to the boil; season to taste and pour over the olives. Add the onion slices, divided into rings, cover and cook in the centre of the oven for 1$\frac{1}{2}$ hours. Remove the strings before serving the beef olives.

Boeuf Stroganoff

1$\frac{1}{2}$ lb. rump steak, thinly sliced
3 level tbsps. seasoned flour
2 oz. butter
1 onion, skinned and sliced thinly
$\frac{1}{2}$ lb. mushrooms, sliced
Salt and pepper
$\frac{1}{2}$ pint soured cream

Beat the steak, trim, cut into strips $\frac{1}{4}$ inch by 2 inches and coat with the seasoned flour. Fry the meat in 1 oz. of the butter till golden-brown – about 5–7 minutes. Cook the onion and mushrooms in the remaining 1 oz. butter for 3–4 minutes, season to taste and add to the beef. Warm the soured cream and stir into the meat mixture. Serve with plain boiled or buttered rice.

Filet de Boeuf en Croûte

2 lb. fillet of beef
Salt and pepper
2 oz. butter
1 tbsp. oil
8 oz. liver pâté
An 11-oz. pkt. of frozen puff pastry (thawed)
1 egg, beaten
Watercress and tomato to garnish

Oven temperature: fairly hot (400 F., mark 6)

Place the meat on a board and, using a sharp knife, trim off and discard all the excess fat and sinewy parts. Sprinkle all over with salt and pepper. Tie some fine string round the meat at intervals to form it into a neat shape; carry the string round the end and across to the other side, as for a parcel, and tie firmly.

Heat 1 oz. butter with the oil in a frying-pan and fry the meat until browned all over, turning it frequently. Put the joint in a roasting tin, and dot with the remaining butter. Cook at the top of the oven for 10 minutes. Remove and leave in a cool place until cold; untie the string.

Mix the pâté in a small basin until smooth, and season to taste. Using a small palette knife, spread pâté over the top and sides of the meat. Roll out the pastry about ⅛ inch thick, into a rectangle large enough to cover the meat well; place the beef, pâté side down, in the centre of the pastry, then spread pâté over the rest of the surface. Brush one long side of the pastry with beaten egg, fold the unbrushed side over the meat, fold the second side over and press together. Cut the top piece of pastry at an angle, then cut straight across, and reserve this piece for decoration. Brush the inner edge of the remaining pastry with egg and fold up, on to the join. Raise the oven temperature to hot (425 F., mark 7). Place the meat join-side down in a roasting tin. Roll out the pastry trimmings and cut into leaves. Brush the pastry surface with beaten egg, arrange the leaves in the centre and brush them with egg. Bake in the centre of the oven for 40 minutes, until the pastry is golden. Arrange on a flat platter, with a garnish of watercress and tomato, and serve hot, accompanied by creamed potatoes and buttered asparagus, or other vegetable. *(Serves 6.)*

Carbonnade of Beef

2 lb. stewing steak, cut into ½-inch cubes
Salt and pepper
2 oz. fat or oil
3 oz. lean bacon, chopped
1½ oz. plain flour
½ pint beer
½ pint stock or water
2–3 tbsps. vinegar
1 lb. onions, skinned and chopped
A clove of garlic, skinned and chopped
A bouquet garni

Oven temperature: cool (300 F., mark 2)

Season the meat and fry in the fat or oil until brown – about 5 minutes. Add the bacon and continue cooking for a few minutes. Remove the meat and bacon from the pan, stir in the flour and brown lightly. Gradually add the beer, stock and vinegar, stirring continuously until the mixture thickens. Fill a casserole with layers of meat, bacon, onion and garlic. Pour the sauce over and add the bouquet garni. Cover and cook for 3½–4 hours towards the bottom of the oven. Add a little more beer while cooking, if necessary. Just before serving, remove the bouquet garni. Serve with plain boiled potatoes.

Boeuf Bourguignonne

2 lb. topside
1½ oz. fat or oil
A 4-oz. piece of streaky bacon, diced
1 level tbsp. flour
3 tbsps. brandy
¼ pint Burgundy or other red wine
¼ pint stock
A pinch of thyme
½ a bay leaf
1 clove of garlic, skinned and chopped
Salt and pepper
6–8 shallots or tiny onions, skinned and left whole

Oven temperature: warm (325°F., mark 3)

Cut the meat into 2-inch squares. Heat 1 oz. of the fat or oil in a large pan and fry the meat until browned, a few pieces at a time; drain and place in a large oven-proof casserole. Fry the bacon in the fat remaining in the pan, add the flour and allow to brown, stirring occasionally. Transfer to the casserole. Warm the brandy, ignite and pour over the meat while it is still flaming. Add the wine and stock, thyme, bay leaf and garlic, and season well. Cover and cook in the centre of the oven for 2 hours. Melt the remaining ½ oz. fat or oil in a small pan, add the shallots and brown them; drain thoroughly and add to the meat. Cook for a further ½ hour in a cool oven (300°F., mark 2) until the meat is tender. Remove the bay leaf before serving.

This classic French dish needs no additional vegetables except creamy mashed potatoes.

Swiss Steak

1 tbsp. oil
2 large onions, skinned and sliced
1½ lb. chuck or blade steak
1 oz. flour
Salt and pepper
8 tomatoes, skinned
A 14-oz. can of tomato juice

Oven temperature: moderate (350°F., mark 4)

Heat the oil and sauté the onions until clear. Cut the steak into 8 portions, dredge with seasoned flour and brown in the oil. Add the tomatoes and tomato juice. Cover, and cook for 1½–2 hours.

(See colour picture facing page 96)

Goulash

1 lb. stewing steak, cut into ½-inch cubes
3 level tbsps. seasoned flour
2 medium-sized onions, skinned and chopped
1 green pepper, de-seeded and chopped
1 oz. fat or oil
2 level tsps. paprika
3 tbsps. tomato paste
A little grated nutmeg
Salt and pepper
2 oz. flour
½ pint stock
2 large tomatoes, skinned and quartered
A bouquet garni
¼ pint beer

Oven temperature: warm (325°F., mark 3)

Coat the meat with seasoned flour. Fry the onions and pepper lightly in the fat or oil for about 3–4 minutes. Add the meat and fry lightly on all sides until golden-brown – about 5 minutes. Add the paprika and fry for about a minute longer. Stir in the tomato paste, nutmeg, seasoning and flour and cook for a further 2–3 minutes. Add the stock, tomatoes and bouquet garni, put into a casserole and cook just below the centre of the oven for 1½–2 hours. Add the beer, cook for a few minutes longer and remove the bouquet garni. Serve with sauerkraut and caraway-flavoured dumplings, or with a green salad.

(See colour picture facing page 97)

Cornish Pasties

12 oz. chuck or blade steak
4 oz. raw potato, peeled and diced
1 small onion, skinned and chopped
Salt and pepper
12 oz. shortcrust pastry *(see Pastry chapter)*

Oven temperature: hot (425°F., mark 7)

Cut the steak into small pieces, add the potato and onion and season well. Divide the pastry into four and roll each piece into a round about 8 inches in diameter. Divide the meat mixture between the pastry rounds, damp the edges, draw the edges of the pastry together to form a seam across the top and flute the edges with the fingers. Place on a baking tray and bake at the top of the oven for 15 minutes to brown the pastry, then reduce the heat to warm (325°F., mark 3) and cook for a further hour. Serve hot or cold.

Hamburgers

1 lb. lean beef, e.g. chuck, shoulder or rump steak
½ an onion, grated (optional)
Salt and pepper
Melted butter or oil for coating or a little fat for shallow frying

Choose lean meat and have it minced finely by the butcher. Mix well with the onion (if used) and a generous amount of salt and pepper. Shape lightly into 6–8 round flat cakes. To cook, brush sparingly with melted butter or oil and grill for 4–6 minutes turning once, or fry in a little fat in a frying pan, turning them once and allowing the same amount of time.

Hamburgers can be served rare or well done, according to personal preference, hence the variation in cooking time.

Hamburgers

Traditionally, hamburgers contain no other ingredients, but they can be varied as follows:

1. Add any of the following when mixing the hamburgers:

2–4 oz. grated cooking cheese
1 tbsp. sweet pickle
1–2 tsps. made mustard
1 level tsp. mixed herbs
1 tbsp. chopped parsley
2 oz. mushrooms, sliced
2–3 tomatoes, skinned and chopped

2. Make the hamburgers into thin cakes and wrap each with a rasher of bacon secured with a cocktail stick, then grill gently, turning them frequently.

Steak and Kidney Pudding

8 oz. suet crust pastry (*see Pastry chapter*)
½–¾ lb. stewing steak, cut into ½-inch cubes
¼ lb. kidney
2 level tbsps. seasoned flour
1 onion, skinned and chopped
Water

Half-fill a steamer or large saucepan with water and put it on to boil. Grease a 1½-pint pudding basin. Cut off a quarter of the pastry to make the lid and roll out the remainder into a round large enough to line the basin. Coat the meat with the seasoned flour. Remove the skin and core from the kidneys, cut into slices and coat with seasoned flour. Fill the basin with the meat, kidney, onion, and 2–3 tbsps. water. Roll out the pastry for the lid to a round the size of the top of the basin and damp the edge of it. Place on top of the meat and seal the edges of the pastry well. Cover with greased greaseproof paper or foil and steam over rapidly boiling water for about 4 hours.

Variation
The meat can be prepared and stewed with the onion for about 2 hours earlier in the day or the previous night before being used for the filling. In this case reduce the steaming time to 1½–2 hours.

Steak and Mushroom Pie

1 lb. stewing steak
2 level tbsps. seasoned flour
1 onion, peeled and sliced thinly
Water
4 oz. mushrooms, sliced
1 pkt. bought puff pastry (4–6 oz., according to size of dish)
Egg to glaze

Oven temperature: hot (425°F., mark 7)

Wipe the meat, cut into small, even pieces and coat with seasoned flour. Put the meat and onions into a pan and just cover with water. Bring to the boil, reduce the heat and simmer for 1½–2 hours, or until the meat is tender. (Alternatively, the meat can be cooked for 2 hours in a covered casserole in the centre of a moderate oven – 350°F., mark 4.)

Put the meat and mushrooms into a dish with enough of the gravy to half-fill it. Roll out the pastry 1 inch larger than the top of the dish. Cut off a ½-inch strip from round the edge of the pastry and put this strip round the damped rim of the dish. Damp the edges of the pastry edge with water and put on the top of the pie, without stretching the pastry; trim if necessary and flake the edges. Decorate if liked and brush with beaten egg. Bake near the top of the oven for 20 minutes. Reduce the heat to moderate (350°F., mark 4) and cook for about a further 20 minutes.

Variations
Replace the mushrooms by one of the following:
1. 4 oz. lamb's kidneys: wipe and core, removing any skin, cut into small pieces and add to the meat in the pie dish before covering with the pastry.
2. 2–3 carrots, peeled and sliced: add to the meat in the pie dish before covering with the pastry.

Cottage Pie *(Shepherd's Pie)*

1 lb. potatoes
2 tbsps. milk
½ oz. butter
Salt and pepper
1 onion, skinned and chopped
A little dripping
8 oz. minced cold beef
Stock
1 tbsp. parsley, chopped, or 1 level tsp. mixed herbs

Oven temperature: fairly hot (375°F., mark 5)

Boil the potatoes, drain and mash them with the milk, butter and seasoning. Fry the onion in a little dripping for about 5 minutes and mix in the minced meat, with a little stock, seasoning and parsley or mixed herbs. Put the prepared meat mixture into an ovenproof dish and cover the top with mashed potato. Mark the top with a fork and bake for 25–30 minutes in the top of the oven, until the surface is crisp and browned.

Variations
1. Add a small can of tomatoes, drained and chopped.
2. Add a small can of baked beans.
3. Mix 1–2 tbsps. of pickle with the meat or put it in a layer at the bottom of the dish.
4. Use 8 oz. fresh minced beef in place of the cooked meat; in this case, add it to the onion in the frying pan and cook for about 10 minutes, stirring well, before adding the stock, etc., and putting the mixture into the ovenproof dish.
5. Top the mashed potatoes with a little grated cheese before baking the pie.

Note: There is much controversy about Cottage and Shepherd's Pies. Some people say that Shepherd's Pie is made only with lamb; others say that Cottage Pie is made with minced meat and Shepherd's Pie with sliced meat.

Steak and Kidney Pudding

Curried Beef

1 lb. stewing steak, cut into ½-inch cubes
2 oz. fat or oil
2 large onions, skinned and chopped
1 cooking apple, skinned and chopped
1 level tbsp. curry powder
1 oz. flour
1 pint stock or water
Salt and pepper
1 tbsp. chutney
2 oz. sultanas
2 tomatoes, skinned and chopped
A squeeze of lemon juice

Oven temperature: moderate (350 F., mark 4)

Fry the meat in the fat or oil until brown. Drain well and put into a casserole. Fry the onions and apple in the remaining fat and add to the meat. Fry the curry powder, add the flour and cook together for 2–3 minutes. Add the stock gradually and bring to the boil; add the seasoning and remaining ingredients and cook for 2–3 minutes, then pour over the meat. Cover the casserole and cook gently in the centre of the oven for 2 hours. Adjust the seasoning as required and serve the curry with boiled rice.

Note: Cold roast beef can be used in a curry. Prepare the sauce as above and add the cubed meat just before putting the dish in the oven; it will need only 30–40 minutes' cooking. Alternatively, make a curry sauce (*see Sauces chapter*), add the meat and simmer for 10–15 minutes until the beef is heated through.

Calcutta Beef Curry

1 level tsp. coriander powder
1 level tsp. turmeric powder
1 level tsp. chilli powder
A pinch of black pepper
A pinch of ground ginger
½ pint coconut milk
1 onion, skinned and sliced
1 clove of garlic, skinned and crushed
1 oz. butter
1 lb. stewing steak, cubed
½ pint stock
Salt and lemon juice

Mix the powdered ingredients and make into a paste with a little of the coconut milk. Fry the onion and garlic in the butter until tender and add the paste, then fry for a further 3–4 minutes. Add the meat and stock, bring slowly to the boil and simmer for about 1 hour. Add the remaining coconut milk, some salt and lemon juice and serve at once, accompanied by boiled rice and a fruit or vegetable sambol.

COCONUT MILK: Traditionally made from fresh coconut, but a good substitute can be gained by infusing 1–2 tbsps. desiccated coconut in about ½ pint boiling water, then squeezing out the liquid through a fine tea strainer.

Curried Mince

1½ oz. fat or oil
2 medium-sized onions, skinned and chopped
1 cooking apple, peeled and chopped
1 tbsp. curry powder
1 level tbsp. flour
½ pint stock
1 tbsp. chutney
2 oz. sultanas
1 lb. raw minced beef
Lemon slices for garnish

Heat 1 oz. of the fat or oil and fry the onions and apple until brown. Remove from the frying pan and put into a saucepan. To the remaining fat add the curry powder and flour and cook together for 2–3 minutes; gradually add the stock, bring to the boil and cook for 1–2 minutes. Stir in the chutney and sultanas, then add to the saucepan and simmer for 20–30 minutes. Cook the mince in the remaining ½ oz. of fat and add to the sauce; continue to simmer the mince for 15 minutes. Serve in a shallow dish with boiled rice and lemon slices to garnish.

Dry Beef Curry

1 level tbsp. coriander powder
1 level tsp. turmeric powder
¼ level tsp. chilli powder
½ level tsp. cumin powder
A pinch of ground cinnamon
2 cloves
1 bay leaf
Tamarind water or diluted vinegar
2 oz. butter
1 onion, skinned and finely chopped
1 clove of garlic, skinned and finely chopped
1 tsp. curry paste
1 lb. stewing steak, cut into ½-inch cubes
½ pint stock or water
Salt to taste

Mix the spices and tamarind water to form a paste. Melt the butter and fry the onion and garlic, then fry the spices and curry paste thoroughly, stirring constantly. Add the meat and cook slowly for about 1 hour, stirring occasionally. Add the stock, cover and cook gently for another hour, till the liquid is absorbed. Adjust the seasoning, if necessary and serve with boiled rice or lentil dhal and with sambols (*see below*).

ACCOMPANIMENTS FOR CURRIES (SAMBOLS)

Boiled rice is a traditional accompaniment but there are also many other side dishes, known as Sambols, without which no curry is considered really complete.

Some can be bought ready to eat and others need

Dry Beef Curry

some preparation. They are usually served in small dishes.

CHAPATTIS: Large unleavened girdle cakes which can sometimes be bought from shops in this country specialising in Eastern foods.

PAPPADUMS: Thin wafer-like biscuits that can be bought in tins. To cook, fry one at a time in a little hot fat until crisp, holding them down with a spoon as they swell in cooking; alternatively heat for 1–2 minutes under a hot grill.

GHERKINS: Use whole or sliced.

MELON: Cut into cubes, removing skin and pips.

BANANAS: Peel and slice thinly. Sprinkle with lemon juice to prevent browning.

GREEN PEPPER: Slice, removing pith and pips.

TOMATOES: Slice thinly.

ONION: Skin and slice thinly.

RELISHES: Such as chutney, guava jelly, preserved ginger, pickled mangoes, olives, grated coconut.

See also the Rice section of the Pasta and Rice chapter for various rice accompaniments.

Meat Loaf

¾ lb. raw minced beef
¼ lb. sausage-meat
1 onion, skinned and finely chopped
1 level tsp. mixed herbs
1 tbsp. tomato ketchup
1 tbsp. table sauce
Salt and pepper
1 oz. white breadcrumbs
1 egg, beaten

Oven temperature: moderate (350° F., mark 4)

Grease a loaf tin measuring 8½ by 4½ inches. Mix together the meats, onion, herbs, sauces and seasoning and add the breadcrumbs. Beat with a fork until well blended, then add the egg and beat again. Pack firmly into the tin and cover with foil or greaseproof paper. Bake in the centre of the oven for 1–1¼ hours, or until the meat is tender and the loaf begins to shrink from the sides of the tin. Serve sliced, either hot with gravy or cold with salad.

Rissoles

8–12 oz. cooked minced beef
½ a small onion, skinned and grated
1 lb. potatoes, boiled and mashed
1 tbsp. sweet pickle or table sauce
Salt and pepper
Beaten egg
Dry breadcrumbs for coating
Shallow fat for frying

Mix the meat, onion and potatoes and add the pickle or sauce and a generous amount of seasoning. Stir until well blended. Turn on to a floured board, form into a roll and cut into slices about 1 inch thick. Shape these into round cakes, coat with the beaten egg and then with crumbs. Fry on both sides in the fat until golden. Drain well on absorbent paper before serving.

Variations
1. Replace the minced meat by a can of corned beef, finely chopped.
2. Omit the pickle or sauce and season with 1 tbsp. chopped parsley, 1 level tsp. mixed dried herbs or 1½–2 level tsps. curry powder.

Chilli con Carne

12 oz. haricot or butter beans
A pinch of bicarbonate of soda
1½ lb. raw minced beef
½ oz. fat or oil
1 large onion, skinned and chopped
1 green pepper, de-seeded and chopped (optional)
A 15-oz. can of tomatoes
Salt and pepper
½–1 level tsp. chilli powder
1 level tsp. sugar

Soak the beans overnight in cold water with the bicarbonate of soda. Fry the beef in the fat or oil until lightly browned, then add the onion and pepper and fry for 5 minutes, until soft. Stir in the drained beans and tomatoes and add the seasoning and chilli powder blended with the vinegar and sugar. Cover and simmer for 2–2½ hours, or until tender.

Notes: Red kidney beans are the traditional kind to use; a 15-oz. can may be used and they should be added 10 minutes before the cooking time is completed.

Add chilli powder very judiciously – some of it is very hot. American chilli powder is generally a milder pre-mixed seasoning, based on ground Mexican chilli, so look for this type.

Aubergine Moussaka

2 aubergines, sliced
3–4 tbsps. olive oil
4–5 medium-sized onions, skinned and sliced
1 lb. minced beef or lamb
4 tomatoes, peeled and sliced
¼ pint stock
¼ pint tomato paste
2 eggs
¼ pint cream
Salt and pepper

Oven temperature: moderate (350° F., mark 4)

Slice the aubergines and fry in 2 tbsps. of the oil for about 4–5 minutes, then arrange them in the bottom of an ovenproof dish. Fry the onions till they are lightly browned – about 5 minutes. Place layers of onion and minced meat on top of the aubergines and lastly add the slices of tomato. Mix the stock and tomato paste and pour into the dish. Bake in the centre of the oven for about 30 minutes. Beat together the eggs and cream, season well and pour this mixture over the meat. Put it back into the oven for 15–20 minutes, until the sauce is set and the mixture is firm and golden brown.

LAMB

CHOICE
1. The younger the animal the paler the flesh; in a young lamb it is light pink, while in a mature animal it is light red.
2. A slight blue tinge to the bones suggests that the animal is young.
3. Imported lamb has a firm white fat, while English lamb (available only in spring and early summer) has creamy-coloured fat.

CUTS AND METHODS OF COOKING
LOIN: A prime cut, usually roasted (or served as chops): can be cooked on the bone or boned, stuffed and rolled.

Allow ¾ lb. on the bone, 4–6 oz. if boned, per person.

LEG: Another good roasting cut.
Allow ¾ lb. on the bone per person.
The meat can be cut from the bone for use in pies, stews, kebabs, and so on.

SHOULDER: A large joint, with more fat but often with more flavour than leg. Usually roasted. Shoulder meat can also be cut from the bone, as for leg.
Allow ¾ lb. on the bone per person.

BEST END OF NECK: The cut next to the loin. Very good roasted, or it can be divided into cutlets.
Allow ¾ lb. per person.

CHOPS: Cut from the loin, those nearest the leg being known as chump chops. Suitable for grilling, frying and casseroles.

Allow 1–2 chops per person.

CUTLETS: From the best end of neck; they have a small 'eye' of lean meat and a long bone; suitable for grilling and frying.

Allow 1–2 cutlets per person.

BREAST: A rather fatty cut, therefore generally quite cheap. Usually boned, stuffed and rolled; it can be slow-roasted or braised, stewed or boiled.

Allow $\frac{1}{2}$–$\frac{3}{4}$ lb. on the bone per person.

MIDDLE AND SCRAG END: Cheap cuts with rather a high proportion of bone and fat, but with a good flavour.

Suitable for stews and casseroles.

Allow $\frac{1}{2}$–$\frac{3}{4}$ lb. on the bone per person.

Accompaniments to Lamb

With roast lamb and grilled chops serve mint sauce or jelly; with roast mutton, red-currant jelly or onion sauce. With boiled leg of mutton, caper sauce is traditional.

Roast Lamb

Oven temperature: hot (425°F., mark 7)

Trim the meat if necessary, then weigh it and calculate the cooking time, allowing 20 minutes per lb. plus 20 minutes. If it is rolled, allow 25 minutes per lb. plus 25 minutes.

Put the meat into a roasting tin with the thickest layer of fat on top and add dripping if the joint is very lean. Put in the middle of the oven and cook uncovered, basting from time to time with the juices from the tin. Cook for the calculated time and serve well done, accompanied by mint sauce, new potatoes (when available), garden peas or any other green vegetables and a slightly thickened gravy.

To roast lamb in a moderate oven (350°F., mark 4) allow 27 minutes per lb. plus 27 minutes for joints on the bone, 35 minutes per lb. plus 35 minutes if boned and rolled.

Crown Roast of Lamb

2 pieces of best end of neck, each with 6–7 cutlets
Dripping if needed
Cutlet frills or potato balls

For the Stuffing
2 oz. onion, skinned and finely chopped
2 oz. celery, finely chopped
8 oz. fresh breadcrumbs, toasted
1 egg, lightly beaten
A pinch of garlic powder
8 oz. cooked rice (approx.) 3 oz. (raw)
1 oz. butter
2 level tsps. curry powder
Salt and pepper

Oven temperature: moderate (350 F., mark 4)

If possible, the pieces of best end should be taken from opposite sides of the animal, though this not essential. They should be chopped, not chined, and sliced between the bones to about half-way down, the ends of the bones being scraped clean. Trim neatly and bend round to form a crown, securing it with skewers and string. Twist some pieces of foil round the exposed bones to prevent them burning. Mix all the ingredients for the stuffing and insert into the prepared crown. Roast in the centre of the oven, allowing 30 minutes to the lb., plus 30 minutes. Before serving, remove the foil and place either small cutlet frills or cooked potato balls on the ends of the bones to form 'jewels.' Garnish with creamed potato baskets filled with peas.
(See colour picture facing page 128)

Alternative Treatments: The above stuffing may be replaced by sausage-meat or sage and onion stuffing. Another way is to leave the centre unstuffed (fill it with foil to keep the shape during the cooking) and to fill it just before serving with cooked vegetables – diced carrots, peas, or small potatoes garnished with parsley butter.

Rolled Stuffed Breast of Lamb

Oven temperature: moderate (350°F., mark 4)

Joints containing a good percentage of bone can be boned (the butcher will usually do this), then rolled and tied into shape before being roasted in the usual way. They can if you wish be stuffed before being rolled – this gives added flavour and helps to make the joints go further.

Spread the boned-out joint flat on a board, sprinkle with salt and pepper and rub the seasonings into the meat. Make up some veal forcemeat or any other suitable stuffing (*see Stuffings chapter*) and spread this over the meat. (The stuffing can be prepared beforehand, but the joint is better stuffed just before cooking.) Roll up the meat loosely, to allow the stuffing to expand during cooking. Tie it in several places with fine string to hold it in shape. Weigh it and calculate the cooking time, allowing 27–30 minutes per lb. plus 27 minutes. Place the meat in the roasting tin, putting it on a grill grid or meat trivet if it is fatty, and cook in the centre of the oven for the calculated time, until well done. Remove the strings and serve sliced fairly thickly, accompanied by a thickened gravy.

Any extra stuffing can be cooked in a separate small dish and served with the joint. Other cuts of lamb suitable for stuffing are shoulder and best end of neck; they are cooked as for breast.

Noisettes of Lamb

These are prepared from a whole best end of neck. Ask the butcher to chine the meat, but not to cut through the rib bones. Remove the chine bones, skin the meat and remove all rib bones. Season the inside of the meat with salt, freshly ground pepper and herbs and roll it up tightly, starting from the thick end towards the flap and wrapping this round. Tie securely at 1½-inch intervals. Using a sharp knife, cut up in portions, with the string coming in the centre of each one. Cook as for chops, allowing 5 minutes longer cooking time. Remove the strings before serving.

Mixed Grill

4 best end of neck lamb chops
½ lb. chipolata sausages
2 lamb's kidneys
4 rashers of bacon
4 tomatoes
4 mushrooms, washed
Salt and pepper
Melted butter or oil

Trim the chops, separate the sausages, skin, halve and core the kidneys, trim the rind from the bacon, halve the tomatoes and trim the ends of the mushroom stalks. Sprinkle the chops, kidneys, tomatoes and mushrooms with salt and pepper. Brush all with fat or oil. Heat the grill and place the tomatoes (cut side up) and the mushrooms (stalks up) in the grill pan, where they will be basted by the juices from the other food and will cook without further attention. Place the grill grid in place and put on the chops, sausages and kidneys. Cook them under a medium heat, allowing 14–16 minutes altogether and turning the food on the grid frequently to ensure even cooking. The kidneys will probably be cooked first, so remove these and keep them warm. Replace them by the bacon rashers and cook for a further 3–5 minutes. If the grill is small and all the food has to be cooked separately, heat the oven to a low temperature to keep the food warm as it cooks.

Serve the food on a large plate, with a simple garnish of watercress. Traditional accompaniments are chipped or matchstick potatoes, and for more formal occasions maître d'hôtel butter.

Note: Small pieces of fillet or rump steak are often substituted for the lamb chop; calf's or lamb's liver is sometimes included in a grill.

Irish Stew

8 middle neck chops
2 lb. potatoes, peeled and sliced
2 large onions, skinned and sliced
Salt and pepper
Chopped parsley

Trim some of the fat from the chops. Place alternate layers of vegetables and meat in a saucepan, seasoning with salt and pepper and finishing with a layer of potatoes. Add sufficient water to half-cover. Cover with a lid and simmer very slowly for 3 hours. Serve sprinkled with chopped parsley.

Alternatively, cook the stew in a casserole in the centre of a fairly hot oven (375°F., mark 5) for 2½–3 hours.

If you use scrag end of neck for Irish Stew it makes an economical dish.

Lamb en Croûte

A 4½-lb. leg of lamb, boned
¼ pint red wine
1 lb. pork sausage-meat
¼ lb. bacon rashers, rinded and chopped
½ oz. pistachio nuts, blanched and chopped
Salt and freshly ground black pepper
1 oz. butter
½ lb. onions, skinned and sliced
A sprig of thyme or a little dried thyme
1 bay leaf
3 parsley stalks
1 clove of garlic, skinned and crushed
A 15-oz. can of consommé
1 lb. ready-made puff pastry
Beaten egg to glaze
Cornflour
Braised celery heads and butter-glazed carrots to garnish

Oven temperature: warm (325°F., mark 3)

Marinate the lamb in the wine for 2–3 hours, turning it occasionally. Combine the sausage-meat, bacon and nuts and season well. Remove the meat from the wine and dry on absorbent paper. Stuff the cavity with the sausage-meat and sew up both ends with string. Fry the meat in the butter to seal the surface, then place in a casserole. Re-heat the butter, add the onions, sauté, and add to the casserole, with the herbs, parsley, garlic, marinade and consommé. Cover, and cook in the centre of the oven for 2 hours. Take the meat from the dish (reserving the juices) and cool it quickly. Roll the pastry out into an oblong about 20 by 10 inches. Brush the meat surface with beaten egg and dust with flour. Place the lamb in the centre and make a parcel by folding the short ends over, sealing them with beaten egg; draw the long edges over and seal. Turn on to a baking sheet, sealed side down. Decorate with the pastry trimmings, brush with beaten egg and bake in a very hot oven (450°F., mark 8) for about 45 minutes, covering with foil if in danger of over-browning. Garnish with braised celery heads and carrots glazed with butter. *(Serves 10.)*

To make gravy, strain the juices and remove the fat with layers of absorbent paper. The yield should be about 1–1¼ pints. Thicken in the usual way with 1½–2 level tbsps. cornflour.

Lamb Paprika

8 middle or best end of neck chops
1½ oz. butter
½ lb. onions, skinned and chopped
1 lb. tomatoes, peeled and sliced
1 tbsp. chopped parsley
1–2 level tsps. paprika pepper
Salt
¼ pint sour cream or yoghourt

Trim off any excess fat from the chops. Heat the butter, brown the chops on both sides and remove from the pan. Fry the onions in the fat until golden-brown – about 5 minutes. Add the tomatoes, parsley, paprika and salt to taste, replace the chops, cover and simmer gently for 1 hour, or bake in a covered casserole in the centre of a warm oven (325°F., mark 3) for 1½ hours. Stir in the cream or yoghourt, re-season and re-heat without boiling.

Lancashire Hot-pot

8 middle neck chops
½ lb. onions, skinned and sliced
2 lamb's kidneys, skinned and diced (optional)
1 lb. potatoes, peeled and sliced
Salt and pepper
½ pint stock
1 oz. lard or dripping

Oven temperature: warm (325°F., mark 3)

Remove any excess fat from the chops and place them in a casserole. Add the onions, the kidneys (if used) and lastly the potato; season well. Pour on the stock and brush the top of the potato with the melted lard or dripping. Cover and cook in the centre of the oven for 2 hours, or until the meat and potatoes are tender. Remove the lid and brown the top layer ot potatoes in a hot oven (425°F., mark 7) for 20 minutes.

Note: Some people prefer to use chunky pieces of potato for the topping instead of the slices suggested in this recipe.

Navarin of Lamb

2–2½ lb. best end of neck or shoulder of lamb
½ oz. fat or oil
1 level tsp. sugar
1 level tbsp. flour
1½ pints stock or water
2 tbsps. tomato paste
Salt and pepper
A bouquet garni
4 onions, skinned and quartered
4 carrots, peeled and sliced
1–2 turnips, skinned and quartered
8 small, even-sized potatoes, peeled
Chopped parsley

This is a traditional dish of French origin.

Trim the meat and cut into serving portions. Fry it lightly on all sides in the fat or oil. (If there is too much fat at this stage, pour off a little to leave 1–2 tbsps.) Stir in the sugar and heat until it browns lightly, then add the flour, stirring until this also cooks and browns. Remove from the heat, stir in the stock gradually, then bring to the boil and add the tomato paste, seasoning and bouquet

garni. Cover, reduce the heat and simmer for about 1 hour. Remove the bouquet garni, add the onions, carrots and turnips and continue cooking for another ½ hour. Finally, add the potatoes and continue cooking for about 20 minutes, until tender.

Serve the meat on a heated serving dish, surrounded by the vegetables and garnished with the parsley.

Note: A small packet of frozen peas can also be added to the mixture about 10 minutes before it is served.

Blanquette D'Agneau

1½ lb. diced lean shoulder of lamb
¼ lb. carrots, peeled and sliced
¼ lb. onions, skinned and sliced
2 sticks of celery, sliced
A small bay leaf
1 level tsp. dried thyme
Salt and pepper
½ pint stock or water
¾ oz. butter, softened
3 level tbsps. flour
1 egg yolk
2 tbsps. cream or milk
Chopped parsley to garnish

Put the meat, carrots, onions, celery, flavourings and seasonings in a large pan. Cover with stock or water, lid and simmer for 1½ hours. Blend together the softened butter and flour; when they are thoroughly mixed, add to the stew in small knobs and stir until thickened; simmer for 10 minutes, adding more liquid if necessary. Blend together the egg yolk and cream, add to the stew and re-heat without boiling. Garnish with parsley before serving.

Kebabs

1lb. minced meat
1 medium-sized onion, grated
1 egg, lightly beaten
Salt
Freshly ground pepper
1 level tsp. marjoram
8 lean rashers, halved
4 slices of fresh pineapple, cored
1 large green pepper, seeded
4 tomatoes, quartered
8 stuffed green olives

Oven temperature: moderate (350°F., mark 4)

Mix together the meat, onion, egg, seasoning and marjoram. Form into 16 small balls and bake in a shallow dish for 20–30 minutes. Allow to cool.

Wrap each meat ball in a half-rasher of bacon. Cut

the pineapple and pepper into small chunks. Alternate the meat balls, tomatoes, pepper and pineapple on 8 kebab skewers. Top each with an olive and bake (or rotate under a moderate grill) for 15–20 minutes. *(Serves 4)*

(See colour picture facing page 129)

VEAL

CHOICE

1. As veal comes from a young animal the flesh should be comparatively light in colour – fine-textured, pale pink, soft and moist; avoid really flabby, wet meat.
2. If the flesh looks bluish or mottled it generally means it comes from an older animal.
3. The fat – of which there is very little – should be firm and pinkish or creamy white.
4. Veal has a lot of bone in proportion to the meat and this makes excellent jellied stock or gravy when it is boiled – it gives the special flavour to veal stews and fricassees.

CUTS OF VEAL AND METHODS OF COOKING

LEG: A prime cut and is usually roasted, being often boned and stuffed before cooking.
    Allow ½ lb. (with bone) for each person.

FILLET: Is usually the most expensive cut, is sold in the piece for roasting; like leg, it is usually boned and stuffed before cooking. It can also be cut into thin slices or escalopes, which are beaten thin and generally fried.
    Allow 4–6 oz. (boned) for each person.

LOIN: Another prime cut for roasting, either on the bone or boned, stuffed and rolled.
    Allow ½ lb. (with bone) for each person.

CHOPS: The loin can be divided into chops, those from the bottom end, which have a small round bone in the centre, being known as chump chops. They are suitable for grilling or frying.
    Allow 1 per person.

CUTLETS: Prime cuts from the top or neck end of the loin; they are grilled, fried or braised.
    Allow 1–2, according to size, for each person.

SHOULDER: An awkward shape and is therefore often quite cheap, although when boned and stuffed it is quite suitable for roasting. Portions of shoulder meat, taken off the bone, are often sold for pies, stews and fricassees.
    Allow 1 lb. (with bone) for each person.

KNUCKLE: This cheap cut from the foreleg is good for boiling and stewing and the meat from it can be used for making pies. It can also be boned, stuffed and then braised.
    Allow 1 lb. (with bone) for each person.

BEST END OF NECK: This fairly cheap cut is good value; it can be boned and stuffed or cooked on the bone. It is suitable for roasting, braising and stewing.
    Allow about 1 lb. (with bone) for each person.

BREAST: A fairly cheap cut, which is usually boned, stuffed and roasted and has a good flavour.
    Allow about 1 lb. (with bone) for each person. It can be served cold as a veal mould.

PIE VEAL: Consists of trimmings and small pieces of shoulder, breast, neck or knuckle, bought ready cut up for use.

Roast Veal

Oven temperature: hot (425°F., mark 7)

Trim the joint, then weigh and calculate the cooking time, allowing 25 minutes per lb. plus 25 minutes if the meat is on the bone, 30 minutes per lb. plus 30 minutes if the joint is boned and rolled. Season well and bake in the centre of the oven for the calculated time, basting frequently; serve well done. Carve in thick slices and serve accompanied by bacon rolls, veal forcemeat and gravy.
    Veal can be a little dry and insipid, so to improve the flavour cover the joint with some strips of streaky bacon or stuff it with forcemeat (*see Stuffings chapter*).
    The meat will be more moist if baked in a closed tin or wrapped in foil, although the appearance is not so good.

Veal Escalopes

When cooking escalopes by any of the three methods described below it is not advisable to have more than 2 in the pan at once as they are difficult to turn over.

Veal Birds

Fried Escalopes (Wiener Schnitzel)

Allow 1 escalope per person and get the butcher to beat it until really thin. Coat with beaten egg and fresh white breadcrumbs, patting them on well. Melt 2 oz. butter in a large frying pan and fry the veal gently (about 5 minutes on each side). Drain well on kitchen paper and serve with wedges of lemon and a green salad.

Escalopes with Parmesan Cheese

Prepare and coat the escalopes as above, then fry gently in butter for about 3 minutes on each side or until just tender. Cover each escalope with a thin slice of cooked ham and 1 level tbsp. grated Parmesan cheese. Spoon a little of the butter over the cheese, cover the pan with a lid or large plate and cook for a further 2–3 minutes, until the cheese just melts. Serve at once.

Escalope with Marsala and Cheese

Coat each escalope with seasoned flour and fry gently in 2 oz. butter until just tender and golden (3 minutes on each side). Stir into the pan 2–3 tbsps. Marsala (or sherry or Madeira) and sprinkle each escalope with 1 level tbsp. grated Parmesan cheese. Spoon some of the butter-wine mixture over, cover the pan with a lid or plate and cook gently for a further 2–3 minutes, until the cheese just melts.

Veal Fricassee

A good standby for all occasions. Add your own personal touch with herbs, or use half stock and half dry white wine for cooking. Alternatively, use half the stated amount of stock for cooking and replace the other half by milk, added at the end.

½ lb. back bacon, cut in 2 thick rashers
1–1½ lb. stewing veal, cubed
1¾ oz. butter
1 tbsp. oil
½ a small onion, skinned and finely chopped
½ pint white stock or water
Salt and pepper
¾ oz. flour
1–2 tbsps. lemon juice

Oven temperature: moderate (350°F., mark 4)

Rind the bacon, trim off any excess fat and cut into pieces the same size as the veal. Fry the veal and bacon very lightly in 1 oz. butter and the oil, but do not colour. Lift them out and place in a 3-pint casserole. Fry the onion in the remaining fat until transparent but not brown and add to the veal. Pour the stock over the meat, season, cover and cook in the centre of the oven for 1½ hours, or until tender. Strain off the liquor and keep the veal and bacon hot in the casserole. Melt the ¾ oz. butter, stir in the flour and cook for 2–3 minutes. Gradually stir in the strained liquor, bring to the boil and boil for 2–3 minutes, stirring all the time. Add the lemon juice and re-check the seasoning. Pour the sauce over the veal.

Osso Bucco

2 lb. shin of veal
Salt and pepper
2 oz. butter
1 medium-sized onion, skinned and finely chopped
1 carrot, peeled and thinly sliced
1 stalk of celery, scrubbed and thinly sliced
¼ pint dry white wine
1 level tbsp. flour
¾ pint stock (make from a bouillon cube)
½ lb. tomatoes, peeled and chopped
A pinch of dried rosemary
1 tbsp. chopped parsley to garnish
1 clove of garlic, skinned and finely chopped
Grated rind of ½ a lemon

Ask your butcher to saw the veal into 2-inch pieces. Season with salt and pepper. Melt the butter, brown the veal all over and remove from the pan. If necessary, add a little more butter and fry the onion, carrot and celery until they are golden-brown. Drain off any excess fat, return the meat to the pan and add the wine. Cover and simmer gently for 20 minutes. Blend the flour with a little stock to a smooth cream, add the remainder of the stock and add to the meat. Add the tomatoes and rosemary, cover tightly and continue to simmer for a further 1½ hours, or until the meat is tender. Arrange in a deep serving dish and sprinkle with a mixture of parsley, garlic and lemon rind. Serve with risotto and a dressed green salad.

Veal Birds

4 veal escalopes
2 rashers of streaky bacon, rinded
½ oz. butter
½ a small onion, skinned and chopped
1 level tbsp. flour
An 8-oz. can of tomatoes

For the Forcemeat
1 thick slice of bread
A pinch of thyme or mixed dried herbs
Salt and pepper
Grated rind of ½ a lemon
Beaten egg or milk to mix

Begin by making the forcemeat. Make the bread into crumbs, add the herbs, salt, pepper and lemon rind and bind with the egg or milk.

Have the escalopes beaten thin, cut each rasher of bacon in half and spread out until thin with the flat of a knife. Lay a piece of bacon on each escalope and add a quarter of the forcemeat. Roll up each escalope and secure by wrapping round with sewing cotton. Fry the 'birds' in the fat until lightly browned (about 4 minutes), remove them and fry the onion lightly, then stir in the flour and the tomatoes made up to ½ pint with water. Add seasoning and bring this sauce to the boil, add the 'birds', cover, then reduce the heat and simmer gently for about 1½ hours, or until tender.

64

Cherry-stuffed Veal

7 lb. breast of veal, boned (approx.) 5 lb. after boning
½ lb. lean back bacon, in a piece
6 oz. glacé cherries
A little rosemary
Oil
Garlic salt (or a clove of garlic and ordinary salt)

Oven temperature: fairly hot (400°F., mark 6)

Lay the veal on a chopping-board. Cut the meat where it tapers and pull back the flap to make an oblong shape. Remove the rind from the bacon, cut the bacon in quarters along the length of the rinded fat, and then in half at right angles to the first cut. Lay the strips of bacon at intervals along the meat, parallel to the width. Position the cherries between the bacon, with the rosemary. Roll up from the short side. Secure in position with skewers before tying neatly and firmly with string. Place in a small roasting tin, brush with oil, dust with garlic salt (or halve the skinned garlic clove and rub it over the skin, then dust with salt). Roast in the centre of the oven for ½ hour, reduce the temperature to moderate (350°F., mark 4) and cook for about a further 2½ hours. Cover with foil or 2 layers of greaseproof paper, previously wetted, if the meat is in danger of over-browning. *(Serves 12.)*

Blanquette of Veal

1–1½ lb. lean veal (from shoulder or knuckle), cubed
2 onions, skinned and chopped
2 carrots, skinned and chopped
A squeeze of lemon juice
A bouquet garni
Salt and pepper
1 oz. butter
1 oz. flour
1 egg yolk
2–3 tbsps. cream
Lemon wedges and bacon rolls to garnish

Put the meat, onions, carrots, lemon juice, bouquet garni and seasoning into a large pan with enough water to cover. Put on the lid and simmer gently for about 1½ hours, until the meat is tender. Strain off the cooking liquid, retaining 1 pint, and keep the meat and vegetables warm. Melt the butter, stir in the flour and cook for 2–3 minutes. Gradually stir in the pint of cooking liquid, bring to the boil and boil for 2–3 minutes, stirring all the time. Adjust the seasoning, remove from the heat and when slightly cooled stir in the egg yolk and cream. Pour over the meat and vegetables and before serving, re-heat without boiling for a further 5 minutes, to allow the flavours to blend. Serve with lemon wedges and bacon rolls.

Raised Veal and Ham Pie

1 lb. hot-water crust *(see Pastry chapter)*
¾ lb. pie veal, diced
¼ lb. ham, chopped
1 tbsp. chopped parsley
Grated rind and juice of 1 lemon
Salt and pepper
A little stock or water
1 hard-boiled egg
Beaten egg to glaze
Jelly stock

Oven temperature: hot (425°F., mark 7)

Make a pastry case as described in the Pastry chapter. Mix the veal, ham, parsley, lemon rind and juice, season with salt and pepper and moisten with a little stock or water. Half-fill the pastry case with this mixture, put the egg in the centre, add the remaining meat mixture, cover and decorate the pie. Glaze the top with a little beaten egg and tie a greaseproof paper band round the pie. Bake in the centre of the oven for 15–20 minutes, then reduce the heat to moderate (350°F., mark 4) and continue cooking for a further 1½ hours or longer, until the meat feels tender when tested with a skewer. Fill the pie up with jelly stock made by dissolving 2 level tsps. gelatine in ½ pint chicken stock (make from a bouillon cube).

PORK

CHOICE
1. The lean part of pork should be pale pink, moist and slightly marbled with fat.
2. There should be a good outer layer of firm, white fat, with a thin, elastic skin; if the joint is to be roasted, get the butcher to score the rind.
3. The bones should be small and pinkish (which denotes a young animal.)
4. Although pork was considered seasonal at one time, it can now be bought all the year round; prices, however, vary considerably, so check up before buying.

CUTS AND METHODS OF COOKING

LEG: Prime joint but rather large, so it is often cut into two. Roasted on the bone, or boned and stuffed.

Allow ½–¾ lb. with bone per person; 4 oz. without bone. To roast on the bone allow 25 minutes per lb. plus 25 minutes over (oven temp. 425°F, mark 7); boned 30–35 minutes per lb. plus 35 minutes (oven temperature 375°F, mark 5)

FILLET: A lean, expensive cut taken from the top of the hind leg, with a central bone. It is best roasted and can

Mushroom Bouillon, *page 24;* Grilled Lamb Cutlets, *page 59;* Cheese board

be cooked on the bone or boned and stuffed.

Pork fillet is also obtainable as fairly thin slices, which can be grilled, fried or casseroled.

Allow $\frac{1}{2}$–$\frac{3}{4}$ lb. with bone per person; 4 oz. without bone.

LOIN: An expensive but prime cut, suitable for roasting; often includes the kidney. It can be cooked on the bone or boned and stuffed.

Allow $\frac{1}{2}$–$\frac{3}{4}$ lb. with bone per person; 4 oz. without bone.

SPARE RIB: Fairly lean and moderately priced. Good for roasting, but can also be cut up for braising and stewing.

Allow $\frac{1}{2}$–$\frac{3}{4}$ lb. with bone per person.

CHOPS: Usually consist of the cut-up loin and often include the kidney. They can be grilled, fried or casseroled.

Allow 1 per person.

CUTLETS: A more unusual cut, these are taken from the sparerib and have little or no bone; they are usually lean.

Cooked as for chops.

Allow 1–2 per person.

BLADE: Another cut for roasting on the bone.

Allow $\frac{1}{2}$–$\frac{3}{4}$ lb. per person.

HAND AND SPRING: The foreleg, suitable for roasting, boiling and stewing.

Allow $\frac{3}{4}$ lb. per person.

BELLY: A fatty cut, sometimes sold salted and usually boiled and served cold.

Allow 4–6 oz. per person.

Accompaniments for Pork

Apple (or gooseberry) sauce is the most usual accompaniment, with sage and onion stuffing when appropriate. Try baked or fried apples or cranberry or redcurrant jelly as an alternative.

Pork Chops with Apple and Prune Stuffing

4 pork chops
Apple and prune stuffing: use about a quarter of the amounts given in recipe in Stuffings chapter, but include at least $\frac{1}{2}$ an egg

Oven temperature: fairly hot (400°F., mark 6)

Trim the chops. Place a portion of stuffing on each chop, put into a greased baking tin and cover with greaseproof paper or foil. Cook near the top of the oven for 1 hour, or until tender.

Grilled Pork Chops with Apple Rings

4 pork chops
Olive oil
1 cooking apple, peeled and cored and sliced

Trim the chops and brush with olive oil. Place the rings of apple in the base of the grill pan and put the chops on the grid. Grill the chops for 8–10 minutes on each side

under a medium grill, making sure that they are well cooked; when they are done, place on a serving dish. Put the apple rings on to the grid and brown very lightly. Arrange between the chops on the serving dish.

Casserole of Pork

8 slices of belly of pork (1$\frac{1}{2}$ lb.)
2 onions, skinned and sliced
1 large cooking apple, peeled, cored and diced
$\frac{1}{2}$ pint stock
Gravy browning, salt, pepper
2 level tbsps. flour
2 carrots, peeled and sliced

Oven temperature: warm (325°F., mark 3)

Trim the excess fat from the belly of pork. Layer the onions and apple in a casserole and overlap the slices of pork on top. Colour the stock with a few drops of gravy browning, add some seasoning and pour over the meat. Cover and cook in the centre of the oven for 2 hours; skin off any excess fat. Blend the flour with a little cold water, stir in the liquid from the casserole and return it to the casserole, with the carrots. Cover and cook for a further hour.

Fried Pork Chops

Trim the chops, removing any extra fat. Fry the chops slowly in a little dripping, oil or lard, turning them frequently, for about 20 minutes.

The chops may first be egg-and-breadcrumbed.

Pork Chops with Orange

4 large pork chump chops, rinded
2 level tbsps. seasoned flour
Oil for frying
2 large thin-skinned oranges
4 level tbsps. soft, light brown sugar
1 level tbsp. cornflour
$\frac{1}{4}$ pint dry white wine
$\frac{1}{2}$ pint orange juice
1 medium-sized onion, skinned and sliced
Watercress to garnish

Oven temperature: moderate (350°F., mark 4)

Coat the chops in seasoned flour. Heat just enough oil in a large frying-pan to cover the base. Fry the chops quickly on either side until well browned. Drain, and place in a shallow casserole, large enough to take the chops in a single layer. Remove the rind and all traces of white pith from the oranges. Slice, discarding the pips, and cut each slice in half; sprinkle with 2 tbsps. sugar. Blend the cornflour with a little wine; add the rest of the wine, the orange juice and sugar. Bring to the boil, stirring, and pour over the chops. Arrange the sliced onion over the chops, cover tightly and cook in the centre of the oven for 1$\frac{1}{4}$–1$\frac{1}{2}$ hours. Remove the lid;

Pork Chops with Apple and Prune Stuffing

arrange the orange slices over the onion and cook for a further 15–20 minutes, basting occasionally. Before serving, reduce the liquor, if you wish, by boiling, then adjust the seasoning and garnish with watercress.

Baked Pork Chops with Pineapple

4 pork chops
Salt and pepper
An 8-oz. can of pineapple rings
Brown sugar

Oven temperature: moderate (350°F., mark 4)

Trim the chops, put in an ovenproof dish and season. Pour in enough pineapple juice to come halfway up the chops, cover with foil and bake in the centre of the oven for about 45 minutes, till tender. Uncover, garnish each chop with a pineapple ring, sprinkle with a little brown sugar and return them to the oven for 5–10 minutes, until the sugar has just melted.

Oriental Pork Chops

4 loin pork chops
2 tbsps. soy sauce
1 tbsp. clear honey
A small clove of garlic, crushed

Oven temperature: fairly hot (375°F., mark 5)

Trim off the surplus fat from the chops.
Blend together the soy sauce, honey and crushed garlic, pour into a shallow dish, and turn the prepared chops in this marinade. Cover the dish and leave for

67

several hours or overnight in the refrigerator or other cold place.

When you are ready to cook the chops, drain them from the marinade and place them in a shallow lidded casserole. Spoon the marinade over and bake in the centre of the oven for 40 minutes. Remove the lid and bake for a further 20 minutes.

Braised Pork Chops

4 thick pork chops
2 oz. fat or oil
1 onion, skinned and thinly sliced
1 carrot, peeled and thinly sliced
A bouquet garni
¼ pint white wine
¼ pint stock
¼ lb. mushrooms, sliced
½ cup milk and water
Salt and pepper
1 level tbsp. plain flour

Oven temperature: moderate (350 F., mark 4)

Trim the chops, brown on both sides in the fat or oil, remove them and lightly fry the onion and carrot for 5 minutes; remove and place in a casserole with the chops on top. Add the bouquet garni, wine and stock and cook in the centre of the oven for 1 hour. Meanwhile put the mushrooms in a pan with the ½ cup milk and water, season, cover and simmer for 5 minutes. Blend the flour with the fat left in the frying pan to make a roux. Drain off the liquid from the casserole and that from the mushrooms and add gradually to the roux, stirring until the sauce has boiled. Add the mushrooms and pour over the chops in the casserole.

Normandy Pork

1½–2 lb. fillet of pork
2 level tbsps. seasoned flour
¼ pint dry white wine
½ lb. button mushrooms, sliced
1½ oz. butter
2 tbsps brandy
2 tbsps. chopped parsley
¼ pint double cream
Salt and pepper

Cut the pork into pieces about the size and shape of potato chips and toss these in the seasoned flour. Bring the wine to the boil, add the mushrooms and simmer, covered, for 10–15 minutes. Brown the pork in the hot butter. Warm the brandy in a small pan, set it alight and when the flames die down, pour it over the meat. Add the wine and mushrooms to the pork and simmer, covered, for ½ hour, or until the meat is tender. Strain the pork and mushrooms, put in a serving dish and keep warm. Add the parsley and cream to the juices in the pan and check the seasoning. Simmer without boiling until the sauce thickens and pour it over the pork. Serve with rice and green salad.

Frikadeller

1 lb. lean pork, cubed
1 small onion, skinned and quartered
1–1½ level tsps. salt
Pepper
2 level tbsps. flour
1 egg, beaten
A little milk
Fat for deep frying

Mince the meat and onion twice. Add the salt and a good shake of pepper and stir in the flour, egg and enough milk to give a mixture that is soft but will hold its shape; roll it into small balls. Heat the fat until it will brown a cube of bread in 1 minute and cook the meat balls until brown, for about 6 minutes. Drain on kitchen paper and serve with a tomato sauce.

Sweet-sour Pork Balls

1 lb. pork, minced
1 clove of garlic, skinned and crushed
1½ oz. flour
2 oz. fresh white breadcrumbs
Salt and pepper
1 egg yolk
1 oz. lard

For the Sauce
3 oz. sugar
4 tbsps. cider vinegar
3 tbsps. soy sauce
1½ level tbsps. cornflour
½ pint water
1 green pepper, blanched and cut in thin strips
½ lb. tomatoes, skinned and quartered
An 11-oz. can of crushed pineapple

Mix the pork, garlic, ½ oz. of the flour, the breadcrumbs, salt and pepper; add the egg yolk and mix well. Form into 24 balls and toss in the remaining flour. Heat the lard in a frying pan, add the balls and fry gently for 20 minutes, turning them frequently until golden.

Meanwhile, put the sugar, vinegar and soy sauce in a saucepan. Blend the cornflour with the water and add to the pan. Bring to the boil, stirring; simmer gently for 5 minutes, then add the green pepper, tomatoes and pineapple. Simmer for a further 5 minutes. To serve, put the pork balls into a warmed casserole and pour the sauce over. Serve with fried rice and a green salad.

Raised Pork Pie

1½–2 lb. pie pork, cubed
¾ pint chicken stock (made from a cube)
½ lb. hot-water crust pastry *(see Pastry chapter)*
1 tbsp. chopped parsley
Salt and pepper

Oven temperature: hot (425°F., mark 7)

Oriental Pork Chops with accompaniments

The Day Before
Put the meat in a pan with the stock, cover and simmer for 1 hour, or until tender. Drain it and leave in a cool place until required. Boil the stock rapidly until it measures ½ pint; cool.

The Next Day
Mould three-quarters of the pastry into a shell about 4 inches in diameter. *(See Pastry chapter.)* Put the cold cooked meat in the pastry case with the parsley and seasoning. Remove any fat from the top of the stock (which should have set to a soft jelly) and add a few tablespoonfuls of the liquid to the meat.

Use the remaining quarter of the pastry to make the lid for the pie. Bake it in the centre of the oven for 15 minutes, reduce the temperature to moderate (350°F., mark 4) and cook for a further 40 minutes. Remove the paper band and cook for another 20 minutes. Leave the pie until cold, then melt the remaining jellied stock and fill it up. (If the stock does not set well, add 1–2 level tsps. powdered gelatine and dissolve it in the stock over a gentle heat.) Leave the pie until quite set before cutting it.

BACON AND HAM

The pigs used for bacon, gammon and ham are specially bred to have the desired proportion of lean and fat. For bacon and gammon the sides of meat are salted down and left to mature for about 3 weeks so that the salt, with its preservative effect, can penetrate right through the meat. The rind is still pale-coloured and the flesh pink; the bacon at this stage is called 'green'. If the green bacon is hung above smouldering sawdust for 2 days the rind turns a deep golden-brown and the flesh a darker pink; the product is then sold as 'smoked' bacon.

Gammon and ham, though both come from the hind leg of the animal, are cured differently. For gammon, the leg from a side of 'green' bacon is cut off square at the top and it is then smoked separately. Ham on the other hand is cut off round the bone before the meat has been salted at all and can be cured and finished in several different ways, according to the local method. Gammon and ham are cooked in exactly the same way, but gammon is cheaper than ham.

One of the best things about bacon and ham joints from the cook's point of view is that they are mostly boned and prepared before being sold, so there is very little waste. Bacon is equally good hot or cold, and the final leftovers make excellent savouries or supper dishes, so once you have cooked the joint it will give several good meals with no extra trouble.

HOW TO CHOOSE BACON

Good bacon has a pleasant, mild smell, the lean is moist but not flabby and wet and the fat is firm and white, with no discoloured patches; the rind should be smooth and thin.

CUTS OF BACON

These vary so much in each part of the country that it is difficult to generalise or to describe all available cuts. However, these are some of the commonest:

BACK: An expensive cut in which there is a good proportion of lean and a distinct layer of fat. Used for frying and grilling and can also be bought in the piece for boiling.

STREAKY: A cut in which lean and fat are mixed. It is good for grilling and frying, provided some fat is not objected to, and can also be boiled in the piece.

BACON CHOPS: are short back bacon, cut $\frac{1}{4}$–$\frac{1}{2}$ inch thick.

GAMMON RASHERS: The leanest and most expensive cut for grilling and frying.

Allow 1 rasher (or $\frac{1}{2}$ rasher if they are very large) for each person.

COLLAR: Prime collar is one of the best boiling and baking joints and is also good for braising. The whole joint weighs about 6 lb., but is usually sold in smaller pieces; end of collar, which weighs about 2 lb., is an inexpensive cut.

Allow 6–8 oz. for each person.

HOCK: A joint which weighs about 5 lb., but is usually sold in two pieces as butt (about $3\frac{1}{2}$ lb.) and fore-slipper ($1\frac{1}{2}$ lb.) the latter being a rather fatty joint but with an excellent flavour. Hock can be boiled, baked and braised.

Allow 6–8 oz. for each person.

GAMMON: A large joint, which is generally divided into several smaller pieces such as hock and slipper; all suitable for boiling, baking and braising.

Allow 6 oz. for each person.

MIDDLE AND CORNER GAMMON: The best of lean joints for boiling; the former weighs about 5 lb. and the latter about 4 lb.

BACON 'IN THE BAG': Joints of bacon are often sold ready packed in hermetically sealed polythene bags, with special instructions for cooking. As the bacon is specially 'mild cured' it can be cooked straight away, without the bag being removed; this has the advantage of keeping the joint a good shape and retaining the natural juices in the meat.

VACUUM-PACKED BACON: For frying and grilling it is specially prepared and of a high quality, but quite expensive. The polythene packs are date-stamped to prevent the sale of bacon which is not in prime condition. Instructions for keeping the bacon after it has been opened are generally printed on the packs.

Rasher Reminders

NUMBERS AND WEIGHT: One pound of bacon cut at No. 6 gives approximately 12–13 top back rashers, 16–17 short back, 28 top streaky, 8 small gammon and 5–6 large gammon rashers (though gammon is best cut much thicker than this).

FAT BACON: Used for larding very lean joints of meat and poultry, is sold cut in strips and is cheaper than ordinary rashers. Failing this, ask for thinly-sliced oddments.

PREPARING: Rind rashers thinly with kitchen scissors or a sharp knife. Thick rashers or chops should be snipped at intervals along the fat edge to help them remain flat and attractive-looking during the cooking process.

If you suspect that chops or other thick bacon or gammon slices are salty, soak them or poach them in water for a few minutes, throw away the water and cook as desired. Very salt bacon should also be blanched before it is used in made-up dishes or the flavour may be too strong.

Frying and Grilling: For frying, lay the bacon rashers in a cold pan, with the lean parts over the fat; for grilling, arrange them in the reverse way. Lean rashers are better brushed with fat or oil for grilling.

Cook quickly to obtain a crisp effect, slowly if you prefer the rashers softer.

GAMMON RASHERS

Grilled Gammon Rashers

Choose rashers not less than $\frac{1}{4}$ inch thick. Cut off the rind with scissors and clip the fat at intervals. Put the rashers on to a lightly greased grill grid, brush with melted butter or a little oil and cook under a medium heat for about 5 minutes. Turn them, brush the second side with butter or oil and continue cooking for a further 5–10 minutes until tender.

Glazed Gammon Rashers

Prepare and cook as above, but spread the second side with any of the following before cooking: melted butter and a sprinkling of brown sugar; marmalade sharpened with a little vinegar or lemon juice; brown sugar mixed with a pinch of dry mustard or ground ginger and moistened with orange or pineapple juice.

Accompaniments for Gammon Rashers

APPLE RINGS: Remove the core of the apple with an apple corer or small cutter and cut across into thick rings. Brush with melted butter, sprinkle with brown sugar and grill lightly alongside the gammon.

PINEAPPLE RINGS: Baste the rings with a little pineapple juice, sprinkle with sugar and grill lightly alongside the ham.

RED-CURRANT AND ORANGE RELISH: Chop 1–2 sticks of celery, peel and chop 1 orange and mix both with 3–4 tbsps. red-currant jelly. Stir until really well blended.

SWEET AND SOUR SAUCE: Mix 2 tbsps. red-currant jelly with 2 tbsps. mango chutney and the grated rind and juice of $\frac{1}{2}$ a lemon. Simmer together for 5 minutes until syrupy; serve hot or cold.

To boil Bacon or Gammon

Weigh the pieces, then calculate the cooking time, allowing 20–25 minutes per lb. plus 20 minutes over. If you are cooking a large joint, e.g. a gammon of 10 lb. or over, allow 15–20 minutes per lb. plus 15 minutes. Cover it with water and allow to soak for about 1 hour. Place the bacon or gammon in a large pan, skin side down, cover with fresh cold water and bring slowly to the boil, skimming off any scum that forms. Time the cooking from this point. Cover and simmer gently until cooked. For extra flavour add 2 onions, quartered, 2 carrots, quartered, 1 bay leaf and 4 peppercorns.

When the bacon or gammon is cooked, cut off the outer skin and serve the joint hot with parsley sauce, or as an accompaniment to roast turkey or chicken. Alternatively, allow it to cool in the cooking liquid, cut off the outer skin and press browned breadcrumbs into

the fat; when the meat is cold, serve with salad or in sandwiches.

To bake Bacon or Gammon

Oven temperature: moderate (350°F., mark 4)

Weigh the bacon, calculate the cooking time and soak as for boiled bacon. Boil for half the cooking time, then drain and wrap in foil. Bake in the centre of the oven until $\frac{1}{2}$ hour before the cooking time is complete. Raise the oven heat to hot (425°F., mark 7). Undo the foil, cut the rind from the bacon, score the fat into diamonds, stud with cloves and sprinkle the surface with 3–4 tbsps. brown sugar for a special effect. Return the joint to the oven until crisp and golden. Serve with cranberry sauce or with canned peaches or apricots.

Alternative Glazes and Finishes

ORANGE AND ALMOND: Spread the fat with orange marmalade and sprinkle with chopped almonds. You can then serve the meat with an orange salad.

FRUIT: Drain the juice from a can of pineapple rings or apricots. Press Demerara sugar over the joint, arrange the fruit over the joint or round it in the tin, pour about $\frac{1}{4}$ pint fruit juice over and baste well. Finish cooking, basting every 10 minutes with the juice, and serve the joint garnished with the fruit.

VIRGINIAN STYLE: Brush the joint with warmed syrup and sprinkle with equal quantities of flour and brown sugar. Serve with a gravy made from the liquid in the tin.

CIDER: Mix 4 oz. brown sugar with 1 level tsp. dry mustard and spread over the joint. Pour $\frac{1}{4}$ pint cider over and continue baking, basting frequently. Honey can be used instead of the brown sugar to give a richer flavour.

OATMEAL OR BREADCRUMBS: After removing the skin, brush the fat with egg white (optional) and press fine oatmeal or breadcrumbs all over the surface of it, then return the ham to the oven for the final $\frac{1}{2}$ hour.

Braised Bacon

A piece of bacon or gammon
1 onion, skinned and sliced
4 carrots, peeled and sliced
$\frac{1}{2}$ turnip, peeled and sliced
2 sticks of celery, scrubbed and sliced
2 oz. fat or oil
Stock
A bouquet garni
Salt and pepper

Oven temperature: moderate (350°F., mark 4)

Soak the bacon or gammon for 1 hour (or overnight if you think it is likely to be very salty). Boil it for half the cooking time, allowing 20–25 minutes per lb. plus 20 minutes over. Lightly fry the vegetables in the hot fat or oil for 3–4 minutes. Put them in a casserole, put the bacon on top and add enough stock to cover the vegetables. Add the bouquet garni and the seasoning, cover and cook in the centre of the oven for the remainder of the cooking time. Half an hour before the bacon is done, remove the rind and continue cooking, uncovered, for the final 30 minutes. Remove the bouquet garni.

Parsley sauce goes well with this, or you can thicken the vegetable liquid with a little cornflour.

Bacon and Egg Pie

6 oz. shortcrust pastry *(see Pastry chapter)*
4 rashers of bacon, chopped
4 eggs
4 tbsps. milk
Salt and pepper
2 tomatoes or 4 mushrooms sliced (optional)

Oven temperature: hot (425°F., mark 7)

Line a 7-inch pie plate with half the pastry; roll out the remaining pastry to form a lid. Spread the bacon over the base. Whisk the eggs and add the milk and seasoning. Pour over the bacon and add the tomatoes or mushrooms (if used). Damp the edges of the pastry on the dish and cover with the lid, pressing the edges well together; flake and scallop the edge. Brush the top of the pie with the little egg that remains in the basin. Bake in the centre of the oven, reducing the temperature after 10 minutes to moderate (350°F., mark 4) and cook for a further 30 minutes. Serve the pie hot or cold.

Note: See also Quiche Lorraine in the Cheese chapter.

Bacon Pasties

1 onion, skinned and chopped
4 tomatoes, peeled and chopped
6 oz. streaky bacon, rinded and chopped
½ level tsp. mixed herbs
Salt and pepper
8 oz. shortcrust pastry *(see Pastry chapter)*
A little milk to glaze

Oven temperature: hot (425°F., mark 7)

Mix together the onion, tomatoes, bacon, herbs and seasoning. Roll out the pastry and cut into 4 rounds, using a small saucepan lid as a cutter. Put a quarter of the meat mixture in the centre of each round of pastry, wet the edges of the pastry, draw them up and press firmly together over the top of the pasty; crimp the edges with your fingers and brush the pasty with milk. Place on a baking tray and cook towards the top of the oven for about 15 minutes, or until the pastry begins to brown, then lower the heat to warm (325°F., mark 3) and bake for another 45–60 minutes, depending on the size of the pasties.

Bacon Fritters

Cut cold cooked bacon into ¼-inch slices. Make a coating batter in the usual way. (¼ pint is sufficient for 4 average slices.) Dip the bacon slices into the batter and fry in shallow fat until crisp and golden-brown on both sides.

Bacon Roly-Poly

8 oz. suetcrust pastry *(see Pastry chapter)*
½ level tsp. salt
¾ lb. cooked bacon, minced or finely chopped
1 onion, skinned and finely chopped
1 level tsp. sage or mixed herbs
1 tbsp. sweet pickle (optional)

Put the pastry on a floured board and roll it out into an oblong 12 inches by 6 inches. Mix the remaining ingredients together (omitting the salt if the bacon is very salty, and binding the mixture if necessary with a beaten egg or a few chopped canned tomatoes). Spread the filling over the pastry to within ½ inch of the edges. Damp the edges and roll up like a Swiss roll, starting from one short end, wrap in greased greaseproof paper or foil and seal well. Steam for 2–2½ hours over rapidly boiling water. Serve with tomato or parsley sauce.

Caramelled Gammon

2 gammon rashers cut ½ inch thick
An 8-oz. can of pineapple rings
1½ oz. butter
4 level tbsps. Demerara sugar

Trim the rashers, snip the fat at intervals and cut each rasher in half. Drain the pineapple rings, retaining the juice. Poach the rashers in a little water for 1–2 minutes and throw away the water. Fry the rashers in the butter until golden-brown on both sides – about 2 minutes. Remove the rashers and cool the remaining butter; add the pineapple juice and sugar, dissolve over a low heat and bring to the boil. Return the rashers to the pan. reduce the heat, cover and simmer for about 20 minutes, or until tender. Arrange the rashers on a serving dish. Reduce the liquor by boiling rapidly. Add the pineapple rings and heat through, arrange them on top of the rashers and pour the glaze over them. Serve with fluffy rice.

Ham Charlotte

2 oz. ham, chopped
3 hard-boiled eggs, sliced
2 oz. mushrooms, finely chopped
2 sticks of celery, scrubbed and chopped
1½ oz. butter
1½ oz. flour
¾ pint milk
Salt and pepper
3–4 tbsps. fresh breadcrumbs

Oven temperature: fairly hot (375°F., mark 5)

Baked Gammon

Put the ham in an ovenproof dish. Slice the eggs and add them to the ham, retaining 2–3 slices for garnish. Fry the mushrooms and celery in 1 oz. butter for 10 minutes, or until soft. Stir in the flour, then remove the pan from the heat and gradually stir in the milk. Return the mixture to the heat, bring to the boil, stirring all the time, and season to taste. Pour the sauce over the eggs, sprinkle with breadcrumbs, dot with shavings of butter and bake uncovered in the centre of the oven for about 20 minutes. Garnish with sliced egg.

Ham and Asparagus Mould

½ pint aspic jelly
A 10½-oz. can of asparagus tips
½ oz. gelatine
2 tbsps. cold water
3 oz. granulated sugar
4 level tsps. dry mustard
½ level tsp. salt
3 eggs, slightly beaten
⅓ pint vinegar
½ pint single cream
¾ lb. cooked ham, cut into 1-inch slivers
Watercress and tomato

Line a 1½-pint mould with aspic jelly (made according to the directions on the packet) and decorate the sides with some asparagus tips. Dissolve the gelatine in the cold water. Mix the sugar, mustard and salt together and add to the eggs. Heat the vinegar just to boiling point and gradually add the egg to it. Return the mixture to the heat and cook slowly till it thickens but does not boil.

Remove from the heat, add the dissolved gelatine and chill, stirring occasionally, until the mixture thickens. Add the cream, the ham and the rest of the asparagus, cut into small pieces. Pour into the prepared mould and chill until firm. Unmould and garnish with watercress and tomato wedges.

Layered Potatoes with Ham

4 tbsps. soured cream
2 tbsps. double cream
1 level tsp. salt
2 oz. butter
1 lb. cold cooked potatoes, thinly sliced
3 hard-boiled eggs, sliced
¼ lb. cooked ham, diced finely
3 oz. fresh breadcrumbs
¼ level tsp. celery salt
2 oz. melted butter

Oven temperature: moderate (350° F., mark 4)

Put the soured cream, double cream and salt in a bowl and mix them. Grease the inside of an ovenproof dish with butter, then put in one-third of the potatoes and cover with the sliced eggs; pour some of the cream mixture over. Add another third of the potatoes in a layer, sprinkle with the diced ham, then pour the remaining cream mixture over. Top with the remaining sliced potatoes. Mix the breadcrumbs and the celery salt with the melted butter and sprinkle this mixture evenly over the potatoes. Bake in the centre of the oven for 30 minutes, or until the topping is bubbly.

OFFAL

There are various parts of an animal which do not fit into the category of 'joints' and a lot of delicious things come under the not very pleasing heading of 'offal'. The favourite is perhaps liver, with kidney and oxtail almost as popular.

LIVER

OX OR BULLOCK LIVER: This is fairly cheap, has a strong flavour and is often rather tough and coarse-textured, so that it is best used in a casserole or stew rather than for frying or grilling.

CALF'S LIVER: The best and most expensive, is very tender and delicate in flavour. It can be lightly grilled or fried, but over-cooking makes it hard and dry.

LAMB'S LIVER: Is a little cheaper than calf's liver and has a stronger flavour. It is excellent for grilling and frying, as well as for casseroles and stews.

PIG'S LIVER: Is cheaper than lamb's or calf's liver, but it has a very pronounced flavour and a soft texture that many people dislike. It is best casseroled or stewed and makes excellent pâté.

Allow 4 oz. liver for each person.

KIDNEY

Delicious grilled with bacon or devilled and served on toast, but equally good made into a rich stew with rice or used as an ingredient in a casserole, pie or pudding.

OX OR BULLOCK KIDNEY: Is usually the cheapest and has a fairly strong flavour. It needs slow, gentle cooking to make it tender, so should be stewed, casseroled, used in curries, pies and so on, rather than fried or grilled. A whole kidney, consisting of many joined lobes, weighs about 1½ lb.

Allow about 4 oz. kidney for each person.

CALF'S KIDNEY: Is more and delicate in flavour than ox kidney, but is used in same ways.

1 kidney will serve 1–2 persons.

LAMB'S KIDNEYS: These are usually the best, being small, well-flavoured and tender enough to grill or fry, either whole or in halves. The thin skin and white 'core' should be removed before cooking.

Allow 2 whole kidneys for each person.

PIG'S AND SHEEP'S KIDNEYS: Are similar to lamb's kidneys, but are slightly larger and generally not quite so tender. They can be halved and grilled or fried, or they may be used in stews, curries or casseroles.

Allow 1–2 per person, depending on their size.

HEART

Though somewhat neglected nowadays, hearts can be used to make a variety of economical and savoury dishes.

BULLOCK OR OX HEART: Is the largest and tends to be rather tough unless cooked long and slowly. It can be par-boiled whole and then roasted, or cut up and braised or used in stews, but in any case it needs strong seasonings and flavourings. When cooked whole, ox heart is often stuffed with a savoury forcemeat.

An ox heart may weigh about 3–4 lb. and is enough for 4–6 people. It can also be bought sliced, by the pound, for use in stews, casseroles and similar dishes.

CALF'S HEART: Is small and more tender, but still needs slow cooking to make it enjoyable. It may be roasted, braised or stewed.

One calf's heart will serve 2 people.

LAMB'S HEART: The smallest kind, one of which serves only 1 person. More tender than calf's or ox heart, it has a finer flavour and is usually stuffed and either roasted or braised.

SWEETBREADS

These take a little time to prepare, but the results are worth the effort. Either fried or braised, they make a delicious change.

BULLOCK'S OR OX SWEETBREADS: Are usually the cheapest and need slow, gentle cooking, in either a stew or a casserole, to make them tender.

CALF'S SWEETBREADS: These are more expensive and more tender, but are also best stewed or casseroled.

LAMB'S SWEETBREADS: The most expensive and tender, with a fine delicate flavour. They can be fried, stewed or casseroled.

Allow 4 oz. sweetbreads per person.

OXTAIL

This has a high proportion of bone and is generally rather fatty, so it is not highly priced. Its flavour is excellent and when cooked long and slowly it makes rich, hearty and delicious stews and soup. Choose an oxtail with bright red flesh and creamy white fat.

One will generally make a good stew for 4 people.

TRIPE

This can be of different texture, known as 'blanket' or 'honeycomb', from the first or the second stomach respectively. Tripe is usually sold 'dressed', that is, cleaned and par-boiled.

Allow 4–6 oz. per person.

TONGUE

Often sold pickled or salted, in which case the cooking time is halved.

OX TONGUE: A single tongue weighs about 4 lb. and is usually salted, cooked whole and served cold and sliced.

CALF'S TONGUE: Weighs 1–2 lb. Usually salted. Several tongues are often pressed together after cooking and served cold and sliced. They can, however, also be served hot.

LAMB'S TONGUES: These weigh only 4–5 oz. each. Usually served hot.

Allow about 4 oz. cooked tongue per person.

BRAINS

Calf's brains are considered the best; they are served poached, with a sauce. Lamb's brains are more often used for stews, etc., but can be cooked separately as for calf's brains.

Allow 1 'set' of brains per person.

Liver and Onions

1 lb. onions, skinned and chopped
1 oz. fat or oil
Salt and pepper
½ level tsp. dried sage or mixed herbs (optional)
¾–1 lb. calf's or lamb's liver

Fry the onions lightly in the hot fat or oil until they begin to colour, then add the seasoning (and the herbs, if used). Cover the frying pan with a lid or large plate and simmer very gently for about 10 minutes until the onions are soft. Meanwhile wash and trim the liver and cut it into thin strips. Add to the onions, increase the heat slightly and continue cooking for about 5–10 minutes, stirring all the time, until the liver is just cooked. Remove it from the pan, drain and serve with boiled rice.

Liver Marsala

1 lb. calf's or lamb's liver
Lemon juice
Seasoned flour
2 oz. butter
3 tbsps. Marsala
¼ pint stock (made with a stock cube)
Whole grilled tomatoes, matchstick potatoes and parsley to garnish

Sprinkle the sliced liver with the lemon juice and coat with seasoned flour. Melt the butter in a frying pan and fry the liver quickly on both sides until lightly browned. Stir in the Marsala and stock and simmer until the meat is just cooked and the sauce syrupy. Arrange the liver on a serving dish and garnish with the tomatoes, potatoes and parsley.

Liver Terrine

1 lb. pig's liver
¼ lb. fat bacon
4 eggs, beaten
1 clove of garlic, crushed
¼ pint thick white sauce
Salt and pepper
12 rashers of streaky bacon, rinded

Oven temperature: warm (325°F., mark 3)

Mince the liver and fat bacon finely, then put the mixture through the mincer again and finally sieve it, to ensure a really smooth result. Mix it with the beaten eggs, crushed garlic, sauce and seasoning to taste. Line a 2-pint terrine with bacon rashers, fill up with the liver mixture and place in a dish containing some cold water. Bake just below the centre of the oven for 2 hours. Cover the top of the liver mixture with greaseproof paper, put a heavy plate or something similar on top and leave for 24 hours in a cold place before serving. Serve cold and sliced, with toast and butter and crisp lettuce.

Grilled Kidneys

Allow 1–2 lamb's or pig's kidneys per person, according to size. Wash the kidneys, cut in half and cut out the core. Thread them on to a skewer, cut side uppermost, brush over with oil and sprinkle with salt and pepper. Cook under a hot grill, uncut side first and then cut side, so that the juices gather in the cut side. Serve on fried bread, with grilled or fried bacon, or with fried or diced potatoes.

Kidneys in Red Wine

2 oz. butter
1 onion, skinned and chopped
4–6 sheep's kidneys
3 level tbsps. flour
¼ pint red wine
¼ pint stock
A bouquet garni
1 tbsp. tomato paste
Salt and pepper
2 oz. mushrooms, sliced

Curried Kidneys

Lambs' kidneys may be cooked in the sauce given for Curried Beef earlier in this chapter, but since they are very rich, a smaller quantity is required, and they should be served in a border of noodles or rice. Use ½ lb. kidneys, finely chopped, and halve the quantities for the sauce ingredients; cook for about ½ hour, or until the kidney is tender.

Melt the butter and fry the onion until golden-brown. Wash, skin and core the kidneys and cut them into small pieces, add to the pan and cook for 5 minutes, stirring occasionally. Stir in the flour, pour in the wine and stock and bring slowly to the boil, then add the bouquet garni, tomato paste and some salt and pepper. Simmer for 5 minutes. Add the mushrooms and simmer for a further few minutes. Remove the bouquet garni before serving and check the seasoning. Serve with plain boiled rice or creamed potatoes.

Stuffed Heart Casserole

4 small lamb's hearts
4 oz. fresh white breadcrumbs
1 medium-sized onion, skinned and finely chopped
3 tbsps. melted butter
2 level tsps. mixed dried herbs
Salt and pepper
2 level tbsps. seasoned flour
1 oz. fat or oil
1 pint stock
1 onion, skinned and sliced
4 sticks of celery, scrubbed and sliced
¼ lb. carrots, peeled and sliced
1 tbsp. cider (optional)

Oven temperature: moderate (350°F., mark 4)

Wash the hearts, slit open, remove any tubes or gristle and wash again. Fill with a stuffing made from the breadcrumbs, onion, melted butter, mixed herbs and seasonings. Tie the hearts firmly into their original shape with string, coat with seasoned flour and brown quickly in the hot fat or oil. Place in a casserole with the stock, cover and bake in the centre of the oven for 2½ hours, turning them frequently. Add the onion, celery, carrots and cider (if used) for the last 45 minutes of the cooking time.

Rich Casseroled Heart

1 ox heart, weighing 2½–3 lb.
2 oz. fat or oil
2 onions, skinned and sliced
1 oz. flour
½ pint stock
½ lb. carrots, peeled and grated
½ a small swede, peeled and grated
Rind of 1 orange
6 walnuts, chopped

Oven temperature: cool (300°F., mark 2)

Cut the heart into ½-inch slices, removing the tubes, and wash it well. Fry the slices of meat in the fat or oil till slightly browned and put into a casserole. Fry the onions and add to the casserole. Add the flour to the remaining fat and brown slightly. Pour in the stock, bring to the boil and simmer for 2–3 minutes, then strain over the slices of heart in the casserole; cover and cook for 3½–4 hours in the oven, adding the carrots and swede after 2½–3 hours. Remove the rind from the orange, shred it finely, cook in boiling water for 10–15 minutes, then drain. Add the walnuts and orange rind to the casserole 15 minutes before the cooking is completed. Alternatively, replace the orange rind and walnuts by an 8-oz. can of tomatoes (chopped up).

Oxtail Casserole

1 oxtail, cut up
1 oz. fat or oil
2 onions, skinned and sliced
1 oz. plain flour
¾ pint stock
A pinch of mixed herbs
A bay leaf
2 carrots, peeled and sliced
2 tsps. lemon juice
Seasoning

Oven temperature: fairly hot (375°F., mark 5)

Fry the oxtail in the fat or oil until golden-brown, then place it in a casserole. Fry the onions and add to the meat. Sprinkle the flour into the fat and brown it, add the stock gradually and bring to the boil, then pour over the meat. Add the herbs, carrots and lemon juice, season, cover and cook in the centre of the oven for ½ hour, then reduce to cool (300°F., mark 1) and simmer very gently for a further 2½–3 hours.

Creamed Sweetbreads

1 lb. sweetbreads (prepared)
½ an onion, skinned and chopped
1 carrot, peeled and chopped
A few parsley stalks
½ a bay leaf
Salt and pepper
1½ oz. butter
1½ oz. flour
½ pint milk
A squeeze of lemon juice
Chopped parsley to garnish

Put the sweetbreads, vegetables, herbs and seasoning in a pan with water to cover and simmer gently until tender – ¾–1 hour. Drain and keep hot, retaining ½ pint of the cooking liquid. Melt the butter, stir in the flour and cook for 2–3 minutes. Remove the pan from the

heat and gradually stir in the sweetbread liquid and the milk. Bring to the boil and continue to stir until it thickens, season well and add a squeeze of lemon juice. Re-heat the sweetbreads in the sauce and serve sprinkled with the parsley.

Fried Sweetbreads

Allow 1 lb. lamb's or calf's sweetbreads for 4 people. Soak them for about 3–4 hours in cold water, drain and put into a pan. Cover them with water and the juice of ½ a lemon, bring slowly to the boil, then simmer for 5 minutes. Drain and leave in cold water until they are firm and cold, then strip off any stringy unwanted tissues.

Press the sweetbreads well between absorbent paper, slice and dip into beaten egg and crumbs. Cut a few rashers of streaky bacon into strips and fry lightly until just crisp; drain and keep hot, then fry the sweetbreads in the same fat until golden. Toss the bacon and sweetbreads together and serve at once, with Tartare or tomato sauce.

Tripe and Onions

1 lb. dressed tripe
3–4 onions, skinned and chopped
1 pint milk
Salt and pepper
½ a bay leaf (optional)
1 oz. butter
1 oz. flour
Chopped parsley

Simmer the tripe, onions, milk, seasonings and bay leaf (if used) in a covered pan for about 2 hours, or until tender. Alternatively, cook in a casserole in the centre of a cool oven (300°F., mark 2) for 3 hours. Strain off the liquid and measure 1 pint. Melt the butter, stir in the flour and cook for 2–3 minutes. Remove the pan from the heat and gradually stir in the cooking liquid. Bring to the boil and continue to stir until it thickens. Add the tripe and onions and reheat. Adjust the seasoning, sprinkle with parsley and serve with pieces of toast or boiled potatoes.

Boiled Ox Tongue

Before cooking a pickled tongue, soak it in cold water for several hours (overnight if the tongue has been smoked). Skewer it into a convenient shape if very large and put it into a pan with water to cover, bring gradually to the boil and drain. Add flavouring ingredients such as peeled and sliced carrot, onion, turnip,

Tripe and Onions

a few peppercorns and a bouquet garni, cover with fresh cold water, bring to the boil and simmer until tender – 2½–3 hours if pickled, 4½–6 hours if fresh; skim from time to time. Plunge it into cold water, then skin it, taking out any bones or pieces of gristle.

TO SERVE COLD: Put the tongue into a convenient-sized cake tin (a 7-inch one is required for a 6-lb. tongue). Fill up with a little of the stock, put a plate on top, weigh down with a heavy object and leave to set. Turn out and garnish.

TO SERVE HOT: Sprinkle the skinned tongue with browned crumbs and garnish with sliced lemon and parsley. Serve with parsley or tomato sauce.

Note: For method of salting a fresh tongue, see paragraph on Pickling Meat in the introduction to this chapter.

Brains in Black Butter Sauce

4 pairs of lamb brains
1 tbsp. vinegar
Salt
4 oz. butter
1 tbsp. wine vinegar
Black pepper
Chopped parsley

Wash the brains and soak for an hour in cold water. Remove as much of the skin and membrane as possible and put the brains into a pan with the vinegar, ½ level tsp. salt and enough water to cover well. Bring to simmering point and cook gently for 15 minutes; put into cold water, then dry on a towel. Heat half of the butter in a frying pan, add the brains, brown on all sides and put on to a very hot dish. Add the rest of the butter and heat it until dark brown, without allowing it to burn. Add the wine vinegar and pour over the brains; sprinkle with salt, pepper and parsley.

Brawn

½ a pickled or fresh pig's head or calf's head
A bouquet garni
6 peppercorns
1 large onion, skinned
Pieces of carrot and turnip, peeled
Salt
Pepper and ground nutmeg
1 hard-boiled egg, sliced

Wash the head thoroughly, making sure the ear and nostrils are clean; soak it in salted water for about 1 hour. Cut off the ear and remove the brains. Scald the ear, scrape it free of hair and wash well. Place the head in a large pan with the ear, bouquet garni, peppercorns, vegetables and 1 level tsp. salt if the head is pickled (allow 2 level tsps. if it is fresh). Cover with water, bring to the boil, skim carefully and allow to cook very slowly until the meat is tender – about 2–3 hours. Strain off the liquid, remove the meat from the bones and cut it into small pieces. Skin the tongue and slice thinly. Cut the ear into strips. Skim off the fat from the remaining liquid, add the brains, tied up in muslin, then boil until the liquid is reduced to half. Chop the brains and add to the meat. Season the mixed meats well with salt, pepper and nutmeg. Garnish the bottom of a mould or cake tin with sliced egg, pack the meat in tightly and pour some of the liquid over. Put a saucer and a weight on it and leave till cold and set. When the brawn is required for use, dip the mould into hot water and turn the brawn out on to a dish.

Pressed Ox Cheek

1 ox cheek
1 cow heel
Salt
A few peppercorns
A bouquet garni
Allspice (optional)

Clean the cheek and cow heel, put in a pan and cover with cold water; bring to the boil and discard the water. Add salt, the peppercorns and bouquet garni and fresh cold water to cover, bring to simmering point and simmer for about 3 hours, till the meat will fall easily from the bone. Drain and shred the meat. Add some seasoning and a little allspice if liked, pack closely into a bowl or mould, cover and weight down. When it is cold, turn it out and serve with salad.

Casserole of Lamb's Tongues

4 lamb's tongues
1 oz. fat or oil
1 onion, skinned and sliced
1 carrot, peeled and grated
4 large tomatoes, skinned and sliced
1 tbsp. chopped parsley
Salt and pepper
Stock

Oven temperature: moderate (350°F., mark 4)

Wash the tongues and trim if necessary. Fry the onion golden-brown in the fat or oil and place it in a casserole. Add the tongues, carrot, tomatoes, parsley and seasoning and just enough stock to cover. Cook in the centre of the oven for 1½ hours. If preferred, the tongues may be skinned and then re-heated in the liquor before serving. Grilled or baked bacon rolls make a good garnish for this dish.

SAUSAGES

The sausage is a convenient way of utilising odd scraps of meat that are too 'bitty' and diverse to make a proper cut or joint. Good-quality, well-flavoured sausages make endless excellent meals or snacks.

Pork and beef sausages are the two commonest types in this country, but there are all kinds of local variations in different regions – black and white 'puddings', smoked sausage, breakfast sausage and so on, some of which are ready-cooked and make good snacks and sandwiches. Supermarkets and delicatessens offer an enormous variety of continental sausages and we give below notes on three of the most popular types.

BEEF AND PORK SAUSAGES: Pork sausages are more expensive and more delicately flavoured than beef, which have a distinctive taste that is not popular with everybody. Each kind is sold both in the normal 8-to-the-pound size and as the thinner 16-to-the-pound chipolatas. The actual mixture is usually the same, but the thick sausages need longer, slower cooking if they are not to split; chipolatas sometimes look more attractive and appeal to those people who like plenty of nice crisp, brown 'outside'.

'SKINLESS SAUSAGES cook quickly and are good for casseroles, pies and made-up dishes and for people who do not like sausage skins, but they are apt to be dry.

SAUSAGE-MEAT, which can be bought by the pound, is very useful for stuffing, for sausage rolls and for such dishes as Scotch eggs.

FRANKFURTERS, sold either loose or canned, are thin, highly seasoned smoked pork sausages which need only a short cooking time (or none at all), and are very suitable for snacks, barbecues, kebabs and so on.

LIVER SAUSAGE, sold by weight, is a soft-textured, rather fatty kind, often with a white skin or casing, made from liver and pork meat and widely used for sandwiches and as an hors d'oeuvre.

SALAMI is a highly seasoned, garlic-flavoured sausage, originally made in Italy.

FRIED SAUSAGES

Melt a little fat in the frying pan, add the sausages and fry for 15–20 minutes, keeping the heat low to prevent their burning and turning them once or twice to brown them evenly.

GRILLED SAUSAGES

Heat the grill to hot, put the sausages on the grill rack in the pan and cook until one side is lightly browned, then turn them; continue cooking and turning them frequently for about 15–20 minutes, until the sausages are well browned.

BAKED SAUSAGES

Heat the oven to fairly hot (400 F., mark 6). Put the sausages in a greased baking tin and cook in the centre of the oven for 30 minutes.

Alternatively, make Kilted Sausages by wrapping rinded streaky rashers round pairs of chipolatas and baking in the same way at 375 F., mark 5.

SAUSAGE CAKES

Mix 1 lb. sausage-meat with 1 grated onion and 1 level tsp. mixed dried herbs. Divide the mixture into 8 and shape each portion into a round cake. Heat 1 oz. fat or oil in a frying pan and fry the cakes over a low heat for 10 minutes; turn them and fry the other side until crisp and brown.

Toad in the Hole

4 oz plain flour
½ level tsp. salt
1 egg
½ pint milk and water
½ lb. skinless sausages

Oven temperature: hot (425°F., mark 7)

Put the flour and salt into a bowl. Add the egg and half the liquid. Gradually stir in the flour and beat until smooth; stir in the remaining liquid. Grease a shallow ovenproof dish or Yorkshire Pudding tin, put in the

sausages and pour in the batter. Bake at the top of the oven for 40–45 minutes, or until the batter is well risen and golden-brown.

Sausage Rolls

8 oz. shortcrust pastry *(see Pastry chapter)*
8 oz. sausage-meat
A little flour
A little milk to glaze

Oven temperature: fairly hot (400°F., mark 6)

Roll the pastry out thinly into an oblong, then cut it lengthwise into 2 strips. Divide the sausage-meat into 2 pieces, dust with flour, and form into 2 rolls the length of the pastry. Lay a roll of sausage-meat down the centre of each strip, brush down the edges of the pastry with a little milk, fold one side of the pastry over the sausage-meat and press the two edges firmly together. Seal the long edges together by tapping horizontally with a knife to give a flaked effect. Brush the length of the two rolls with milk, then cut each into slices 1½–2 inches long. Place on a baking tray and bake towards the top of the oven for 15 minutes; to cook the meat thoroughly, reduce the temperature to moderate (350°F., mark 4) and bake for a further 15 minutes.

Good sausage rolls can be made with bought puff pastry, fresh or frozen. Use a 4-oz. packet and allow it to reach room temperature (which will take about 2 hours) before rolling it out, then it will be easier to handle. Make the rolls as above, but heat the oven to moderate (350 F., mark 4) and bake for a further 15 minutes.

Sausage Flan

4 oz. shortcrust pastry (see Pastry chapter)
1 onion, skinned and chopped
½ green pepper, de-seeded and chopped
4 oz. streaky bacon, rinded and chopped
½ oz. fat
¾ lb. sausage-meat
1 egg, beaten
1 level tsp. mixed herbs
Salt and pepper

Oven temperature: fairly hot (375°F., mark 5)

Line a 7-inch metal pie plate or sandwich cake tin with the pastry, making a double edge. Fry the onion, pepper and bacon in the fat for 5 minutes, until soft. Drain well and add to the sausage-meat, binding the mixture with the egg and adding the herbs and seasoning. Turn it into the pastry case and bake near the top of the oven for 30–40 minutes, until the filling is cooked and begins to shrink slightly from the pastry.

This flan can be served either hot or cold. As it is fairly rich it is best accompanied by tomatoes, a green vegetable or perhaps a mixed salad.

Sausage Casserole

Sausage Pie

2 onions, skinned and chopped
2–3 potatoes, peeled and thinly sliced
Salt and pepper
½–¾ lb. sausage-meat
1 level tsp. dried sage or mixed herbs
4 oz. shortcrust pastry *(see Pastry chapter)*

Oven temperature: fairly hot (400°F., mark 6)

Put the vegetables into salted water, cover and bring slowly to the boil, then drain. Put them into a 7-inch pie plate, and cover with the sausage-meat, divided into small pieces, then add a generous amount of seasoning and the herbs. Roll out the pastry to form a lid and cover the pie with it, making a double edge so that it will not brown too much. Bake near the top of the oven for about 10–15 minutes, until the pastry begins to brown, then reduce the heat to moderate (350°F., mark 4) and cook for about 30 minutes longer, until the vegetables and meat are tender.

Sausage Casserole

¼ lb. streaky bacon
½ lb. chipolata sausages
½ lb. apples, peeled, cored and sliced
¼–½ lb. tomatoes, skinned and sliced
1 green pepper, de-seeded and sliced
2–3 tbsps. stock or water
Seasoning

Oven temperature: fairly hot (400°F., mark 6)

Cut the rind off the bacon and wrap each slice around 2 sausages, fry them (or brown lightly under the grill) and place in a casserole. Arrange the apples, tomatoes and pepper in layers on top of the sausages and bacon, add the stock and seasoning and cook in the centre of the oven for about 40 minutes.

Poultry

Poultry includes chickens (fowls), guinea fowls, ducks, geese and turkeys. Quite a lot of it is frozen, which means there is a good all-the-year-round supply (*see notes below on frozen poultry*). Most poultry is sold cleaned, plucked and trussed. Both fresh and frozen chicken and ducks, and occasionally turkeys, are available in joints as well as whole.

HANGING AND STORING

Poultry should be hung for 2–3 days after killing before it is cooked. In cold weather it can if necessary be hung for about a week, but unlike game it is not kept until it is 'high'. Poultry is usually plucked before hanging (*see below*), though this is not essential, but the inside should be left in.

Hang the bird by the feet in a cool, airy larder and protect it from flies, using muslin if the larder is not fly-proof.

If poultry is to be put in a refrigerator, remove the inside and wrap the bird loosely or put it in a covered dish.

PLUCKING AND SINGEING

Poultry is usually plucked, or at least rough-plucked, immediately after killing, as the feathers are much easier to remove while the bird is warm. If many feathers remain, spread a piece of old sheeting or a large piece of paper on the floor or table; hold the bird firmly, take 2–3 feathers at a time and pull them sharply towards the head – that is, in the opposite direction to the way they lie. Don't try to pluck handfuls at a time, or you may tear the skin. Large wing feathers are firmly attached and need to be plucked singly, with pliers if necessary. After the actual feathers have all been plucked, down (such as that on a goose) and any hairs can be singed off. Hold the bird over an open flame (gas burner, lighted taper or a piece of burning paper), turning it quickly.

DRAWING

In older birds the leg sinews need removing. Cut a small slit with a sharp-pointed knife in the leg just above the claw and parallel with the leg bone, exposing the sinews. Slip a skewer under one of them, then, holding the foot firmly, pull on the skewer to draw out the sinew from the flesh. There are 4–5 sinews in each leg and they must be taken out singly.

Unless the bird is very young it is usual to cut off the feet and the easiest way of doing this is to sever the leg at the joint; bend the foot back, insert the knife in the joint and cut through. (The feet can be added to giblet stock.)

To cut off the head, first cut through the skin of the neck about 2 inches from the body. Slip back the skin and cut off the neck close to the trunk. (The neck is kept for stock, but the head is discarded.)

Slit the skin of the neck a little way down the back of the bird – far enough to let you get your fingers inside and to loosen the windpipe and gullet, which simplifies the drawing process. Cut round the vent at the tail end with scissors or a sharp knife, taking care not to puncture the entrails. Make the hole large enough to get your fingers inside the body. Take hold of the gizzard (the large, oval, muscular organ containing food and grit) and draw out all the entrails, including the lungs, windpipe and gullet. Reserve the giblets (heart, gizzard and liver) and any fat – there is always plenty in a goose. Discard the rest of the entrails, burning them if possible. Wipe out the inside of the bird with a clean, damp cloth.

THE GIBLETS

Cut out the gall-bladder from the liver, keeping it intact, and discard it; discard also the flesh on which it rested, as this may have a bitter flavour. Carefully cut through the flesh of the gizzard up to but not through the crop, peel off the flesh and discard the crop.

Giblet Stock

Wash the liver, gizzard and heart. Wash and scald the

feet, remove the scales and nip off the claws. Put all in a saucepan, cover with water and stew gently for $\frac{3}{4}$–1 hour, to make a stock that can be used for gravy or soup.

BONING
To bone a chicken for a galantine or similar purpose, first cut off the neck and feet as above and cut off the end joints of the wings. Commence boning at the neck. Using a small, sharp knife and keeping it close to the bone, separate the flesh from the bone. To bone the wings, cut through from inside where the wing joins the body, then work down the bone, scraping the flesh from it and turning the wing inside out; repeat with the other wing. Continue to work down the body, boning the legs in the same manner as the wings. Finally, turn the bird right side out.

STUFFING AND TRUSSING
The object of trussing is to keep the bird a good shape so that it will be easy to carve. A trussing needle (a long needle with an eye large enough to take fine string) is useful, but failing this, use a skewer and some fine string. First fold the neck skin under the body and fold the tips of the wings back towards the backbone so that they hold the neck skin in position; set the bird on its back and press the legs well into the side, thus raising the breast. Make a slit in the skin above the vent and put the tail (the 'parson's nose') through this.

Thread the needle with a length of string and insert it close to the second joint of the right wing; push it right through the body, passing it out so as to catch the corresponding joint on the left side. Insert the needle again in the first joint of the left wing, pass it through the flesh at the back of the body, catching the tips of the wings and the neck skin, and pass it out through the first joint of the wing on the right side. Tie the ends of the string in a bow. To truss the legs, re-thread the needle and insert it through the gristle at the right side of the 'parson's nose'. Pass the string over the right leg, over the left leg, through the gristle at the left side of the 'parson's nose', carry it

behind the 'parson's nose' and tie the ends of the string firmly to keep all in place.

When using a skewer, insert it right through the body of the bird just below the thigh bone and turn the bird over on to its breast. First, catching in the wing tips, pass the string under ends of skewer and cross it over the back.

Turn the bird over and tie the ends of the string together round the tail, at the same time securing the drumsticks.

FROZEN POULTRY
Deep-frozen poultry should be allowed to thaw out at room temperature; the time required depends on the size of the joint or bird – single joints take up to 6 hours in the fridge; a 3-lb. bird takes 15–18 hours in the fridge; and large turkeys up to 4 days. If you need to speed up the defrosting process, hold the bird under cold (not hot) running water, but this is only an emergency measure.

The giblets are usually wrapped in polythene and placed inside the body cavity, so remove them before cooking the bird. Frozen birds are usually sold trussed, ready for stuffing.

CARVING POULTRY
Place the bird so that one wing is towards your left hand, with the breast diagonally towards you. Hold the wing with the fork and cut through the outer layer of the breast, judging the direction of the cut so that the knife enters the wing joint. Gently ease the wing away from the body of the bird and firmly cut through the joint gristle. Repeat for the other wing.

Steadying the bird with the flat of the knife held against the breast, prise the leg outwards with the fork, thus exposing the thigh joint – one clean cut through the joint will then sever the leg. It is usual to divide the thigh from the drumstick by cutting through the joint and in a big bird the thigh is further divided. Cut the breast in thin slices, parallel with the breastbone. When stuffing has been cooked in a bird, it is sliced from the front of the breast; the rest is scooped out with a spoon.

CHICKEN

When buying a fresh (non-frozen) bird, feel the tip of the breast-bone with the thumb and finger. In a young bird this is soft and flexible; if it is hard and rigid the bird is probably too old to roast satisfactorily and will have to be steamed or boiled. Look at the feet also – in a young bird they are smooth with small (not coarse) scales and with short spurs.

Many different terms have been used at times to classify chickens, but the main categories seen nowadays are:

Poussins
Very small chickens, 1–2 lb.; 6–8 weeks old; one serves 1–2 people.

Broilers
Small birds, $2\frac{1}{2}$–$3\frac{1}{2}$ lb.; 12 weeks old; one serves 3–4 people. (Frozen chickens are usually broilers.)

Large Roasters
Generally young cockerels or hens, but may be capons. 'Young roasters' are 4–5 lb. and one serves 5–6 people;

capons weigh up to 8 lb. and one serves 6–10 people.

Boiling Fowls
Older, tougher birds; 4–7 lb. They should be 18 months old, but may in some cases be older. Usually served in casseroles, etc.; allow 3–4 oz. meat per person.

Bacon Rolls: Roll up rashers of streaky bacon, thread on a skewer and grill until crisp – 3–5 minutes.

Thin Gravy: Pour off all the fat except 1 tbsp. from the roasting tin. Sprinkle in 4 level tbsps. flour and stir in about $\frac{1}{2}$ pint giblet stock (*see above*). Bring to the boil, stirring, season with salt and pepper and add a touch of gravy browning, if necessary. The finely chopped chicken liver may be included to give a richer flavour.

Roast Chicken

Oven temperature: fairly hot (400°F., mark 6)

If the bird is frozen, allow it to thaw out completely, then remove the bag of giblets. Wash the inside of the bird and stuff it at the neck end before folding the neck skin over. To add flavour you can put an onion, a thick lemon wedge or a knob of butter in the body of the bird. Brush the chicken with melted butter or oil and sprinkle with salt and pepper. Put in a shallow roasting tin. A few strips of streaky bacon may be laid over the breast to prevent it from becoming too dry.

Bake in the centre of the oven, basting from time to time and allowing 20 minutes per lb. plus 20 minutes. Put a piece of paper over the breast if the flesh shows signs of becoming too brown. Alternatively, wrap the chicken in foil before roasting; allow the same cooking time, but open the foil for the final 15–20 minutes, to allow the bird to brown.

Serve with roast potatoes and a green vegetable or – for a change – a tossed green salad. Bacon rolls, forcemeat balls, small chipolata sausages, bread sauce and thin gravy are the usual accompaniments.

Chicken Kiev

4 large chicken leg joints or breasts, skinned
4 oz. butter
Grated rind of $\frac{1}{2}$ a lemon
1 tbsp. lemon juice
Salt and pepper
1 tbsp. chopped parsley
1 clove of garlic, skinned and crushed
1 oz. seasoned flour
1 egg, beaten
4 oz. fresh white breadcrumbs
Oil for deep frying

Choose large leg joints which have a good portion of breast attached. Using a small, sharp knife, carefully work the flesh off the bone; the tip of the bone can be left in if wished, in which case crack it towards the tip. Don't split the flesh. With a slightly damped heavy knife beat out each piece.

Work together the butter, lemon rind, juice, salt, pepper, parsley and garlic. Place on a sheet of non-stick or waxed paper, form into a roll and chill until firm. Cut into 4 pieces and place one on each piece of chicken; roll up, folding the ends in to enclose the butter completely, and secure with cocktail sticks. Coat in seasoned flour, then egg and crumb, patting the crumbs well in. Chill till required.

Heat the oil to 325°F. Place 2 chicken portions in a frying basket and carefully lower into the oil; fry for about 15 minutes and drain. Fry the remaining chicken. Serve at once, on a bed of savoury rice.

Chicken Maryland

A 2$\frac{1}{2}$–3 lb. chicken, jointed
3 level tbsps. seasoned flour
1 egg, beaten
Dry breadcrumbs
2 oz. butter
1–2 tbsps. oil
4 bananas
Sweet corn fritters
4 rashers of streaky bacon

Divide the chicken into fairly small portions, coat with seasoned flour, dip in beaten egg and coat with breadcrumbs. Fry the chicken in the butter and oil in a large frying pan until lightly browned. Continue frying gently, turning the pieces once, for about 20 minutes, or until tender. Alternatively, fry them in deep fat for 5–10 minutes. (The fat should be hot enough to brown a 1-inch cube of bread in 60–70 seconds.) Serve the chicken with fried bananas, corn fritters and bacon rolls.

Fried Bananas
Peel and slice the bananas lengthways and fry gently for about 3 minutes in a little hot butter or lard, until lightly browned.

Corn Fritters
Make up a batter from 4 oz. flour, a pinch of salt, 1 egg and $\frac{1}{4}$ pint milk (*see Batter recipe in Hot Puddings chapter*). Fold in 1 small packet of frozen corn kernels (thawed). Fry in spoonfuls in a little hot fat until crisp and golden, turning them once. Drain well on crumpled kitchen paper.

Chicken and Walnuts

A roasting chicken (3$\frac{1}{2}$–4 lb.), jointed (or 6 chicken joints)
2 tbsps. sherry
2 level tsps. caster sugar
3 tbsps. oil
8 oz. button mushrooms
A 6-oz. can of water chestnuts
1 pint chicken stock
2 level tbsps. cornflour
4 oz. halved walnuts
1 oz. butter

Oven temperature: moderate (350°F., mark 4)

Chicken and Walnuts with accompaniments

Place the chicken in a dish, pour the sherry and caster sugar over it and leave it to marinade for 1–2 hours.

Heat the oil in a frying pan and brown the chicken pieces. Slice the mushrooms, drain and dice the chestnuts and place them all in a large casserole. Arrange the chicken pieces on top, pour the chicken juices and chicken stock into the casserole, cover and bake in the centre of the oven for 2 hours. Drain off the liquor, keep the chicken hot and thicken the liquor with the cornflour. Brown the walnuts in melted butter for 4–5 minutes and drain. Dish up the chicken and vegetables, pour some of the gravy over them (serving the rest separately) and garnish with the browned walnuts.

Chicken Ramekins

½ oz. butter
4 oz. cooked chicken, minced
2 mushrooms, chopped
2 eggs, separated
2 tbsps. cream
Salt and pepper

Oven temperature: moderate (350°F., mark 4)

Grease 4 ramekins with the butter. Mix the chicken and mushrooms and bind with the egg yolks and cream; season to taste with salt and pepper. Whisk the egg whites stiffly and fold into the chicken mixture. Divide this mixture between the ramekins, place the ramekins on a baking tray and cook in the centre of the oven for 15–20 minutes. Serve at once.

The chicken mixture need not be cooked in separate dishes, but can be put into a greased 1-pint soufflé dish, baked just above the centre of a fairly hot oven (400°F., mark 6) for 25–30 minutes and served as a savoury.

Poussins in a Basket

4 poussins
4 oz. melted butter
Salt and pepper
2 onions, skinned and sliced (optional)
Watercress

Split the birds down the back. Trim off the legs and the wings at the first joint, open out the birds and flatten as much as possible. Brush all over with melted butter and season lightly. Grill under a medium heat, turning once or twice, for about 20 minutes, or until the poussins are tender. Serve on a napkin in a basket, garnished with the onion rings and watercress.

Chicken Fricassee

A 2½-lb. boiling chicken, jointed
2 medium onions, skinned and finely chopped
2 carrots, peeled and finely sliced
¼ lb. mushrooms, sliced
Water
A bouquet garni
Salt and pepper
2 oz. butter
2 oz. flour
4 rashers of streaky bacon, rolled
1 egg yolk
3 tbsps. cream
Juice of ½ a lemon

Place the chicken joints, vegetables, just enough water to cover and the bouquet garni in a large saucepan. Add salt and pepper and bring slowly to the boil; simmer gently for 1 hour, or until the chicken is tender. When the chicken is cooked, remove it from the heat, strain

off the stock and put it on one side. Remove the chicken meat from the bones and cut it into cubes. Melt the butter, stir in the flour, cook for 2–3 minutes and remove from the heat. Measure off 1 pint of the strained stock, gradually stir it into the cooked fat and flour, bring to the boil and continue to stir until the sauce thickens. Add the meat and vegetables and heat through for about 2 minutes.

Grill the bacon rolls. Blend together the egg yolk and cream, add a little of the sauce to the mixture and blend to a smooth cream. Return the blended mixture to the sauce and heat through gently, without boiling. Add the lemon juice. Pour the fricassee into a serving dish and garnish with the bacon rolls and chopped parsley.

Chicken à la King

2 oz. butter
4 oz. mushrooms, sliced
½ a green pepper, chopped (or 1 small canned pimiento, chopped)
1½ oz. flour
¾ pint milk or milk and chicken stock, mixed
Diced cooked chicken (8–12 oz.)
Salt, pepper, paprika or ground nutmeg
1–2 tbsps. sherry (optional)

Melt the butter and fry the mushrooms and pepper until soft. Stir in the flour, cook for 2–3 minutes, remove from the heat and stir in the milk gradually. Bring the sauce to the boil and continue to stir until it thickens. Add the chicken, season to taste and add the sherry, if used. Serve with boiled rice or buttered noodles or as a snack with toast or crisp rolls.

Chicken à la King can be bought in cans and kept as a standby for a quick meal; serve as suggested above.

Chicken Marengo

4 chicken joints
3–4 tbsps. oil
2 carrots, peeled and sliced
1 stick of celery, scrubbed and chopped
1 onion, skinned and chopped
2 oz. streaky bacon, chopped
3 level tbsps. flour
½ pint chicken stock
A 15-oz. can of tomatoes
2 tbsps. sherry
Salt and pepper
A bouquet garni
¼ lb. mushrooms, sliced
Chopped parsley

Oven temperature: moderate (350 F., mark 4)

Fry the chicken joints in the oil for about 5 minutes, until golden-brown, remove them from the pan and put into a casserole. Fry the vegetables and bacon in the oil for about 5 minutes until golden-brown, remove them from

Chicken Marengo

the pan. Stir the flour into the remaining fat, cook for 2–3 minutes and gradually stir in the stock; bring to the boil and continue to stir until it thickens. Return the vegetables to the pan and add the tomatoes, sherry, salt and pepper. Pour this sauce over the chicken joints, add the bouquet garni and sliced mushrooms and cook in the centre of the oven for ¾–1 hour, until the chicken joints are tender. Remove them to a warm serving dish. Strain the sauce from the casserole over them and sprinkle with chopped parsley.

Coq au Vin

3 oz. bacon, rinded and chopped
6 oz. mushrooms, washed and sliced
16 button onions, skinned
½ oz. butter
1 tbsp. oil
1 small roasting chicken
4 tbsps. brandy
3 level tbsps. flour
½ bottle red wine
¼ pint stock
1 level tbsp. sugar
A bouquet garni
A pinch of ground nutmeg
Salt and pepper

Oven temperature: moderate (350°F., mark 4)

Fry the bacon, mushrooms and onions in the butter and oil for about 3–4 minutes, until lightly browned; remove from the pan.

Fry the chicken on its breast and underside for 8–10 minutes, until golden-brown. Pour the brandy over the chicken, remove the pan from the heat and 'flame' it by igniting the liquid in the saucepan with a match. Remove the chicken when the flames have died down and place it in a casserole.

Stir the flour into the fat remaining in the pan and cook for 2–3 minutes. Stir in the wine and stock gradually, bring to the boil and continue to stir until the mixture thickens; add sugar, herbs and seasonings. Add the cooked vegetables to the casserole and pour the sauce over the chicken. Cover and cook in the centre of the oven for ¾–1 hour, until tender. Before serving, remove the bouquet garni.

Curried Chicken

1 chicken, jointed and skinned
2 level tbsps. seasoned flour
2 onions, sliced and skinned
2 oz. butter
1 apple, cored and chopped
2 level tsps. curry powder
¼ pint stock
A little lemon juice
2 level tsps. sweet chutney

Coat the chicken with flour. Lightly fry the onions in the butter, then add the chicken and fry until golden-brown. Add the apple, curry powder and remaining flour, stir well and fry for 1–2 minutes. Add the stock, lemon juice and chutney and mix together. Cover the pan and simmer till the chicken is cooked and the sauce thickens – about 40 minutes. Serve with rice or a pilau (*see Pasta and Rice chapter*) and garnish with tomato slices.

If you use cooked chicken, omit the preliminary frying.

Galantine of Chicken

1 boiling chicken
Salt and pepper
12 oz. sausage-meat
2 hard-boiled eggs, shelled and sliced
2 oz. cooked ham, chopped
2 oz. cooked tongue; chopped
¼–½ pint aspic jelly
Sliced cucumber, olives, egg, etc., to garnish

Bone the bird as described at the beginning of the chapter. When all the bones are removed, spread out the bird and sprinkle the flesh with salt and pepper. Cover the body of the bird with the sausage-meat, pushing it inside the wings and legs so that they regain their original shape. Arrange the sliced eggs, ham and tongue over the sausage-meat and season again. Wrap the cut ends of the skin over one another to make a neat shape, as like that of the original bird as possible. Using a large bodkin or trussing needle and a piece of string, sew the skin in place.

Wrap the bird in a clean cloth, tie firmly, put in a large pan and cover with salted water. Put on the lid and simmer for about 2 hours, or until tender. When the chicken is cooked, remove from the pan and re-shape. When it is cold, remove the cloth, coat with aspic jelly (made according to the manufacturer's instructions), decorate with slices of cucumber, stuffed olives, hard-boiled egg, etc., and cover with more aspic jelly; leave to set. Serve sliced with salad.

Chicken Mousse

¼ pint aspic jelly
Slices of cucumber and thin strips of tomato and lemon rind
   to garnish
12 oz. cooked chicken, minced
¼ pint Béchamel sauce
2–3 tbsps. mayonnaise
½ pint cream, whipped

Line a 1½-pint mould or some individual moulds with a little aspic jelly and allow to set. Decorate with a few slices of cucumber and strips of tomato and lemon rind, spoon a little more jelly over and allow to set. Mix the chicken, Béchamel sauce and mayonnaise and add the remainder of the aspic jelly. When the mixture is on the point of setting, fold in the whipped cream. Turn the mixture into the mould or moulds and leave to set. When it is cold and firm, turn out and garnish with slices of cucumber and strips of tomato and lemon rind.

Chicken Chaudfroid

¼ pint aspic jelly
A cooked chicken
¼ pint Béchamel sauce *(see Sauces chapter)*
Cucumber, pickled walnuts, radish and strips of lemon rind to garnish

Make up the aspic as directed on the packet and leave

it until it has almost reached setting point. Place the chicken on a cooling rack over a tray or large plate. Add half the aspic to the Béchamel sauce, stir in lightly and allow to thicken but not set. (Keep the remaining aspic in a basin which is standing in a bowl of warm water.) Coat the chicken by pouring the sauce steadily over it to give a smooth, even surface; allow the excess to run off and collect in the tray. Decorate the chicken with strips of cucumber skin, pieces of pickled walnut, slices of radish and strips of lemon rind, then carefully spoon over it the remaining aspic (which should be at setting point), so that the coated bird is completely covered but the decoration is not disturbed.

GUINEA FOWL

These are available all the year round, but are at their best from February to June. A guinea fowl has grey plumage and white spots and is usually of about the same size as a pheasant, though it can be as large as a small chicken. When choosing one, look out for the same points as in a fresh chicken, especially a plump breast and smooth-skinned feet. An average-sized bird will serve 4 people. Guinea fowl needs to be hung for some time after killing. All methods for cooking chicken or pheasant *(see Game chapter)* are applicable, especially

braising or casseroling, but take care to use plenty of fat when roasting it, otherwise the flesh will be dry.

Roast Guinea Fowl

Singe, draw and wipe the bird *(see beginning of chapter)* and truss it for roasting. Roast in a fairly hot oven (400 F., mark 6) for 45–60 minutes, or longer, according to size, basting frequently with butter or dripping. Garnish with watercress and serve with thin gravy and orange or mixed green salad or with bread sauce.

DUCK

The name 'duckling' applies to a bird up to 8 weeks old.
Choose a young bird with soft, pliable feet; the feet and the bill should be yellow.
Allow about 1 lb. dressed weight per person.

Roast Duck

Oven temperature: fairly hot (400°F., mark 6)

Pluck, draw and truss in the usual way *(see beginning of this chapter)*, except that the wings are not drawn across the back; tie the legs with fine string.
A young duckling does not require stuffing, but it is usual to stuff an older bird with sage and onion stuffing at the tail end. Sprinkle the breast with salt and pepper. Cook just above the centre of the oven, allowing 20 minutes per lb. Remove the trussing strings and skewers; serve the bird garnished with watercress and accompanied by apple sauce, potatoes, peas and thin brown

gravy. Orange salad is also a favourite accompaniment for roast duck.
(See colour picture facing page 160)
WILD DUCK: *See Game chapter.*

Duck with Cherries

1 roasting duck
½ oz. butter
Salt
½ pint stock
1 orange
3–4 lumps of sugar
1½ oz. caster sugar
1 wineglass port
1 lb. red cherries, stoned
1 pint Espagnole sauce or good gravy

Oven temperature: hot (425°F., mark 7)

Rub the breast of the duck with the butter and sprinkle with salt. Put the duck in the roasting tin with the stock and cook in the centre of the oven for 15 minutes per lb., basting occasionally with the liquid. Meanwhile, rub the skin of the orange with sugar lumps to obtain the zest and put the lumps in a pan with the caster sugar and the port. Squeeze the orange and add the juice to the sugar in the pan; allow the sugar to dissolve slowly, add the cherries, cover and simmer gently for about 5 minutes.

The duck should still be slightly pink when cooked; remove it from the oven and cut into joints. Place the joints on a serving dish and keep hot. Strain the syrup from the cherries and keep the fruit hot. Add the syrup to the Espagnole sauce and spoon some of the mixture over the duck. Arrange the cherries at either end of the serving dish and serve the remaining sauce separately.

Duck in Red Wine

1 duck (about 5–6 lb.)
½ a clove of garlic, crushed
2 oz. flour
¾ pint red wine
2 oz. mushrooms, sliced
A bay leaf
Sprigs of parsley
½ level tsp. dried thyme
1 level tsp. salt
1 lb. small onions, skinned
1 lb. small carrots, scraped

Oven temperature: moderate (350°F., mark 4)

Remove the skin and fat from the duck and put them with the giblets into a pan; cover with water and simmer for 1 hour. Skim off the fat from the surface and let the stock cool. Cut the duck into joints. Heat 2 tbsps. of the duck fat in a pan, then brown the duck joints on all sides. Remove them from the fat and put in a casserole. Add the crushed garlic to the fat, fry for 1 minute and stir in

the flour. Add the wine, mushrooms, herbs and salt. Bring to the boil, stirring constantly until the sauce thickens. Put the onions, carrots and duck joints into the casserole, pour the sauce over, cover and cook in the centre of the oven for ¾–1 hour, until tender.

Duck and Orange Casserole

1 duck, jointed
Seasoned flour
½ oz. fat
¼ lb. mushrooms, sliced
2 onions, skinned and chopped
1–2 oz. flour
¾ pint stock
¼ pint orange juice
1 orange

Oven temperature: moderate (350°F., mark 4)

Coat the duck joints with the seasoned flour. Fry the duck in the fat for 8–10 minutes, until well browned, and transfer to a casserole. Fry the mushrooms and onions lightly in the hot fat for about 3 minutes, remove from the pan and add to the casserole. Stir the flour into the remaining fat and brown over a very low heat, stirring all the time. Remove from thee heat, gradually stir in the stock and orange juice and bring to the boil; continue to stir until it thickens. Pour over the duck, cover and cook in the centre of the oven for 1 hour, until the duck is tender.

Peel off the coloured part of the orange rind with a vegetable peeler and cut it into very thin strips. Divide the orange itself into segments, removing any pith or pips. Simmer the strips of rind in water until tender – about 5 minutes; drain well and sprinkle over the cooked duck joints. Garnish with the orange segments before serving.

GOOSE

Geese are available all the year round, but are at their best from December to March. A 10-lb. bird will serve 7–8 people.

A young bird, which has more tender flesh, is recognised by soft, yellow feet and a yellow bill; the fat should be yellow and the flesh pinkish in colour.

Roast Goose

Oven temperature: fairly hot (400°F., mark 6)

PREPARATION AND TRUSSING: Pluck the bird (*see beginning of this chapter*) and remove the stumps from the wings. Cut off the feet and the wing tips at the first joint. Cut off the head, then, forcing back the neck skin, cut off the neck where it joins the back. Draw the bird as described for other poultry and clean the inside with a cloth wrung out in hot water. Put a thick fold of cloth over the breast-bone and flatten it with a mallet or rolling pin. Stuff with sage and onion stuffing or a fruit stuffing.

Working with the breast side uppermost and tail end away from you, pass a skewer through one wing, then

Roast Duck and Orange

through the body and out again through the other wing. Pass a second skewer through the end of the wing joint on one side, through the thick part of the leg, through the body and out the other side in the same way. Pass a third skewer through the loose skin near the end of the leg, through the body and out the other side in the same way. Enlarge the vent, pass the tail through it and fix with a small skewer. Wind string round the skewers, keeping the limbs firmly in position, but avoid passing the string over the breast of the goose. Tuck the neck skin in under the string.

COOKING AND SERVING: Sprinkle the bird with salt, put in a baking tin on a rack or trivet (as goose tends to be fatty) and cover with the fat taken from inside, then with greased paper. A sour apple put in the roasting tin during the cooking adds flavour to the gravy.

Roast for 15 minutes per lb. plus 15 minutes, basting frequently. To cook by the slow method, roast in a moderate oven (350°F., mark 4) for 25–30 minutes per lb. Remove the paper for the last 30 minutes, to brown the bird.

Serve with giblet gravy (made in the roasting tin after the fat has been poured off) and apple or gooseberry sauce. Apple rings which have been dipped in lemon juice, brushed with oil and lightly grilled. also make an attractive garnish.

TURKEY

Turkeys are now available all the year round, but are of course especially abundant at Christmas time.

Choose a bird that is plump and white-fleshed; short spurs and smooth black legs are signs that it is young.

A 10–13 lb. turkey will serve 13–15 people.

A 16–20 lb. turkey will serve 20–30 people.

A frozen turkey of 9 lb. dressed weight is equivalent to a non-frozen one of 12 lb. undressed weight.

For general preparation, see the notes at the beginning of the chapter.

Roast Turkey

It is usual to stuff the neck end of a turkey with veal forcemeat or chestnut stuffing; allow 1 lb. made stuffing for a bird of up to 14 lb.; twice this amount for a larger bird. For the body cavity, sausage-meat or sausage stuffing is generally used – allow 1–2 lb., according to size. *(Recipes will be found in the Stuffings chapter.)*

Make the turkey as plump and even in shape as possible, then truss it with the wings folded under the body and the legs tied together. Before cooking the bird, spread it with softened dripping or butter; the breast may also be covered with strips of fat bacon. If you are going to cook it by the quick method (*see below*) it is best to wrap the bird in aluminium foil to prevent the flesh drying and the skin hardening. Foil is not recommended for the slow method of cooking, as it tends to give a steamed rather than a roast bird.

For the slow method cook in a warm oven (325°F., mark 3); for the quick method cook in a very hot oven (450°F., mark 8), calculating the time according to the chart below.

WEIGHT IN LBS.	HOURS, SLOW METHOD	HOURS, QUICK METHOD
6–8	3–3½	2¼–2½
8–10	3½–3¾	2½–2¾
10–12	3¾–4	2¾
12–14	4–4¼	3
14–16	4¼–4½	3–3¼
16–18	4½–4¾	3¼–3½

Unless the bird is cooked in foil, baste it regularly, turning it round once to ensure even browning. Foil, if used, should be unwrapped for the last ½ hour, so that the bird may be well basted and then left to become crisp and golden.

Frozen Turkeys

These should first be allowed to thaw out completely, preferably slowly. Allow 20–30 hours in a cool larder for a bird up to 12 lb. Over this weight it takes from 2–4 days.

Garnish and Accompaniments

Small sausages, forcemeat balls, rolls of bacon and watercress may be used to garnish the turkey. Serve it with brown gravy and bread sauce. Cranberry or some other sharp sauce can also be served. Sliced tongue or ham is a favourite accompaniment.

Devilled Turkey Drumsticks

Cut the drumsticks from a cooked turkey. (Other fair-sized portions can be used in the same way.) Score with a sharp knife, then brush with melted butter. To prepare the devilled mixture, mix on a plate 1 level tsp. each of French and English mustard, 2 level tsps. finely chopped chutney, a pinch of ground ginger and a little pepper, salt and cayenne. Spread this mixture over and into the cuts and leave the turkey legs for 1 hour or longer. Grill them on a greased grid under a medium heat until crisp and brown, turning them regularly to ensure even cooking. Serve garnished with watercress.

Blanquette of Turkey

½ lb. cooked turkey
1 medium-sized onion, skinned and chopped
1½ oz. butter
3 level tbsps. flour
¾ pint chicken stock
Salt and pepper
A pinch of mace
1 egg yolk
2 tbsps. cream
2 tsps. lemon juice

Remove all the skin and bone from the turkey meat and cut it into cubes. Cook the onion lightly in the butter for 5 minutes without colouring; stir in the flour and cook for a further 2–3 minutes. Gradually stir in the stock, bring to the boil and continue stirring until it thickens. Add the turkey meat, season well, add the mace and heat the turkey thoroughly. Remove the sauce from the heat. Blend the egg yolk, cream and lemon juice to a smooth cream; stir in a little of the sauce, return the blended mixture to the pan and reheat without boiling. Turn the blanquette into a serving dish and serve with small triangles of fresh toast.

Game

Game is a name given to wild birds and animals which are hunted and killed for food, but which at certain times of the year are protected by law. For convenience' sake we also deal in this chapter with pigeons (though strictly speaking only wood or wild pigeons count as game), with protected birds and with rabbits, since they so closely resemble hares from the cookery point of view.

Availability of Game

We give here the period when the bird or animal is most likely to be available in the shops – not necessarily the formal open season.

BLACK GAME: Late August–early December.

CAPERCAILZIE: August–February.

DUCK, WILD (including Teal, Widgeon): August–February.

GROUSE: Mid-August–early December.

HARE: September–February.

PARTRIDGE: September–early February.

PHEASANT: October–January.

PLOVER: Generally imported – variable.

PTARMIGAN: September–December.

QUAIL: Domestically produced; all year.

SNIPE: September–February.

VENISON: At its best October–March.

WOODCOCK: September–February.

Buying Game and other Birds

Try to choose a young bird. The plumage is a guide, as all young birds have soft, even feathers. With pheasants and partridge, the long wing feathers are V-shaped in a young bird, as distinct from the rounded ones of an older bird. Smooth, pliable legs, short spurs and a firm, plump breast are other points to look for. Ask whether the bird has been hung (*see below*), as some poulterers do this.

Hanging and preparation

All game birds need to be hung up by the legs, without being plucked or drawn, before being cooked, or the flesh will be tough and tasteless. The time for hanging depends on the weather and on your taste, varying from a week in 'muggy' weather to 2–3 weeks in frosty weather.

Keep the bird in a cold, dry, airy place and examine it from time to time, especially any that has been shattered when shot, or has got wet, or has been packed up for any length of time before hanging, as such birds do not keep so well. For most people the bird is sufficiently mature when the tail or breast feathers will pluck out easily. With a pheasant, the flesh on the breast begins to change colour and the bird smells 'gamey'.

Pluck, draw and truss the bird as for poultry (*see Poultry chapter*), but leave the feet on and don't draw the sinews from the legs. Some birds, such as snipe, have the head left on and are not drawn before being roasted – *see the individual recipes*. The larger birds may be jointed like a chicken before being cooked.

Cooking

Generally speaking, the more simply the game is cooked, the better. For a young bird, there is no better way than roasting, but for older birds, which are likely to be tough if plainly roasted, braising or casseroling is a better method.

Game birds lack fat, so it is usual to cover the breast before roasting with pieces of fat bacon (this is called 'barding') and to baste frequently with butter during the cooking. When the bird is nearly cooked, the bacon can be removed; the breast is then dredged with flour

Swiss Steak, *page 52*

and basted in order to brown it. Sometimes a knob of butter or a piece of juicy steak is put inside the bird before roasting.

Accompaniments

THIN GRAVY: Served with roast game. To make it, add ¼ pint water or meat stock to the roasting tin and with a spoon rub down any cooking juices left in the tin; bring to the boil and boil for 2–3 minutes. Remove all grease from the surface with a metal spoon, season to taste and strain before serving.

FRIED CRUMBS: Fry 2–4 oz. fresh white breadcrumbs in 1 oz. butter until golden-brown.

GAME CHIPS: *See Potato section of Vegetables chapter.*

Carving Game

A pheasant or other game bird, if large, is carved in the same general manner as a chicken. Partridges, pigeons and birds of similar size are usually cut in half. If very small, the whole bird may be served as one portion; woodcock, snipe and quail are among the birds which are served whole, on the toast on which they were cooked. Special scissors (rather like small secateurs) are available for cutting birds in half; failing these, use the game carver or a short, pointed kitchen knife, by inserting the point of the knife in the neck end of the breast and cutting firmly through the bird in the direction of the breast-bone and tail.

Roast Grouse

Oven temperature: fairly hot (400°F., mark 6)

After hanging, pluck, draw and truss the bird, season inside and out and lay some fat bacon over the breast. Put a knob of butter inside the bird and place it on a slice of toast. Roast in the centre of the oven for 40 minutes, basting frequently. After 30 minutes' roasting, remove the bacon, dredge the breast with flour and baste well.

Remove the trussing strings before serving the bird on the toast on which it was roasted. Garnish with watercress and serve with thin gravy, bread sauce, fried crumbs and game chips. A lettuce or watercress salad may also be served.

Roast Partridge

Oven temperature: very hot (450°F., mark 8)

Select a young bird; pluck, draw and truss it, season the inside with pepper and salt, replace the liver and add a knob of butter. Cover the breast with pieces of fat bacon.

Roast the bird in the centre of the oven for 10 minutes, then reduce the oven to fairly hot (400°F.,

mark 6) and roast for a further 20–30 minutes, according to size; partridge must be well-done.

The usual accompaniments are fried crumbs and game chips and a tossed salad or bread (or orange) sauce. A garnish of lemon quarters and watercress (seasoned and sprinkled with a few drops of vinegar) is often added.

Casserole of Partridge

2 medium onions, skinned and sliced
2 sticks of celery, scrubbed and sliced
¼ lb. mushrooms, washed and sliced
4 oz. bacon, rinded and chopped
1 tbsp. oil
1 oz. butter
2 partridges, plucked, drawn and jointed
3 level tbsps. flour
¾ pint stock
A 15-oz. can of tomatoes
Salt and pepper
¼ pint red wine

Oven temperature: moderate (350°F., mark 4)

Fry the onions, celery, mushrooms and bacon in the oil and butter for about 5 minutes, until golden-brown. Remove from the pan with a slotted spoon and line the bottom of a casserole with them. Fry the partridge joints in the oil and butter for about 5 minutes, until golden-brown. Remove from the pan with the slotted spoon and put in the casserole on the bed of vegetables. Stir the flour into the fat remaining in the pan and cook for 2–3 minutes. Gradually stir in the stock, bring to the boil and continue to stir until it thickens. Add the tomatoes, salt, pepper and wine, pour the sauce over the partridge joints, cover and cook in the centre of the oven for 1 hour, until the partridge joints are tender.

Roast Pheasant

Pheasant requires to be well hung, otherwise the flesh is dry and tasteless; it needs on an average 10–11 days – rather less should the weather be 'muggy', up to 3 weeks if frosty.

Oven temperature: very hot (450°F., mark 8)

Pluck, draw and truss the bird and cover the breast with strips of fat bacon. Roast in the centre of the oven for 10 minutes, then reduce the heat to fairly hot (400°F., mark 6) and continue cooking for 30–40 minutes, according to the size of the bird, basting frequently with butter. About 15 minutes before the cooking is completed, remove the bacon, dredge the breast of the bird with flour, baste well and finish cooking. Remove the trussing strings, put the pheasant on a hot dish and garnish with watercress. Serve with thin gravy, bread sauce, fried crumbs and game chips; a tossed green salad may also be served.

Goulash, *page 53*

BLACKGAME (Blackcock, Grey-hen): Cook as for Grouse.

Roast Pigeon

Oven temperature: very hot (450°F., mark 8)

Select young birds for roasting. Pluck and draw them, singe if necessary and truss them. Spread with some softened butter and tie a piece of fat bacon over the breasts. Roast in the centre of the oven for 15–20 minutes, according to size, basting well and removing the bacon before cooking is completed, to allow the breast to brown.

Add a garnish of watercress and serve gravy or a sauce separately. If liked, the pigeons may be halved before serving.

Pigeons à la Française

4 large pigeons
Salt and pepper
4 tbsps. cooking oil
6 tbsps. dry sherry
6 oz. button onions, skinned
1 lettuce, washed and shredded
A 1-lb. pkt. of frozen peas
¼ tsp. mint (not peppermint) essence
½ oz. butter
2 level tsps. flour

Oven temperature: warm (325°F., mark 3)

Halve the pigeons and season with salt and pepper. Fry them in the oil, flesh side down, until golden-brown. Drain, and place in a flameproof casserole. Pour the sherry over, add the onions, cover tightly and cook in the centre of the oven for about 1½ hours. About ½ hour before the end of the time add the lettuce, peas and mint essence. Return the dish to the oven and cook until the peas are tender. Thicken the juices with the butter and flour creamed to a paste and added a little at a time; bring to the boil, stirring. Serve with sauté potatoes and baked tomatoes.

Failing mint essence, use minted peas or add a little fresh mint.

Quail

Allow 1 quail per person.

Oven temperature: hot (425°F., mark 7)

Pluck and singe the birds but do not draw, as they are eaten whole. Cut off the head and neck and take out the crop. Place each bird on a round of fried bread and cover the breast with thin rashers of fat bacon. Roast in the centre of the oven for about 25 minutes, basting with butter. Serve on the bread with the bacon; thin

gravy, fried crumbs and chipped potatoes are usual accompaniments.

Creamed Quail Casserole

4 quail
Seasoned flour
2 oz. butter
4 oz. button mushrooms
4 tbsps. dry sherry
Salt and pepper
¼ pint soured cream
Chopped parsley

Oven temperature: fairly hot (375°F., mark 5)

Coat the quail in the seasoned flour. Melt the butter in a flameproof casserole and brown the birds evenly. Add the mushrooms and sauté them, then add the sherry and seasoning. Cover and cook in the centre of the oven for 40 minutes. Stir in the soured cream, adjust the seasoning and serve sprinkled with chopped parsley.

Capercailzie (Capercailye, Wood Grouse)

A game bird, also called 'Cock of the Woods' or 'Mountain Cock'. It is similar to grouse and may be cooked in the same way.

Ptarmigan

A small bird of the grouse family; it has not such a good flavour as grouse, but may be cooked in the same way.

Wild Duck

A teal will serve 1–2 people; other wild duck as a rule will serve 2–3 people.

Oven temperature: hot (425°F., mark 7)

Hang for a short time only, then pluck, draw and truss like a domestic duck. Stuff with a roughly chopped mixture of 1 sour apple, 1 orange and 1 onion for each duck, otherwise the flesh may taste 'fishy'. Spread with softened butter and roast in the centre of the oven, basting frequently. Allow 20 minutes for teal, 30 minutes for mallard and widgeon – they should on no account be over-cooked. At half time, pour a little port or orange juice over the birds. Garnish with watercress and serve with thin gravy and orange salad or with Bigarade sauce.

Woodcock, Snipe, Plover

Allow 1 bird per person.

Oven temperature: fairly hot (375°F., mark 5)

Pluck and singe the birds. Don't draw them, but skin the head and neck and remove the eyes before trussing. Cover each bird all over with softened butter, then put

Roast Partridges

it on a round of toast. Cover the breast with rashers of fat bacon and roast in the centre of the oven for 15–20 minutes. Serve the birds on the toast, garnished with lemon and watercress. Thin gravy, fried crumbs and game chips (or if preferred, a salad) are the usual accompaniments.

Roast Hare

Oven temperature: moderate (350°F., mark 4)

Very young hares may be roasted whole, but for larger hares the body alone is used, being known as saddle or baron of hare. Cut off the saddle close to the shoulders

(reserve the rest of the hare to jug or make into soup). Prepare some veal forcemeat (*see Stuffings chapter*). If liked, the heart, liver and kidneys may be added to the forcemeat; wash them well, put into a pan of cold water, bring to boiling point, strain and chop finely. Stuff the hare, fold the skin over and sew in position. Lay slices of fat bacon over the back, cover with greased grease-proof paper, put in a tin with some knobs of dripping and roast in the centre of the oven for 1½–2 hours, according to size. Baste frequently, as the flesh is apt to be dry. Fifteen minutes before the cooking is completed, remove the paper and bacon, baste the hare and allow to brown. Remove the skewers and string before dishing up. Serve with thick gravy and red-currant or guava jelly.

Jugged Hare

1 hare
2 oz. bacon, rinded and chopped
1 oz. lard or dripping
1 onion, skinned and stuck with 2 cloves
1 carrot, peeled and sliced
1 stick of celery, scrubbed and sliced
1½ pints stock
A bouquet garni
Juice of ½ a lemon
3 level tbsps. flour
1 tbsp. red-currant jelly
1 glass of port or red wine (optional)

Oven temperature: warm (325°F., mark 3)

Prepare the hare as described, retaining the blood; wipe and joint. Fry the joints with the bacon in the lard until they are lightly browned (about 5 minutes). Transfer to a deep casserole and add the vegetables, enough stock to cover the joints, the bouquet garni and lemon juice. Cover and cook in the centre of the oven for 3–4 hours, or until tender.

A few minutes before serving, blend the flour with a little cold water to a smooth cream, stir in the blood of the hare and add to the casserole, with the jelly and wine (if used). Re-heat without boiling and serve with red-currant jelly and forcemeat balls (*see Stuffings chapter*).

Stuffings and Sauces

STUFFINGS

Stuffing, sometimes called forcemeat, serves a triple purpose – it fills up the cavity in a boned joint or in a bird, helping to retain its good shape; it adds flavour; it makes a small joint or bird go further.

Assemble the ingredients well ahead, but don't mix with liquid or egg or stuff the meat or bird until you want to cook it: it is not safe to leave stuffing around – even in the refrigerator – for more than 2–3 hours.

Most stuffings start with a base of one of the following:

SAUSAGE-MEAT

BREADCRUMBS
Make these from bread 2–3 days old.

RICE
Boil it in salted water, rinse and dry before using.

To this basis add a fat (butter, dripping, oil or, most commonly, chopped suet); a little moisture and/or egg to bind; herbs and seasonings to give flavour and perhaps vegetables or fruits of various kinds.

Reminders
Don't have the stuffing too wet or it becomes stodgy, nor yet too dry, or it will become crumbly and fall apart. Season a stuffing very well.

Don't stuff a joint or bird too tightly, for when the stuffing absorbs juices from the flesh during the cooking, it expands and might burst the skin or come out. It is better to cook any surplus stuffing in a separate casserole or baking tin. Sometimes it is rolled into small balls and cooked round a joint.

Roll a stuffed joint such as breast of lamb firmly and tie in several places with fine string to hold the shape during cooking. In the case of a leg or shoulder that has been boned and stuffed, press it into the correct shape and if necessary tie with fine string. (Remove all strings before carving.)

When stuffing a bird, put the forcemeat in loosely at the neck end, under the flap of skin, taking care to give the breast a plump, rounded shape. Put an onion, a knob of butter or a wedge of lemon in the body of the bird to keep the flesh moist. Truss the bird firmly.

Veal Forcemeat *(Made with Meat)*

4 oz. lean veal
3 oz. lean bacon
1 onion, skinned and finely chopped
1 oz. butter
3 oz. fresh white breadcrumbs
1 large mushroom, washed and chopped
1 level tsp. finely chopped parsley
Salt, pepper, cayenne and mace
1 egg, beaten

Pass the mixed veal and bacon twice through a mincer, then beat them well in a bowl. Lightly fry the onion in a little of the butter, until soft but not coloured – 2–3 minutes; add to the meat. Add the breadcrumbs, mushroom, the remaining butter, parsley and seasonings and lastly the beaten egg. Mix well; if the mixture is too stiff, add a little milk.

Use for veal or lamb; double the quantities for a 14-lb. turkey.

Sage and Onion Stuffing

2 large onions, skinned and chopped
1 oz. butter
4 oz. fresh breadcrumbs
2 level tsps. dried sage
Salt and pepper

Sage and Onion Stuffing with Pork

Put the onions in a pan of cold water, bring to the boil and cook until tender – about 10 minutes. Drain well, add the other ingredients and mix well.

Use with pork.

Chestnut Stuffing

2 oz. bacon, rinded and chopped
4 oz. fresh white breadcrumbs
1 level tsp. chopped parsley
1 oz. butter, melted
Grated rind of a lemon
8 oz. chestnut purée *(see note)*
Salt and pepper
1 egg, beaten

Fry the bacon gently in its own fat for about 3–5 minutes, until crisp. Drain and add the rest of the ingredients, binding with the beaten egg.

This stuffing is suitable for a 10-lb. turkey.

Note: Chestnut purée may be made from fresh chestnuts. Boil 1 lb. chestnuts for 2 minutes to soften the skins, remove from the heat and peel them while they are hot. Simmer the peeled chestnuts in milk for about 40 minutes, until soft. Sieve them or put them in an electric blender.

Sausage Stuffing

1 large onion, skinned and chopped
1 lb. pork sausage-meat
2 level tsps. chopped parsley
1 level tsp. mixed herbs
1 oz. fresh breadcrumbs
Salt and pepper

Mix all the ingredients together.

Use with chicken, or turkey, adapting the quantities as necessary.

Apple and Prune Stuffing

4 oz. prunes, soaked and stoned
8 oz. cooking apples, peeled and cored
4 oz. rice, cooked
2 oz. shredded suet
2 oz. almonds, blanched and shredded
Salt and pepper
Juice and grated rind of ½ a lemon
1 egg, beaten

Cut the prunes into quarters and roughly chop the apples. Mix the fruit, rice, suet and nuts, season to taste, add the lemon rind and juice and bind with beaten egg.

Use for pork.

Apple and Celery Stuffing

2 oz. bacon, rinded and chopped
1 oz. butter
2 onions, skinned and chopped
2 sticks of celery, scrubbed and chopped
4 medium cooking apples, peeled, cored and sliced
3 oz. fresh white breadcrumbs
2 level tbsps. chopped parsley
Sugar to taste
Salt and pepper

Fry the bacon in the butter for 2–3 minutes until golden-brown and remove from the pan with a slotted spoon. Fry the onions and celery for 5 minutes and remove from the pan with the slotted spoon. Fry the apples for 2–3 minutes, until soft. Mix all the ingredients together.

Use with duck or pork, or make double the quantity and use for goose.

Apricot Stuffing

6 oz. fresh white breadcrumbs
4 oz. dried apricots, finely chopped
2 oz. salted peanuts, finely chopped
1 tbsp. chopped parsley
2 oz. butter
6 oz. onion, skinned and finely chopped
Juice and grated rind of 1 small orange
¾ level tsp. curry powder
¼ level tsp. salt
Freshly ground black pepper
1 small egg, beaten

Place the breadcrumbs in a bowl and add the apricots, peanuts and parsley. Melt the butter in a small sauce, add the onion and orange rind, cover and cook gently until soft. Remove from the pan and add to the breadcrumbs. Sprinkle in the curry powder and cook gently for 1 minutes. Pour 3 tbsps. orange juice over and bubble gently for 30 seconds. Blend the curried orange juice into the breadcrumbs. Season well with salt and pepper, and bind all together with beaten egg.

This is ideal with duck or goose, and also good with other birds.

SAUCES

A well-made sauce – which can be quite simple – improves the flavour and appearance of many dishes. Sometimes, indeed, the sauce *makes* the dish, as in Eggs Mornay.

For white sauces the liquid used is usually milk or milk and white stock; for brown sauces meat stock and/or vegetable water give a good flavour; for a sauce to serve with fish the fish bones can be used to make a stock which is used in combination with milk. The method of making stocks is given in the Soups chapter; however, nowadays a chicken or beef bouillon cube is often used to make a quick substitute for traditional stock.

When a sauce is thickened with flour it may be made in one of two ways, known as the roux and the blended methods:

A roux is made by melting the butter (or other fat), adding the flour, mixing thoroughly and cooking until they are well combined; in the case of a brown sauce the roux is cooked until it is an even golden-brown colour, but for a white sauce it is not allowed to colour. The liquid is then added gradually, the sauce being stirred and cooked after each addition, until it has reached the required consistency. (Beginners will find it easier if they take the pan off the heat to add the liquid.)

With the blended method, the flour (or cornflour) and a little of the cold liquid are blended to a creamy mixture, the rest of the liquid is brought to the boil and stirred gradually into the blended flour and the sauce is then cooked and stirred for a few minutes.

The White Sauce recipe below shows how to vary the proportion of ingredients to give sauces of different consistencies for different purposes.

You can prepare a sauce early in the day (pressing a piece of damped greaseproof paper on to its surface to prevent a skin forming) and re-heat it when needed.

Vast as the number of individual savoury sauces may be, most of them can be divided into White (simple or rich), Brown and Egg sauces, plus a group of Miscellaneous ones such as Mint Sauce.

Simple White Sauce – Roux Method

I – Pouring Consistency

¾ oz. butter
¾ oz. (2 level tbsps. approx.) flour
½ pint milk or milk and stock
Salt and pepper

Melt the fat, add the flour and stir with a wooden spoon until smooth. Cook over a gentle heat for 2–3 minutes, stirring until the mixture (called a roux) begins to bubble. Remove from the heat and add the liquid

gradually, stirring after each addition to prevent lumps forming. Bring the sauce to the boil, stirring continuously, and when it has thickened, cook for a further 1–2 minutes. Add salt and pepper to taste.

II – Coating Consistency

1 oz. butter
1 oz. (3 level tbsps.) flour
½ pint milk or milk and stock
Salt and pepper

Make the sauce as above.

For a thick coating sauce increase the quantities to 1½ oz. each of butter and flour.

III – Binding Consistency (Panada)

2 oz. butter
2 oz. (6 level tbsps.) flour
½ pint milk or milk and stock
Salt and pepper

Melt the fat, add the flour and stir well. Cook gently for 2–3 minutes, stirring, until the roux begins to bubble and leave the sides of the pan. Add the liquid gradually, bring to the boil, stirring all the time, and cook for 1–2 minutes after it has thickened; add salt and pepper to taste.

This very thick sauce is used for binding mixtures such as croquettes.

Simple White Sauce – Blending Method

I – Pouring Consistency

½ oz. (1½ level tbsps.) cornflour or flour
½ pint milk
A knob of butter
Salt and pepper

Put the cornflour in a basin and blend with 1–2 tbsps. of the milk to a smooth cream. Heat the remaining milk with the butter until boiling; pour onto the blended mixture, stirring all the time to prevent lumps forming. Return the mixture to the pan and bring to the boil, stirring continuously with a wooden spoon. Cook for 1–2 minutes after the mixture has thickened, to make a white glossy sauce. Add salt and pepper to taste before serving.

II – Coating Consistency

Increase the quantity of cornflour to 2 level tbsps.

Variations on Simple White Sauce
A white sauce made by either of the above two methods can be used as the basis of many other

Cheese Sauce served with Boiled Onions

savoury sauces – for example; to each ½ pint of white sauce add:

ANCHOVY SAUCE (made with ½ fish stock and ½ milk): Anchovy essence to taste, a squeeze of lemon juice and red colouring (if desired) to make sauce a dull pink. Serve with fish.

CAPER SAUCE: 1 tbsp. capers, 1–2 tsps. vinegar from capers or lemon juice, season well. Serve with boiled mutton.

EGG SAUCE: 1 hard-boiled chopped egg, 1–2 tsps. chopped chives. Serve with poached or steamed fish or kedgeree.

FISH SAUCE (made with ½ milk and ½ fish liquid): Any additional flavouring.

LEMON SAUCE (½ fish or chicken stock and ½ milk): Use liquid in which lemon rind has been simmered for 5 minutes. When thickened stir in juice of 1 lemon and 1–2 level tsps. sugar. Season.

CHEESE SAUCE: Remove sauce from the heat and add 2–4 oz. strong cheese, grated, pinch of dry mustard, pinch of cayenne pepper (optional). Season. Serve with vegetables, eggs, fish or pasta.

MUSHROOM SAUCE: 2–3 oz. button mushrooms, sliced and gently fried in butter. Season. Serve with fish, meat or eggs.

MUSTARD SAUCE: 1 level tbsp. dry mustard, 2 level tsps. sugar, 1 tbsp. vinegar, blended. Serve with fish.

Béchamel Sauce

½ pint milk
Small piece of onion, skinned
Small piece of carrot, peeled
½ a stick of celery, scrubbed and cut up
½ a bay leaf
3 peppercorns
1 oz. butter
1 oz. (3 level tbsps.) flour
Salt and pepper

Put the milk, vegetables and flavourings in a saucepan and bring slowly to the boil. Remove from the heat, cover and leave to infuse for about 15 minutes. Strain the liquid and use this with the butter and flour to make a roux sauce (see page 105). Season to taste before serving.

RICH WHITE SAUCES

Variations on Béchamel

AURORE: Add to ½ pint of Béchamel sauce 1–2 level tbsps. tomato paste, 1 oz. butter, added a little at a time, seasoning. Serve with eggs, fish or chicken.

MORNAY: 2 oz. Parmesan or Gruyère cheese. Serve with eggs, fish or chicken.

SOUBISE: ½ lb. skinned chopped onions cooked gently in 1 oz. butter and a small amount of stock or water for about 10–15 minutes, sieved. Season. Serve with meat.

Chaudfroid Sauce (White)

¼ an envelope of aspic jelly powder
¼ pint hot water
¼ oz. gelatine (2 level tsps.)
½ pint Béchamel sauce
⅛–¼ pint single cream
Salt and pepper

Put the aspic jelly powder in a small basin and dissolve it in the hot water. Stand the basin in a pan of hot water, sprinkle in the gelatine and stir until it has dissolved, taking care not to overheat the mixture. Stir into the warm Béchamel sauce, beat well and add the cream and extra salt and pepper if necessary. Strain the sauce and leave to cool, stirring frequently so that it remains smooth and glossy. Use when at the consistency of thick cream, for coating chicken, fish or eggs.

Note: A simpler Chaudfroid sauce can be made by adding ¼ pint melted aspic jelly to ½ pint warm Béchamel sauce; beat well, strain, cool and use as above.

Velouté Sauce

¾ oz. butter
¾ oz. (2 level tbsps. approx.) flour
¾ pint chicken or other light stock
2–3 tbsps. single cream
A few drops of lemon juice
Salt and pepper

Melt the butter, stir in the flour and cook gently, stirring well, until the mixture is pale fawn colour. Stir in the stock gradually, bring to the boil, stirring all the time, and simmer until slightly reduced and syrupy. Remove from the heat and add the cream, lemon juice and seasoning.

Serve with poultry, fish or veal.

Suprême Sauce (*below*) is one of the commonest variations of Velouté Sauce.

Suprême Sauce

¼ pint Velouté Sauce
1–2 egg yolks
2–3 tbsps. single or double cream
½–1 oz. butter
A squeeze of lemon juice
Salt and pepper

Make the Velouté sauce, remove from the heat and stir in the egg yolks and cream. Add the butter a little at a time, the lemon juice and seasoning to taste. Re-heat if necessary but don't re-boil, or the sauce will curdle.

Serve with poultry or fish. Suprême sauce is sometimes used in meat and vegetable dishes.

BROWN SAUCES

The main kinds are Gravy (which is really a simple brown sauce), Espagnole Sauce and its variations, and Demi-Glace Sauce, again with variations.

Gravy

A rich brown gravy is served with all roast joints – thin with roast beef and thick with other meats. If the gravy is properly made in the baking tin, there should be no need to use extra colouring.

Remove the joint from the tin and keep it hot while making the gravy.

THIN GRAVY: Pour the fat very slowly from the tin, draining it off carefully from one corner and leaving the sediment behind. Season well with salt and pepper and add ½ pint hot vegetable water or stock (which can be made from a bouillon cube). Stir thoroughly with a wooden spoon until all the sediment is scraped from the tin and the gravy is a rich brown; return the tin to the heat and boil for 2–3 minutes. Serve very hot.

This is the 'correct' way of making thin gravy, but some people prefer to make a version of the thick gravy given below, using half the amount of flour.

THICK GRAVY: Leave 2 tbsps. of the fat in the tin, add 1 level tbsp. flour (preferably shaking it from a flour dredger, which gives a smoother result), blend well and cook over the heat until it turns brown, stirring continuously. Carefully mix in ½ pint hot vegetable water or stock and boil for 2–3 minutes. Season well, strain and serve very hot.

Notes: 1. If the gravy is greasy (due to not draining off enough fat) or thin (due to adding too much liquid), it can be corrected by adding more flour, although this weakens the flavour.
2. When gravy is very pale, a little gravy browning may be added.

3. Meat extracts are sometimes added to give extra taste; however, they do tend to overpower the characteristic meat flavour. A sliced carrot and onion cooked with the meat in the gravy will give extra 'body' to the taste without impairing it. A tbsp. of cider or wine added at the last moment does wonders.

Espagnole Sauce

1 oz. streaky bacon, chopped
1 oz. butter
1 shallot, skinned and chopped (or a small piece of onion, chopped)
1 oz. mushroom stalks, washed and chopped
1 small carrot, peeled and chopped
¾–1 oz. (2–3 level tbsps.) flour
½ pint beef stock
A bouquet garni
2 level tbsps. tomato paste
Salt and pepper

This classic brown sauce is used as a basis for many other savoury sauces.

Fry the bacon in the butter for 2–3 minutes, add the vegetables and fry for a further 3–5 minutes, or until lightly browned. Stir in the flour, mix well and continue frying until it turns brown. Remove from the heat and gradually add the stock (which if necessary can be made from a stock cube), stirring after each addition. Return the pan to the heat and stir until the sauce thickens; add the bouquet garni, tomato paste and salt and pepper. Reduce the heat and allow to simmer very gently for 1 hour, stirring from time to time to prevent it sticking; alternatively, cook in the centre of a warm oven (325°F., mark 3) for 1½–2 hours. Strain the sauce, re-heat and skim off any fat, using a metal spoon. Re-season if necessary.

1 tbsp. sherry may be added just before the sauce is served.

Demi-Glace Sauce

¼ pint clear beef gravy or jellied stock from under beef dripping
¼ pint Espagnole sauce

Add the gravy to the sauce and boil (uncovered) until the sauce has a glossy appearance and will coat the back of the spoon with a shiny glaze.

This is a simplified version of the classic demi-glace, but gives quite a satisfactory result for ordinary use.
Serve with dishes made from beef.

VARIATIONS OF ESPAGNOLE AND DEMI-GLACE SAUCES

Bigarade Sauce

½ pint Espagnole sauce
Juice of 1 orange
Juice of 1 lemon
2–3 tbsps. port
A pinch of sugar
Salt and pepper

Heat the Espagnole sauce, stir in the fruit juices and port and simmer (uncovered) for 10 minutes; add a little sugar if the sauce is too sharp and extra seasoning if necessary.
Serve with roast duck.

Réforme Sauce

3–4 tbsps. vinegar
6 peppercorns
½ pint Espagnole sauce
2–3 tbsps. port
1 tbsp. red-currant jelly

Put the vinegar and peppercorns into a pan and boil rapidly (uncovered) until reduced by a half. Stir in the Espagnole sauce, port and jelly, simmer for 10–15 minutes and strain.
Serve with lamb cutlets or fillet of beef.

Madeira or Marsala Sauce

Add up to ¼ pint Madeira or Marsala to ½ pint Espagnole sauce and re-heat but don't re-boil. The juice and extractives from the meat tin can also be reduced and added, to give extra flavour.
Serve with any meat or game.

Chaudfroid Sauce – Brown

½ an envelope of aspic jelly powder
¼ pint hot water
¼ oz. gelatine (2 level tsps.)
¾ pint Espagnole sauce
Madeira, sherry or port to taste
Salt and pepper

Put the aspic jelly powder in a small basin, dissolve in the hot water and stand the basin in a pan of hot water. Sprinkle in the gelatine and stir over a gentle heat until it dissolves. Warm the Espagnole sauce and beat in the aspic and gelatine mixture. Add wine to taste and extra salt and pepper if necessary. Strain the sauce and allow to cool, beating it from time to time so that it remains smooth and glossy. When it reaches the consistency of thick cream, use to coat game, duck or cutlets.

EGG SAUCES

Hollandaise

2 tbsps. wine or tarragon vinegar or lemon juice
1 tbsp. water
2 egg yolks
3–4 oz. butter
Salt and pepper

Put the vinegar and water in a small pan and boil until reduced to about 1 tbsp.; cool slightly. Put the egg yolks in a basin and stir in the vinegar. Put over a pan of hot water and heat gently, siirring all the time, until the egg mixture thickens (never let the water go above simmering point). Divide the butter into small pieces and gradually whisk into the sauce; add seasoning to taste. If the sauce is too sharp add a little more butter – it should be slightly piquant, almost thick enough to hold its shape and warm rather than hot when served. Serve with salmon and other fish dishes, asparagus, or broccoli.

Béarnaise Sauce

4 tbsps. wine or tarragon vinegar
1 shallot, skinned and chopped
A few sprigs of tarragon, chopped
2 egg yolks
3 oz. butter
Salt and pepper

Place the vinegar, shallot and tarragon in a small saucepan over a gentle heat and reduce to about 1 tbsp. Stir into the egg yolk in a basin and cook over a pan of simmering water until slightly thickened (*as for Hollandaise sauce, above*). Whisk in the butter a little at a time, then season to taste. The sauce should be slightly thicker than Hollandaise and with a more piquant flavour.
    Serve with steaks or grills.

Note: 1 tbsp. vinegar can be replaced by 1 tbsp. water – this gives a slightly less piquant sauce which is preferred by some people.

Mayonnaise

This is strictly speaking an egg sauce, but as it is served with salads, the recipes is given under Salad Dressings in the Salads chapter.

Tartare Sauce

¼ pint mayonnaise or salad cream
1 tsp. chopped tarragon or chives
2 tsps. chopped capers
2 tsps. chopped gherkins
2 tsps. chopped parsley
1 tbsp. lemon juice or tarragon vinegar

Mix all the ingredients well, then leave the sauce to stand at least 1 hour before serving, to allow the flavours to blend.
    Serve with fish.

OTHER SAVOURY SAUCES

Apple Sauce

1 lb. cooking apples, peeled and cored
1 oz. butter
A little sugar (optional)

Slice the apples and simmer gently in a covered saucepan with 2–3 tbsps. water until soft – about 10 minutes. Beat to a pulp with a wooden spoon, then sieve or put in an electric blender. Stir in the butter and add a little sugar if the apples are very tart.
    Serve with pork or sausages.

Bread Sauce

1 medium-sized onion
2 cloves
¾ pint milk
Salt
A few peppercorns
⅜ oz. butter
3 oz. fresh white breadcrumbs
½ a small bay leaf

Peel the onion and stick the cloves into it, place in a saucepan with the milk, salt and peppercorns, bring almost to boiling point and leave in a warm place for about 20 minutes, in order to extract the flavour from the onion. Remove the peppercorns and add the butter and breadcrumbs. Mix well and allow to cook very slowly for about 15 minutes, then remove the onion.
    If liked, remove the onion before adding the bread-crumbs, but a better flavour is obtained by cooking it with the crumbs, as this allows the taste of the onion to penetrate them.
    Serve with roast chicken, turkey or pheasant.

Barbecue Sauce

2 oz. butter
1 large onion, skinned and chopped
1 level tsp. tomato paste
2 tbsps. vinegar
2 level tbsps. demerara sugar
2 level tsps. dry mustard
2 tbsps. Worcestershire sauce
¼ pint water

Melt the butter and fry the onion for 5 minutes, or until soft. Stir in the tomato paste and continue cooking for a further 3 minutes. Blend the remaining ingredients to a smooth cream and stir in the onion mixture. Return the sauce to the pan and simmer for a further 10 minutes.
    Serve with chicken, sausages, hamburgers or chops.

Cranberry Sauce

½ lb. sugar
½ pint water
½ lb. cranberries

Dissolve the sugar in the water and boil for 5 minutes. Add the cranberries and simmer for about 10 minutes. Cool before serving. A little port can be added for additional flavour.
    Serve with turkey.

Tomato Sauce *(Made from fresh tomatoes)*

1 small onion, skinned and chopped
1 small carrot, peeled and chopped
1 oz. butter
½ oz. flour
1 lb. cooking tomatoes, quartered
½ pint chicken stock (made from a cube)
½ bay leaf
1 clove
1 level tsp. sugar
Salt and pepper

Lightly fry the onion and carrot in the butter for 5 minutes. Stir in the flour and add the tomatoes, the stocks, flavourings, etc. Bring to the boil and simmer for 30–45 minutes, or until the vegetables are cooked. Sieve, re-heat and re-season if necessary.

Serve with croquettes, cutlets, réchauffés or any savoury dish.

Notes: You can add 2 level tsps. tomato paste to give a full flavour and better colour.

1–4 tbsps. white wine or sherry can also be added just before serving.

Tomato Sauce *(Made from canned tomatoes)*

½ an onion, skinned and chopped
2 rashers of bacon, chopped
½ oz. butter
½ oz. flour
A 15-oz. can of tomatoes
1 clove, ½ a bay leaf, a few sprigs of rosemary (or 1 level tsp. mixed dried herbs)
Salt and pepper

Fry the onion and bacon in the butter for 5 minutes. Stir in the flour and gradually add the tomatoes, also the flavourings and seasoning. Simmer gently for 15 minutes, then sieve and if necessary re-season.

Serve with made-up meat dishes such as beef olives or stuffed peppers.

Mint Sauce

A small bunch of mint, washed
2 level tsps. sugar
1 tbsp. boiling water
1–2 tbsps. vinegar

Put the mint leaves only with the sugar on a board and chop finely. Put in a sauceboat, add the boiling water and stir until the sugar is dissolved. Stir in vinegar to taste. The sauce should be left for 1 hour before being served.

Mint sauce is served with lamb.

Curry Sauce

2 medium-sized onions, skinned
1 oz. dripping or butter
1 level tbsp. curry powder
1 level tsp. curry paste
1 level tbsp. rice flour or ordinary flour
A clove of garlic
⅓ pint stock or coconut milk
Salt
A little Cayenne pepper
2 level tbsps. chutney
1 tbsp. single cream (optional)

Slice the onions and chop finely. Melt the fat, fry the onions golden-brown and add the curry powder, paste and rice (or ordinary) flour. Cook for 5 minutes, then add the garlic, pour in the stock or coconut milk and bring to the boil. Add the seasonings and chutney, then simmer for 30–40 minutes. This sauce is much improved by the addition of 1 tbsp. cream immediately before use and less curry powder may be used for those who prefer a 'mild' dish.

Note: The rice flour and ordinary flour can be omitted, since a curry is thickened by reduction of the liquid and by long, slow simmering.

Cooked Salad Cream

3 level tbsps. flour
1 level tbsp. sugar
2 level tsps. dry mustard
1 level tsp. salt
¼ pint milk
2 eggs, beaten
2 oz. butter
¼ pint vinegar
¼ pint oil

Mix all the dry ingredients and blend to a smooth cream with the milk. Bring to the boil, stirring all the time, cook for 1 minute and then cool. Beat in the eggs and butter, return the pan to the heat and cook until thick, but don't boil. Beat in the vinegar gradually and finally stir in the oil.

This salad dressing can be used as for mayonnaise. It can also be bottled and kept for a few days in a refrigerator – in this case, shake it well before using, as it tends to separate out on standing.

Egg Cookery

EGGS

To Test for Freshness

There is always a small air space inside an egg and this increases as the egg ages. The fresher the egg, therefore, the fuller it is, and that is the basis of the following test. Place the egg in a tumbler of cold water. If fresh and full, it lies flat at the bottom of the glass. If the egg tilts slightly, it is probably not fresh enough to boil, but will fry or scramble satisfactorily; if it floats, it is very likely to be quite bad.

Ducks' Eggs

Ducks' eggs are larger and richer than hens' eggs. They need to be thoroughly cooked to be safe, at least 10 minutes being allowed for boiling. They can be included in cakes (except sponge mixtures) and puddings, but they should not be used for making meringues or any sweet which is cooked for only a short time or at a low temperature, nor should they be preserved or stored.

Turkey and Goose Eggs

These are as delicate in flavour as hens' eggs, but they are of course much larger. They can be cooked by any of the methods given for hens' eggs and can be used for all cakes and puddings. Allow a longer time for boiling – for soft-boiled eggs allow about 7 minutes. One goose egg will make sufficient scrambled egg for 4 people.

Gull, Plover, Pheasant and Guinea Fowl Eggs

These are usually served hard-boiled as an hors d'oeuvre. Cook them for 10–15 minutes.

BOILED EGGS

Eggs should be simmered rather than boiled. Put them into boiling water, using a spoon, lower the heat and cook for 3 minutes for a light set and up to 4½ minutes for a firmer set. Alternatively, put them in cold water and bring slowly to the boil – they will then be lightly set. The water in each case should be just sufficient to cover the eggs.

Fresh eggs tend to take a little longer to cook than those which are a few days old.

Hard-Boiled Eggs

Put the eggs into boiling water, bring back to the boil and cook for 10–12 minutes.

Hard-boiled eggs should be placed at once under running cold water and left until they are cold; this prevents a discoloured rim forming round the outside of the yolk and enables the shell to be easily removed. Crack the shell all round by tapping on a firm surface, then peel it off.

Coddled Eggs

Place the eggs in boiling water, cover, remove from the heat and keep in a warm place for 8–10 minutes; they will then be lightly set.

POACHED EGGS

The eggs may be cooked in a special poaching pan or in a frying pan, with the aid of round pastry cutters. To use an egg poacher, half-fill the lower container with water, place a small piece of butter in each cup and put over the heat; when the water boils, break the eggs into the cups, season lightly and cover the pan with the lid. Simmer gently until the eggs are set and loosen them with a knife before turning out.

To use a frying pan, half-fill it with water, adding a pinch of salt or a few drops of vinegar to help the eggs keep their shape and give added flavour. Grease the required number of plain pastry cutters. Bring the water to the boil, put in the cutters and break an egg into each; cook gently until lightly set and lift out with a slotted spoon or fish slice.

Drain the eggs before serving.

FRIED EGGS

Melt a little drippping or lard in a frying pan. Break

each egg separately into a cup and drop carefully into the hot fat. Cook gently and use a spoon to baste with the fat, so that the eggs cook evenly on top and underneath. When they are just set, remove them from the pan with a fish slice or broad palette knife. If the eggs are to be served with fried bacon, cook this first, then remove the rashers and keep them hot while frying the eggs in the hot bacon fat.

BAKED EGGS

Oven temperature: moderately hot (350°F., mark 4)

Place the required number of individual ovenproof dishes or cocottes on a baking sheet, with a knob of butter in each dish. Put them in the oven for 1–2 minutes, until the butter has melted. Break an egg into each dish, sprinkle with a little salt and pepper, place in the centre of the oven and leave until the eggs are just set – about 5–8 minutes. Garnish if desired and serve at once.

SCRAMBLED EGGS

Melt ½ oz. butter in a strong pan. Whisk 2 eggs with 2 tbsps. milk or water and some salt and pepper. Pour into the saucepan and stir slowly over a gentle heat until the mixture begins to thicken. Remove from the heat and stir until creamy. Pile on to hot buttered toast and serve immediately.

Scrambled Egg Variations
Add to a 4-egg mixture one of the following ingredients:
2 oz. lightly fried sliced mushrooms.
2 peeled tomatoes, chopped and lightly fried with a diced rasher of bacon.
2 oz. chopped ham, tongue or other cooked meat.
2 oz. sliced cooked pork sausages.
2 oz. Finnan haddock (or other smoked fish), cooked, freed of bones and skin and flaked.
2 oz. picked shrimps.
2–3 oz. grated cheese.
½ level tsp. dried herbs or 1 level tbsp. finely chopped mixed fresh herbs.
   Alternatively, pile scrambled egg onto one half of a slice of buttered toast and on the other half pile hot cooked mushrooms, tomatoes, green peppers or flaked boned fish.

Scrambled Eggs Archiduchesse

3 oz. butter
6 eggs, beaten
Salt and paprika pepper
2–3 tbsps. cream
2 oz. cooked ham, chopped
1 oz. mushrooms, sliced and lightly fried
Fried bread
1 dozen cooked asparagus heads (or 1 small can of asparagus)

Melt the butter and add the eggs, seasonings and cream. Cook very slowly, stirring gently. As the mixture starts

to thicken, add the ham and mushrooms. Serve on fried bread, topped with the asparagus heads.

Plain Omelette

Allow 2 eggs per person. Whisk them lightly, season with salt and pepper and add 1 tbsp. water. Place the pan over a gentle heat and when it is hot add a knob of butter to grease it lightly. Pour the beaten eggs into the hot fat. Stir gently with the back of the prongs of a fork, drawing the mixture from the sides to the centre as it sets and letting the liquid egg from the centre run to the sides. When the egg has set, stop stirring and cook for another minute until it is golden underneath. Tilt the pan away from you slightly and use a palette knife to fold over a third of the omelette to the centre, then fold over the opposite third. Turn the omelette out on to the warmed plate, with the folded sides underneath, and serve at once. Don't overcook or the omelette will be tough.

Omelette Fillings

FINES HERBES: Add 1 level tsp. mixed dried herbs to the beaten egg mixture before cooking.

CHEESE: Grate 1½ oz. cheese and mix 1 oz. of it with the eggs before cooking; sprinkle the rest over the omelette after it is folded.

TOMATO: Peel and chop 1–2 tomatoes and fry in a little butter in a saucepan for 5 minutes, until soft and pulpy. Put in the centre of the omelette before folding.

MUSHROOM: Wash and slice 2 oz. mushrooms and cook in butter in a saucepan until soft. Put in centre of omelette before folding.

BACON: Rind and chop 2 rashers of bacon and fry in a saucepan until crisp. Put in the centre of the omelette before folding.

KIDNEY: Skin, core and chop 1–2 sheep's kidneys, add 1 tsp. finely chopped onion and fry lightly in a little butter in a saucepan until tender. Put in the centre of the omelette before folding.

HAM OR TONGUE: Add 2 oz. chopped meat and 1 tsp. chopped parsley to the beaten egg before cooking.

FISH: Flake some cooked fish and heat gently in a little cheese sauce. Put in the centre of the omelette before folding.

SHRIMP OR PRAWN: Thaw out 2 oz. frozen shrimps or prawns and sauté in melted butter in a saucepan, with a squeeze of lemon juice. Put into the centre of the omelette before folding.

Soufflé Omelette

2 eggs
1 level tsp. caster sugar (or salt and pepper to taste for a
savoury omelette)
2 tbsps. water
½ oz. butter

Separate the yolks from the whites of the eggs, putting them in different bowls. Whisk the yolks until creamy. Add the sugar (or seasoning) and the water and beat again. Whisk the egg whites as stiffly as possible. At this point place the pan containing the butter over a low heat and let the butter melt without browning. Turn the egg whites into the yolk mixture and fold in carefully, using a spoon, but don't over-mix. Grease the sides of the pan with the butter by tilting it in all directions and then pour in the egg mixture. Cook over a moderate heat until the omelette is golden-brown on the under-side. Now place the pan in a moderate oven (350°F., mark 4) or under the grill until the omelette is browned on the top. Remove at once when it is ready, as over-cooking tends to make it tough. Run a spatula gently round the edge and underneath the omelette to loosen it, make a mark across the middle at right angles to the pan handle, add any required filling – *see suggestions below* – and double the omelette over. Turn it gently onto a hot plate and serve at once. (Makes 1 serving.)

Soufflé Omelette Fillings

JAM: Spread the cooked omelette with warmed jam, fold it over and sprinkle with sugar.

RUM: Add 1 tbsp. rum to the egg yolks before cooking. Put the cooked omelette on a hot dish, pour 3–4 tbsps. warmed rum round it, ignite and serve immediately.

APRICOT: Add the grated rind of an orange or tangerine to the egg yolks. Spread some thick apricot pulp over the omelette before folding it and serve sprinkled with caster sugar.

SAVOURY: Any of the fillings already given for plain omelettes can be used for soufflé omelettes.

Oven Omelette

4 rashers of streaky bacon, rinded and chopped
½ an onion, skinned and chopped
2 level tsps. seasoned flour
1 tbsp. chopped parsley
4 eggs
¼ pint milk
4 oz. cheese, grated

Oven temperature: moderate (350°F., mark 4)

Fry the chopped bacon and drain it with a slotted spoon, leaving the fat in the frying pan. Put the bacon into a deep pie plate. Add the chopped onion to the bacon fat in the pan and fry until golden; add the flour and stir. Spread this mixture over the bacon and sprinkle with the chopped parsley. Whisk together the eggs and

milk, pour them over the onion mixture and sprinkle the cheese on top. Bake in the centre of the oven for 30 minutes, until firm.

Basic Soufflé Mixture

3 eggs
1 oz. butter
1 oz. flour
¼ pint milk
Salt and pepper
Filling *(see below)*

Oven temperature: fairly hot (400°F., mark 6)

Grease a 7-inch soufflé dish. Separate the eggs. Melt the butter, stir in the flour and cook for 2–3 minutes. Gradually stir in the milk and bring to the boil, stirring all the time. Cool slightly and add the filling. Add the egg yolks one at a time, beating well, and season. Stiffly whisk the egg whites, fold these into the mixture and put it into the soufflé dish. Bake in the centre of the oven for about 35 minutes, until well risen and brown. (Sufficient for 4 servings.)

Soufflé Fillings and Flavourings

Don't use too great a weight of filling or the soufflé will be heavy.

HAM: 3 oz. cooked ham, finely chopped.

FISH: 3 oz. cooked smoked haddock, finely flaked.

MUSHROOM: 3–4 oz. mushrooms, chopped and cooked in butter until tender.

CHEESE: Make the basic sauce from 1 oz. butter, ½ oz. flour and ¼ pint milk; add 3 oz. finely grated cheese.

SWEET: *See Hot Puddings chapter; for cold soufflés, see Cold Puddings.*

Eggs à la Mornay

1½ oz. butter
1 oz. flour
½ pint milk
Salt and pepper
2 oz. cheese, grated
4 eggs, hard-boiled and sliced
Chopped parsley

Melt 1 oz. butter, stir in the flour and cook for 2–3 minutes. Remove the pan from the heat and gradually stir in the milk, bring to the boil and continue to stir until the sauce thickens. Season well and stir in 1 oz. of the cheese. Lay the eggs in a fireproof dish, reserving a few slices for garnish. Pour the sauce over them, sprinkle the remaining cheese over the top, dot with shavings of butter and brown under a hot grill for a few minutes. Garnish with the slices of egg and a little chopped parsley.

Scrambled Eggs Archiduchesse

Curried Eggs

2 oz. butter
1 onion, skinned and finely chopped
½ an apple, peeled and finely chopped
2 level tsps. curry powder
3 level tbsps. flour
¼ pint stock or water
Salt and paprika
2 tsps. lemon juice
4 eggs
4 oz. rice, freshly cooked
Chopped parsley

Melt the butter in a saucepan and lightly fry the onion until golden. Add the apple, curry powder and flour and cook for a few minutes, stirring occasionally. Add the stock gradually and season with salt and lemon juice. Bring to the boil, stirring all the time, cover and simmer for about 30 minutes. Hard-boil the eggs during the last 10 minutes of the time, shell and halve them. Place them in a hot dish and pour the sauce over.

Surround with the rice and garnish with chopped parsley and paprika pepper.

Scotch Eggs

4 eggs, hard-boiled and shelled
2 level tsps. seasoned flour
Worcestershire sauce
½ lb. sausage-meat or skinless sausages
1 egg, beaten
Dry breadcrumbs
Deep fat
Parsley

Dust the eggs with the seasoned flour. Add a few drops of Worcestershire sauce to the sausage-meat and divide it into 4 equal portions. Form each quarter into a flat cake and work it round an egg, making it as even as possible, to keep the egg a good shape and making sure there are no cracks in the sausage-meat. Brush with beaten egg and toss in breadcrumbs. Heat the fat until it will brown a cube of bread in 40–50 seconds. (As the sausage-meat is raw, it is essential that the frying should not be hurried unduly, so the fat must not be too hot.) Fry the eggs for about 7–8 minutes. When they are golden-brown on the outside, remove them from the fat and drain.

Cut the eggs in half lengthways, garnish each half with a small piece of parsley and serve either hot with tomato sauce (*see Sauces chapter*) or cold with a green salad.

Croque-monsieur

4 slices of bread, generously buttered
4 slices of cheese
4 thin rashers of bacon, rinded
4 tomatoes, halved
Salt
4 eggs

Toast the bread on the buttered side until it is golden. Lay a slice of cheese on each piece of bread and grill until bubbly and golden in colour. Lightly grill the rashers of bacon and put on top of the cheese. Arrange the slices of bread and the tomatoes in an ovenproof dish and sprinkle with salt. Turn the grill low and put the dish under it until the tomatoes are soft and the bacon crisp. Fry the eggs, lift out from the pan, using a slotted spoon to drain off any fat, and serve on top of the bacon.

Egg and Vegetable Flan

4 oz. shortcrust pastry
1 oz. butter
1 oz. flour
½ pint milk
3 oz. cheese, grated
Salt and pepper
3 eggs, hard-boiled and sliced
1 pkt. of frozen mixed vegetables

Oven temperature: fairly hot (400°F., mark 6)

Line a 7-inch flan ring or pie plate with the pastry and bake 'blind'. Cool.

Melt the fat, stir in the flour and cook for 2–3 minutes. Remove the pan from the heat and gradually stir in the milk, bring to the boil and continue to stir until the sauce thickens. Stir in 2 oz. of the cheese and salt and pepper to taste. Arrange the sliced eggs in the cooled flan case. Cook the frozen vegetables according to the directions on the packet, mix them with the cheese sauce and pour into the flan case. Sprinkle with the remaining cheese and brown under the grill.

Cheese Cookery

Cheese on Toast

8 oz. firm cheese, grated
1 level tsp. dry mustard
Salt and pepper
$\frac{1}{2}$–1 tsp. Worcestershire sauce
Milk to mix
Buttered toast

Mix the cheese and seasonings and bind to a paste with milk. Spread on the toast and cook under a hot grill until golden and bubbling.

Welsh Rarebit

8 oz. Cheddar cheese, grated
1 oz. butter
1 level tsp. dry mustard
Salt and pepper
3–4 tbsps. brown ale
Toast

Place all the ingredients in a thick-based pan and heat very gently until a creamy mixture is obtained. Pour over the toast and put under a hot grill until golden and bubbling.

BUCK RAREBIT: This is Welsh Rarebit topped with a poached egg.

Cheese Pudding

4–6 slices of white bread (4 oz.)
4 tbsps. dry white wine (optional)
1 oz. butter, melted
2 eggs, beaten
$\frac{1}{2}$ pint milk
Salt and pepper
4 oz. cheese, grated

Oven temperature: fairly hot (375°F., mark 5)

Cut the bread into cubes and place in a $1\frac{1}{2}$-pint greased ovenproof dish with the wine (if used) and the butter. Mix the eggs and milk, season well and pour over the bread mixture. Sprinkle with the cheese and bake towards the top of the oven for about 30 minutes, until golden and well risen. Serve at once.

Cheese and Vegetable Tart

4 oz. short crust pastry
1 pkt. of mixed frozen vegetables
1 oz. butter or margarine
1 oz. flour
$\frac{1}{2}$ pint milk
4 oz. cheese, grated
Salt and pepper

Oven temperature: hot (425°F., mark 7)

Line an 8-inch flan ring or pie plate with the pastry. Bake 'blind' near the top of the oven for 15–20 minutes, until the pastry is cooked but light in colour. Meanwhile cook the vegetables according to the manufacturer's instructions. Melt the fat, stir in the flour and cook for 2–3 minutes. Remove the pan from the heat and gradually stir in the liquid. Bring to the boil and continue to stir until the sauce has thickened. Remove from the heat and stir in 3 oz. of the cheese, the drained cooked vegetables and seasoning to taste. Pour into the pastry case and sprinkle the remaining cheese over. Brown under a hot grill or at the top of the oven before serving.

Cheese and Asparagus Tart

Use the same ingredients as above, substituting 1 can of asparagus spears for the mixed vegetables. Place the drained asparagus in the pastry case, retaining a little for decoration, pour the sauce over, and finish as above.

Cheese and Asparagus Tart

Cheese and Rice Soufflé

2 oz. long-grain rice
A small can of tomatoes, drained
1 oz. butter
1½ oz. flour
½ pint milk
6 oz. cheese, grated
3 eggs, separated
Salt and pepper

Oven temperature: fairly hot (400°F., mark 6)

Cook the rice in the usual way until just soft. Put the tomatoes into a greased 1½-pint soufflé dish or well-greased large ovenproof dish. Melt the fat, stir in the flour and cook for 2–3 minutes. Remove the pan from the heat and gradually stir in the milk. Bring to the boil, stirring all the time and when the sauce has thickened, remove from the heat, stir in the cooked rice, cheese, egg yolks and seasoning to taste. Finally whisk the egg whites stiffly and fold in lightly. Pour over the tomatoes and bake in the centre of the oven for 30–35 minutes until well risen and golden. Serve immediately.

Variation
1 small sliced onion and 3–4 chopped rashers of bacon can be sautéed lightly and used with or instead of the tomatoes.

Fondue

1 clove of garlic, crushed
$\frac{1}{4}$ pint dry white wine and a squeeze of lemon juice
8 oz. cheese, cut in thin strips (half Gruyère and half Emmenthal)
2 level tsps. cornflour
1 liqueur glass of Kirsch
A little pepper and grated nutmeg

Rub the inside of a flameproof dish with the garlic, place the dish over a gentle heat and warm the wine and lemon juice in it. Add the cheese and continue to heat gently, stirring well until the cheese has melted and begun to cook. Add the cornflour and seasonings, blended to a smooth cream with the Kirsch, and continue cooking for a further 2–3 minutes; when the mixture is of a thick creamy consistency, it is ready to serve.

Traditionally, fondue is served at the table in the dish in which it was cooked, kept warm over a small spirit lamp or dish-warmer. To eat it, provide cubes of crusty bread which are speared on a fork and dipped in the fondue.

An anglicised version of fondue can be made using a strong-flavoured Cheddar cheese, cider instead of white wine and brandy instead of Kirsch.

Cheese and Onion Pie

2 onions, skinned and chopped
8 oz. cheese, grated
1 egg, beaten
Salt and pepper
8 oz. bought flaky pastry

Oven temperature: fairly hot (400°F., mark 6)

Cook the onions in boiling salted water for 5 minutes, drain well and mix with the cheese. Add nearly all the egg and season to taste. Roll out half the pastry, line a 7–8 inch metal pie plate with it and pour the cheese filling into the centre. Roll out the remaining pastry to form a lid. Damp the edges of the pastry on the dish and cover with the lid, pressing the edges well together. Flake and scallop the edge and brush with the remaining egg. Bake towards the top of the oven for about 30 minutes.

Fluffy Cheese Flan

4 oz. shortcrust pastry
1 oz. butter or margarine
1 oz. flour
$\frac{1}{2}$ pint milk
4 oz. cheese, grated
Salt and pepper
2 eggs, separated

Oven temperature: hot (425°F., mark 7)

Make the pastry and use it to line a 7–8 inch pie plate or plain flan ring. Bake this case 'blind' near the top of the oven for 15–20 minutes or until cooked but still pale in colour. Melt the fat, stir in the flour and cook for 2–3 minutes. Remove pan from the heat and gradually stir in the milk. Bring to the boil and continue to stir until the sauce thickens. Remove from the heat and stir in 3 oz. of the cheese, the seasoning and egg yolks; pour into the pastry case. Whisk the egg whites stiffly, pile on top of the flan and sprinkle with the remaining cheese. Reduce the oven to moderate (350°F., mark 4) and return the flan for about 10 minutes, or until it is heated through and the meringue is golden.

Variations

Add 1 small skinned and chopped onion (lightly boiled), 2 oz. sliced mushrooms, lightly fried, or 2 skinned and chopped tomatoes to the sauce before putting it in the case.

Pizza with Tomatoes and Cheese

$\frac{1}{4}$ pint milk (approx.)
1 level tsp. sugar
$\frac{1}{4}$ oz. (2 level tsps.) dried yeast
8 oz. plain flour
1 level tsp. salt
2 oz. butter
1 egg, beaten
1 lb. tomatoes, skinned and sliced
A small piece of onion, skinned and chopped
1 level tbsp. freshly chopped marjoram or oregano (or 2 level tsps. mixed dried herbs, marjoram or oregano)
1–2 tbsps. olive oil
3 oz. Bel Paese or Port Salut cheese
2 oz. stuffed olives
1 can of anchovy fillets

Oven temperature: moderate (350°F., mark 4)

Warm the milk to blood heat and dissolve the sugar in it. Sprinkle the yeast on and leave in a warm place until frothy. Mix the flour and salt, rub in the fat and stir in the yeast, milk and eggs, to give a fairly soft dough. Knead well on a floured board, then cover and leave to rise until doubled in size.

Meanwhile, fry the tomatoes, onion and herbs gently in the oil for 5 minutes, without browning; cool and drain off the excess liquid.

Knead the dough lightly, put in a well-oiled 8-inch round cake tin and cover with the tomato mixture. Sprinkle with the cheese, sliced olives and anchovy fillets, cover and leave to prove for about 15 minutes. Brush with a little oil and bake uncovered towards the top of the oven for about 30 minutes. Serve cut in wedges, with a green salad.

As a pizza is quite filling, this size will serve 4–6 persons, according to appetite.

Savoury Cheese Slice

8 oz. self-raising flour
3 oz. butter or margarine
5 oz. cheese, grated
1 egg, beaten
A little milk (if needed)
1 small onion, skinned and finely chopped
4 oz. streaky bacon, chopped
½–1 level tsp. mixed herbs
Seasoning

Oven temperature: fairly hot (400°F., mark 6)

Rub 2 oz. of the fat into the flour until it resembles breadcrumbs. Stir in 3 oz. of the cheese, then mix to a fairly soft dough with egg and some milk if necessary. Fry the onion and bacon gently for about 5 minutes in the remaining 1 oz. fat. Divide the dough into 2 pieces and roll out each piece into an 8-inch square. Place one piece on a greased baking sheet, cover with the onion and bacon and sprinkle with the herbs and seasoning. Wet the edges and cover with the second piece of dough, pressing the edges together. Brush with milk and sprinkle with the remaining cheese. Bake towards the top of the oven for about 20 minutes, until crisp and golden. Serve cut in fingers or wedges; you can eat it hot or cold.

Variation

Fry 2–3 skinned and chopped tomatoes with the onion and bacon.

Cheese Puffs

1 oz. butter or margarine
4 oz. self-raising flour
Salt, pepper and cayenne pepper
½ cup boiling water
4 oz. Bel Paese cheese, sliced
Fat for deep frying

Rub the fat into the flour and seasonings, pour in the boiling water and mix to a pliable dough. Beat until smooth, turn the dough on to a floured board and knead lightly. Leave for a few minutes to become firm enough to handle, roll out fairly thinly and cut into 2-inch squares. Put a triangle of cheese on each square, wet the edges of the pastry, fold over into a triangle and seal the edges by pressing with a fork. Fry in deep fat until crisp and golden. Drain well on crumpled kitchen paper and serve hot.

Quiche Lorraine

4 oz. ready-made flaky pastry
3–4 oz. lean bacon, chopped
3–4 oz. Gruyère cheese, thinly sliced
2 eggs, beaten
¼ pint single cream or creamy milk
Salt and pepper

Oven temperature: fairly hot (400°F., mark 6)

Roll out the pastry and line a 7-inch plain flan ring or sandwich cake tin, making a double edge. Cover the bacon with boiling water and leave for 2–3 minutes, then drain well. Put into the pastry case with the cheese, mix the eggs and cream, season well and pour into the case. Bake towards the top of the oven for about 30 minutes, until well risen and golden.

There are many variations on this traditional dish – it can be made with bacon or cheese or both as shown. The cheese and bacon given above may be replaced by 3 oz. blue cheese mixed with 6 oz. cream cheese. In some recipes lightly boiled rings of onions or leeks are used instead of, or as well as, the bacon. Milk can be used instead of cream.

Roquefort Quiche

4 oz. shortcrust pastry
3 oz. Roquefort or other blue cheese
6 oz. cream cheese
2 eggs, beaten
¼ pint single cream
1–2 level tsps. grated onion (or 1 level tbsp. chopped chives)
Salt and pepper

Oven temperature: hot (425°F., mark 7)

Make the pastry and use it to line a 7–8 inch flan case or metal pie plate. Bake 'blind' near the top of the oven for 10 minutes, until the pastry is just set. Cream the two kinds of cheese and stir in the eggs, cream, onion and seasoning. Pour into the pastry case, reduce the oven temperature to fairly hot (375°F., mark 5) and cook for about 30 minutes, until well risen and golden. Serve at once.

This is a rich dish which will serve 4–6 people. Have a green salad as accompaniment.

Cheesecake 1

For the Pastry
6 oz. plain flour
3 oz. butter
1 level tsp. sugar
½–1 egg, beaten

For the Filling
2 oz. butter
3 oz. sugar
2 eggs, separated
1½ oz. ground almonds
1 oz. semolina
8 oz. cream or cottage cheese
Grated rind and juice of 1 lemon
2 oz. raisins, stoned

Oven temperature: moderate (350°F., mark 4)

Rub the fat into the flour, add the sugar and mix to a firm dough with the beaten egg. Knead lightly, then roll out the pastry and line an 8-inch sandwich cake tin or fairly deep metal pie place.

For the filling, cream the butter and sugar, add the egg yolks, almonds, semolina, cheese, lemon rind and juice and raisins and mix well. Fold in the stiffly whisked egg whites and pour into the pastry case. Bake in the centre of the oven for about 50 minutes, until the filling is set, reducing the oven to cool (300°F., mark 2) if the filling is browning too quickly. Serve hot or cold.

This cake always tends to sink on cooling.

Note: If cottage cheese is used, sieve it before adding it to the mixture.

Cheesecake 2

5 oz. butter
5 oz. cream cheese
5 oz. ground almonds
5 oz. sugar
Grated rind and juice of 1 lemon
5 eggs, separated
1 oz. flour

Oven temperature: hot (425°F., mark 7)

Grease and line an 8-inch cake tin. Cream together the butter, cheese, almonds, sugar, rind, juice and egg yolks. Fold in the flour and finally the stiffly whisked egg whites. Pour into the prepared tin and bake in the centre of the oven for 15 minutes, then reduce the heat to moderate (350°F., mark 4) and cook for a further 45 minutes, or until the cake is dry inside when tested with a skewer. Turn out and cool.

Salads

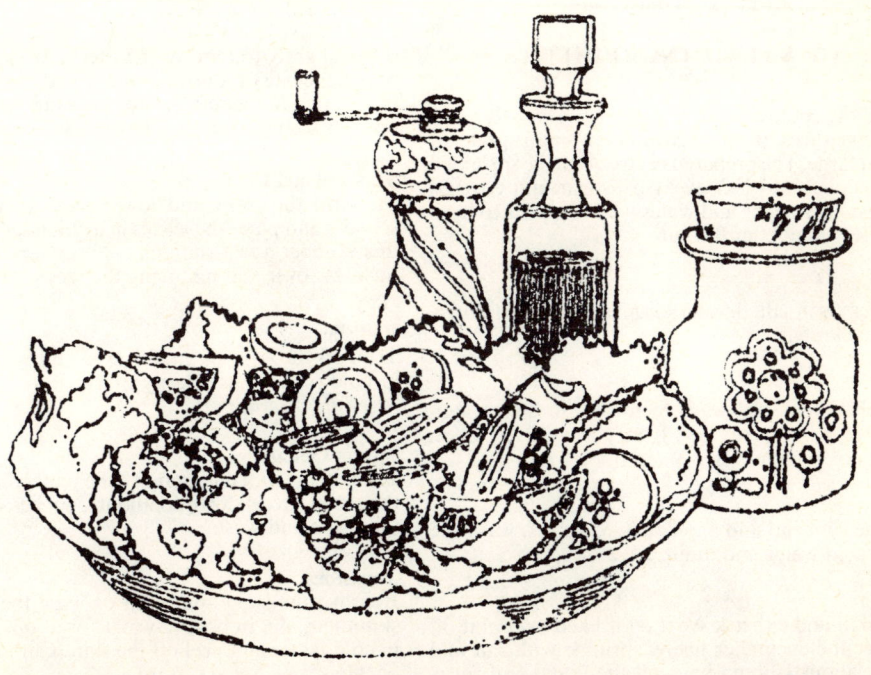

Salads are always most enjoyable for their freshness, crispness and taste, and also because they so often complement the main course (and in many cases a substantial salad can be served when the main course is very simple). They provide us with vitamin C and some mineral salts.

Storing Salads
Trim and wash the salad plants, shake them free of surplus moisture and keep them in the salad drawer of a refrigerator, or loosely wrapped in a polythene bag at the bottom of the refrigerator. Alternatively, store them in a covered saucepan set in a cool place.

PREPARING SALAD INGREDIENTS

Beetroot
Thinly peel the cooked beetroot (*see Vegetables chapter*). Cut into thin slices, if the beetroots are small; grate or dice them if large. The prepared beetroot can be sprinkled with salt, pepper and 1–2 level tsps. sugar and covered with vinegar or vinegar and water – this helps it to keep and also gives it a better flavour.

Cabbage
Wash the leaves in salted water, drain and cut into shreds with a sharp knife.

Celery
Separate the sticks and wash them well in cold water, scrubbing to remove any dirt from the grooves. Slice, chop or make into curls (*see Salad Garnishes*).

Chicory
Trim off the root end and any damaged leaves, wash the chicory in cold water and drain.

Cucumber
Wipe the skin and either leave it on if liked or peel it off thinly. Slice the cucumber finely, sprinkle with salt and leave it for about 1 hour; pour off the liquid and rinse.

Alternatively, you can soak the cucumber in a little vinegar, with salt and a pinch of sugar. If you like the cucumber crisp use it when freshly sliced.

Endive
Trim off the root end, remove the coarse outer leaves, separate remaining leaves, wash and drain well.

Lettuce
Remove the outer coarse leaves. Separate the inner leaves and wash them under a running cold tap or in a bowl of cold water. Drain them in a sieve or colander or shake them in a clean tea towel.

To 'revive' a withered lettuce, wash it in cold water, shake slightly to remove the excess moisture, place in a polythene bag or a bowl covered with a plate and put in the bottom of the refrigerator or in any cool place. In an hour or so the leaves will have crisped up.

Mustard and Cress
Trim off the roots and lower parts of the stems with scissors and place the leaves in a colander or sieve. Wash them (under a fast-running cold tap if possible), turning the cress over and removing the seeds.

Radishes
Trim off the root end and leaves and wash the radishes in cold water. Slice thinly or cut into 'lilies' or 'roses' (*see Salad Garnishes*).

Spring Onions
Trim off the root end, remove the papery outer skin, trim the green leaves down to about 2 inches of green above the white and wash.

Tomatoes
Remove the stem and wash or wipe the tomatoes. To skin them, dip in boiling water for about $\frac{1}{2}$ minute, then in cold water and peel off the skin. Cut in wedges, slices or 'lilies' (*see Salad Garnishes*).

Watercress
Trim the coarse ends from the stalks, wash the watercress and drain well before using.

Dressing the Salad
The dressing can make or mar a salad. The most usual mistake is to use too much dressing, swamping the salad instead of making it appetising. No surplus dressing should be seen at the bottom of the bowl – there should be just sufficient clinging to the salad ingredients to flavour them.

Herbs in Salads
Parsley is an addition to any salad. Do not chop it very finely but snip it with scissors straight on to the salad, just before serving. A few leaves of fresh mint, sage, thyme, dill or tarragon (one at a time, not all together) can be chopped and sprinkled over a salad. Some people like verbena or rosemary, but don't be too liberal with these slightly scented flavours unless you know the tastes of the people you are serving.

Garlic
Many of those who say they dislike garlic don't really know how to use it. True, it is pungent and needs using with discretion – you will find one 'clove' ample for the average bowl of salad.

First remove the papery outside skin of the garlic clove, then crush the clove with a broad-bladed knife (do this on a plate, unless you have a board that you keep specially for onion-chopping). Scrape the crushed garlic into the salad bowl or add it to the dressing. Alternatively, use a garlic press, if you have one.

TO MAKE SALAD GARNISHES

Celery Curls
Cut a celery stick into strips about $\frac{1}{2}$ inch wide and 2 inches long. Make cuts along the length of each, close together and to within $\frac{1}{2}$ inch of one end. Leave the pieces in cold or iced water for 1–2 hours, until the fringed strips curl. Drain well before using.

Cucumber Cones
Use thin slices of cucumber. Make a cut in each slice from the centre to the outer edge, then wrap one cut edge over the other to form a cone.

Crimped Cucumber
Run a fork down the sides of the cucumber to remove strips of peel and slice the cucumber thinly in the usual way – this gives the slices an attractive deckled edge.

Gherkin Fans
Use whole gherkins, choosing long, thin ones. Cut each lengthwise into thin slices, but leave these joined at one end. Fan out the strips of gherkins so that they overlap each other.

Radish Roses
Trim the radishes. Make 4 or 8 small, deep cuts, crossing in the centre at the root end. Leave the radishes in cold or iced water for 1–2 hours, till the cuts open to form 'petals'.

Tomato Lilies
Choose firm, even-sized tomatoes. Using a small sharp-pointed knife, make a series of V-shaped cuts round the middle of each, cutting right through to the centre. Carefully pull the halves apart.

Quick Garnish
Sprinkle finely chopped parsley on potato salad; finely chopped onion on beetroot; chopped spring onion on tomato; chopped mint, chives, tarragon or parsley on green salad

ACCOMPANIMENT SALADS

Green Salad

Use two or more green salad ingredients, such as lettuce, cress, watercress, endive, chicory, cabbage and so on. Wash and drain them and just before serving toss lightly in a bowl with French dressing, adding a little finely chopped onion if liked.

Sprinkle with chopped fresh parsley, chives, mint, tarragon or other herbs, as available.

Endive Salad

Endive, washed and trimmed
French dressing
1 hard-boiled egg, finely chopped

Prepare the endive and chill it, toss it in the dressing and sprinkle with egg. Use as an alternative to green salad.

Cucumber Salad

$\frac{1}{4}$ of a cucumber
French dressing
Chopped parsley

Wipe the cucumber, peel if liked and slice thinly. Put the cucumber in a dish, cover with the dressing and allow to stand for about $\frac{1}{4}$ hour; serve sprinkled with the parsley.

Tomato Salad

4 tomatoes
A small piece of onion (or 2–3 small spring onions)
Salt and pepper
French dressing
Chopped parsley or chives

Wipe the tomatoes, skin them if liked and cut in thin slices. Skin and finely chop the onion (or spring onions). Arrange the tomatoes in a dish, sprinkle with the onion and seasoning and pour the dressing over. Allow to stand for a short time and serve sprinkled with the chopped herbs.

Onion and Tomato Salad

2 onions, skinned and sliced
3 firm tomatoes, skinned and sliced
3–4 tbsps. French dressing
Chopped chives

Arrange the onions and tomatoes alternately in a shallow dish. Pour the dressing over and serve sprinkled with the chives.

Potato Salad

Leftover boiled potatoes
A small piece of raw onion, skinned and finely chopped
Salad cream to bind
Finely chopped parsley or chives

The potatoes must be firm and cold. Cut them in $\frac{1}{2}$-inch dice, mix with the onion and add salad cream to bind the mixture together. Pile into a dish and sprinkle with parsley or chives. Allow to stand for about $\frac{1}{2}$ hour before serving, so that the flavours can blend.

Mushroom Salad

4 oz. open mushrooms
1 tbsp. lemon juice or cider vinegar
3 tbsps. salad oil
1 tbsp. finely chopped parsley
A little freshly ground black pepper
Salt

Wash and dry the mushrooms but don't peel them; remove the stalks (keeping them to use in a stew, sauce, etc.). Slice the mushrooms very thinly into a serving dish and add the lemon juice, oil, parsley and pepper. Marinade in the dressing for $\frac{1}{2}$ hour and salt lightly just before serving.

This is a good accompaniment salad with fish.

Orange Salad

2 oranges, peeled
Chopped tarragon or mint
French dressing

Divide the oranges into sections, removing all the skin, pith and pips, or cut across in thin slices, using a saw-edged knife. Put the slices into a shallow dish, sprinkle with the tarragon or mint and pour the dressing over; allow to stand for a short time before serving.

This salad can be served on a bed of watercress, small cress or endive.

Salade Niçoise

$\frac{1}{2}$ lb. tomatoes, peeled and skinned
$\frac{1}{2}$ a small cucumber, thinly sliced
Salt and freshly ground black pepper
1 tsp. chopped basil
1 tsp. chopped parsley
Grated rind of 1 lemon
4 oz. cooked French beans
2 oz. black olives
$\frac{1}{2}$ a clove of garlic, finely crushed
French dressing
8 anchovy fillets, halved
Brown bread and butter
Quarters of lemon

Slice the tomatoes, put in layers with the cucumber on a shallow dish, season well and sprinkle with the herbs and lemon rind. Pile the French beans in the centre of the dish, scatter the stoned and chopped olives over and season again. Add the garlic to the dressing and pour over the salad. Arrange the anchovy fillets in a lattice pattern over the salad and allow to stand for about $\frac{1}{2}$ hour before serving, so that the flavours blend. Serve with the bread and butter and lemon.

Rice Salad

$\frac{1}{4}$ lb. tomatoes, skinned and quartered
$\frac{1}{2}$ lb. long-grain rice, cooked and drained
$\frac{1}{4}$ lb. French beans, cooked
$\frac{1}{4}$ lb. frozen peas, cooked
2 sticks of celery, scrubbed and chopped
1 small dessert apple, chopped
2 tsps. chopped parsley
2 tsps. chopped chives or 1 tsp. chopped onion
French dressing (well flavoured with mustard)
2 bunches of watercress, trimmed and washed

Remove the seeds from the tomatoes, strain off any juice and cut the flesh into quarters. Put the rice (which should be quite dry) into a bowl and add the beans, peas, celery and apple. Stir with a fork, adding the parsley, chives, tomato juice and enough dressing to moisten nicely. Pile up in the centre of a dish and arrange the tomato quarters round the sides, with the watercress at each end.

Cole Slaw

$\frac{1}{2}$ a hard white cabbage, washed and finely shredded
A small piece of onion, skinned and finely chopped
$\frac{1}{2}$–1 tbsp. chopped parsley (optional)
4 tbsps. salad cream (approx.)
1 level tsp. sugar
Salt and pepper
A few drops of vinegar or lemon juice

Combine the cabbage, onion and parsley (if used) in a large bowl. Mix the salad cream with the sugar, salt and pepper and add enough vinegar or lemon juice to sharpen the flavour. Toss with the salad in the bowl until lightly coated, adding a little more salad cream if necessary.

Mixed Vegetable Salad

A good way of using up leftover cooked vegetables.

Use an assortment such as carrots, peas, potatoes, cauliflower, beetroot and turnip. Cut into even-sized pieces, toss in enough salad cream to bind the mixture and serve sprinkled with chopped parsley, chives or other fresh herbs.

MAIN-DISH SALADS

Cheese Salad

French dressing
1 tsp. made mustard
½–1 small onion, skinned and finely chopped
¼ lb. Gruyère cheese, cut in thin strips
Lettuce or watercress, washed and trimmed

Make the French dressing, add the mustard and onion and mix with the cheese. Allow to stand for 1 hour and serve on a bed of lettuce or watercress.

Cream Cheese and Celery

3 sticks of celery, scrubbed and chopped
½ lb. cream cheese
1 bunch of watercress, washed and trimmed
Paprika

Mix the celery and cream cheese together. Arrange the watercress on a plate, pile the cheese mixture on top and serve sprinkled with a little paprika.

This simple cream cheese salad can be varied by reducing the amount of celery to 1–2 sticks and adding any of the following: 1 red-skinned apple, cored and chopped; a few canned pineapple chunks or segments of mandarin orange, drained; ½–1 oz. chopped walnuts; 1 oz. sultanas.

Salmon and Rice Salad

6 oz. long-grain rice
An 8-oz. can of salmon
½ lb. tomatoes, skinned and chopped
4 tbsps. finely chopped chives
2–3 tbsps. double cream, whipped
6 tbsps. mayonnaise
1 level tsp. celery seeds (optional)
Grated rind of 1 lemon
A little salt and pepper
Lettuce and radishes

Cook the rice in the usual way and allow to cool. Drain the salmon, remove the skin and bones and flake the fish; add with the tomatoes and chives to the rice and mix lightly. Fold the whipped cream into the mayonnaise and add the celery seeds (if used), with the lemon rind

and salt and pepper to taste. Fold in the rice mixture and press into a 2-pint ring mould (or jelly mould). When set, turn out on to a plate lined with lettuce and garnish with sliced radishes.

Tahitian Salad

1 small lettuce, washed
4 pineapple rings
8 oz. cream cheese
Chopped chives
Grated coconut

Arrange the lettuce on a plate, place the rings of pineapple on it and divide the cream cheese evenly between them. Sprinkle with chopped chives and grated coconut.

Caribbean Salad
Replace the pineapple rings by peeled and sliced bananas (dipped in lemon juice to prevent discoloration).

Stuffed Tomato Salad

8 firm tomatoes
2 eggs, hard-boiled and shelled
4 tbsps. cooked peas
1–2 tbsps. thick salad cream
Lettuce or small cress, washed and trimmed

Wipe the tomatoes and cut a slice from the top of each; remove the pulp with a small spoon, and turn the cases upside-down to drain. Chop one of the eggs and mix with the peas and salad cream. Pile into the tomato cases and serve on a bed of lettuce or cress. Cut the other egg into long wedge-shaped slices and use as a garnish.

Egg Mayonnaise

4 hard-boiled eggs, shelled
A few lettuce leaves
¼ pint mayonnaise
Chopped parsley or paprika

Cut the eggs lengthways into halves or quarters. Wash and drain the lettuce and put on a shallow dish. Serve the eggs on the lettuce, cut side down; coat with the mayonnaise and garnish with parsley or paprika.

Mixed English Salad

Mixed English Salad

A small bunch of radishes, washed and trimmed
A bunch of spring onions, washed and trimmed
1 lettuce, washed
A bunch of watercress (or a box of small cress), washed and trimmed
4 tomatoes, wiped and skinned
1 cooked beetroot, peeled and diced
1 small piece of cucumber, wiped and skinned (if liked)
2–4 hard-boiled eggs, shelled and sliced
2–4 oz. firm cheese, grated

Cut the radishes into 'roses' *(see Salad Garnishes)*. Make fine cuts down the length of the onion tops. Put the radishes and onions in iced water and leave until the radishes open and the onions curl. Put a bed of lettuce and watercress or cress on a shallow plate and arrange the remaining ingredients on top, in rows or groups.

Shrimp Salad

3–4 tbsps. mayonnaise
8–12 oz. shelled shrimps
1 small lettuce, shredded
½ a cucumber, sliced
Lemon wedges

Stir the mayonnaise into the shrimps and serve on the lettuce, garnished with cucumber and lemon wedges.

If frozen shrimps are used, allow them to thaw completely and drain well before using.

Grapefruit and Shrimp Salad

Lettuce, washed
1 grapefruit, peeled
½ a cucumber, peeled and diced
½ pint picked shrimps (or 8 oz. frozen shrimps, thawed)
French dressing

Arrange a bed of lettuce in a shallow salad bowl. Remove the pith from the grapefruit and divide it into segments; cut each segment into three and put the juice and grapefruit flesh into a basin. Add the cucumber and the shrimps, pour on some French dressing and mix lightly with a spoon and fork. Pile the mixture on the lettuce and garnish with a few shrimp heads (if available).

Lobster Mayonnaise

1 medium-sized lobster, cooked
1 lettuce, washed
¼ pint mayonnaise
1 hard-boiled egg, sliced

Remove the meat from the lobster, retaining the flesh from the claws and any coral for garnishing. Flake the remaining flesh with a fork or divide it into neat pieces. Arrange the shredded outer leaves of the lettuce in a salad bowl. Mix the lobster meat with the mayonnaise and pile lightly on the lettuce leaves in the bowl. Garnish with slices of egg, the lettuce heart, divided into quarters, the claw meat of the lobster and the coral (if present).

Crab can be served in the same way.

Crown Roast of Lamb, *page 59*

Jellied Salad Ring

Aspic jelly powder
1 hard-boiled egg, shelled
2–3 tomatoes, skinned and diced
A few cooked green peas
8 oz. cooked meat, poultry, fish, shellfish, etc.

Make up 1 pint of aspic jelly, following the printed instructions; when it is cold, pour a little into a 1½-pint ring mould; turn it until the sides are coated with jelly. Put in some slices of hard-boiled egg and tomato and a few peas (or other vegetables as available) to make a design. Pour in enough aspic to cover the pattern and leave to set. Cut up the meat or poultry or flake the cooked fish and free it from skin and bones; use prawns or shrimps whole and lobster or crabmeat loosely flaked. Put into the ring, with any remaining peas, egg or tomato, which should be cut small; fill up with the jelly. Leave in a cool place until set, then turn out, garnish with peas and serve with a green or mixed summer salad.

Russian Salad – 1 *(Using aspic jelly)*

1 small cauliflower, cooked
1–2 envelopes of aspic jelly powder
4 tbsps. cooked peas
2 tbsps. cooked diced carrot
2 tbsps. cooked diced turnip
3 potatoes, cooked and diced
1 small beetroot, cooked and diced
2 tomatoes, skinned and diced
2 oz. ham or tongue, diced
2 oz. shrimps or prawns, cooked
2 oz. smoked salmon, cut in strips (optional)
3 gherkins, chopped
1 tbsp. capers
A few lettuce leaves, shredded
2–3 tbsps. salad cream
4 olives
4 anchovy fillets

Divide the cauliflower into small sprigs. Make up the aspic jelly following the manufacturer's instructions. When it is cold, pour a little into a ring mould and turn this round until the sides are coated with jelly. Decorate with a little of the peas and diced vegetables

and allow to set. Set layers of vegetables, meat, fish, gherkins and capers alternately with layers of jelly in the mould, but don't use up all the vegetables. When the mould is set, turn it out. Toss the lettuce and remaining vegetables in the salad cream and pile into the centre of the mould. Decorate with olives and anchovy fillets.

Note: Failing a ring mould, use an ordinary jelly one; the remaining salad can be served in a border round the jellied salad.

Russian Salad – 2 *(Without aspic jelly)*

Prepare vegetables, meat and fish as above; put layers of them in a salad bowl, season with salt, pepper and a pinch of caster sugar and cover each layer with salad cream. Decorate with beetroot, olives, capers, anchovies and salmon (if used).

Curried Chicken Salad

6 oz. long-grain rice
½ a cooked chicken
1 small cauliflower, washed and trimmed
3 tbsps. French dressing
¼ pint mayonnaise
2 tbsps. milk or cream
3 level tsps. curry powder
Salt and pepper
1 small green pepper, de-seeded and cut into strips
2 sticks of celery, chopped
1–2 small onions, skinned and finely sliced
1 lettuce, washed

Cook the rice in the usual way and leave to cool. Cut the chicken meat into chunks. Divide the cauliflower into small sprigs and toss with the rice in the French dressing. Combine the mayonnaise, milk or cream, curry powder, salt and pepper in a large bowl, add the chicken and toss together. Add the rice mixture, the green pepper, the celery and the onions and serve on a bed of lettuce.

Shredded coconut, salted peanuts, pineapple cubes, tomato wedges and red-currant jelly, served in small dishes, make good accompaniments.

SALAD DRESSINGS

French Salad Dressing (Sauce Vinaigrette)

¼ level tsp. salt
⅛ level tsp. pepper
⅛ level tsp. dry mustard
¼ level tsp. sugar
1 tbsp. vinegar
2 tbsps. oil

Put the salt, pepper, mustard and sugar in a bowl, add the vinegar and stir until well blended. Beat in the oil gradually with a fork. Use at once – the oil separates out on standing, so if necessary whip the dressing immediately before use. A good plan is to store it in a salad-cream bottle, shaking it up vigorously just before serving.

Note: The proportion of oil to vinegar varies with individual taste, but use vinegar sparingly. Malt, wine,

Kebabs, *page 61*

tarragon or any other vinegar may be used.

Variations of French Salad Dressing
To the above dressing add any of the following:
A clove of garlic, crushed
1–2 tsps. chopped chives
½–1 level tsp. curry powder
2 tsps. chopped parsley, ½ tsp. dried marjoram and a
 pinch of dried thyme
1 tsp. chopped parsley, 1 tsp. chopped gherkins or
 capers, 1 tsp. chopped olives
1–2 tsps. sweet pickle
1 tbsp. finely sliced or chopped stuffed olives
1–2 tsps. Worcestershire sauce
1–2 tsps. chopped mint
1 tbsp. finely chopped anchovies
A pinch of curry powder, ½ a hard-boiled egg, shelled
 and finely chopped, 1 tsp. chopped onion (this is called
 Bombay dressing)
1 oz. blue-vein cheese, crumbled

Classic Mayonnaise

1 egg yolk
½ level tsp. dry mustard
½ level tsp. salt
¼ level tsp. pepper
½ level tsp. sugar
¼ pint (approx.) oil
1 tbsp. white vinegar

Put the egg yolk into a basin with the seasonings and
sugar. Mix thoroughly, then add the oil drop by drop,
stirring briskly with a wooden spoon the whole time or
using a whisk, until the sauce is thick and smooth. If
it becomes too thick add a little of the vinegar. When
all the oil has been added, add the vinegar gradually
and mix thoroughly.
    If liked, lemon juice may be used instead of the
vinegar.

Notes: To keep the basin firmly in position, twist a damp
cloth tightly round the base – this prevents it from
slipping.
    In order that the oil may be added 1 drop at a time,
put into the bottle-neck a cork from which a small
wedge has been cut.
    Should the sauce curdle during the process of making,
put another egg yolk into a basin and add the curdled
sauce very gradually, in the same way as the oil is added
to the original egg yolks.

Variations of Mayonnaise
Using ¼ pint mayonnaise as a basis, add a flavouring
as follows:

CAPER: Add 2 tsps. chopped capers, 1 tsp. chopped
pimiento and ½ tsp. tarragon vinegar. Goes well with
fish.

CELERY: Add 1 tbsp. chopped celery and 1 tbsp. chopped
chives.

CREAM: Add 4 tbsps. whipped cream. Goes well with
salads containing fruit, chicken or rice.

CUCUMBER: Add 2 tbsps. finely chopped cucumber and
½ level tsp. salt. Goes well with fish salads, especially
crab, lobster and salmon.

HERBS: Add 2 tbsps. chopped chives and 1 tbsp. chopped
parsley.

HORSERADISH: Add 1 tbsp. horseradish sauce.

PIQUANT: Add 1 tsp. tomato ketchup, 1 tsp. chopped
olives and a pinch of paprika pepper.

TOMATO: Add ½ a tomato, skinned and diced, 1 spring
onion, chopped, ¼ level tsp. salt and 1 tsp. vinegar or
lemon juice.

BLUE CHEESE: Add 1 oz. crumbled blue cheese.

Note: All these variations can also be made using a basis
of bought salad cream.

Cream Dressing

Salt
Cayenne pepper
¼ pint double cream
1–2 tbsps. vinegar

Season the cream to taste and whip until thick; add the
vinegar very gradually and chill before using.

Lemon and Oil Dressing

2–3 tbsps. oil
Pepper and salt
1 tbsp. lemon juice

Add the oil gradually to the salt and pepper and when
they are well blended, whisk in the lemon juice with a
fork.

Vegetables

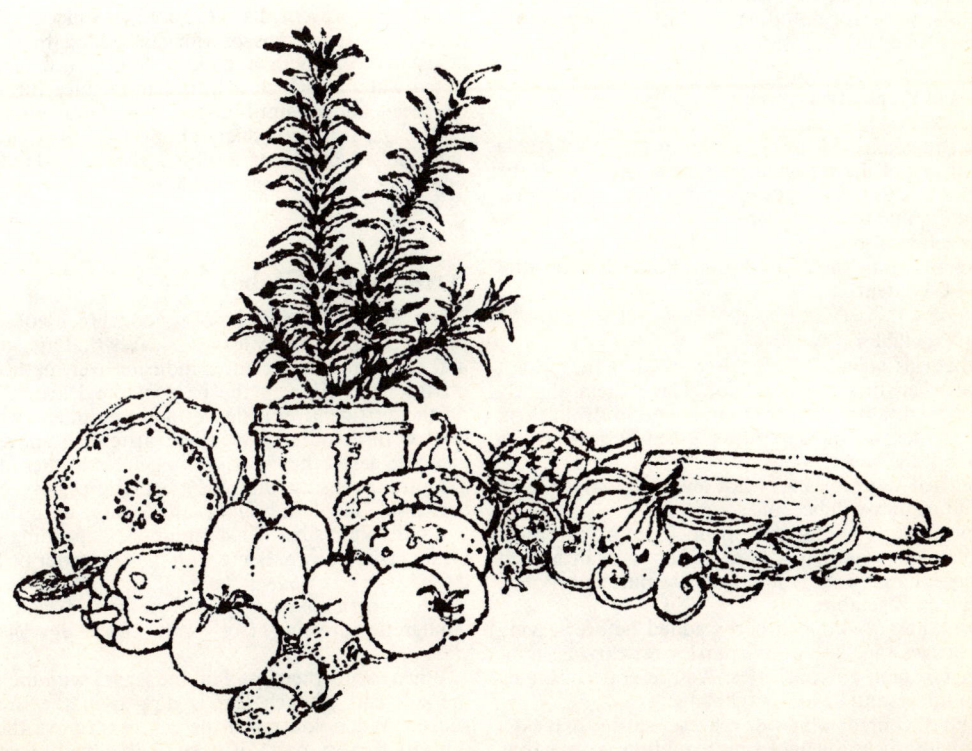

Vegetables add interest and flavour to the day's meals and many of them are also a good source of Vitamins A or C. For example, a helping of potatoes and one of some green vegetable will supply most (sometimes all) of the daily Vitamin C requirement.

Most vegetables are served as an accompaniment to other dishes, but some (for instance, globe artichokes) make a good appetiser and there are various dressed vegetables which can form a course in themselves, either after the roast at a formal meal (e.g., dressed asparagus) or as a main dish for an informal lunch or supper (e.g. cauliflower cheese).

Storing and Preparation
Keep vegetables in a cool, airy place – for example, in a vegetable rack placed in a cool larder or in the vegetable compartment of the refrigerator. Green ones should be used as soon as possible after gathering, while their Vitamin C value is at its highest.

All vegetables should be prepared as near to the time of cooking as possible, to retain both flavour and Vitamin C content.

Serving Vegetables
Serve them as soon as they are cooked – they don't improve when they are kept hot. Have them slightly under-cooked rather than over-cooked, and drain them well, if boiled. (You can press green vegetables to squeeze out the water.)

Serve fried vegetables very hot and don't cover them with a lid or they will become soggy.

A sprinkling of salt and pepper improves most vegetables – especially fried ones, where no salt is used in the cooking process. Add a knob of butter to boiled and steamed vegetables.

A sprinkling of chopped herbs added before serving also improves vegetables – try parsley on carrots, mint on peas, tarragon on courgettes. A little grated nutmeg gives an interesting flavour to cabbage.

A well-flavoured white or cheese sauce makes a change with such vegetables as cauliflower, marrow, leeks and onions, broad beans and carrots. (*For recipes see the Sauces chapter.*)

Artichoke (Jerusalem)
Scrub the artichokes; using a stainless knife or peeler, peel them quickly and immediately plunge them into cold water, keeping them under the water as much as possible to prevent discoloration. A squeeze of lemon juice (or a few drops of vinegar) added to the water helps to keep them a good colour. Cook in boiling salted water to which a little lemon juice (or vinegar) has been added, until just soft – about 30 minutes. Drain, garnish with finely chopped parsley and serve with melted butter or a white, cheese or Hollandaise sauce (*see Sauces chapter*). Allow 6–8 oz. per portion.

Artichokes (Globe)
The artichokes should be of a good green colour, with tightly clinging, fleshy leaves – leaves that are spreading and fuzzy, purplish centres indicate over-maturity. Cut off the stem close to the base of the leaves and take off the outside layer of leaves and any others which are dry or discoloured. As globe artichokes have close-growing leaves, they need soaking in cold water for about $\frac{1}{2}$ hour, to ensure that they are thoroughly cleaned; drain well. Cook in boiling salted water until the leaves will pull out easily – 20–40 minutes, depending on size. Drain upside-down. Serve with melted butter or Hollandaise sauce (*see Sauces chapter*).

Globe artichokes may also be served cold, with a vinaigrette dressing (*see Salad Dressings in Salads chapter*).

When eating them, pull off the leaves with the fingers; the soft end of each leaf is dipped in the sauce and sucked. When you reach the centre, remove the choke (or soft flowery part), if it has not already been taken out, and eat the bottom, which is the chief delicacy, with a knife and fork.

Allow 1 artichoke per person.

Asparagus

Cut off the woody end of the stalks and scrape the white part lightly, removing any coarse spines. Tie in bundles with all the heads together and place upright in a saucepan of boiling salted water. Boil for 10 minutes, then lay them flat and continue cooking until just soft – a further 10–15 minutes. Alternatively, lay the bundles in the bottom of a saucepan with the heads all pointing in the same direction and have one side of the pan slightly off the heat, so that the heads are in the cooler part; allow about 15 minutes.

Don't overcook asparagus – it is better to have to discard more of the stem part than to have the tips mushy.

Drain and untie the bundles before serving with melted butter or Hollandaise sauce (see Sauces chapter). To eat, hold a stick by the stem end and dip the tip in the butter or sauce. It is not usual to eat the stem end.

Asparagus may also be served cold, with a vinaigrette dressing (see Salad Dressings) or with mayonnaise.

Allow 8–12 stems per portion.

Aubergine or Egg Plant

A long, oval-shaped vegetable with a shiny purple skin. Aubergines should be of uniform colour, firm, smooth and free from blemishes. Cut off the stem and small 'leaves' which surround it; wash the vegetables and if necessary, peel them. Aubergines are usually fried or stuffed and baked.

Allow about 6 oz. per portion.

Stuffed Aubergines

2 medium-sized aubergines
2 oz. ham, diced
1 tbsp. chopped parsley
1 tomato, skinned and chopped
2 oz. fresh breadcrumbs
½ an onion, skinned and grated
Salt and pepper
4 oz. Cheddar cheese, grated
A little stock or beaten egg to bind (if necessary)

Oven temperature: fairly hot (400°F., mark 6)

Wash the aubergines and remove the stalks. Cut in half lengthways and scoop out the flesh from the centre of each, leaving a ¼-inch thick 'shell'.

Make the stuffing by combining the ham, parsley, tomato, crumbs, onion, seasoning and 2 oz. of the cheese with the roughly chopped aubergine flesh. Moisten with a little stock or beaten egg and fill the aubergine shells. Sprinkle with the remaining grated cheese, cover with a lid or foil and bake in the centre of the oven for 15–20 minutes, until cooked. Uncover

and cook for a further 5–10 minutes, until crisp and brown on top. Serve hot with a cheese or tomato sauce (see Sauces chapter).

Ratatouille Niçoise

2 onions, cut into rings
2 red peppers, seeded and sliced
2 green peppers, seeded and sliced
1 tbsp. oil
2 aubergines, diced
½ a marrow, peeled and diced (or 5 courgettes, sliced)
3 tomatoes, skinned and chopped
Salt and pepper
Chopped parsley

Oven temperature: moderate (350°F., mark 4)

Fry the onions and peppers in the oil. Add the aubergines and marrow, mix well, then add the tomatoes and seasoning. Put into a casserole, cover and bake for 20–30 minutes. Garnish with parsley before serving. (Serves 4)

(See colour picture facing page 192)

Beans *(Broad)*

Shell and cook in boiling salted water until soft – 20–30 minutes. If liked, serve with parsley sauce.

When broad beans are very young and tender – that is, when the pods are only a few inches long and the beans inside very small – the whole pods may be cooked and eaten.

Allow ½–¾ lb. beans per portion (weight as bought).

Beans *(French and Runner)*

Top, tail and string the beans. Slice runner beans thinly; French beans may be left whole. Cook in boiling salted water until soft – 15–20 minutes. Remove any scum that rises to the top with a spoon. Drain and toss with salt and pepper and a knob of butter before serving.

Allow ¼–½ lb. per portion.

Beetroot

Cut off the stalks 1 inch or so above the root, then wash the beetroots, taking care not to damage the skin or they will 'bleed' when boiled. Boil in salted water until soft; the time depends on the age and freshness, but 2 hours is the average. When they are cooked, peel off the skin and cut the beets into cubes or slices. Serve hot, coated with a white sauce, or cold, sliced and in a little vinegar.

Beetroots can be cooked in a much shorter time if peeled and sliced when raw and cooked until tender in a small amount of liquid in a covered saucepan. Again, the time taken varies, the average being ½ hour. Serve

133

in the liquor in which the beetroots were cooked, or use the liquor to make a sauce, instead of milk.

Allow 4–6 oz. when served as an accompaniment.

Glazed Beetroots

12 small beetroots, cooked
1 oz. butter
1 tsp. sugar
Salt and pepper
Grated rind of 1 lemon
1 tsp. chopped chives
2 tsps. chopped parsley
Juice of $\frac{1}{2}$ a lemon
1 tbsp. capers

Remove the skin, stalks and root end from the beetroots. Melt the butter in a saucepan and add the beetroots, sugar, salt, pepper and lemon rind. Toss the beetroots in the pan over a medium heat until they are well coated; add the remaining ingredients, heat through and serve.

Broccoli

There are several varieties of this vegetable, the chief ones being:

White broccoli, with a fairly large flower head, which is cooked and served in the same way as cauliflower. Buy by the head, judging by size.

Purple broccoli and Calabrese (a green sprouting broccoli), which have a more delicate flavour. They are cooked like cauliflower, but take only 15–20 minutes. Serve plain, buttered or with Hollandaise sauce (*see Sauces chapter*). Allow 6–8 oz. per serving.

Brussels Sprouts

Wash the sprouts, removing any discoloured leaves, and cut a cross in the stalks. Cook in boiling salted water until soft – 10–20 minutes. Drain, return them to the pan and re-heat with salt and pepper and a knob of butter.

Allow 4–6 oz. per person.

Cabbage – Savoy and Dutch

Remove the coarse outer leaves, cut the cabbage in half and take out the hard centre stalk. Wash thoroughly, shred finely and cook rapidly in about 1 inch of boiling salted water for about 5–10 minutes, or until cooked.

Drain well and toss with a knob of butter, a sprinkling of pepper and a pinch of grated nutmeg (optional). Serve at once.

Allow 4 oz. per portion.

Spring Greens

Separate the leaves and cut off the base of any thick stems. Wash well and shred thoroughly. Cook as for cabbage.

Allow $\frac{1}{2}$ lb. per portion.

Bubble and Squeak

Leftover mashed potatoes
Leftover cooked cabbage, chopped
Salt and pepper
Butter

Mix the potatoes and cabbage together, with seasoning to taste. Heat some butter in a frying pan, put in the vegetable mixture, smooth it over and flatten with a palette knife. Fry it until it is nicely browned underneath, then turn it over and brown the underside, allowing it to heat through thoroughly.

Other cooked vegetables, such as carrot, celery and parsnip, may be added, also small cubes of cooked meat or poultry.

Red Cabbage

Cook as for Savoy or Dutch Cabbage (*above*), but add 1 tbsp. vinegar to the water to improve the flavour; allow 15–20 minutes.

For pickled red cabbage, see the chapter on Chutneys, Pickles and Sauces.

Carrots

NEW: Trim off the leaves, then scrape lightly with a sharp knife. As they are small, new carrots are usually cooked whole. Simmer in salted water for about 15 minutes, or until cooked. Serve tossed with a little butter, pepper and chopped parsley.

OLD: Peel thinly and cut in one of these ways:
1. Into $\frac{1}{4}$- or $\frac{1}{2}$-inch lengthways strips.
2. Into strips and then across to small squares.
3. Into thin rounds.

Cook and serve as for new carrots, but simmer for about 20 minutes.

Allow 4–6 oz. per portion.

Carrots Cooked by the Conservative Method

1 lb. carrots, trimmed and scraped
1 oz. butter or margarine
$\frac{1}{2}$ level tsp. salt
Up to $\frac{1}{4}$ pint boiling water
Chopped parsley

Slice the carrots thinly if old, leave whole if young. Melt the butter, add the carrots and cook over a low heat with the lid on the pan, shaking frequently, until all the fat is absorbed – about 10 minutes. Now add the salt and the liquid (using less for young carrots) and simmer gently until the carrots are cooked – 15–30 minutes, according to age.

Serve hot, with the small amount of liquid remaining, and garnish with parsley.

Corn on the Cob

Glazed Carrots

2 oz. butter
1 lb. young carrots, scraped and left whole
3 lumps of sugar
$\frac{1}{4}$ level tsp. salt
A little stock
Chopped parsley

Melt the butter in a saucepan. Add the carrots, sugar, salt and enough stock to come half-way up the carrots. Cook gently without a lid, shaking the pan occasionally, until soft; remove the carrots and keep them hot. Boil the liquid rapidly until it is reduced to a rich glaze. Replace the carrots in it a few at a time, turning them until all sides are well coated with glaze.

Serve sprinkled with parsley.

Cauliflower

Remove the coarse outside leaves, cut a cross in the stalk end and wash the cauliflower. Cook it stem side down in fast-boiling salted water for about 20–30 minutes, depending on size. Drain well and serve coated with white or cheese sauce (*see Sauces chapter*).

The cauliflower can be divided into individual florets and cooked in fast-boiling salted water for about 15 minutes. Drain well and serve tossed with butter and a sprinkling of pepper or coated with sauce.

A medium-sized cauliflower serves 4 people.

Celeriac *(The root of Turnip-rooted Celery)*

Peel the celeriac fairly thickly: small roots may be cooked whole, but larger ones should be sliced thickly or cut into dice. Cook in boiling salted water or stock until soft – 1 hour or even longer. Drain well and serve with melted butter or a Béchamel or Hollandaise sauce.

Celeriac may also be braised or served au gratin.

Allow $\frac{1}{4}$–$\frac{1}{2}$ lb. per portion.

Celery

Wash, scrub and cut into even lengths. Cook in boiling salted water until tender – $\frac{1}{2}$–1 hour, depending on the coarseness of the celery. Drain well and serve with a white, parsley or cheese sauce (*see Sauces chapter*).

Allow 1 head of celery per portion if small, 2–3 sticks if large.

Braised Celery

4 small heads of celery, trimmed and scrubbed
2 oz. butter
Stock
Salt and pepper

Oven temperature: moderate (350 F., mark 4)

Tie each head of celery securely to hold the shape. Fry

135

lightly in $1\frac{1}{2}$ oz. butter for 5 minutes, until golden-brown. Put in an ovenproof dish, add enough stock to come half-way up the celery, sprinkle with salt and pepper and add remaining butter. Cover and cook for $1–1\frac{1}{2}$ hours in the centre of the oven. Remove strings and serve with the cooking liquid poured over.

Corn on the Cob

Choose the cobs when they are plump, well formed and of a pale golden-yellow colour and cook them while still really fresh.

Remove the outside leaves and silky threads, put the cobs into boiling unsalted water (salt toughens corn) and cook for 12–20 minutes, depending on their size – overcooking also makes them tough. Drain well and serve with melted butter, salt and freshly-ground pepper.

Allow 1–2 cobs per portion.

Courgettes

These are a variety of small vegetable marrow. They are normally cooked unpeeled, being either left whole or cut into rounds. They may be boiled (allow 15–20 minutes), steamed or fried and are served with melted butter and chopped parsley or tarragon.

Allow $\frac{1}{4}$ lb. per portion, when served as an accompaniment.

Cucumber

Although cucumber is usually eaten raw as a salad vegetable, it may also be cooked. To do this, peel the cucumber, cut it in half lengthwise, then into pieces about 2 inches long (or cut into dice) and cook very gently in butter in a covered pan for 10–15 minutes. Serve with white sauce or melted butter.

Allow 4–6 oz. per portion for cooked cucumber.

Endive

There are two types, the 'Curly' Endive, which has very crinkly leaves, and the 'Batavian' Endive, with much smoother leaves. Both are very pale green in colour – almost white at the heart – and of somewhat bitter flavour. In this country they are generally eaten raw as salad plants, but in France (where they are called Chicorée) they are often served braised, like lettuce.

Allow 1 medium-sized head of endive per person, when it is cooked; for salad use, 1 endive will serve 4 people.

Fennel

The fennel which is eaten as a vegetable is of the 'Florence' variety. It has solid white stems with a swollen base, which rather resembles celery. Whole fennel may be cooked in the same way as celery and served hot. The young, tender side stems can be eaten raw as an hors d'oeuvre or with cheese – they are merely washed, peeled and thinly sliced. Fennel has a slight but distinctive aniseed flavour.

Allow 1 head of fennel per person.

Kale

A green, curly-leaved vegetable of the cabbage family, which does not, however, form a head; it has a good flavour when picked young. Prepare and cook it like cabbage.

Kohl Rabi

A vegetable with a stem enlarged to a turnip-like globe which grows above the ground, topped with curly green leaves. These enlarged stems should be eaten while they are small and young. Cut off the leaves and peel thickly. If the globes are small, leave them whole, otherwise cut them into thick slices or cubes. Cook in a little boiling water until soft – $\frac{1}{2}$–1 hour, according to size. Serve coated with a white sauce (*see Sauces chapter*) or glaze with butter and toss in chopped parsley.

Kohl rabi can also be served cold with vinaigrette dressing.

Allow 4–6 oz. per portion.

Leeks

Remove the coarse outside leaves and cut off the tops and roots. Wash the leeks very thoroughly, splitting them down the centre to within 1 inch or so of the base, to ensure that all grit is removed – if necessary cut them through completely to achieve this. Cook in boiling salted water until soft – 20–30 minutes. Drain very thoroughly. Serve coated with a white or cheese sauce (*see Sauces chapter*).

Allow 1–3 leeks per portion, or $\frac{1}{2}$–$\frac{3}{4}$ lb., depending on the amount of waste.

Braised Leeks

Cook as for Braised Celery; allow 2–3 leeks per person.

Lettuce

Lettuces, both the cabbage and the cos varieties, are used chiefly as salad vegetables. They can, however, be cooked in various ways – for example, braised.

Allow 1 medium-sized lettuce per person, when it is cooked. For salad use, a medium-sized one will serve 4 people.

Vegetable Marrow

Large marrows must be peeled, the seeds removed and the flesh cut into even-sized pieces. Cook in boiling salted water until soft – about 20 minutes – and drain well. Serve coated with a white or cheese sauce (see Sauces chapter). Marrow can also be roasted in the dripping round the meat or stuffed and baked, either whole or in rings.

Allow 6 oz. per portion when marrow is served as an accompaniment.

Stuffed Marrow

1 vegetable marrow (about 2 lb.)
¾ lb. minced meat
4 tbsps. fresh breadcrumbs
1–2 level tsps. mixed herbs or 1 level tbsp. chopped parsley
1 onion, skinned and finely chopped
Salt and pepper
1 egg, beaten
Tomato sauce

Oven temperature: moderate (350° F., mark 4)

Wash the marrow, peel, cut in half and scoop out the seeds. Mix the meat, crumbs, herbs, onion and seasoning with a fork and add enough beaten egg to bind the mixture together. Put this stuffing into the two halves of the marrow and place them together again. Wrap in greased greaseproof paper, put in an ovenproof dish and bake in the centre of the oven for about 1 hour, until the marrow is done. Remove the paper and serve the marrow with a tomato sauce (see Sauces chapter).

Alternatively, cut the marrow into slices 1½–2 inches thick, remove the seeds, stand the pieces upright on a greased ovenproof dish and fill each with the same stuffing as used above. Cover the dish with foil and bake at the same temperature for about 15–20 minutes.

Mushrooms

The majority of mushrooms bought today are cultivated and require only washing and draining before being used. Cut off and discard the earthy end of each stalk; the rest of the stalk can be included in the dish or as an ingredient in a stuffing. Field mushrooms need skinning and should be washed thoroughly to remove any mud or grit.

Allow 1–3 oz. per portion depending on whether the mushrooms are to be used as a garnish or a vegetable.

Onions

Onions vary considerably in both size and flavour. The small white 'cocktail' onion is not much bigger than a large pea. Shallots are smaller than the average true onion, but have a stronger flavour. Spanish onions are larger but milder in flavour than the English variety.

Both the leaves and the bulbs of the young plants, known as spring onions, may be eaten in salads, but in the case of ordinary mature onions the leaves are discarded.

Allow 4–6 oz. per portion for cooked onions.

Parsnips

Wash the parsnips, peel off the skin, quarter and remove the hard centre cores. Cut into slices, strips or dice and leave in water till required for cooking. Cook in boiling salted water for 30–40 minutes, until soft. Drain and toss in butter, salt, pepper and a little grated nutmeg.

To roast parsnips, par-boil them for 5 minutes in salted water, drain and place in the fat round the joint to cook for 1 hour.

Allow 6–8 oz. per portion.

Peas

The season for fresh peas lasts for about 6 weeks only, but they are sold preserved in various ways – canned, bottled, dried, dehydrated and frozen. Dehydrated and frozen peas are very similar to the fresh ones when they are properly cooked and presented.

Quantities to Allow
For one average serving reckon:
8 oz. fresh peas (as bought)
3 oz. canned, bottled or frozen peas
2 oz. dehydrated peas

Preparation and Cooking

FRESH PEAS: Shell and wash, place in boiling salted water with about 1 level tsp. sugar and a sprig of mint and cook until tender – 20–30 minutes. Drain them, remove the mint and if liked toss the peas with a knob of butter before serving.

PETITS POIS: This particularly small and sweet type of pea is much used on the Continent. The peas are generally cooked with the addition of a little chopped onion and some butter.

FROZEN, DEHYDRATED AND CANNED PEAS: Follow the manufacturer's directions.

Potatoes

Peel potatoes as thinly as possible, using either a special potato peeler or a sharp, short-bladed knife. New potatoes are scraped or brushed. Cook the potatoes as soon as you can after the peeling or scraping; if it is necessary to let them stand for a while, keep them under water, to prevent discoloration.

Allow 6–8 oz. per portion.

BOILED: Cut the prepared potatoes into even-sized pieces, put into cold water, add ½ level tsp. salt per lb., bring to the boil and simmer until tender but unbroken – 15–20 minutes for new potatoes, 20–30 minutes for old. Drain well, add a knob of butter if liked and serve sprinkled with chopped parsley.

MASHED: Boil old potatoes in the usual way, drain and dry over a low heat, then mash with a fork or a potato masher.

CREAMED: Mash the cooked potatoes with a knob of butter, salt and pepper to taste and a little milk. Beat them well over a gentle heat with a wooden spoon until fluffy. Serve in a heated dish, mark with a fork and sprinkle with chopped parsley.

BAKED OR 'JACKET' POTATOES: Choose even-sized old potatoes, scrub well, dry and prick all over with a fork. Bake near the top of a fairly hot oven (400°F., mark 6) for about $\frac{3}{4}$–1 hour for small potatoes, 1–1$\frac{1}{4}$ hours for large ones, or until soft when pinched. Cut a cross in the top of each potato and put in a knob of butter or a spoonful of sour cream.

To cut down the baking time the potatoes can either be boiled first for 10 minutes – they then bake in about 30 minutes – or they can be threaded on a metal skewer and baked for 40 minutes.

ROAST: Using old potatoes, peel in the usual way and cut into even-sized pieces. Cook in salted water for 5–10 minutes – depending on the size – and drain well. Transfer them to a roasting tin containing 4 oz. of hot lard or dripping, baste well and bake near the top of a hot oven (425°F., mark 7) for about 20 minutes; turn them and continue cooking until soft inside and crisp and brown outside – about 40 minutes altogether. Drain well on kitchen paper and serve in an uncovered serving dish, sprinkled with salt.

If preferred, do not parboil the potatoes to begin with – in this case they will take about 50–60 minutes to cook.

They can also be cooked in the roasting tin around the joint, when little or no extra fat will be needed.

SAUTÉ: Boil the potatoes until they are just cooked and cut into slices $\frac{1}{4}$ inch thick. Fry slowly in a little hot butter or lard, turning them once so that they are crisp and golden on both sides. Drain well on kitchen paper and serve with a little chopped parsley or chives.

CHIPPED OR FRENCH FRIED: Cut peeled old potatoes into $\frac{1}{4}$–$\frac{1}{2}$-inch slices and then into strips $\frac{1}{4}$–$\frac{1}{2}$-inch wide. (For speed, several slices can be put on top of one another and cut together.) Place in cold water and leave for at least $\frac{1}{2}$ hour; drain well and dry with a cloth.

Heat a deep fat fryer of oil to 375°F., or until when one chip is dropped in, it rises to the surface at once, surrounded by bubbles. Put enough chips into the basket to about quarter-fill it and lower carefully into the fat. Cook for about 6–7 minutes. Remove the chips and drain on absorbent paper. Follow the same procedure until all the chips have been cooked. Just before serving, re-heat the fat, test to make sure it is hot enough and fry the chips rapidly for about 3 minutes, until crisp and brown. Drain well on kitchen paper and serve in an uncovered dish, sprinkled with salt.

Pulses

DRIED PEAS, SPLIT PEAS, HARICOT AND BUTTER BEANS: Should be soaked overnight in cold water. To cook, put into fresh cold water, add salt, bring to the boil and boil gently until soft; the time varies considerably. For extra flavour, add a ham bone, bay leaf or bouquet garni. Serve tossed in butter or with white cheese or tomato sauce (*see Sauces*).

LENTILS: May be soaked overnight, though this is not essential. To cook, cover with cold water, bring to the boil and simmer very gently until they are soft and the liquid is absorbed – about $\frac{1}{2}$–1 hour; add more liquid if necessary. Allow 1–2 oz. pulses (dry weight) per portion.

Table of Cooking Times

After soaking		
	Dried Peas	25 minutes
	Split Peas	30 minutes
	Haricot Beans	45 minutes
	Butter Beans	60 minutes
Unsoaked	Lentils	25 minutes

Salsify

A whole root vegetable, similar to parsnip in shape. Scrub the roots and scrape them quickly, placing at once in cold water to which a few drops of lemon juice or vinegar have been added; this helps to keep them a good colour. Cut into short lengths and cook in boiling salted water until soft – about 30–40 minutes. Serve coated with a white sauce or re-heat in a Béchamel sauce (*see Sauces chapter*).

Allow 4–6 oz. per portion.

Seakale

This resembles thin celery stalks in appearance; it is bleached and forced in the same way as celery. Wash well, cut off ends and tie into neat bundles. Cook until soft in boiling salted water to which a squeeze of lemon juice has been added (this is to preserve the white colour) for 20–30 minutes. Drain well and remove the strings before serving. If liked serve coated with a Béchamel or Hollandaise sauce (*see Sauces chapter*).

Seakale may also be braised or served au gratin. Cold, it may be served with a vinaigrette dressing or added to a salad. It is also eaten raw with cheese and in salads.

Allow 4–8 oz. per portion.

Sorrel

A leafy plant with a strong acid flavour, used in small quantities to add flavour to lettuce and other salads and to sauces. It may also be puréed like spinach for serving with poached eggs, sweetbreads and some meat dishes and can be mixed with spinach to improve its flavour. The French make a soup with it. Sorrel should be picked when young and fresh.

Allow 6–8 oz. per portion.

Stuffed Peppers

Spinach

Wash well in several waters to remove all grit and strip off any coarse stalks. Pack into a saucepan with only the water that clings to the leaves. Heat gently, turning the spinach occasionally, then bring to the boil and cook gently until soft – 10–15 minutes. Drain thoroughly and re-heat with a knob of butter and a sprinkling of salt and pepper.

Allow $\frac{1}{2}$ lb. per portion.

Swedes *(Swedish Turnips)*

A large root vegetable with yellow flesh and tough skin, obtainable from late autumn to spring. Swedes can be served as a separate vegetable and used in soups or in savoury dishes combined with bacon or cheese.

Swedes should be peeled thickly so that all the tough outer skin is removed. They may be sliced, diced or cut into fancy shapes. Keep them covered with water and cook as soon as possible after peeling. Boil till soft in a little salted water with the lid on for about 30–60 minutes (according to size and age), drain and mash with a little salt, pepper and grated nutmeg and a knob of butter. Alternatively, roast them as follows: cut in chunks or fingers and cook round the joint or in a separate tin with dripping, allowing 1–1¼ hours, according to the size of the pieces. Serve round the joint.

Allow 4–6 oz. per portion.

Sweet Peppers

Sweet peppers, both red and green, can be eaten raw as a salad vegetable. Being quite strong-flavoured, they should be sliced or chopped and only a small quantity added to the salad. Small amounts of raw peppers (again sliced or chopped) may be included in savoury dishes made with rice and macaroni. Peppers may be fried or stuffed and baked.

To prepare them, cut off the stalks, cut in half lengthwise and remove the seeds and any stringy membrane. If required for flavouring, they may then be sliced or chopped.

Allow 1 medium-sized pepper per portion for cooked dishes such as stuffed or fried peppers.

Stuffed Peppers

4 green peppers, halved lengthways and seeded
1 onion, skinned and chopped
4 oz. bacon, chopped
1½ oz. butter
4 tomatoes, skinned and sliced
4 oz. rice, boiled
Salt and pepper
4 level tbsps. Cheddar cheese, grated
2 oz. fresh breadcrumbs
¼ pint stock

Oven temperature: fairly hot (375°F., mark 5)

Put the halved peppers in an ovenproof dish. Lightly fry the onion and bacon in 1 oz. of the butter until golden-brown. Add the tomatoes, cooked rice, seasoning and half the cheese. Mix the rest of the cheese with the breadcrumbs. Put the bacon stuffing into the cases and sprinkle with the breadcrumb mixture. Pour the stock round the cases, top each with a knob of butter and cook just above the centre of the oven for 15–20 minutes, or until the the pepper cases are cooked.

Sweet Potatoes

Sweet potatoes are no relation to ordinary potatoes and have a sweet, slightly perfumed flesh. They may be boiled or roasted. In America, where they are very popular, they are also served as a sweet, cooked with sugar or molasses and flavoured with cinnamon.

Allow ½ lb. per portion.

Swiss Chard *(Also known as Silver Beet or Seakale Beet)*

These different names are given to a variety of beets cultivated for their 'chards' or broad mid-ribs, instead of for their roots. They are almost two vegetables in one,

as the leaves and mid-ribs can be treated separately. Trim the mid-ribs free of all green leaf, scrape, removing the stringy parts, cut into 3-inch pieces and cook as for celery.

The green leafy part is cooked as for spinach. Alternatively, keep the leaves whole and cook in boiling salted water for about ½ hour.

Allow 6–8 oz. leaves per portion or 2–3 ribs per portion.

Tomatoes

Although strictly speaking a fruit, the tomato is nearly always used as a vegetable and has come to be classed under that heading.

The characteristic flavour is probably best enjoyed when tomatoes are picked ripe and eaten raw as a salad, but they are very useful in cookery, making soups and many light savoury dishes (e.g. stuffed tomatoes) and giving a good flavour to such things as stews and cheese dishes. Grilled, baked and fried tomatoes make a colourful garnish for hot dishes and raw tomatoes can be used in various ways for decoration. Tomato juice is a popular refreshing drink.

To remove the skins from tomatoes, plunge them for a minute into boiling water, then lift them out and put them immediately into cold water; when they are cool, the skins will peel off easily with a knife. Alternatively, spear a tomato on the prongs of a fork and turn it gently over a gas jet until the skin bursts, then peel it off with a knife.

Turnips

Peel thickly to remove the outer layer of skin and put under water to prevent discoloration. Young turnips can be left whole, older ones should be sliced or diced. Cook in salted water for 20–30 minutes. If they are used whole, toss in butter or a little top of the milk, with added seasoning, or serve in a white sauce (*see Sauces chapter*). Old ones are mashed with salt, pepper and a knob of butter.

Allow 4–6 oz. per portion.

Watercress

Watercress is usually eaten raw as a salad plant or used as a garnish, but may also be cooked as for spinach and makes a good soup.

Allow 1 bunch for 4–6 people, for salad use.

Pasta and Rice

TYPES OF PASTA

STRING OR TUBULAR: These are round in cross-section and come in many different diameters, the large ones being hollow tubes. Some of the best-known are:

SPAGHETTINI AND VERMICELLI: Very fine.

SPAGHETTI: Probably the commonest of the fine pastas.

SPAGHETTONI: Slightly thicker than spaghetti.

BUCHATINI, MACHERONI, MEZZA ZITE, ZITA: Large types of hollow tubular pasta, the commonest being MACHERONI (or macaroni, as it is spelt here).

FANCY-SHAPED: The basic paste used for string and tubular pasta is often made into fancy shapes, e.g. bows (FARFALETTE).

RIDGED: These are mainly tubular, marked with ridges and cut in lengths of about 1½–3 inches. Some are straight, while others are curved, e.g. RIGATTONI, MANICHE, CANNERONI (in this country often wrongly called canneloni). They are usually stuffed, coated with a sauce and baked. Some are also made in fancy shapes, e.g. large shells.

RIBBON: These are long, flat pasta in varying widths and include TAGLIATELLE (¼-inch), FETTUCCINE (⅛-inch) and LASAGNE (½-inch).
    Nouilles, or noodles as they are called in English, are the French version of the Italian tagliatelle and are usually made from a richer paste which includes eggs.

STUFFED: Stuffed pastas are made from two thin sheets of pasta sandwiched with a savoury filling and cut up into small shapes. RAVIOLI (the commonest form) and TORTELLI are cut into squares. Other forms include small hat shapes (Capelletti), small coils of paste with a rich stuffing (TORTELLINI). CANNELLONI consist of squares of pasta cooked lightly, then stuffed and rolled up. (In

this country, as mentioned above, the name is often given to large tubular pasta.)

SOUP PASTAS: These are made in small fancy shapes such as stars, letters, melon seeds, rings and shells, and are meant to be added to soup and broth – they are not served as a dish in themselves.

COOKING AND SERVING PASTA

Italians would reckon about 3–4 oz. per person, but in this country 1½–2 oz. is considered sufficient by most people. The pasta should be cooked in a large quantity of fast-boiling salted water (*see chart for times*) until *al dente*, or just resistant to the teeth – pasta should never be mushy or slimy. Drain as soon as it is cooked and serve on a heated dish. A knob of butter or a little olive oil is usually stirred in just before serving and grated Parmesan cheese can be stirred into the pasta or served separately, according to taste.

Cooking times for Pasta

The times given below cater for the English rather than the Continental taste, for in Italy pasta tends to be eaten while still almost chewy. Remember that different kinds of pasta will require slightly different cooking times; if the pasta has been stored for some time, a slightly longer cooking time is likely to be needed.

STRING AND TUBULAR

Vermicelli, spaghettini	5 minutes
Spaghetti	9–12 minutes
Macaroni	15–20 minutes

FANCY-SHAPED

Farfalette	10 minutes

RIDGED

Canneroni, large shells	20 minutes

RIBBON
Tagliatelle, noodles	10 minutes
Lasagne	10–15 minutes

STUFFED
Ravioli	15–20 minutes

SOUP
Letters, stars, wheels, etc.	8–10 minutes

Spaghetti al Burro *(Spaghetti with butter and Parmesan cheese)*

Have ready a large pan of boiling water. Allow 3 oz. spaghetti per person; hold the end of the bunch of spaghetti in the water and as it softens, coil it round in the pan. Boil rapidly for 9–12 minutes, moving the spaghetti occasionally to prevent sticking, until it is just cooked. Drain well and return it to the pan with 1–2 oz. butter and a good sprinkling of grated Parmesan cheese. Stir and leave for a few minutes for the butter and cheese to melt. Serve with more grated cheese in a separate dish.

Any form of tubular or ribbon pasta can be cooked and served in this way.

Spaghetti alla Bolognese *(Using a traditional Italian meat sauce)*

8 oz. spaghetti
Grated Parmesan cheese to serve

For the Sauce
2 oz. bacon, chopped
½ oz. butter
1 small onion, skinned and chopped
1 carrot, peeled and chopped
1 stick of celery, scrubbed and chopped
8 oz. minced beef, raw
4 oz. chicken livers, chopped (optional)
1 level tbsp. tomato paste
¼ pint dry white wine
½ pint beef stock
Salt and pepper
Powdered nutmeg

Make the sauce first. Fry the bacon lightly in the butter for 2–3 minutes, add the onion, carrot and celery and fry for a further 5 minutes until lightly browned. Add the beef and brown lightly. Stir in the chicken livers, if used. After cooking them for about 3 minutes, add the tomato paste and wine, allow to bubble for a few minutes and add the stock, seasoning and nutmeg. Simmer for 30–40 minutes, until the meat is tender and the liquid in the sauce is well reduced. Adjust the seasoning if necessary.

Meanwhile cook the spaghetti in the usual way in fast-boiling water for about 9–12 minutes. Drain and serve on a heated dish with the sauce poured over. Serve the cheese sprinkled over the sauce or in a separate dish.

Canneloni with Cheese Sauce

6 large canneloni
Salt
¼ lb. mushrooms, chopped
2 oz. butter
A 6½-oz. can of pimientos
A 10-oz. can of peas, drained
2 cloves of garlic, skinned and crushed
A 7½-oz. can of salmon
2 oz. fresh breadcrumbs

For the Sauce
2 oz. butter
1½ oz. flour
1 pint milk
6 oz. Cheddar cheese, grated
Salt and pepper

Oven temperature: fairly hot (400°F., mark 6)

Cook the canneloni in salted water for the time directed on the packet; drain well. Meanwhile sauté the mushrooms in the butter; add 2 caps of pimiento (diced), the peas, garlic, salmon and breadcrumbs. Cook over a low heat for 5 minutes, stirring. Make up the sauce in the usual way, using 5 oz. of the cheese. Stuff the canneloni with the salmon filling so that it protrudes slightly at each end. Arrange side by side in an ovenproof dish. Pour the sauce over. Garnish with the remainder of the pimiento, cut in strips, and scatter the rest of the cheese over. Bake in the centre of the oven for 30 minutes, until bubbly and golden-brown.

Carnival Macaroni Cheese

4 oz. macaroni
1½ oz. butter
3 oz. button mushrooms
2 tbsps. chopped canned pimiento
2 tbsps. sliced green pepper
1 oz. flour
1 level tsp. salt
A dash of pepper
¾ pint milk
6 oz. Cheddar cheese, grated
Buttered breadcrumbs

Oven temperature: moderate (350°F., mark 4)

Cook the macaroni in boiling salted water for 15 minutes. Meanwhile, melt the butter in a saucepan, then add the mushrooms, pimiento and green pepper (reserving a little of each for garnish) and brown lightly. Stir in the flour, salt and pepper. Add the milk gradually and cook until thickened, stirring constantly. Add the cheese, stirring well to make a smooth sauce.

Rinse the macaroni in warm water and drain well. Fold it into the cheese sauce, pour into a casserole, top with breadcrumbs and garnish. Bake in the oven for about 25 minutes.

Variations:
Instead of the mushrooms, pimiento and green pepper

143

Pasta with Mediterranean Sauce

use any of the following:

1 small onion, skinned, chopped and boiled
4 oz. bacon or ham
1 medium sized can of salmon or tuna, drained and flaked

(See colour picture facing page 193)

Macheroni alla Carbonara *(Macaroni with Ham and Eggs)*

6 oz. macaroni, in short lengths
1 oz. butter
4 oz. cooked ham
2–3 eggs, beaten
Salt and pepper
2 tbsps. grated Parmesan cheese

Cook the macaroni in the usual way in fast-boiling water for 15–20 minutes, until soft, and drain it well. Fry the ham lightly for 2–3 minutes in the butter, until heated through, and stir in the drained macaroni, beaten eggs and seasoning. Stir over a gentle heat until the mixture is well blended and the eggs are just beginning to thicken. Add the cheese, mix well and serve straight away.

Quick macaroni can also be used – cook as directed on the packet.

Pasta With Mediterranean Sauce

Any type of pasta
2 medium onions, skinned and chopped
1½ oz. butter or 2–3 tbsps. oil
1 clove of garlic, crushed
A 15-oz. can of Italian tomatoes
A 2½-oz. can of tomato paste
1 level tsp. dried marjoram or rosemary
1 level tsp. sugar
Salt and pepper
4 oz. mushrooms, sliced

Cook the pasta in the usual way. Fry the onions gently in 1 oz. of the butter for 5 minutes, until soft but not coloured. Stir in the garlic, tomatoes, tomato paste, herbs, sugar and seasoning, cover and simmer for 30 minutes, until the sauce is thick. Fry the mushrooms gently for about 3 minutes in the remaining ½ oz. butter and add to the sauce. Adjust the seasoning and serve as a sauce over the pasta.

Semolina Gnocchi alla Romana

1 pint milk
4 oz. semolina
Salt, pepper
A pinch of grated nutmeg
1–2 eggs, beaten
3 oz. grated Parmesan cheese
A little butter and extra cheese for topping

Bring the milk to the boil, sprinkle in the semolina and seasonings and stir over a gentle heat until the mixture is really thick. Beat well until smooth and stir in the eggs and cheese. Spread this mixture, about ¼–½ inch thick, on a shallow buttered dish and allow to cool. Cut into 1-inch rounds or squares and arrange in a shallow greased oven-proof dish. Put a few knobs of butter over the top, sprinkle with a little extra cheese and brown under the grill or towards the top of a fairly hot oven (400°F., mark 6). Serve with more cheese and tomato sauce *(see Sauces chapter)*.

Cream Cheese Gnocchi

½ lb. cream cheese (traditionally Ricotta) sieved
2 oz. butter
4 level tbsps. grated Parmesan cheese
2 eggs, beaten
2–3 oz. flour
Salt, pepper, a little grated nutmeg
Melted butter and grated cheese to serve

Mix all the ingredients together, beat until smooth, then form into small balls or cork shapes. Roll these in flour and poach a few at a time in boiling salted water – this takes about 5 minutes, and they are ready when they rise to the top of the pan. Serve tossed in melted butter and sprinkled with grated Parmesan cheese.
Gnocchi is the name given to several different dishes, based on semolina, maize meal, cooked potatoes, cheese-flavoured choux pastry and even cream cheese.

RICE

SHAPES OF GRAIN
There are three main kinds of rice grain – long, medium and short.

The long grains are fluffy and separate when cooked so they are ideal for made-up savoury rice dishes and for rice used as an accompaniment to savoury dishes such as curries and stews. Medium and short-grain rice have moister, stickier grains. The medium grains are very suitable for savoury dishes where the rice needs to be moulded or bound together (e.g. rice rings, stuffings and croquettes). Short-grain rice is usually used for rice puddings and other sweet rice dishes. *(See chapters on Hot and Cold Puddings.)*

TYPES OF RICE
REGULAR WHITE RICE: The hulls, germs, outer bran and most of the inner bran layers are removed. The rice is white in colour, with only a bland, very slight flavour when cooked.

BROWN RICE: Whole unpolished grains of rice with only the inedible outer hull removed. It takes longer to cook than white rice and apart from its fawn colour when cooked; differs from white rice by having a more chewy texture and quite a nutty flavour. It is used in savoury dishes.

PAR-BOILED RICE: Cooked before milling by a special steam pressure process, which helps to retain the natural food value. It takes longer to cook than white rice, but more easily produces a perfect result, with grains that are fluffy, separate and plump when cooked.

PRE-COOKED RICE (often referred to as Instant Rice): This is completely cooked and only needs soaking in boiling water for about 5 minutes. It is a very good standby for snacks and quick rice dishes, both savoury and sweet.

WILD RICE: This is not actually rice, but seeds from a wild grass, used for savoury dishes. It is expensive and not widely available, but delicious for special occasions, particularly with game.

Preparing and Cooking Rice
Rice sold in unbranded packs or loose should be washed before it is cooked. Put it in a strainer and rinse it under the cold tap until all the loose starch (white powder) is washed off – it is this loose starch which prevents rice drying out into separate grains when cooked.

Boiled Rice – the 1-2-1 Method
Place 1 cup of long-grain rice in a saucepan with 2 cups water and 1 level tsp. salt. Bring quickly to the boil, stir well and cover with a tight-fitting lid. Reduce the heat and simmer gently for 14–15 minutes. Remove from the heat and before serving separate out the grains gently, using a fork. (The rice will not need draining.)

If a drier effect is required, leave the rice covered for 5–10 minutes after it has been cooked. The grains should then be tender, but dry and quite separate.

The one cup of rice gives 3–4 servings.

Here are some points to remember when using the 1-2-1 method:

Don't increase the amount of water or the finished rice will be soggy.

Don't uncover the rice whilst it is cooking or the steam will escape and the cooking time will be increased.

Don't stir the rice while it is simmering – it breaks up the grains and makes them soggy.

When the rice is cooked, don't leave it longer than 10 minutes before serving, or the grains will stick together.

Oven-cooking Rice by the 1-2-1 Method
Place 1 cup rice in an ovenproof dish. Bring 2 cups water and 1 level tsp. salt to the boil, pour over the rice and stir well. Cover tightly with a lid or foil and bake in the centre of a moderate oven (350°F., mark 4) for 35–40 minutes, or until the grains are just soft and the cooking liquid has all been absorbed by the rice.

Fried Rice

4 oz. long-grain rice
2 eggs, beaten
4 tbsps. oil
½ level tsp. salt
½ an onion, skinned and finely chopped
2 oz. mushrooms, thinly sliced
2 tbsps. frozen peas
2 oz. cooked ham, diced
2 tsps. soy sauce

Boil the rice. Make a plain omelette from the eggs, cut it into thin strips and set aside. Fry the drained rice for about 5 minutes in 2 tbsps. of very hot oil with the salt, stirring all the time; remove from the pan and set aside. Clean the pan and add the remaining oil. Fry the onion for about 3 minutes, till lightly browned, add the remaining vegetables and the ham and fry lightly for a further 3 minutes, stirring well. Slowly add the rice and when well mixed, stir in the soy sauce and shredded omelette; serve the mixture as soon as it is hot, to accompany chicken.

Curried Rice

1 onion, finely chopped
1 oz. butter
1 cup long-grain rice
1–2 oz. currants or stoned raisins
½ level tsp. curry powder
2½ cups chicken or beef stock (made from a cube)
Salt and pepper
1 oz. blanched almonds, slivered and browned (optional)

Fry the onion in the butter for about 5 minutes, until soft. Add the rice and fry for a further 2–3 minutes, stirring all the time. Add the fruit, curry powder, stock and seasoning and bring to the boil. Stir and cover with a lid, reduce the heat and simmer gently for 14–15 minutes. Stir in the almonds (if used) and serve.

Good with meat or chicken.

Risotto alla Milanese

1 onion, skinned and finely chopped
3 oz. butter
8 oz. long-grain rice
¼ pint dry white wine
1½ pints boiling chicken stock (make from a cube)
Salt and pepper
2–3 level tbsps. grated Parmesan cheese

Fry the onion gently for about 5 minutes in 2 oz. of the butter, until it is soft and just beginning to turn golden. Add the rice and continue frying, stirring all the time, until the rice looks transparent. Pour in the wine and allow to bubble briskly until well reduced. Add about ½ pint of the stock and the seasoning and cook over a moderate heat in the open pan until the stock has been absorbed. Continue adding the stock until it is all used and the rice is just soft – 15–20 minutes. Add the remaining butter and stir in well. The cheese can also be stirred in until it melts, or if preferred it can be served separately. Traditionally, 1–2 oz. of beef marrow is included, being fried after the onion is soft; the rice is coloured with saffron, which is dissolved in a little of the stock and added towards the end of the cooking time. If these two ingredients are omitted, the risotto should strictly speaking be called a *Risotto bianco*.

Basic Pilau

8 oz. long-grain rice
2 oz. butter
3 pints boiling chicken stock (made from a cube)
Salt and pepper

Fry the rice gently in the melted butter for about 5 minutes, stirring all the time, until it looks transparent. Add the stock, pouring it in slowly, as it will tend to bubble rather a lot at first. Add the seasoning, stir well, cover with a tight-fitting lid and leave over a very low heat for about 15 minutes, until the water is absorbed and the rice grains are just soft. (The idea is that the rice should cook in its own steam, so don't stir it while it is cooking.)

Remove the lid, cover the rice with a cloth, replace the lid and leave in a warm place to dry out for at least 15 minutes before serving. (This is a traditional part of making a pilau, although not included in many European versions of this dish.)

To serve, stir lightly with a fork to separate the grains, add a knob of butter and serve at once.

Chicken Pilau

½ a boiling chicken or 2–3 good-sized chicken portions (uncooked)
3 oz. butter
2 small onions, skinned and finely chopped
1 stick of celery, scrubbed and finely chopped
1 clove of garlic, crushed (optional)
1 green pepper, seeded and finely chopped
2 oz. mushrooms, sliced
2 oz. bacon or ham, chopped
¼ pint dry white wine
Chicken stock
Salt and pepper
Chopped fresh herbs as available (e.g. marjoram, thyme or basil)
8 oz. long-grain rice
Grated Parmesan cheese

Skin the chicken, bone it and cut the flesh in strips. Melt 1 oz. of the butter and fry one of the onions gently for 5 minutes, until soft. Add the chicken, the remaining vegetables and the bacon or ham and fry for a further few minutes, stirring all the time. Add the wine and let it bubble until well reduced; just cover with chicken stock and add the seasoning and herbs. Put on the lid and leave to simmer for about 1 hour, until the chicken is really tender.

Fry the remaining onion in 1 oz. of the remaining butter for about 5 minutes, until soft. Add the rice and stir until transparent. Add about ½ pint of chicken stock and cook over a moderate heat, uncovered, until the stock has been absorbed; continue to cook adding more stock as required, until the rice is just soft (15–20 minutes). Pour in the chicken mixture, stir well and continue cooking until the two mixtures are well blended and the liquid all absorbed. Stir in the remaining butter and some Parmesan cheese and serve.

Mutton Pilau

1–1½ lb. loin or best end of neck of mutton
1½ pints chicken stock (from a cube)
6 oz. long-grain rice
A pinch of ground cinnamon
A pinch of ground cloves
Salt and pepper
2 oz. currants or stoned raisins
2 oz. butter

Trim the meat and cut into even-sized pieces. Cover with the stock and stew until tender, then lift out, drain and keep on one side. Wash the rice well and sprinkle into the

Curried Rice

liquid in which the meat was cooked; add the spices, seasoning and currants. Bring to the boil, then cover and simmer very gently for about 15 minutes, until all the liquid is absorbed and the rice is just soft. Remove from the heat and leave covered for about 15 minutes to dry out. Fry the meat in half the butter until lightly browned and stir the remaining butter into the rice mixture. Serve the rice piled on a dish with the meat in the centre. This dish can be garnished with wedges of tomato or fried onion rings.

Liver Pilau

½ lb. calf's liver, cut in strips
2 oz. butter
2 onions, skinned and finely chopped
1 oz. shelled peanuts or almonds
6–8 oz. long-grain rice
Salt and pepper
A pinch of mixed spice
2 oz. currants
2 tomatoes, skinned and chopped
1½–2 pints chicken or meat stock (boiling)
A little chopped parsley

Fry the liver lightly in the butter for 2–3 minutes and remove it from the fat with a slotted spoon. Fry the onions for 5 minutes in the same fat until soft but not brown. Add the nuts and rice and fry for a further 5 minutes, stirring all the time. Add the seasoning, spice, currants, tomatoes and stock, stir well, cover with a tight-fitting lid and simmer for about 15 minutes, until all the liquid has been absorbed. Stir in the liver and parsley, cover again and before serving leave for 15 minutes in a warm place (but without further cooking). The liver may if preferred be replaced by cooked leftover chicken or lamb.

Paella

1 small chicken
3 tbsps. olive oil
1 onion, skinned and chopped
1 clove of garlic, skinned and chopped
8 oz. long-grain rice
½ level tsp. saffron
¾ pint chicken stock
Salt and pepper
2 oz. shrimps
1 small pkt. of frozen peas
1 red pimiento, seeded and chopped

Cut the flesh from the chicken, cut into small pieces and fry in the oil until golden. Remove from the pan and fry the onion and garlic until browned. Add the rice and cook until transparent. Add the saffron, chicken, stock, salt and pepper and bring to the boil. Add the shrimps, peas and pimiento, cover and simmer for 15–20 minutes, adding a little more stock if necessary and stirring from time to time. Serve immediately. *(Serves 6)*

(See colour picture facing page 224)

Hot Puddings

BAKED SPONGE PUDDINGS

Plain Baked Sponge

3 oz. butter or margarine
3 oz. caster sugar
1 egg, beaten
5 oz. self-raising flour
$\frac{1}{2}$ tsp. vanilla essence
Milk to mix

Oven temperature: moderate (350 F., mark 4)

Grease an ovenproof dish. Cream the fat and sugar until pale and fluffy. Add the egg a little at a time, beating after each addition. Fold in the flour with the essence and a little milk to give a dropping consistency. Put into the prepared dish and bake towards the top of the oven for 30–40 minutes, until well risen and golden. Serve with syrup sauce or custard.

This sponge pudding can be varied in several ways – for instance:

Jam Sponge
Put 2–3 tbsps. jam in a layer over the bottom of the greased dish before adding the sponge mixture. Serve with a jam or a sweet white sauce.

Baked Castle Puddings
Grease 8 individual foil dishes or dariole moulds and put 1–2 tsps. jam in the bottom of each. Divide the mixture between the dishes or moulds, bake for 20 minutes and serve with jam sauce.

Orange and Lemon Sponge
Add the grated rind of an orange or lemon to the creamed mixture and replace the milk by the fruit juice. Serve with an orange or lemon sauce.

Spicy Fruit Sponge
Sift $\frac{1}{2}$–1 level tsp. mixed spice with the flour. Add 3–4 oz. sultanas or currants and 1–2 oz. chopped glacé cherries or cut mixed peel with the flour. Serve with white sauce or custard.

Chocolate Sponge
Add 1 oz. cocoa, sifted with the flour, or stir 1 oz. chocolate 'Polka Dots' into the mixture. Serve with chocolate sauce.

Coconut Sponge
Replace 1 oz. of the flour by 1 oz. desiccated coconut; omit the vanilla essence.

Ginger Sponge
Sift $\frac{1}{2}$ level tsp. ground ginger with the flour, or add 2 pieces of preserved ginger, finely chopped, and 2 tsps. of the ginger syrup to the mixture. Serve with a sauce made from golden syrup, thinned down with hot water.

Eve's Pudding

1 lb. cooking apples, peeled and cored
3 oz. Demerara sugar
Grated rind of 1 lemon
1 tbsp. water
3 oz. butter or margarine
3 oz. caster sugar
1 egg, beaten
4 oz. self-raising flour

Oven temperature: moderate (350°F., mark 4)

Slice the apples thinly into a greased ovenproof dish and sprinkle the Demerara sugar and grated lemon rind over them. Add the tbsp. of water. Cream the fat and caster sugar together until pale and fluffy. Add the beaten egg a little at a time, beating well after each addition. Fold in the flour with a metal spoon and spread the mixture over the apples. Bake in the centre of the oven for 40–45 minutes, until the apples are tender and the sponge mixture cooked.

Lemon Layer Pudding

Pineapple Upside-down Pudding

2 oz. butter for topping
2 oz. brown sugar
1 small can of pineapple rings, drained
4 oz. butter or margarine
4 oz. caster sugar
2 eggs, beaten
6 oz. self-raising flour
2–3 tbsps. pineapple juice or milk

Oven temperature: moderate (350°F., mark 4)

Grease a 7-inch round cake tin. Cream together the butter and brown sugar and spread it over the bottom of the tin. (Alternatively, use 2–3 tbsps. golden syrup.) Arrange the rings of pineapple on this layer in the bottom of the tin. Cream together the remaining fat and sugar until pale and fluffy. Add the beaten egg a little at a time and beat well after each addition. Fold in the flour, adding some pineapple juice or milk to give a dropping consistency, and spread on top of the pineapple rings. Bake in the centre of the oven for about 45 minutes. Turn out on to a dish and serve with a pineapple sauce made by thickening the remaining juice with a little cornflour.

Chocolate Pear Upside-down Pudding
Use canned halved pears instead of pineapple. Substitute 1 oz. cocoa powder for 1 oz. of the flour in the sponge mixture.

Ginger Upside-down Pudding
Cut $\frac{1}{2}$–$\frac{3}{4}$ lb. trimmed rhubarb into 1-inch lengths (or peel, core and thinly slice 2 cooking apples). Arrange the fruit over the layer of creamed fat and sugar or syrup. Make up the cake mixture, using soft brown sugar instead of white, and sift 1–2 level tsps. powdered ginger with the flour.

Lemon Layer Pudding

Juice and grated rind of 1 lemon
2 oz. butter
4 oz. sugar
2 eggs, separated
$\frac{1}{2}$ pint milk
2 oz. self-raising flour

Oven temperature: fairly hot (400°F., mark 6)

Add the lemon rind to the butter and sugar and cream the mixture until pale and fluffy. Add the egg yolks and beat well. Stir in the milk, lemon juice and flour. Whisk the egg whites stiffly, fold in and pour the mixture into a fairly large greased ovenproof dish – about $2\frac{1}{4}$ pints. Stand the dish in a shallow tin of water and cook near the top of the oven for about 45 minutes, or until the top is set and firm to the touch.

Note

This pudding separates out in the cooking into a custard layer with a sponge topping.

PASTRY SWEETS

Syrup Tart

4 oz. shortcrust pastry *(see Pastry chapter)*
5–6 tbsps. golden syrup
2 oz. fresh white breadcrumbs
Grated rind of ½ a lemon

Oven temperature: hot (425°F., mark 7)

Roll out the pastry and line a 7-inch pie plate. Mix together the syrup, breadcrumbs and lemon rind. Spread the mixture in the pastry case, keeping the border free. Make cuts down the border at 1-inch intervals and fold over each strip to form a triangle. Cook towards the top of the oven for about 20 minutes or until golden-brown. Serve hot or cold.

Fruit Pie

1½ lb. cooking apples, plums or rhubarb
4 oz. sugar
1–2 tbsps. water
4–6 oz. shortcrust pastry *(see Pastry chapter)*

Oven temperature: hot (425 F., mark 7)

Prepare the fruit as for stewing and layer it with the sugar into a pie dish (1½–2 pint size). Add the water. Roll out the pastry ¼-inch thick to the shape of the pie dish and about 1 inch larger all round. Cut off a strip of pastry wide enough to cover the rim, wet this and press the strip on. Moisten the strip of pastry and cover with the lid, pressing the edges well together. Trim, flake and scallop the edges. Bake for 15–20 minutes towards the top of the oven, until the pastry is lightly browned, then reduce the temperature to moderate (350 F., mark 4) and bake for a further 20–30 minutes, until the fruit is cooked. Dredge with a little sugar before serving.

Variations
1. A spice can be added with the sugar, e.g. 1 level tsp. powdered ginger with rhubarb, 1 level tsp. powdered cinnamon with gooseberries or plums.
2. Fruits such as apple can be given more flavour and colour by mixing them with blackberries or raspberries, when in season.

Apple Dumplings

8 oz. shortcrust pastry
4 even-sized cooking apples
2 oz. sugar
Milk to glaze
Caster sugar

Oven temperature: hot (425 F., mark 7)

Divide the pastry into four and roll out each piece into a round 8–10 inches across. Peel and core the apples, place one on each round and fill the centre with some of the sugar. Moisten the edges of the pastry with water, gather the edges to the top, pressing well to seal them together, and turn the dumplings over. If liked, decorate with leaves cut from any trimmings of pastry. Brush the tops with milk. Bake on a greased baking tray towards the top of the oven for 10 minutes, then reduce the temperature to warm (325 F., mark 3) and continue to cook for a further 30 minutes, until the apples are soft. Dredge with caster sugar and eat hot or cold, with custard or cream.

Dutch Apple Pie

1½ lb. cooking apples, peeled and quartered
4–6 tbsps. water
4 oz. soft brown sugar
1 level tbsp. cornflour or arrowroot
½ level tsp. salt
1 level tsp. powdered cinnamon
2 tbsps. lemon juice
1 oz. butter or margarine
½ tsp. vanilla essence
6 oz. shortcrust pastry
A little milk to glaze

Oven temperature: hot (425 F., mark 7)

Simmer the apples with the water until soft. Mix together the sugar, cornflour or arrowroot, salt and cinnamon and add to the cooked apples. Stir in the lemon juice and cook, stirring, until fairly thick. Remove from the heat, stir in the butter and essence and cool. Roll out half of the pastry and line a 7-inch pie plate; put the cooked apples in the pastry case. Roll out the remaining pastry to make a lid. Damp the edges of the pastry on the dish and cover with the lid, pressing the edges well together; flake and scallop the edges. Brush the top with milk and bake towards the top of the oven for 10 minutes, then reduce the temperature to fairly hot (375°F., mark 5) and continue to cook for a further 20–25 minutes, until the fruit is soft. Serve hot or cold, with cream or custard.

Lemon Meringue Pie

4 oz. shortcrust pastry *(see Pastry chapter)*
3 level tbsps. cornflour
¼ pint water
Juice and grated rind of 2 lemons
4 oz. sugar
2 eggs, separated
3 oz. caster sugar
Glacé cherries and angelica

Oven temperature: hot (425 F., mark 7)

Roll out the pastry and line a 7-inch flan case or deep pie plate. Trim the edges and bake blind towards the top of the oven for 15 minutes. Remove the paper and baking beans and return the case to the oven for a further 5 minutes. Reduce the oven temperature to moderate (350°F., mark 4). Mix the cornflour with the water in a saucepan, add the lemon juice and grated rind and bring slowly to the boil, stirring until the mixture thickens, then add the sugar. Remove from the heat, cool the mixture slightly and add the egg yolks. Pour into the pastry case. Whisk the egg whites stiffly, whisk in half the caster sugar and fold in the rest. Pile the meringue on top of the lemon filling and bake in the centre of the oven for about 10 minutes, or until the meringue is crisp and lightly browned. Decorate before serving.

Apfel Strudel

The dough for this popular Austrian dish should tradition-ally be pulled out until it is thin enough to read through!

8 oz. plain flour
½ level tsp. salt
1 egg, slightly beaten
2 tbsps. oil
4 tbsps. lukewarm water
1½ oz. seedless raisins
1½ oz. currants
3 oz. caster sugar
½ level tsp. powdered cinnamon
2½ lb. cooking apples, peeled and grated
1½ oz. butter, melted
4 oz. ground almonds
Icing sugar

Oven temperature: fairly hot (375°F., mark 5)

Put the flour and salt in a large bowl, make a well in the centre and pour in the egg and oil. Add the water gradually, stirring with a fork to make a soft, sticky dough. Work the dough in the bowl until it leaves the sides, turn it out on to a lightly floured surface and knead for 15 minutes. Form into a ball, place on a cloth and cover with a warmed bowl. Leave to 'rest' in a warm place for an hour.

Mix thoroughly the raisins, currants, sugar, cinnamon and apples.

Warm the rolling pin. Spread a clean old cotton table-cloth on the table and sprinkle lightly with 1–2 tbsps. flour. Place the dough on the cloth and roll out into a rectangle about ⅛ inch thick, lifting and turning it to prevent its sticking to the cloth. Gently stretch the dough, working from the centre to the outside and using the backs of the hands, until it is paper-thin. Trim the edges to form a rectangle about 27 by 24 inches. Leave to dry and 'rest' for 15 minutes.

Arrange the dough with one of the long sides towards you, brush it with melted butter and sprinkle with ground almonds. Spread the apple mixture over the dough, leaving a 2-inch border uncovered all round the edge. Fold these pastry edges over the apple mixture, towards the centre. Lift the corners of the cloth nearest to you up and over the pastry, causing the strudel to roll up, but stop after each turn, to pat it into shape and to keep the roll even.

BAKED FRUIT PUDDINGS

Baked Apples

4 medium-sized cooking apples
4 tbsps. water
Demerara sugar
Butter

Oven temperature: fairly hot (400°F., mark 6)

Wipe the apples and make a shallow cut through the skin round the middle of each. Core the apples and stand them in an ovenproof dish. Pour the water round them, fill each apple with sugar and top with a small knob of butter. Bake in the centre of the oven till the apples are soft – ¾–1 hour.

Variations
1. Stuff the centre of the apples with mincemeat instead of Demerara sugar.
2. Stuff the apples with currants, sultanas, stoned raisins,

chopped dried apricots, mixed peel or glacé fruits or with a mixture of chopped dates and walnuts or other nuts.
3. Put a marshmallow on each apple just before the end of the cooking and return the apples to the oven to brown the topping.

Apple and Blackberry Charlotte

1 lb. apples, peeled
1 lb. blackberries
Rind and juice of ½ lemon
¼ level tsp. ground cinnamon
2 oz. melted butter
6 slices from a 2-lb. white loaf
6–8 oz. sugar
2 tbsps. bread or cake crumbs

Oven temperature: fairly hot (375°F., mark 5)

Fruit Cobbler

Quarter the apples and remove the cores. Wash and pick over the blackberries. Stew the fruit in a pan with the lemon rind, juice and cinnamon. Brush a charlotte mould or a 5-inch cake tin generously with melted butter. Cut the crusts off the bread. Trim one piece to a round the same size as the base of the tin, dip it into the melted butter and fit into the bottom of the tin. Dip the remaining slices of bread in the butter and arrange closely around the side of the tin, reserving one piece for the top. Add the sugar and crumbs to the stewed fruit, mix well and fill the tin. Cover with the remaining slice of bread, trimmed to fit the top of the mould. Cook in the centre of the oven for about 1 hour, turn out and serve with custard or cream.

This is the traditional Charlotte recipe. It is often made with apples alone; any other stewed fruit, or a mixture, may be used in the same way.

Fruit Crumble

1½ lb. raw fruit (apples, plums)
3 oz. margarine
6 oz. plain flour
3 oz. caster sugar

Oven temperature: fairly hot (400°F., mark 6)

Prepare the fruit as for stewing and put it in an oven-proof dish. Rub the fat into the flour until the mixture is the texture of fine crumbs; stir in the sugar. Sprinkle the mixture on top of the prepared fruit and bake in the centre of the oven for 30–40 minutes. Alternatively, stew the fruit before putting it in the dish and bake for 20–30 minutes. Serve with custard or cream.

Variations
1. Add 1 level tsp. powdered cinnamon, mixed spice or

ginger to the flour before rubbing in the fat.

2. Add 2 oz. chopped crystallised ginger to the crumb mixture before sprinkling it over the prepared fruit.

3. Add the grated rind of an orange or lemon to the crumb mixture before sprinkling it on the fruit.

Fruit Cobbler

8 oz. self-raising flour
A good pinch of salt
2 oz. butter or margarine
1 oz. caster sugar
$\frac{1}{4}$ pint milk (approx.)
Sweetened cooked fruit, e.g. plums, blackberries and apples, apricots, gooseberries
Milk to glaze

Oven temperature: hot (425°F., mark 7)

Sift the flour and salt, rub in the fat to the texture of fine crumbs and stir in the sugar. Make a well in the centre and add sufficient milk to give a fairly soft dough. Turn it on to a lightly floured board and roll out the dough to $\frac{1}{2}$ inch thick; cut out rounds with a $1\frac{1}{2}$-inch fluted cutter. Place the cooked fruit in an ovenproof dish, arrange the rounds overlapping round the edge of the dish and glaze them with a little milk. Bake towards the top of the oven for 10–15 minutes, until the topping is golden-brown.

STEAMED PUDDINGS

GENERAL RULES FOR STEAMING

1. Put on the steamer with the base half-filled with water so that this is boiling by the time the pudding is made. If you have no steamer, half-fill a large saucepan with water, bring this to the boil and stand the pudding basin in it.

2. Grease the pudding basin well.

3. Cut double greaseproof paper or a piece of foil to cover the pudding basin and grease well.

4. Fill the basin not more than two-thirds full with mixture.

5. Cover the basin tightly with the paper or foil to prevent steam or water entering.

6. Keep the water in the steamer boiling rapidly all the time and have a kettle of boiling water ready to top it up regularly, or the steamer will tend to boil dry.

Plain Sponge Pudding

4 oz. butter or margarine
4 oz. caster sugar
2 eggs, beaten
A few drops of vanilla essence
6 oz. self-raising flour
A little milk to mix

Half-fill a steamer or large saucepan with water and put it on to boil. Grease a $1\frac{1}{2}$-pint pudding basin. Cream together the fat and sugar until pale and fluffy. Add the beaten egg and the essence a little at a time and beat well after each addition. Using a metal spoon, fold in half the sifted flour, then fold in the rest, with enough milk to give a dropping consistency. Put the mixture into the basin, cover with greased greaseproof paper or foil and secure with string. Steam for $1\frac{1}{2}$ hours. Serve with jam sauce.

This basic recipe can be varied as follows:

Jam Sponge Pudding

Put 2 level tbsps. jam into the bottom of the greased pudding basin before adding the pudding mixture. Serve with a custard sauce or jam sauce.

Syrup Sponge Pudding

Put 2 level tbsps. golden syrup into the bottom of the basin before adding the mixture.

Fruit Sponge Pudding

Put a layer of drained canned fruit or a layer of stewed fruit in the basin before adding the pudding mixture.

Mincemeat Surprise Pudding

Line the bottom and sides of the basin with a thin layer of mincemeat and fill with the pudding mixture. When the pudding is cooked, turn it out carefully so that the outside remains completely covered with the mincemeat. This pudding is sometimes known as Mock Christmas Pudding and makes a less rich alternative to the traditional version.

Chocolate Sponge Pudding

Blend 1 oz. cocoa powder to a smooth cream with 1 tbsp. hot water; add gradually to the creamed fat and sugar. Serve with a chocolate or rum sauce.

Jamaica Pudding

Add 2–4 oz. chopped preserved ginger with the flour. Serve with a syrup sauce.

Lemon or Orange Sponge

Add the grated rind of 1 orange or lemon when creaming the fat and sugar. Serve with an orange lemon or marmalade sauce.

Cherry Sponge Pudding

Add 2–3 oz. halved glacé cherries with the flour. Serve with custard or sweet white sauce.

Steamed Castle Puddings

Prepare an ordinary steamed sponge mixture and divide it between greased individual pudding basins or dariole moulds. Fill two-thirds full, cover each mould with greased foil and secure with string. Steam for 30–45 minutes (depending on size) over rapidly boiling water. Turn out on to a dish and serve with jam sauce.

Steamed Suet Pudding – Basic Mixture

6 oz. self-raising flour
A pinch of salt
3 oz. shredded suet
2 oz. caster sugar
$\frac{1}{4}$ pint milk (approx.)

Half-fill a steamer or large saucepan with water and put on to boil. Grease a 1$\frac{1}{2}$-pint pudding basin. Mix the flour, salt, suet and sugar. Make a well in the centre and add enough milk to give a soft dropping consistency. Put into the greased basin, cover with greased greaseproof paper or foil and secure with string. Steam over rapidly boiling water for 1$\frac{1}{2}$–2 hours. Serve with a jam, golden syrup sauce or fruit sauce.

Variations

For a lighter pudding use 3 oz. self-raising flour and 3 oz. fresh breadcrumbs. For a richer pudding, use 1 beaten egg and about 6 tbsps. milk instead of the $\frac{1}{4}$ pint milk.

JAM: Put 2 level tbsps. red jam in the bottom of the greased pudding basin before adding the mixture.

APPLE: Add to the dry ingredients $\frac{1}{2}$ lb. cooking apples, peeled and finely chopped or grated. Serve the pudding with a white sauce flavoured with a pinch of nutmeg.

DATE: Add to the dry ingredients 4 oz. chopped dates and the grated rind of a lemon; reduce the sugar to 1 oz. Serve with lemon sauce.

APRICOT: Add to the dry ingredients 2 oz. chopped dried apricots, 4 oz. apple, peeled and finely chopped, and the grated rind of 1 lemon; reduce the sugar to 1 oz.

RICH FIG: Add to the dry ingredients 4 oz. chopped dried figs, 1–2 oz. chopped blanched almonds and the grated rind of 1 lemon; reduce the sugar to 1 oz. Mix to a soft dropping consistency with 2 beaten eggs and 2 tbsps. sherry or milk. Serve with lemon sauce or custard.

Spotted Dick

3 oz. self-raising flour
A pinch of salt
3 oz. fresh breadcrumbs
3 oz. shredded suet
2 oz. caster sugar
6 oz. currants
4–6 tbsps. milk (approx.)

Put the steamer or a large saucepan on to boil. Mix together the flour, salt, breadcrumbs, suet, sugar and currants in a bowl. Make a well in the centre and add enough milk to give a fairly soft dough. Form into a roll on a well-floured board, wrap loosely in greased greaseproof paper and then in foil, sealing the ends well. Steam over rapidly boiling water for 1$\frac{1}{2}$–2 hours. Unwrap the pudding, put in a hot dish and serve with custard or with a white sauce flavoured with cinnamon or grated lemon rind.

Alternatively, make the mixture of a soft dropping consistency and steam it for 1$\frac{1}{2}$–2 hours in a greased 1$\frac{1}{2}$-pint basin.

Christmas Pudding

12 oz. fresh breadcrumbs
12 oz. plain flour
1 level tsp. salt
$\frac{1}{2}$ level tsp. powdered mace
$\frac{1}{2}$ level tsp. powdered ginger
$\frac{1}{2}$ level tsp. powdered nutmeg
$\frac{1}{2}$ level tsp. powdered cinnamon
12 oz. shredded suet
8 oz. caster sugar
8 oz. soft brown sugar
8 oz. mixed candied peel
12 oz. currants
8 oz. sultanas
1 lb. 4 oz. raisins, stoned
6 oz. almonds, blanched and chopped
$\frac{1}{2}$ lb. apples, peeled and chopped
Grated rind and juice of 1 lemon
Grated rind and juice of 1 orange
4 tbsps. brandy
3 large eggs, beaten
$\frac{1}{4}$ pint milk (approx.)

Mix together in a large mixing bowl all the dry ingredients, the almonds, apples and orange and lemon rind. Mix the lemon and orange juice and the brandy with the beaten eggs and add to the dry ingredients, with enough milk to give a soft dropping consistency. Cover the mixture lightly and leave overnight. Half-fill 3 saucepans with water and put them on to boil. Grease a 1-pint, 1$\frac{1}{2}$-pint and 2-pint pudding basin. Stir the mixture before turning it into the prepared basins, cover with greased greaseproof paper and with a clean dry cloth or foil.

Steam over rapidly boiling water as follows:

1-pint pudding	5 hours
1$\frac{1}{2}$-pint pudding	7 hours
2-pint pudding	9 hours

When the puddings are cooked, remove them from the pans and allow to cool. Re-cover them with a fresh cloth, foil or greaseproof paper and store in a cool place.

On the day of serving renew the covering (cloth, greased greaseproof paper or foil) and steam the pudding as follows:

1-pint pudding	2 hours
1½-pint pudding	3 hours
2-pint pudding	3 hours

Turn out on to a hot dish and serve with brandy or rum butter or a sweet white sauce flavoured with rum.

Note: Don't put the aluminium foil directly on to the pudding, as the fruit eats into it after some weeks; this does no harm to the pudding, but the foil ceases to be watertight.

Bread and Butter Pudding

3–4 thin slices of bread and butter
1–2 oz. currants or sultanas
½ oz. caster sugar
¾ pint milk
2 eggs
Ground nutmeg

Oven temperature: moderate (350°F., mark 4)

Cut the bread and butter into strips and arrange, buttered side up, in layers in a greased ovenproof dish, sprinkling the layers with the fruit and sugar. Heat the milk, but do not allow it to boil. Whisk the eggs lightly and pour the milk on to them, stirring all the time. Strain the mixture over the bread, sprinkle some nutmeg on top and let the pudding stand for ¼ hour. Bake in the centre of the oven for 30–40 minutes, until set and lightly browned.

Queen of Puddings

¾ pint milk
1 oz. butter
Grated rind of ½ a lemon
2 eggs, separated
2 oz. caster sugar
3 oz. fresh white breadcrumbs
2 level tbsps. red jam

Oven temperature: moderate (350°F., mark 4)

Warm the milk, butter and lemon rind. Whisk the egg yolks and 1 oz. of the sugar lightly and pour on the milk, stirring well. Strain over the breadcrumbs, pour into a greased 2-pint ovenproof dish and leave to stand for ¼ hour. Bake in the centre of the oven for 25–30 minutes, until lightly set; remove from the oven. Warm the jam and spread it over the pudding. Whisk up the egg whites stiffly and add half the remaining sugar; whisk again and fold in the remaining sugar. Pile the meringue on top of the jam and bake for a further 15–20 minutes, until the meringue is lightly browned.

(See colour picture facing page 225)

HOT SOUFFLÉS

Vanilla Soufflé

1 oz. butter
½ oz. flour
¼ pint milk
1–2 tsps. vanilla essence
1 level tbsp. caster sugar
3 eggs, separated

Oven temperature: fairly hot (400°F., mark 6)

Grease a 7-inch soufflé dish. Melt the butter in a large saucepan, stir in the flour and cook for 2–3 minutes. Gradually stir in the milk and bring to the boil, stirring all the time until the mixture thickens. Stir in the vanilla essence and sugar and cool slightly. Add the egg yolks one at a time, beating well. Stiffly whisk the egg whites, fold into the mixture and pour into the soufflé dish.

Bake in the centre of the oven for about 35 minutes, until well risen and brown. Serve at once.

Chocolate Soufflé
Dissolve 1½ oz. plain chocolate in the milk and omit the vanilla essence. Otherwise make the soufflé as above. Serve with chocolate sauce.

Orange Soufflé
Put the thinly peeled rind of 2 oranges with the milk in a saucepan and bring slowly to the boil; remove from the heat, cover and leave to stand for 10 minutes, then strain. Make the soufflé as above, adding 2–3 tbsps. Grand Marnier or Cointreau after the addition of the egg yolks. Decorate with icing sugar and with thin strips of orange rind, cooked until soft, then marinaded in 1 tbsp. Grand Marnier for 1–2 hours.

BATTERS

Pouring Batter

4 oz. plain flour
A pinch of salt
1 egg
½ pint milk or milk and water

Mix the flour and salt, make a well in the centre and break in the egg. Add half the liquid and beat the mixture until it is smooth. Add the remaining liquid gradually and beat until well mixed.

Rich Pancake Batter

Follow the above recipes, but add ½ oz. melted butter with the liquid.

Variations
1. Add 1–2 level tsps. icing sugar to the flour before mixing.
2. Add the grated rind of ½ a lemon or orange to the flour before mixing.
This batter can be used as the basis of Crêpes Suzette.

Coating Batter

4 oz. plain flour
A pinch of salt
1 egg
¼ pint milk or milk and water

Make a well in the centre of the flour and salt and break in the egg. Add half the liquid and beat the mixture until smooth. Gradually add the rest of the liquid and beat until well mixed.

Pancakes

½ pint pouring batter
Lard
Caster sugar
Lemon wedges

Make up the batter mixture in the usual way. Heat a little lard in a frying pan until really hot, running it round to coat the sides of the pan; pour off any surplus. Pour or spoon in just enough batter to cover the base of the pan thinly and cook quickly until golden-brown underneath. Turn with a palette knife or by tossing and cook the second side until golden. Turn out on to sugared paper, sprinkle with sugar and a squeeze of lemon juice and serve at once, with extra sugar and lemon wedges.

If you are cooking a large number of pancakes, keep them warm by putting them as they are made between 2 plates in a warm oven. Finally, roll up all the pancakes and serve at once.

Cooked pancakes will keep for up to a week if wrapped in greaseproof paper and stored in a refrigerator. Re-heat them in a hot frying pan, without any fat, turning them over once.

Crêpes Suzette

Butter for frying
¼ pint rich pancake mixture
2 oz. sugar
2 oz. butter
Juice of 2 oranges
Grated rind of 1 lemon
3 tbsps. Cointreau
2 tbsps. brandy

Heat a little butter in a small, thick-based frying pan, pour off the excess and cook the pancakes in the usual way; keep them flat between 2 plates in a warm place. Clean the pan, put in the sugar and heat gently, shaking the pan occasionally until the sugar has melted and turned golden-brown. Remove the pan from the heat and add the butter and the orange juice. Fold each pancake in half and then in half again to form a quarter-circle. Add the Cointreau to the fruit juice, replace all the crêpes in the pan and simmer for a few minutes until re-heated, spooning the sauce over them. Warm the brandy, pour it over the crêpes, ignite it and serve at once.

Apple Fritters

Peel and core 3–4 cooking apples and cut into rings ¼-inch thick. Dip in coating batter (use either recipe) and fry until golden in some deep fat which is hot enough to brown a 1-inch cube of bread in 60–70 seconds. Drain on crumpled kitchen paper, toss in caster sugar and a little powdered cinnamon and serve straight away.

Variations

PINEAPPLE FRITTERS: Use drained canned pineapple rings.

BANANA FRITTERS: Use small bananas, peeled and cut in half lengthways.

FRUIT FRITTERS WITH LIQUEUR: Soak some pineapple rings in Kirsch or some apricot halves in rum before making into fritters.

Cold Puddings

Fruit Salad

4 oz. sugar
½ pint water
Juice of ½ a lemon
A selection of fruit, e.g. 2 red-skinned apples; 2 oranges;
  2 bananas; 4 oz. black or green grapes

Make a syrup by dissolving the sugar in the water over a gentle heat and boil for 5 minutes; cool and add the lemon juice. Prepare the fruits as required (*see page*) and put them into the syrup as they are ready. Mix all together and if possible leave to stand for 2–3 hours before serving, to blend the flavours. Any other combinations of fresh fruits can be used, such as dessert pears, strawberries, raspberries, cherries and melon.

To give additional flavour, add to the syrup:
1. ¼ level tsp. ground cinnamon or nutmeg.
2. 1–2 tbsps. fruit liqueur, brandy or rum.

Fruit salad can be served in a hollowed-out melon or pineapple; in either case the flesh which has been removed should be cut into chunks and used in the salad.

Canned fruit such as peach slices and pineapple chunks can also be used in fruit salads, and so can the more exotic kinds such as canned guavas and lychees.

Gooseberry Fool

1 lb. gooseberries (or a 1 lb. 4 oz. can, drained)
Sugar to taste
¼ pint custard
¼ pint double cream, whipped
Chopped nuts

Stew the fruit in a little water, with sugar as required (unless canned fruit is used). Sieve the fruit (or put it into an electric blender), fold the purée into the custard and cream and sweeten to taste. Pour into glasses and decorate with chopped nuts. Serve with shortbread,

sponge fingers or a plain sweet biscuit. This sweet can also be made with blackberries, raspberries, apricots, rhubarb or damsons.

Summer Pudding

2 tbsps. water
5 oz. sugar
1 lb. mixed black-currants, stringed and washed, and blackberries, picked over and washed
4–6 oz. white bread, cut in thin slices
Whipped cream or custard

Stir the water and sugar together and bring slowly to the boil, add the fruits and stew gently, until they are soft but retain their shape. Cut the crusts from the bread and line a 1½-pint pudding basin with the slices. Pour in the fruit and cover with more slices of bread. Place a saucer with a weight on it on top of the pudding and leave overnight in a cool place. Turn out and serve with whipped cream or custard.

Other soft fruits (or a mixture) may be used in Summer Pudding, providing that they have a rich, strong colour – for example, raspberries, red-currants, damsons. A proportion of apple can also be included.

Ginger Meringue Creams

2 large egg whites
4 oz. caster sugar
A small carton double cream
2 tbsps. finely chopped stem ginger

Oven temperature: very cool (250°F., mark ¼)

Line a baking tray with silicone (non-stick) paper. Whisk the egg whites until stiff, whisk in half the sugar until the mixture is stiff, then fold in the remaining sugar. Spoon the meringue into 4 heaps on the prepared baking tray, keeping well apart. Make into flan shapes, with a hollow in the centre of each. Put the cases towards the

Roast Duck, *page 91*

Fruit Salad

bottom of the oven and dry out for about 2½–3 hours. Remove from the paper and when cool store in an airtight tin. To finish the sweet, whip the cream lightly and fold in half the chopped ginger; divide the mixture between the meringue shells and top with the remaining chopped ginger.

Strawberry Shortcake

3 oz. butter or margarine
8 oz. self-raising flour
¼ level tsp. salt
3 oz. sugar
1 egg, beaten
1–2 tbsps. milk
¾–1 lb. strawberries
3–4 level tbsps. sugar for filling
¼ pint double cream

Oven temperature: fairly hot (375°F., mark 5)

Grease a deep 8-inch sandwich tin.

Rub the fat into the flour and salt until the mixture resembles fine breadcrumbs; stir in the sugar. Add the egg a little at a time to the rubbed-in mixture until this begins to bind together; use a little milk as well if necessary. Knead the mixture lightly into a smooth, fairly firm dough.

Turn the dough on to a floured board, form into a round and roll out until it is 8 inches across. Press it evenly into the tin and bake near the top of the oven for 20 minutes, or until golden and firm. Turn the cake out of the tin on to a cooling tray.

Wash the stawberries and remove the hulls and stems. Keep about a dozen berries whole for decorating and crush the rest with a fork in a basin, sprinkling with 2–3 level tbsps. of the sugar. Whisk the cream and stir in the remaining sugar. Split the cake, spread with half of the cream and all the crushed fruit and replace the top. Pile the remaining cream on the top of the cake and decorate with whole berries.

161

Summer Salads, *pages 123-130*

MILKY AND CUSTARD SWEETS

Rice Variations

2 oz. short-grain rice
1 pint milk
1 oz. sugar
Flavouring or other addition *(see below)*

Put the rice, milk and sugar into a thick-based pan or in the top of a double boiler, cover and cook for $1\frac{1}{2}$–2 hours, until creamy. Remove the lid after $\frac{3}{4}$ hour and cook uncovered for the remainder of the time, stirring the pudding occasionally. Allow to cool and finish in one of the following ways –

Creamy Rice

Beat $\frac{1}{4}$ pint cream and fold into the pudding just before serving.

Fudge Rice

Beat 2 oz. chopped fudge into the pudding just before serving.

Honey Pudding

When making the pudding, use 1 oz. honey instead of sugar; serve topped with chopped nuts.

Fruit Rice

Fold the drained contents of a small can of fruit into the pudding just before serving.

Chocolate Rice

Fold 2 oz. coarsely grated chocolate or 2 oz. chocolate chips into the cooled rice pudding and top with more chocolate.

Peach Condé

A 1-pint rice pudding, made as above
A 15-oz. can of peach halves
8 level tbsps. red-currant jelly
1 tbsp. water
Lemon juice

Divide the rice pudding between 4 sundae glasses. Drain the peach halves thoroughly and arrange the halves on top of the rice, cut side down. Heat the red-currant jelly with the water and lemon juice, stirring until smooth and somewhat thickened. Pour over the peaches and leave to cool before serving.

Simple Junket

1 pint milk
1–2 level tbsps. caster sugar
1 tsp. rennet
Flavouring *(see below)*

Warm the milk to blood heat (that is, just warm to the finger) and stir in the sugar until it is dissolved. Add the rennet, stir, pour the mixture at once into serving dishes and put in a warm place to set. Chill lightly before serving.

Flavourings for Junket

NUTMEG: Sprinkle a little grated or ground nutmeg over the surface of the junket.

VANILLA, ALMOND, RASPBERRY: Add a few drops of the essence to the milk, with a few drops of the appropriate vegetable colouring.

RUM: Add 1–2 tsps. rum to the milk.

Caramel Custard

$4\frac{1}{2}$ oz. sugar
$\frac{1}{4}$ pint water
1 pint milk
4 eggs

Oven temperature: warm (325°F., mark 3)

Put 4 oz. of the sugar and the water into a small pan and dissolve the sugar slowly; bring to the boil and boil without stirring until it caramelises, i.e. becomes a rich golden-brown colour. Pour the caramel into a 6-inch cake tin which has been heated slightly, turning the tin until the bottom is completely covered. Warm the milk, pour on to the lightly whisked eggs and remaining sugar and strain over the cooled caramel. Place the tin in a shallow tin of water and bake just below the centre of the oven for 40–45 minutes, until set.

To serve hot: Allow to stand for a few minutes, then turn out on to a hot dish and serve at once.

To serve cold: Leave in the tin until quite cold (preferably until the next day) before turning out – it is easier to turn the custard out when it is really cold.

Syllabub made with Wine

2 egg whites
4 oz. caster sugar
Juice of $\frac{1}{2}$ a lemon
$\frac{1}{4}$ pint sweet white wine
$\frac{1}{2}$ pint double cream, whipped
Crystallised lemon slices

Whisk the egg whites stiffly and fold in the sugar, lemon juice, wine and cream. Pour the mixture into individual glasses and chill for several hours before serving. Decorate with the lemon slices.

Note: It is quite correct for this mixture to separate out.

Ginger Meringue Cream

Syllabub made with Brandy

Juice and grated rind of 1 lemon
3 oz. caster sugar
1–2 tbsps. brandy
2 tbsps. sherry
½ pint double cream, whipped

Soak the lemon rind in the juice for 2–3 hours, then add the sugar, brandy and sherry. Add to the whipped cream, mixing until it is all evenly blended. Serve with sponge fingers or spoon it over crushed macaroons.

Cornflour Mould

1½ oz. cornflour
1 pint milk
A strip of lemon rind
1–2 oz. sugar

Blend the cornflour to a smooth cream with 1–2 tbsps. of the milk. Boil the remaining milk with the lemon rind and strain it on to the blended mixture, stirring well. Return the mixture to the pan and bring to the boil, stirring all the time, until it thickens. Cook for a further 2–3 minutes and add sugar to taste. Pour into a wetted jelly mould and leave to set. Turn out when cold and serve with fruit or jam sauce.

ORANGE MOULD: Substitute orange for lemon rind.

CHOCOLATE MOULD: Mix 1 level tbsp. cocoa with the blended cornflour *or* add 2 oz. melted chocolate to the cooked mixture. Omit the lemon rind and add a few drops of vanilla essence.

COFFEE MOULD: Add 1–2 tbsps. coffee essence or 1–2 level tsps. instant coffee to the cooked mixture. Omit the lemon rind.

Syllabub

Sherry Trifle

8 small sponge cakes
Jam
2–3 wineglasses of sherry
6 macaroons, crushed
¾ pint custard
½ pint double cream, whipped
Sugar and flavouring
Glacé cherries, angelica and cream to decorate

Split the sponge cakes, spread them with jam and arrange in a glass dish, then pour the sherry over and leave to soak for ½ hour. Sprinkle the macaroons over the sponge cakes and pour on the custard. Sweeten and flavour the cream to taste and spread or pipe most of it over the custard. Decorate with cherries and angelica (or with ratafias, almonds, etc.) and pipe with the remaining cream.

Fruit juice may replace some or all of the sherry, if preferred.

Choc-au-Rhum

6 oz. dark chocolate
3 large eggs, separated
1 tbsp. rum
¼ pint double cream, whipped
Grated chocolate or finely chopped nuts

Melt the chocolate in a bowl over a pan of hot water. Beat the yolks into the melted chocolate and add the rum. Whisk the whites until stiff and carefully fold into the chocolate mixture. Chill and serve in sundae glasses, topped with whipped cream and grated chocolate or chopped nuts.

Milk Jelly

2 oz. caster sugar
3 thin strips of lemon rind
1 pint milk
½–¾ oz. gelatine
3 tbsps. water

Add the sugar and lemon rind to the milk and allow to infuse for 10 minutes over a gentle heat. Let it cool. Dissolve the gelatine in the water over a gentle heat and add the cooled milk. Strain into a wetted mould and leave to set.

ICE CREAMS

Rich Vanilla Ice Cream

¼ pint milk
1½ oz. sugar
1 egg, beaten
½–1 tsp. vanilla essence
¼ pint double cream, half-whipped

Heat the milk and sugar and pour on to the egg, stirring. Return the mixture to the saucepan and cook it over a gentle heat, stirring all the time until the custard thickens; strain it and add the vanilla essence. Allow to cool, fold in the half-whipped cream, pour into a freezing tray and freeze.

Variations

CHOCOLATE: Add 1½ oz. melted chocolate.

COFFEE: Add 2 level tsps. powdered coffee, dissolved in 1 tsp. hot water.

BANANA: Add 2 small bananas, mashed or puréed.

GINGER: Add 1½ oz. preserved ginger, chopped, and 1 tbsp. ginger syrup.

Lemon Water Ice

8 oz. caster sugar
1 pint water
Rind and juice of 3 lemons
1 egg white, whisked

Dissolve the sugar in the water over a low heat, add the thinly pared lemon rind and boil gently for 10 minutes; leave to cool. Add the lemon juice and strain the mixture into the ice cube tray. Place in the freezing compartment of the refrigerator, turned to 'coldest', and leave to half-freeze. Turn the mixture into a bowl, fold in the egg white, mixing thoroughly, replace in the tray and re-freeze.

MOUSSES

Traditionally, a mousse is made from a mixture of fruit purée and whipped cream, blended together and frozen. Stiffly whisked egg whites are added to lighten the texture and egg yolks can be added to enrich the purée.

Black-currant Mousse

½ lb. fresh black-currants (or a 15-oz. can of black-currants, drained)
Caster sugar to taste
4 egg yolks
¼ pint double cream, whipped
2 egg whites, whisked

Sieve the fruit to make ¼ pint purée. Put the purée, sugar and egg yolks into a large bowl, stand this over a saucepan of hot water and whisk until thick and creamy – the mixture should be stiff enough to retain the impression of the whisk for a few seconds. Remove from the heat and whisk until cool. Fold in the whipped cream and the egg whites, pour the mixture into a shallow dish or some individual soufflé dishes and freeze it in the usual way.

Note: For a plainer mousse, omit the egg yolks and mix the fruit purée with ¼ pint custard (*see Sauces chapter*) without heating. Then fold in the cream and egg whites and continue as above.

COLD SOUFFLÉS

To Prepare the Soufflé Dish

Cut a strip of double greaseproof paper long enough to go right round the soufflé dish with the ends over-lapping slightly and deep enough to reach from the bottom of the dish to about 3 inches above the top. Tie the paper round the outside of the dish with string, so that it fits closely to the rim of the dish and prevents any mixture escaping. The soufflé will then set at least 1 inch above the rim and after the paper is removed will appear to have risen like a baked soufflé.

To take off the paper when the soufflé has set, remove the string and ease the paper away from the mixture with a knife dipped in hot water.

Milanaise Soufflé

Note: The ingredients are listed in numbered groups to make it easier to refer to them in the instructions for making and also in the variations on the basic recipe that follow.

Prepare a 5-inch soufflé dish.

Stage 1
3 egg yolks
3 oz. caster sugar
Grated rind and juice of 2 lemons

STAGE 1: Put the Stage 1 ingredients in a bowl, stand this over a pan of hot water and whisk until thick and creamy. Remove the bowl from the hot water and continue whisking until the mixture is cool.

Stage 2
2 level tsps. powdered gelatine
2 tbsps. water

STAGE 2: Put the gelatine and water in a basin, stand this in a pan of hot water and heat gently until the gelatine is dissolved; allow to cool slightly. Pour into the lemon mixture in a steady stream, stirring the mixture all the time.

Stage 3
¼ pint double cream, whipped

STAGE 3: Stir in the ¼ pint cream until evenly mixed.

Stage 4
3 egg whites

STAGE 4: Whisk the egg whites in a clean bowl until stiff and then fold them into the mixture. It is important that the mixture should be evenly blended, but take care that it is not over-mixed, or the soufflé will be flat and leathery. Pour the mixture into the soufflé case and allow it to set.

Stage 5
Finely chopped nuts or cake crumbs
Crystallised lemon slices or halved walnuts
Double cream, whipped

STAGE 5: Remove the paper and decorate the sides of the soufflé with the chopped nuts or cake crumbs. To do this, stand the case on a piece of paper and press the nuts or crumbs on to the sides of the soufflé with a broad-bladed knife, letting any loose ones fall on to the paper; repeat until the sides are completely coated. Decorate the top with segments of crystallised lemon or halved walnuts and pipe the edge with whipped cream.

Variations

In the set of variations below only small alterations are made. In the second set, where the alterations are more extensive, the ingredients are numbered in the same way as in the basic Milanaise recipe, which should be followed for the method of making. It will be noticed that in some cases there are now two or more ingredients where previously there was only one.

ORANGE: Use the grated rind and the juice of 1½ medium-sized oranges instead of the lemon rind and juice. Decorate with orange slices, nuts and cream.

TANGERINE: Use the grated rind and the juice of 3 tangerines and the juice of 1 lemon instead of the lemon rind and juice. Decorate with tangerine segments of crystallised orange slices, nuts and cream.

LIME: Use the grated rind and the juice of 3 fresh limes instead of the lemon rind and juice. Decorate with nuts, cream and frosted grapes. (To make these, dip grapes in lightly whisked egg white, then in caster sugar, and dry on a cooling rack until crisp on the outside.)

COFFEE: Use 5 tbsps. strong black coffee instead of the lemon rind and juice. Decorate with chocolate drops, nuts and cream.

MISCELLANEOUS

Strawberry Yog

1½ lb. fresh ripe strawberries
¼ lb. cottage cheese
¼ pint fat-free yoghurt
Liquid sweetener

Divide the strawberries between 6 glasses. Beat to-gether the cottage cheese and yoghurt, adding sweetener to taste. Pour over the strawberries and chill. *(Serves 6)*

(See colour picture facing page 32)

Spiced Pear Grill

1 lb. dessert pears, peeled and sliced
¼ pint water
Finely grated rind of ½ a lemon
A small piece of cinnamon
Artificial sweetener
2 oz. cornflakes
1 oz. butter

Cook the pears in the water with the lemon rind and the cinnamon. Add sweetener to taste. Place in a shallow flameproof dish, sprinkle with cornflakes and dot with butter. Place under a moderate grill for 5 minutes. *(Serves 4)*

Charlotte Russe

½ pkt. of yellow or red jelly
Glacé cherries and angelica or fresh fruit
1 pkt. of sponge fingers
¼ pint double cream, whipped
½ pint custard (cold)
1–2 tbsps. Kirsch or Cointreau (optional)
½ oz. gelatine
3 tbsps. water
Whipped cream to decorate (optional)

Make up the jelly and set ¼ inch of it in the bottom of a straight-sided mould. When it is set, decorate with pieces of cherry and angelica or fresh fruit, carefully cover with a little more jelly and allow to set.

If necessary, trim the sides of the sponge fingers, then brush the edges with liquid jelly. Line the sides of the mould with the fingers, pressing them closely together. Combine the cream, custard and liqueur, if used. Dissolve the gelatine in the water and add to the cream mixture. When this is on the point of setting, pour it into the centre of the mould and allow to set. Trim off any surplus from the top of the sponge fingers.

When the cream mixture is set, dip the bottom of the mould in hot water and turn the Charlotte out on to a serving dish. Put chopped jelly round it and if you wish, pipe whipped cream between the biscuits. Tie a ribbon round the Charlotte before serving.

As a variation, make a fruit-flavoured cream for the centre – add ¼ pint fruit purée to the mixture before adding the dissolved gelatine.

Chocolate Refrigerator Cake

24–26 soft sponge fingers
6 oz. caster sugar
2 level tbsps. cornflour
¾ pint milk
½ pint double cream
2 oz. unsweetened chocolate
2 egg yolks
1 oz. butter
1 level tsp. powdered gelatine
2 tsps. water
Toasted flaked almonds to decorate

Use a loaf tin measuring about $7 \times 5 \times 2\frac{1}{2}$ inches; line with non-stick paper. Arrange a layer of sponge fingers to cover base and sides. Blend the sugar and cornflour in a saucepan; gradually stir in the milk and half the cream. Break up the chocolate, add to the milk and bring slowly to the boil, stirring. Boil gently for 2–3 minutes, stirring, cool for a few minutes and beat in the egg yolks. Cook for 1 minute and beat in the butter. Sprinkle the gelatine over the water and stir into the mixture. Cool, stirring occasionally. When the mixture is beginning to thicken, pour half of it over the sponge fingers. Cover with another layer of sponge fingers, then spoon the remaining mixture over these. Trim the tops of the fingers level with the filling and use the trimmings to make a final layer. Leave overnight in the refrigerator. To serve, turn out on to a flat dish. Whip the rest of the cream, cover the top of the cake with it and strew with the almonds.

GÂTEAUX AND PASTRIES

Gâteau St. Honoré

4 oz. shortcrust or flan pastry
Choux pastry, using 2½ oz. plain flour
1 egg, beaten, to glaze
2 egg yolks
2 oz. caster sugar for filling
½ oz. plain flour
½ oz. cornflour
½ pint milk
1 tsp. vanilla essence
3 egg whites, stiffly whisked
¼ pint double cream, whipped
3 level tbsps. caster sugar for syrup
3 tbsps. water
Angelica and glacé cherries

Oven temperature: fairly hot (375 F., mark 5)

Make the two kinds of pastry in the usual way (*see Pastry chapter*). Roll the shortcrust or flan pastry into a 7-inch round, prick well and put on a lightly greased baking tray. Brush a ½-inch band round the edge with beaten egg. Using a ½-inch plain nozzle, pipe a circle of choux paste round the edge of the pastry and brush it with beaten egg. With the remaining choux paste pipe about 20 walnut-sized rounds on to the baking tray. Brush these with beaten egg and bake both the flan and the choux balls in the centre of the oven for about 35 minutes, or until well risen and golden-brown. Cool on a rack.

Meanwhile prepare the pastry cream filling. Cream the egg yolks with the caster sugar until pale, add the flours, with a little of the milk, and mix well. Heat the remainder of the milk with the vanilla essence almost to boiling point; pour on to the egg mixture, return this to the pan and bring to the boil, stirring all the time. Boil for a further 2–3 minutes, then turn the mixture into a bowl to cool. Whisk with a rotary beater till smooth, then fold in the egg whites. Pipe some whipped cream inside the cold choux paste buns, reserving a little for the top of the gâteau.

Dissolve the sugar in the water and boil until the edge just begins to turn straw-coloured. Dip the tops of the choux paste buns in this syrup, using a skewer or tongs.

Use the remainder of the syrup to stick the buns on to the choux pastry border. Fill the centre of the gâteau with the pastry cream mixture and cover this with the remaining cream. Decorate with angelica and cherries.

Mille-Feuilles Slices

4 oz. puff or rough puff pastry
Raspberry jam
Whipped cream
Glacé icing (see Party Cakes chapter)
Chopped nuts

Oven temperature: very hot (450 F., mark 8)

Roll the pastry into a strip $\frac{1}{2}$ inch thick, 4 inches wide and the length of the baking tray. Brush the baking tray with water, lay the pastry on it and cut it from side to side in strips 2 inches wide, but don't separate the slices. Bake towards the top of the oven for 10 minutes. Separate the strips and cool them; split each into two and sandwich them together in threes or fours with jam and cream. Cover the tops with icing and sprinkle chopped nuts at each end.

Profiteroles

Choux pastry, using 2$\frac{1}{2}$ oz. plain flour
$\frac{1}{4}$ pint double cream, whipped
Icing sugar
Chocolate sauce

Oven temperature: hot (425 F., mark 7)

Using a $\frac{1}{2}$-inch plain vegetable pipe, force small balls of pastry about the size of a walnut on to wetted baking sheets. Bake towards the top of the oven until crisp – 15–20 minutes. Allow to cool.

Split the profiteroles and fill with whipped cream. Dust with icing sugar and pile into a pyramid. Pour a little chocolate sauce over and serve the rest separately. Use the recipe given under Ice Cream Sauces, or melt $\frac{1}{4}$ lb. Menier chocolate over a very low heat, gradually stir in a small can of evaporated milk and beat well.

FLANS AND FLAN CASES

Pastry Flan Cases

Use shortcrust of flan pastry and bake it blind in a 7-inch flan ring or on a pie plate.

Sponge Flan Cases

Grease a 7-inch sponge flan tin and dust it with a mixture of flour and caster sugar. If you wish you can place a round of greased greaseproof paper on the raised part of the flan tin to prevent sticking. Make a sponge cake mixture, using 2 eggs, 2 oz. caster sugar and 2 oz. plain flour; pour it into the tin and bake in the centre of a fairly hot oven (400°F., mark 6) for 15 minutes, until well risen, golden and just firm to the touch. Loosen the edge carefully, turn the flan case out on to a wire rack and leave to cool. For a larger flan case make a 3-egg mixture and bake it in a fairly hot oven at a slightly lower temperature (375°F., mark 5) for about 20 minutes.

Biscuit Crust Flan Cases

6 oz. wheatmeal or plain biscuits
3 oz. butter, melted

Grease a shallow 7- or 8-inch pie plate or sandwich cake tin. Crush the biscuits with a rolling pin and bind together with the melted butter. Line the plate or tin with the mixture, pressing it firmly into place. Chill or leave in a cool place until set.

Variations

1. Replace 1 oz. of the crumbs by 1 oz. desiccated coconut or chopped nuts.
2. Add the grated rind of 1 lemon.
3. Add 1–2 level tsps. ground ginger or mixed spice.
4. Bind the crumbs with 3–4 oz. chocolate and a walnut-sized knob of butter, melted together.
5. Use gingernut biscuits and bind with melted plain chocolate.

Cornflake Crust Flan Case

3 oz. cornflakes
2 oz. butter
2 oz. sugar
1 tbsp. golden syrup

Grease a shallow 7- or 8-inch pie plate or sandwich tin. Crush the cornflakes roughly in your hands. Heat remaining ingredients until melted and bubbling, pour over the cornflakes in a basin and stir until well blended. Line the plate or tin with the mixture, pressing it firmly into place. Chill or leave in a cool place until set.

Chocolate Peppermint Crisp Flan

Fresh Fruit Flan Filling

$\frac{1}{2}$ lb. approx. fresh fruit (e.g. strawberries, raspberries)
Red-currant jelly or $\frac{1}{2}$ a tablet of red jelly

Pick over the fruit, wash it if necessary and arrange in the flan case. Make a glaze by melting 2–3 level tbsps. red-currant jelly with about 1 tbsp. water or by making up $\frac{1}{2}$ a tablet of table jelly; pour the glaze over the fruit when it begins to thicken.

Canned Fruit Flan Filling

A 15-oz. can of fruit
3 level tsps. cornflour
$\frac{1}{4}$ pint fruit juice

Arrange the fruit in the flan case, filling it well. Blend the cornflour with a little of the fruit juice to a smooth cream. Boil the rest and stir into the blended cornflour. Return this mixture to the pan and bring to the boil, stirring until a clear thickened glaze is obtained. Spoon over the fruit to coat it evenly.

Chocolate Peppermint Crisp Flan

3 egg yolks
4 oz. caster sugar
2 tbsps. crème de menthe
2 level tsps. gelatine
2 tbsps. water
A few drops of green colouring
$\frac{1}{4}$ pint double cream, whipped
A biscuit crust case made with gingernuts and chocolate
 (see above)

Whisk the egg yolks, add the sugar and crème de menthe and continue whisking until the mixture thickens. Put the gelatine and water in a basin, stand this in a pan of hot water and heat gently until the gelatine has dissolved; allow to cool slightly and gradually whisk into the egg mixture. Fold in the colouring and cream. When the filling is beginning to set, pour into the biscuit crust case. Chill before serving.

Frangipane Flan

A 7½-inch shortcrust flan case
1 oz. cornflour
¾ pint milk
4 egg yolks
1 oz. caster sugar
3 oz. ground almonds
Almond essence

For the Fruit Layer and Topping
¼ lb. white grapes, skinned, halved and seeded
2 oranges, peeled and segmented
1 banana, peeled and sliced
Caster sugar
2 oz. flaked almonds, toasted

Make the flan case in the usual way. Mix the cornflour to a smooth paste with a little of the milk. Put the remainder on to heat; stir in the cornflour paste and cook, stirring, until thick and smooth. Remove from the heat and beat in the egg yolks one at a time. Continue cooking over a gentle heat until the mixture thickens. Remove from the heat and stir in the caster sugar, ground almonds and a few drops of almond essence. Cover, and leave until cold.

Arrange the fruits in the pastry case. Spread the frangipane cream mixture over and pile into a pyramid shape. Dust thickly with caster sugar. With a red-hot skewer, brand the sugar to caramelise it – re-heat the skewer after marking each line. Sprinkle with the almonds.

Pastry

Shortcrust Pastry

4 oz. plain flour
A pinch of salt
1 oz. lard
1 oz. margarine
4 tsps. water (approx.)

Mix the flour and salt together. Cut the fat into small knobs and add it. Using both hands, rub the fat into the flour between finger and thumb tips. After 2–3 minutes there will be no lumps of fat left and the mixture will look like fresh breadcrumbs.

Add the water a little at a time, stirring with a round-bladed knife until the mixture begins to stick together. With one hand, collect it together and knead lightly for a few seconds, to give a firm, smooth dough. The pastry can be used straight away, but is better allowed to 'rest' for 15 minutes. It can also be wrapped in polythene and kept in the refrigerator for a day or two.

When the pastry is required, sprinkle a very little flour on a board or table and roll out the dough evenly, turning it occasionally. The usual thickness is about $\frac{1}{8}$ inch; don't pull or stretch it. Use as required.

The usual oven temperature is hot (425°F., mark 7).

Flan Pastry

4 oz. plain flour
A pinch of salt
3 oz. butter or margarine and lard
1 level tsp. caster sugar
1 egg, beaten

Mix the flour and salt together and rub in the fat with the fingertips, as for shortcrust pastry, until the mixture resembles fine crumbs. Mix in the sugar. Add the egg, stirring until the ingredients begin to stick together, then with one hand collect the mixture together and knead very lightly to give a firm, smooth dough. Roll out as for shortcrust pastry and use as required.

This pastry should be cooked in a fairly hot oven (400°F., mark 6).

Cheese Pastry

4 oz. plain flour
A pinch of salt
2 oz. butter or margarine and lard
2 oz. Cheddar cheese, finely grated
A little beaten egg or water

Mix the flour and salt together and rub in the fat, as for shortcrust pastry, until the mixture resembles fine crumbs in texture. Mix in the cheese. Add the egg or water, stirring until the ingredients begin to stick together, then with one hand collect the dough together and knead very lightly to give a smooth dough. Roll out as for shortcrust pastry. Use as required.

The usual temperature for cooking cheese pastry is fairly hot (400°F., mark 6).

Rich Cheese Pastry

3 oz. butter or margarine and lard
3 oz. Cheddar cheese, finely grated
4 oz. plain flour
A pinch of salt

Cream the fat and cheese together until soft. Gradually work in the flour and salt with a wooden spoon or a palette knife until the mixture sticks together; with one hand collect it together and knead very lightly until smooth. Cover with greaseproof or waxed paper and leave in a cool place. Use as required. Bake as for the first cheese pastry, above.

Suetcrust Pastry

8 oz. self-raising flour
$\frac{1}{2}$ level tsp. salt
4 oz. shredded suet
8 tbsps. cold water (approx.)

Mix together the flour, salt and suet. Add enough cold water to give a light, elastic dough and knead very lightly until smooth. Roll out to $\frac{1}{4}$ inch in thickness.

This pastry may be used for both sweet and savoury

dishes and can be steamed, boiled or baked; the first two are the most satisfactory methods, as baked suet-crust pastry is inclined to be hard.

'Fork-Mix' Pastry *(made with oil)*

2½ tbsps. oil
1 tbsp. cold water
4 oz. plain flour
A pinch of salt

Put the oil and water into a basin and beat well with a fork to form an emulsion. Mix the flour and salt together and add gradually to the mixture to make a dough. Roll this out on a floured board or between greaseproof paper.

This is a slightly more greasy pastry than one made with solid fat, so it is more suitable for savoury dishes than for sweet tarts and so on.

Bake in a fairly hot oven (400°F., mark 6).

'FLAKED' PASTRIES

Flaky
Probably the commonest of the flaked types, this can be used in many savoury and sweet dishes. The instructions may appear rather complicated at first reading, but are less difficult than they appear and if you follow them carefully, you should be able to obtain really good results.

Rough Puff
This is similar in appearance and texture to flaky pastry; though perhaps not so even, but it is quicker and easier to make and can be used instead of flaky in most recipes.

Puff
The richest of all the pastries, puff gives the most even rising, the most flaky effect and the crispest texture, but because of the time it takes, is made only occasionally. It requires very careful handling and whenever possible should be made the day before it is to be used, so that it has time to become firm and cool before it is shaped and baked.

Bought puff pastry is very satisfactory, but remember to roll it out to a thickness of $\frac{1}{16}$ inch only, as it rises very well.

'First rollings' are used for vol-au-vents, bouchées, and patties, where appearance is important. 'Second rollings' and trimmings can be used for other dishes, such as sausage rolls, where you might otherwise have used rough puff or flaky pastry.

Flaky Pastry

8 oz. plain flour
A pinch of salt
6 oz. butter or a mixture of butter and lard
8 tbsps. cold water to mix (approx.)
A squeeze of lemon juice
Beaten egg to glaze

Mix together the flour and salt. Soften the fat by 'working' it with a knife on a plate; divide it into 4 equal portions. Rub one quarter of the softened fat into the flour and mix to a soft, elastic dough with the water and lemon juice. On a floured board, roll the pastry into an oblong 3 times as long as it is wide. Put another quarter of the fat over the top two-thirds of the pastry in flakes, so that it looks like buttons on a card. Fold the bottom third up and the top third of the pastry down and give it half a turn, so that the folds are now at the sides. Seal the edges of the pastry by pressing with the rolling pin. Re-roll as before and continue until all the fat is used up.

Wrap the pastry loosely in greaseproof paper and leave it to 'rest' in a refrigerator or cool place for at least ½ an hour before using. This makes the handling and shaping of the pastry easier and gives a more evenly flaked texture.

Sprinkle a board or table with a very little flour. Roll out the pastry $\frac{1}{8}$-inch thick and use as required. Brush with beaten egg before baking, to give the characteristic glaze.

The usual oven for cooking flaky pastry is hot (425°F., mark 7).

Rough Puff Pastry

8 oz. plain flour
A pinch of salt
6 oz. fat (butter or margarine and lard mixed)
8 tbsps. cold water to mix (approx.)
A squeeze of lemon juice
Beaten egg to glaze

Mix the flour and salt; cut the fat (which should be quite firm) into cubes about $\frac{3}{4}$ inch across. Stir the fat into the flour without breaking up the pieces and mix to a fairly stiff dough with the water and lemon juice. Turn on to a floured board and roll into a strip 3 times as long as it is wide. Fold the bottom third up and the top third down, then give the pastry half a turn so that the folds are at the sides. Seal the edges of the pastry by pressing lightly with a rolling pin. Continue to roll and fold in this way 4 times altogether. Leave to 'rest' wrapped in greaseproof paper for about ½ an hour before using. Roll out and use as for flaky pastry.

Rough puff gives a similar result to flaky pastry, but the flakes are not usually as even, so where even rising and appearance are particularly important, e.g. with patties and vol-au-vents, it is better to use flaky pastry. On the other hand, rough puff has the advantage of being quicker to make.

The usual oven for cooking rough puff is hot (425°F., mark 7).

Puff Pastry

8 oz. plain flour
A pinch of salt
8 oz. butter (preferably unsalted)
8 tbsps. cold water to mix (approx.)
A squeeze of lemon juice
Beaten egg to glaze

Mix the flour and salt. 'Work' the fat with a knife on a plate until it is soft, then rub about $\frac{1}{2}$ oz. of it into the flour. Mix to a fairly soft, elastic dough with the water and lemon juice and knead lightly on a floured board until smooth. Form rest of fat into an oblong and roll the pastry out into a square. Place fat on one half of the pastry and enclose it by folding the remaining pastry over and sealing the edges with a rolling pin. Turn the pastry so that the fold is to the side, then roll out into a strip 3 times as long as it is wide. Fold the bottom third up and the top third down and seal the edges by pressing lightly with the rolling pin. Cover the pastry with waxed or greaseproof paper and leave to 'rest' in a cool place or in the refrigerator for about 20 minutes. Turn the pastry so that the folds are to the sides and continue rolling, folding and resting until the sequence has been completed 6 times altogether.

After the final resting, shape the pastry as required. Always brush the top surfaces with beaten egg before cooking, to give the characteristic glaze of puff pastry.

The usual oven for cooking puff pastry is very hot (450°F., mark 8).

Choux Pastry

2 oz. butter or margarine
$\frac{1}{4}$ pint water
2$\frac{1}{2}$ oz. plain flour, sifted
2 eggs, lightly beaten

Melt the fat in the water and bring to the boil; remove from the heat and quickly tip in the flour all at once. Beat until the paste is smooth and forms a ball in the centre of the pan. (Take care not to over-beat or the mixture becomes fatty.) Allow to cool slightly. Beat in the eggs gradually, adding just enough to give a smooth, glossy mixture of piping consistency. Use as required.

The usual oven is fairly hot (400°F., mark 6).

Hot-Water Crust Pastry

1 lb. plain flour
2 level tsps. salt
4 oz. lard
$\frac{1}{4}$ pint plus 4 tbsps. milk or milk and water

Mix the flour and salt. Melt the lard in the liquid, then bring to the boil and pour into a well made in the dry ingredients. Working quickly, beat with a wooden spoon to form a fairly soft dough. Turn it out on to a lightly floured board and knead until smooth. Use as required. Recipes for Raised Veal and Ham Pie, Raised Pork Pie and Raised Game Pie appear in the Meat and the Game chapters respectively. See the directions below for the method of shaping a raised pie by hand and in a cake tin. Keep the part of the dough that is not actually being used covered with a cloth or an up-turned basin, to prevent it hardening before you can use it.

Family Cakes

Cherry Cake

4 oz. butter or margarine
8 oz. self-raising flour
A pinch of salt
4 oz. sugar
4–6 oz. glacé cherries, washed, dried and quartered
1 egg, beaten
½ tsp. vanilla essence
About 5 tbsps. milk to mix

Oven temperature: moderate (350°F., mark 4)

Grease and line the base of a loaf tin measuring 8½ by 4½ inches (top measurements; 2¼-pint capacity).

Rub the fat into the flour and salt until the mixture resembles fine breadcrumbs. Stir in the sugar and the cherries. Make a well in the centre, pour in the egg, essence and some of the milk and gradually work in the dry ingredients, adding more milk if necessary to give a dropping consistency. Put the mixture into the tin and level the top. Bake in the centre of the oven for about 1¼ hours, until well risen, golden-brown and firm to the touch.

Fruit Cake

4 oz. butter or margarine
8 oz. self-raising flour
A pinch of salt
4 oz. sugar
2 oz. currants
2 oz. sultanas
1 oz. candied peel, chopped
2 eggs, beaten
About 4 tbsps. milk to mix

Oven temperature: moderate (350°F., mark 4)

Line a 7-inch cake tin.

Rub the fat into the flour and salt until the mixture resembles fine breadcrumbs. Stir in the sugar, fruit and peel. Make a well in the centre, pour in the egg and some of the milk and gradually work in the dry ingredients, adding more milk if necessary to give a dropping consistency. Put the mixture into the tin and level the top. Bake in the centre of the oven for about 1 hour, until the cake is golden-brown and firm to the touch.

Variations

SULTANA CAKE: Make as above, using 5 oz. sultanas instead of the mixture of fruit.

SEED CAKE: Make as above, using 1 oz. of caraway seeds instead of the fruit.

Plain Buns

4 oz. butter or margarine
8 oz. self-raising flour
A pinch of salt
4 oz. sugar
1 egg, beaten
1–2 tsps. vanilla essence
Milk to mix

Oven temperature: fairly hot (375°F., mark 5)

Spread out 18–20 paper bun cases on a baking tray.

Rub the fat into the flour and salt until the mixture resembles fine breadcrumbs; stir in the sugar. Make a well in the centre, pour in the egg, vanilla essence and some of the milk and gradually stir in the dry ingredients, adding more milk if necessary to give a soft dropping consistency. Put a good teaspoon of the mixture in each baking case and bake towards the top of the oven for about 15–20 minutes, until the buns are well risen, golden-brown and firm to the touch. When they are cold, decorate if liked with glacé icing (*see Party Cakes chapter*).

Variations

FRUIT BUNS: Add 2 oz. dried fruit with the sugar.

LEMON CHERRY BUNS: Add 2 level tsps. grated lemon rind with the sugar. Decorate with lemon-flavoured glacé icing and a piece of glacé cherry.

ORANGE BUNS: Add 2 level tsps. grated orange rind with the sugar. Decorate if liked with orange glacé icing and a piece of crystallised orange.

COCONUT BUNS: Replace 2 oz. of the flour by desiccated coconut and add with the sugar. Decorate with glacé icing, sprinkle generously with desiccated coconut and add a halved glacé cherry.

CHOCOLATE BUNS: Use 7 oz. flour and 1 oz. cocoa and add ½ tsp. vanilla essence. Decorate with white glacé icing and flaked chocolate, chocolate vermicelli or chocolate drops.

CHERUB CAKES: Make plain buns as above and allow to cool. Meanwhile make a filling by creaming 4 oz. butter until soft, gradually beating in 6 oz. icing sugar and adding a few drops of almond essence. When the cakes are quite cold, cut a slice from the top of each and pipe or fork in some filling. Cut each cake slice in half and replace at an angle in the cream, to represent the cherub's wings.

Rock Buns

4 oz. butter or margarine
8 oz. self-raising flour
A pinch of salt
½ level tsp. mixed spice
Grated rind of ½ a lemon
4 oz. sugar
4 oz. mixed dried fruit
½ oz. mixed peel, chopped
1 egg, beaten
Milk to mix

Oven temperature: fairly hot (400°F., mark 6)

Grease two baking trays.

Rub the fat into the flour, salt and spices until the mixture resembles fine breadcrumbs. Stir in rind, sugar, fruit and peel. Make a well in the centre, pour in the egg and a little milk and stir in the dry ingredients, adding more milk if necessary to give a stiff dough. Spoon the mixture in small piles on to the try and bake towards the top of the oven for 15–20 minutes.

Variation

Replace the dried fruit and peel by 4 oz. chopped stoned dates and ½ oz. chopped crystallised ginger.

Victoria Sandwich Cake

4 oz. butter or margarine
4 oz. caster sugar
2 eggs, beaten
4 oz. self-raising flour
1–2 rounded tbsps. jam
Caster sugar to dredge

Oven temperature: fairly hot (375°F., mark 5)

Grease two 7-inch sandwich tins and line the base of each with a round of greased greaseproof paper.

Cream the fat and sugar until pale and fluffy. Add the egg a little at a time, beating well after each addition. Fold in half the flour, using a tablespoon, then fold in the rest. Place half the mixture in each tin and level it with a knife. Bake both cakes on the same shelf, just above the centre of the oven, for about 20 minutes, or until they are well risen, golden, firm to the touch and beginning to shrink away from the sides of the tins.

When the cakes are cool, sandwich them together with jam and sprinkle the top with caster sugar.

Variations

CHOCOLATE: Replace 1 oz. of the flour by 1 oz. cocoa. Sandwich together with vanilla or chocolate butter cream.

ORANGE OR LEMON: Add 2 level tsps. grated orange or lemon rind to the mixture. Sandwich the cakes together with orange or lemon curd or orange or lemon butter cream. Use the juice of the fruit to make glacé icing.

COFFEE: Add 2 tsps. instant coffee dissolved in a little warm water to the creamed mixture with the egg.

Victoria Sandwich Cake made with Oil

5 oz. self-raising flour
1 level tsp. baking powder
A pinch of salt
4½ oz. caster sugar
7 tbsps. cooking oil
2 eggs
2½ tbsps. milk
A few drops of vanilla essence
Jam

Oven temperature: moderate (350°F., mark 4)

Grease two 7-inch sandwich cake tins and line the base of each with greased greaseproof paper.

Sift the flour, baking powder and salt into a bowl and stir in the sugar. Add the oil, eggs, milk and essence and stir with a wooden spoon until the mixture is blended and creamy—not less than 2 minutes. Put into the tins and bake near the centre of the oven for 35–40 minutes. When cold, sandwich together with jam.

Madeira Cake

4 oz. plain flour
4 oz. self-raising flour
6 oz. butter
6 oz. caster sugar
1 tsp. vanilla essence
3 eggs, beaten
About 1–2 tbsps. milk
2–3 thin slices of citron peel

Oven temperature: moderate (350°F., mark 4)

Line a 7-inch cake tin.
 Sift the flours. Cream the butter, sugar and essence until pale and fluffy. Beat in the egg a little at a time. Fold in the flour, adding a little milk if necessary to give a dropping consistency. Put into the tin and bake just below the centre of the oven. After $\frac{1}{2}$ hour, put the citron peel across the cake and continue to cook for a further 1–1$\frac{1}{4}$ hours. Cool on a wire rack.

Variations

ORANGE CAKE: Add the grated rind of 2 oranges to the butter and sugar.

RICH SEED CAKE: Add 2 level tsps. caraway seeds with the flour. Omit the citron peel.

DREAM CAKE: Add 3 oz. chopped walnuts and 3 oz. quartered glacé cherries with the flour. Omit the citron peel.

Chocolate Cake

3 oz. self-raising flour
1 oz. ground rice
4 oz. plain chocolate, grated
4 oz. butter or margarine
3 oz. caster sugar
1–2 tsps. vanilla essence
2 eggs, beaten
Chocolate butter icing
Chocolate glacé icing
Crystallised violets and mint leaves

Oven temperature: moderate (350°F., mark 4)

Line a 6-inch cake tin.
 Mix the flour and ground rice. Put the grated chocolate into a small basin, place over a saucepan of hot water and heat gently to melt the chocolate. Cream the fat, sugar and essence until pale and fluffy. Add the melted chocolate (which should be only just warm) to the creamed mixture and mix lightly together. Beat in the egg a little at a time. Fold in the flour, put into the tin and bake just above the centre of the oven for 1–1$\frac{1}{4}$ hours. When cold, split in half and fill with butter icing. Ice with glacé icing and decorate with violets and mint leaves. Alternatively, fill and decorate with coffee butter icing.

DIVORCE CAKE: Sandwich with rum butter (*see Sauces chapter*) and dust the top with caster sugar.

Dundee Cake

4 oz. currants
4 oz. raisins, stoned
4 oz. sultanas
4 oz. candied peel
2 oz. whole almonds, blanched
10 oz. plain flour
8 oz. butter or margarine
8 oz. soft brown sugar
Grated rind of 1 lemon
4 eggs, beaten

Oven temperature: warm (325°F., mark 3)

Line an 8-inch cake tin.
 Prepare the fruit and chop the peel and nuts (leaving a few nuts whole for decorating the cake). Mix with the flour. Cream the fat, sugar and lemon rind until pale and fluffy. Beat in the egg, fold in the dry ingredients, put into the tin and hollow the centre slightly; arrange the almonds on top. Bake just below the centre of the oven for 2$\frac{1}{2}$–3 hours. Cover the top with brown paper if the cake is browning too fast. When quite firm to the touch, remove from the tin and cool on a rack.

Coburg Cakes

6 oz. plain flour
$\frac{1}{2}$ level tsp. bicarbonate of soda
$\frac{1}{2}$ level tsp. allspice
$\frac{1}{2}$ level tsp. ground ginger
$\frac{1}{2}$ level tsp. cinnamon
3 oz. butter or margarine
3 oz. sugar
2 eggs, beaten
1 tbsp. warm water
1 tbsp. syrup

Oven temperature: fairly hot (400°F., mark 6)

Grease 12–18 patty tins.
 Sift the flour, bicarbonate of soda and spices. Cream the fat and sugar until pale and fluffy. Add the egg a little at a time, beating well after each addition. Add the mixed water and syrup alternately with the flour, folding in lightly. Three-quarters fill the patty tins and bake in the middle of the oven for 15–20 minutes.
 If one large cake is required, put the mixture in 2 greased 7-inch sandwich tins and bake in a moderate oven (350°F., mark 4) for about 30 minutes.

Sponge Cake

3 eggs
4$\frac{1}{2}$ oz. caster sugar
3 oz. plain flour

Oven temperature: fairly hot (375°F., mark 5)

Grease two 7-inch sandwich tins and dust with flour and sugar.

Madeira Cake

Put the eggs and sugar in a large bowl, stand this over a pan of hot water and whisk until light and creamy – the mixture should be stiff enough to retain the impression of the whisk for a few seconds. Remove from the heat and whisk until cold. Sift half the flour over the mixture and fold in very lightly, using a tablespoon. Add the remaining flour in the same way. Pour the mixture into the tins and bake near the top of the oven for 20–25 minutes.

Swiss Roll

3 eggs
4 oz. caster sugar
4 oz. plain flour
1 tbsp. hot water
Caster sugar to dredge
Warm jam

Oven temperature: hot (425°F., mark 7)

Line a Swiss roll tin (9 by 12 inches).

Put the eggs and sugar in a large bowl, stand it over a pan of hot water and whisk until light and creamy: the mixture should be stiff enough to retain the impression of the whisk for a few seconds. Remove the bowl from the heat and whisk until cool. Sift half the flour over the mixture and fold in very lightly, using a tablespoon. Add the remaining flour in the same way and lightly stir in the hot water.

Pour the mixture into the prepared tin, allowing it to run over the whole surface. Bake near the top of the oven for 7–9 minutes until golden-brown, well risen and firm.

Meanwhile, have ready a sheet of greaseproof paper liberally sprinkled with caster sugar. To help make the sponge pliable, you can place the paper over a tea towel lightly wrung out in hot water. Turn the cake quickly out on to the paper, trim off the crusty edges with a sharp knife and spread the surface with warmed jam. Roll up with the aid of the paper, making the first turn firmly so that the whole cake will roll evenly and have a good shape when finished, but roll more lightly after this first turn. Dredge the cake with sugar and cool on a cake rack.

Madeleines

4 oz. butter or margarine
4 oz. caster sugar
2 eggs, beaten
4 oz. self-raising flour
Red jam
Desiccated coconut
Glacé cherries and angelica

Oven temperature: moderate (350°F., mark 4)

Grease 12 dariole moulds.

Cream the fat and sugar until pale and fluffy. Add the egg a little at a time, beating well after each addition. Fold in half the flour, using a tablespoon, then fold in the rest. Three-quarters fill the moulds and bake towards top of oven for about 20 minutes, or until firm and browned. Trim off the bottoms, so that the cakes stand firmly and are of even height. When they are nearly cold, brush with melted jam, holding them on a skewer, then roll them in coconut. Top each madeleine with a glacé cherry and 2 small angelica 'leaves'.

Note: For the traditional French madeleine, Genoese Sponge is baked in special fluted shell-shaped tins.

Genoese Sponge

3 oz. butter
2 oz. plain flour
½ oz. cornflour
3 large eggs
4 oz. caster sugar

Oven temperature: fairly hot (375°F., mark 5)

Grease and line two 7-inch sandwich tins.

Heat the butter gently until it is melted, remove it from the heat and let it stand for a few minutes, for the salt and any sediment to settle. Sift the flour and cornflour. Put the eggs and sugar in a large bowl, stand this over a saucepan of hot water and whisk until light and creamy – the mixture should be stiff enough to retain the impression of the whisk for a few seconds. Remove from the heat and whisk until cool. Pour the tepid fat round the edge of the mixture, taking care not to let the salt and sediment run in. Fold in lightly, using a tablespoon, until almost all the fat is worked in. Sift half of the flour over the surface of the mixture and fold in very lightly. Add the rest in the same way. Mix very lightly or the fat will sink to the bottom and cause a heavy cake. Pour the mixture into the tins and bake near top of oven until golden-brown and firm to the touch – 20–25 minutes. Use as required, for layered cakes and iced cakes.

Everyday Gingerbread

1 lb. plain flour
1 level tsp. salt
1 level tbsp. ground ginger
1 level tbsp. baking powder
1 level tsp. bicarbonate of soda
8 oz. brown sugar
6 oz. butter or margarine
6 oz. treacle
6 oz. golden syrup
½ pint milk
1 egg, beaten

Oven temperature: Warm (325°F., mark 3)

Line an 8-inch square tin.

Sift the flour, salt, ginger, baking powder and bicarbonate of soda. Warm the sugar, fat, treacle and syrup until melted, but do not allow to boil. Mix in the milk and the egg. Make a well in the centre of the dry ingredients, pour in the liquid and mix very thoroughly. Pour the mixture into the tin and bake in the centre of the oven for about 1½ hours, or until firm to the touch.

For smaller cake, use half quantities, with a 7-inch square tin; bake for about 1 hour.

Maids of Honour

1 pint milk
A pinch of salt
1 tsp. rennet
3 oz. butter, softened
2 eggs
1 tbsp. brandy
1 oz. blanched almonds, chopped
2 level tsps. sugar
8 oz. puff pastry
A few currants (optional)

Oven temperature: hot (425°F., mark 7)

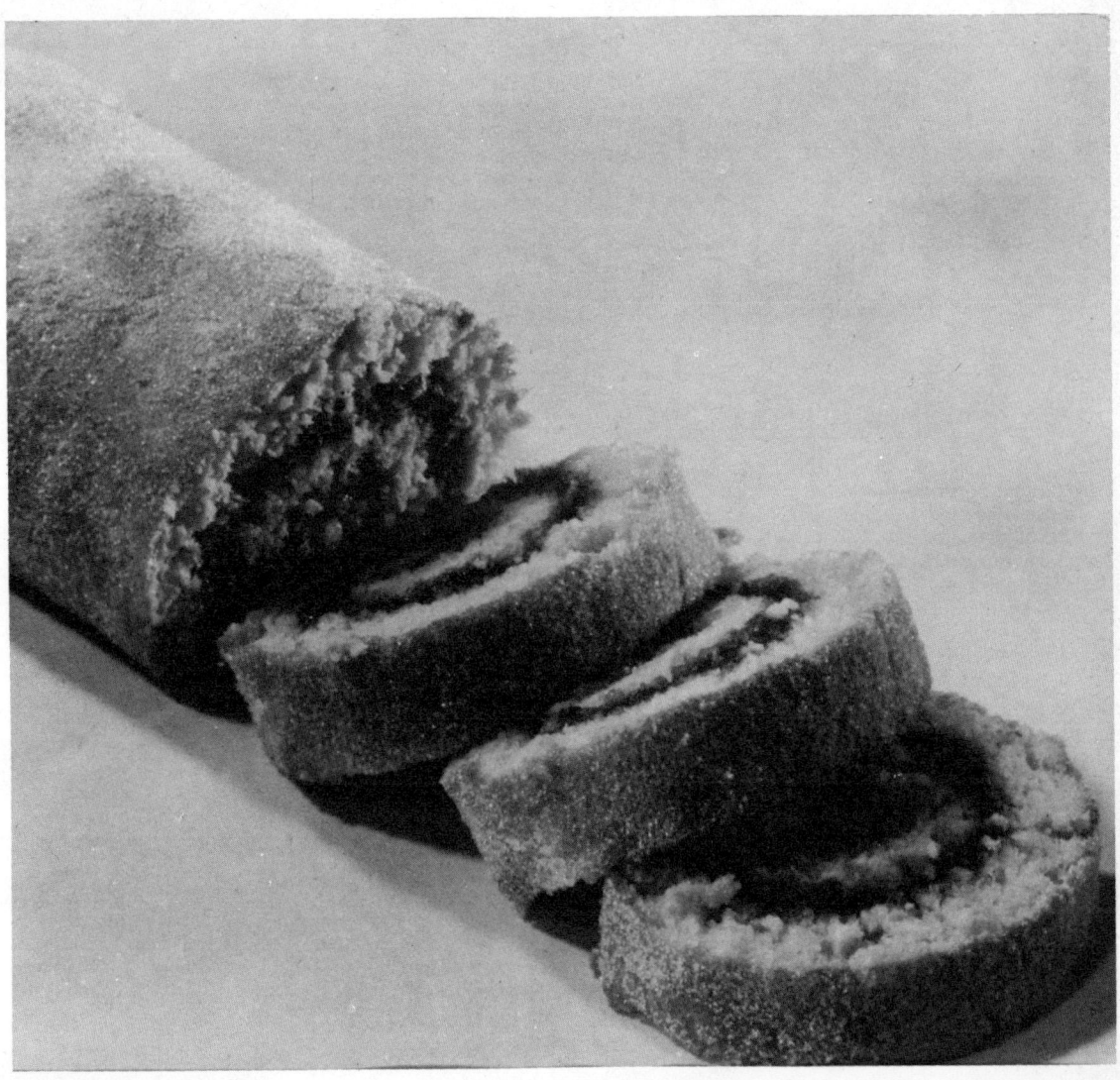

Swiss Roll

Warm the milk until it feels just warm to a finger, add the salt and rennet and leave to set; when firm, put into a piece of fine muslin, secure with a piece of string and hang it up over a bowl. Allow to drain overnight.

The next day, rub the curds and the butter through a sieve. Whisk the eggs and brandy together and add to the curds, with the almonds and sugar. Line some deep patty tins with the pastry, half-fill with the curd mixture and if liked sprinkle currants over the top. Bake in the centre of the oven for 15–20 minutes.

One-Stage Fruit Cake

8 oz. self-raising flour
2 level tsps. mixed spice
1 level tsp. baking powder
4 oz. soft margarine
4 oz. soft brown sugar
8 oz. dried fruit
2 eggs
2 tbsps. milk

Oven temperature: warm (325°F., mark 3)

Grease a 7-inch round cake tin and line the base with a round of greased greaseproof paper.

Sift the flour, spice and baking powder into a large bowl, add the rest of the ingredients and mix until thoroughly combined. Put into the tin and bake in the centre of the oven for 1¾ hours.

One-Stage Sandwich Cake

4 oz. self-raising flour
1 level tsp. baking powder
4 oz. soft margarine
4 oz. caster sugar
2 eggs
Jam or lemon curd to fill

Oven temperature: warm (325°F., mark 3)

Grease two 7-inch sandwich tins and line each base with a round of greased greaseproof paper.

Sift the flour and baking powder into a large bowl. Add the other ingredients, mix well, then beat for about 2 minutes. Put evenly into the tins. Bake in the centre of the oven for 25–35 minutes. When cool, sandwich with jam or lemon curd.

For a more lavish decoration, sandwich together with butter cream and pour chocolate icing over the top, letting it trickle down the sides. (*See Party Cakes chapter for icings.*)

Variations

ORANGE: Add the grated rind and juice of 1 orange.

MOCHA: Sift 2 level tbsps. cocoa and 1 level tbsp. instant coffee with 3 oz. flour.

CHOCOLATE, CHERRY AND NUT CAKE: Omit 1 oz. sugar and add 1 oz. grated plain chocolate, 3 oz. chopped glacé cherries and ½ oz. chopped walnuts.

SMALL BUNS: Make into 18–20 buns and bake near the top of a fairly hot oven (400°F., mark 6) for 15–20 minutes.

Oven Scones

1–2 oz. butter or margarine
8 oz. self-raising flour
½ level tsp. salt
¼ pint (approx.) milk

Oven temperature: very hot (450°F., mark 8)

Grease and flour a baking tray.

Rub the fat into the flour and salt until the mixture resembles fine breadcrumbs. Make a well in the centre and stir in enough milk to give a fairly soft dough. Turn it on to a floured board, knead very lightly if necessary to remove any cracks, then roll out lightly to about ¾ inch thick, or pat it out with the hand. Cut into 10–12 rounds with a 2-inch cutter (dipped in flour) or cut into triangles with a sharp knife. Place on the baking tray,

brush if liked with beaten egg or milk and bake near the top of the oven for 8–10 minutes, until brown and well risen. Cool the scones on a rack.

Alternative Raising Agents

If plain flour and baking powder are used instead of self-raising flour, allow 3 level tsps. baking powder to ½ lb. flour and sift them together before using. If you use cream of tartar and bicarbonate of soda in place of baking powder, allow 2 level tsps. cream of tartar and 1 level tsp. bicarbonate of soda.

Fruit Scones

EVERYDAY FRUIT SCONES: Add 2 oz. currants, sultanas, stoned raisins or chopped dates (or a mixture of fruit) to the dry ingredients in the basic recipe.

RICH AFTERNOON TEA SCONES: Follow the basic recipe, adding 1–2 level tbsps. caster sugar to the dry ingredients and using 1 beaten egg with 1–2 tbsps. water or milk; 2 oz. dried fruit may also be included.

Girdle Scones

1½ oz. butter or margarine
8 oz. self-raising flour
A pinch of salt
1 oz. sugar
¼ pint milk or milk and water

Rub the fat into the flour and salt until the mixture resembles fine breadcrumbs. Stir in the sugar. Mix to a fairly soft dough with the liquid, then turn it on to a floured board and knead it very lightly if necessary to remove any cracks. Roll out ½ inch thick and cut into 10–12 triangles or rounds. Cook steadily on the hot girdle for about 5 minutes, until well risen and pale brown underneath; turn them and cook for a further 5 minutes until the other side is browned and the centre is dry.

Scotch Pancakes or Drop Scones

4 oz. self-raising flour
1 oz. sugar
1 egg, beaten
¼ pint milk

Mix the flour and sugar. Make a well in the centre and stir in the egg, with enough of the milk to make a batter of the consistency of thick cream. The mixing should be done as quickly and lightly as possible – don't beat. If a thin pancake is wanted, add slightly more milk.

Drop the mixture in dessertspoonfuls on to a hot, lightly greased girdle; for round pancakes, drop it from the point of the spoon, for oval ones, from the side. Keep the girdle at a steady heat and when bubbles rise to the surface of the pancakes and burst – after 2–3

Madeleines

minutes – turn the cake over, using a palette knife. Continue cooking until golden-brown on the other side – a further 2–3 minutes. Place the finished pancakes on a clean tea towel, cover with another towel and place on a rack to cool. (This keeps in the steam and the pancakes do not become dry.) Serve with butter or with whipped cream and jam. Makes about 15–18 pancakes.

Simple Doughnuts

8 oz. plain flour
½ level tsp. bicarbonate of soda
1 level tsp. cream of tartar
A pinch of ground cinnamon
1 oz. butter
2 oz. sugar
1 egg, beaten
Milk
Deep fat for frying

Sift the flour, bicarbonate of soda, cream of tartar and cinnamon and rub in the butter until the mixture resembles fine breadcrumbs. Stir in the sugar. Make a well in the centre, pour in the egg and gradually work in the dry ingredients, adding a little milk if necessary to give a soft dough. Heat the fat so that when a cube of bread is dropped in it takes 60–70 seconds to brown. Drop small balls of the mixture into the fat and fry until a light brown colour, turning them frequently. Lift out, drain on crumpled kitchen paper and sprinkle with sugar. Alternatively, the dough may be made stiffer, turned out on to a floured board and lightly kneaded until free from cracks, then rolled out until ½-inch thick, cut into rings with two round cutters and fried as before. *For doughnuts made with yeast see chapter on Bread, Rolls and Buns.*

Party Cakes

Butter Cream

3 oz. butter
6 oz. icing sugar, sifted
Vanilla essence (or other flavouring)
1–2 tbsps. milk or warm water

Cream the butter until soft and gradually beat in the sugar, adding a few drops of essence and the milk or water.

This amount will coat the sides of a 7-inch cake, or give a topping and a filling. If you wish both to coat the sides and give a topping or filling, increase the amounts of butter and sugar to 4 oz. and 8 oz. respectively.

ORANGE OR LEMON BUTTER CREAM: Omit the vanilla essence and add a little finely grated orange or lemon rind and a little of the juice, beating well to avoid curdling the mixture.

WALNUT BUTTER CREAM: Add 2 tbsps. finely chopped walnuts; mix well.

ALMOND BUTTER CREAM: Add 2 tbsps. very finely chopped toasted almonds; mix well.

COFFEE BUTTER CREAM: Omit the vanilla essence and flavour with 2 level tsps. instant coffee powder or 1 tbsp. coffee essence.

CHOCOLATE BUTTER CREAM: Flavour either by adding 1–1½ oz. melted chocolate or by adding 1 level tbsp. cocoa dissolved in a little hot water (this should be cooled before it is added to the mixture).

MOCHA BUTTER CREAM: Dissolve 1 level tsp. cocoa and 2 level tsps. instant coffee powder in a little warm water; cool before adding to the mixture.

Glacé Icing

Put 4 oz. sifted icing sugar and (if liked) a few drops of any flavouring essence in a basin and gradually add 1–2 tbsps. warm water. The icing should be thick enough to coat the back of a spoon. If necessary, add more water or sugar to adjust the consistency. Add a few drops of colouring if required and use at once.

For icing of a finer texture, put the sugar, water and flavouring into a small pan and heat, stirring, until the mixture is warm – don't make it too hot. The icing should coat the back of a wooden spoon and look smooth and glossy.

This amount is sufficient to cover the top of a 7-inch cake.

ORANGE ICING: Substitute 1–2 tbsps. strained orange juice for the water in the above recipe.

LEMON ICING: Substitute 1 tbsp. strained lemon juice for the water.

CHOCOLATE ICING: Dissolve 2 level tsps. cocoa in a little hot water and use to replace the same amount of plain water.

COFFEE ICING: Flavour with either 1 tsp. coffee essence or 2 level tsps. instant coffee powder, dissolved in a little water.

MOCHA ICING: Flavour with 1 level tsp. cocoa and 2 level tsps. instant coffee powder, dissolved in a little water.

LIQUEUR ICING: Replace 2–3 tsps. of the water by liqueur as desired.

Fondant Icing

Make the fondant as described in the recipe in the Home-made Sweets chapter and prepare it for use as follows:

186

Decorating a Sponge Cake

Put the required amount in a basin (the full amount given makes a generous coating for a 7-inch cake); stand the basin over hot water and melt over a very gentle heat. Take care not to over-heat the fondant, as this makes the texture rough and destroys the gloss. Dilute the melted fondant with sugar syrup (*see below*) or with plain water to the consistency of double cream – or until the mixture will just coat the back of a wooden spoon.

To make sugar syrup, dissolve $\frac{1}{2}$ lb. sugar in $\frac{1}{2}$ pint water, then boil without stirring to 220°F.; cool before using.

Cakes which are to be coated with fondant icing should be glazed completely with apricot glaze (*see below*) and then coated with almond paste, to give a really professional appearance.

To ice small cakes or pastries, spear them on a fork or skewer and dip them in the prepared fondant.

To ice a large cake, put it on a wire tray with a plate below and pour the icing quickly all over the cake. Don't touch the icing with a knife or the gloss finish will be spoilt. Add any desired decoration and leave the cake to set.

To give a thick topping of fondant, as seen in pâtisserie cakes, follow this method: pin a band of double grease-proof paper closely round the cake so that it comes an inch above the top. Prepare half the amount of fondant (i.e. make it with $\frac{1}{2}$ lb. sugar and thin with syrup made with $\frac{1}{4}$ lb. sugar); pour it on to the top of the cake. When the topping is set, ease off the paper collar, using the back of a knife blade and dipping this frequently into hot water.

Apricot Glaze

For use under fondant icing and almond paste

Place $\frac{1}{2}$ lb. apricot jam and 2 tbsps. water in a saucepan over a low heat and stir until the jam softens. Sieve the mixture, return it to the pan and bring to the boil, boiling gently until the glaze is of a suitable coating consistency.

This glaze can be potted as for jam and kept for future use.

DECORATING A SPONGE CAKE

Here are nine easy ways of 'dressing up' a pair of 7-inch cakes, using plain ones for some versions and chocolate or coffee-flavoured cakes for others. Following these recipes come a couple of slightly more elaborate decorated cakes.

1. Sandwich the cakes together with lemon curd. Make some lemon butter cream (4 oz. butter, 8 oz. icing sugar) and roughly spread it over the cake and down the sides. Decorate the top of the cake with mimosa balls and pieces of cut angelica.

2. Make some orange or lemon butter cream (4 oz. butter, 8 oz. icing sugar). Use half to sandwich the cakes together and the rest to cover the top. Mark the top with a fork and decorate with small pieces of crystallised orange or lemon slices.

3. Drain a can of pineapple, mandarins or peaches. Sandwich the cakes together with apricot jam. Make some butter cream (4 oz. butter, 8 oz. icing sugar, including a little of the fruit juice) and spread it round the sides of the cake and over the top. Press chopped almonds round the sides and mark the top with a fork. Decorate with pieces of the drained fruit.

4. Make some coffee butter cream (3 oz. butter, 6 oz. icing sugar) and an equal amount of chocolate butter cream. Sandwich the cakes with some coffee butter cream. Spread some chocolate butter cream round the sides and mark with a fork. Spread the remaining chocolate butter cream over the top. Use the remaining coffee butter cream to pipe whirls on the top. (This cake is even nicer if made with a coffee-flavoured Victoria sandwich.)

5. Sieve 6 tbsps. apricot or raspberry jam. Sandwich the cake with some jam and use the rest to brush round the sides. Holding the cake on its side, roll it in desiccated coconut or chopped nuts until an even layer sticks to the jam. Cover the top with glacé icing (4 oz. icing sugar) and decorate with chocolate drops, halved nuts or small sweets.

6. Sandwich the cakes together with walnut butter cream (2 oz. butter, 4 oz. icing sugar). Cover the top with chocolate glacé icing (4 oz. icing sugar) and decorate with chopped or halved walnuts.

7. Sandwich 2 chocolate cakes together with chocolate butter cream (4 oz. butter, 8 oz. icing sugar) and spread the rest round the sides. Roll the sides in chocolate vermicelli. Cover the top of the cake with chocolate glacé icing (4 oz. icing sugar). Melt 1 oz. plain chocolate and pour in a thin stream from a spoon to form a 'scribble' pattern.

8. Make some chocolate butter cream (4 oz. butter, 8 oz. icing sugar); use some of this to sandwich the cakes and spread the rest roughly round the sides. Cover the top of the cake with white glacé icing (4 oz. icing sugar) and decorate with chocolate drops.

9. Sandwich the cakes together with a little frosting and pour the rest over the cake, allowing it to flow down the sides. Using a warm round-bladed knife, swirl the frosting decoratively.

Victoria Sandwich Slab Cake

Oven temperature: moderate (350°F., mark 4)

Line a meat tin (about 10 by 12 inches). Make a Victoria sandwich from 10 oz. butter, 10 oz. sugar, 5 eggs and 10 oz. self-raising flour (or use twice the amounts given for the Victoria sandwich cake with oil *(see page 000)*. Bake just above the centre of the oven for 40–50 minutes, until well-risen, golden-brown and firm to the touch.

Coffee Diagonals

Coat the top of the cake with coffee glacé icing (10 oz. icing sugar) and when this is nearly set, use stiff coffee icing (10 oz. icing sugar and half the usual amount of water) to pipe double lines $1\frac{1}{2}$ inches apart across the cake; in between sprinkle grated chocolate. Trim the cake with a knife dipped in hot water, then cut it into $1\frac{1}{2}$-inch strips; cut the strips across diagonally.

Lemon Gâteau

6 oz. self-raising flour
2 oz. cornflour
A pinch of salt
8 oz. butter
8 oz. sugar
Juice and finely grated rind of 1 lemon
2 eggs, lightly beaten
6 tbsps. apricot jam
Decoration as desired

For the Frosting
2 egg whites
12 oz. caster sugar
A pinch of salt
2 tbsps. water
2 tbsps. lemon juice
Finely grated rind of 1 lemon
A pinch of cream of tartar
Yellow colouring

Oven temperature: moderate (350°F., mark 4)

Grease and flour three 8-inch sandwich tins. Sift the flour, cornflour and salt on to a plate. Cream the fat, sugar and lemon rind until light and fluffy and gradually add the eggs, beating well. Fold in the flour and lightly stir in the lemon juice. Divide the mixture evenly between the tins and bake in the oven for about 30 minutes, till golden-brown and springy to the touch. When the cakes are quite cold, spread jam evenly over 2 and sandwich all 3 layers together.

To make the frosting, whisk all the ingredients (except the colouring) lightly together; place the bowl over hot water and whisk until the mixture thickens sufficiently to hold peaks. Add a few drops of colouring, to tint it pale lemon-yellow. Using a palette knife, spread frosting over top and sides of cake. Rough up the surface and decorate with angelica and mimosa balls, or as desired.

(See colour picture facing page 256)

Coffee Diagonals

Éclairs

Choux pastry made with 2½ oz. flour *(see Pastry chapter)*
Whipped cream or flavoured custard
Chocolate or coffee glacé icing (4 oz. icing sugar) or 2 oz. melted chocolate

Oven temperature: fairly hot (400°F., mark 6)

Put the choux paste into a forcing bag with a plain round pipe of ½-inch diameter and force in fingers 3½–4 inches long on to the baking tray, keeping the lengths very even and cutting the paste off with a wet knife against the edge of the pipe. Bake towards the top of the oven for about 35 minutes, until well risen, crisp and of a golden-brown colour. Remove from the tin, slit down the sides with a sharp-pointed knife to allow the steam to escape and leave on a cake rack to cool. When the éclairs are cold, fill with whipped cream or flavoured custard, then ice the tops with a little chocolate or coffee glacé icing or dip them in melted chocolate.
Makes about 12.

Meringues

2 egg whites
1½–2 oz. granulated sugar
1½–2 oz. caster sugar
¼ pint whipped cream

Oven temperature: very cool (250°F., mark ¼)

Line a baking try with a sheet of greaseproof paper and rub a trace of olive oil over the surface or line it with silicone (non-stick) paper.

Whisk the egg whites very stiffly, add the granulated sugar and whisk again until the mixture regains its former stiffness. Lastly, fold in the caster sugar very lightly, using a metal spoon. Pipe through a forcing bag (or put in spoonfuls) on to the baking sheet and dry off in the oven for several hours, until the meringues are firm and crisp but still white; if they begin to brown, prop the oven door open a little. When they are cool, sandwich them together with whipped cream.
Makes 12–16 meringue shells.

Variations
1. Tint pink by adding 1–2 drops of red colouring with the sugar.
2. To make coffee meringues, use coffee essence, adding 1 tsp. to each egg white when the sugar is folded in.
3. For chocolate meringues, add cocoa with the caster sugar, allowing 1 level tsp. per egg white.
4. Add finely chopped nuts, melted chocolate or a liqueur to the filling.

Cream Puffs

Choux paste made with 2½ oz. flour *(see Pastry chapter)*
Whipped cream
Melted chocolate or icing sugar

Oven temperature: hot (400°F., mark 6)

Pipe the paste into rounds 1½–2 inches in diameter 3 inches apart on 2 damp baking sheets and cover with Yorkshire pudding or cake tins. Bake in the centre of the oven for 45–50 minutes. It is very important not to remove the covering tin during the cooking or the puffs will collapse; to test them, shake the tin gently – if the puffs move about freely, they are cooked. Split them and cool on a rack. When they are cold, fill with whipped cream and dip the tops in melted chocolate or dust with icing sugar.

Makes 8–10.

Palmiers

4 oz. puff pastry
Caster sugar
Sweetened whipped cream or jam
Icing sugar

Oven temperature: hot (425°F., mark 7)

Roll the pastry out evenly until it is $\frac{1}{8}$ inch thick ($\frac{1}{16}$ inch if bought pastry) and about 20 inches long, then sprinkle it generously with caster sugar. Fold the ends over to the centre until they meet and press down firmly. Sprinkle generously with more sugar and fold the sides to the centre again; press and sprinkle with sugar. Place the two folded portions together and press; then with a sharp knife, cut into $\frac{1}{4}$-inch slices. Place cut edge down on a baking sheet, allowing room to spread, and bake towards the top of the oven for 6–7 minutes, until golden-brown. Turn them and bake for a further 6–7 minutes. Cool on a rack and just before serving, spread sweetened whipped cream on half of the slices, sandwich with the remaining slices and dredge with icing sugar. (If preferred, jam may be used in place of cream.)

Makes about 12.

Rich Christmas Cake

1 lb. 2 oz. currants
8 oz. sultanas
8 oz. raisins, stoned
4 oz. mixed peel, chopped
6 oz. glacé cherries, halved
10 oz. plain flour
A pinch of salt
$\frac{1}{2}$ level tsp. mixed spice
$\frac{1}{2}$ level tsp. ground cinnamon
10 oz. butter
10 oz. soft brown sugar
Grated rind of $\frac{1}{2}$ a lemon
6 eggs, beaten
3 tbsps. brandy

Oven temperature: cool (300°F., mark 1–2)

Line a 9-inch cake tin, using 2 thicknesses of greaseproof paper. Tie a double band of brown paper round the outside.

Clean the fruit if necessary. Mix the prepared currants, sultanas, raisins, peel and cherries with the flour, salt and spices. Cream the butter, sugar and lemon rind until pale and fluffy. Add the eggs a little at a time, beating

well after each addition. Fold in half the flour and fruit, using a tablespoon, then fold in the rest and add the brandy. Put into the tin, spread the mixture evenly, making sure there are no air pockets, and make a dip in the centre. Stand the tin on a layer of newspaper or brown paper in the lower part of the oven and bake for about $4\frac{1}{2}$ hours. To avoid over-browning the top, cover it with several thicknesses of greaseproof paper after $2\frac{1}{2}$ hours.

When the cake is cooked, leave it to cool in the tin and then turn it out on to a wire rack. To store, wrap it in several layers of greaseproof paper and put it in an airtight tin. If a large enough tin is not available, cover the wrapped cake entirely with aluminium foil If you like, you can prick the cake top all over with a fine skewer and slowly pour 2–3 tbsps. brandy over it before storing.

Light Christmas Cake

6 oz. glacé cherries, halved
6 oz. currants
6 oz. sultanas
4 oz. glacé pineapple
4 oz. mixed candied peel, chopped
8 oz. butter or margarine
8 oz. caster sugar
2 oz. ground almonds
4 eggs, beaten
8 oz. self-raising flour
Grated rind and juice of 1 lemon
3 tbsps. brandy

For those who prefer a cake different from the traditional richly-fruited type; it should be made 1–2 weeks before eating.

Oven temperature: warm (325°F., mark 3)

Line a 9-inch cake tin, using a double thickness of greaseproof paper.

If the cherries are very syrupy, wash them and dry well. Clean the currants and sultanas if necessary. Cut the glacé pineapple into small cubes.

Cream the butter and sugar until pale and fluffy and stir in the ground almonds. Add the eggs a little at a time, beating well after each addition. Add 3 tbsps. of the flour to the fruits and peel, mixing well. Fold these ingredients, alternately with the rest of the flour, the grated lemon rind and the lemon juice, into the creamed mixture. Lastly, stir in the brandy. Put the mixture into the tin and bake in the centre of the oven or just below the centre for about $2\frac{1}{2}$ hours, or till risen and just firm to the touch. Cool and store as for the Rich Christmas Cake.

Note 1: If a firmer cake is preferred, use 4 oz. self-raising flour and 4 oz. plain.

Note 2: As an alternative, use twice the amount of ingredients given for Genoa Cake and bake in a 9-inch round tin.

White Fruit Cake

4 oz. plain flour
4 oz. self-raising flour
2 oz. cornflour
4 oz. glacé pineapple
6 oz. glacé cherries
4 oz. mixed glacé fruits
2 oz. crystallised ginger
2 oz. mixed chopped peel
2 oz. angelica
2 oz. blanched almonds
2 oz. shelled walnut
8 oz. butter or margarine
5 oz. caster sugar
4 large eggs
3 tsps. lemon juice
3–4 tbsps. milk

Oven temperature: warm (325°F., mark 3)

Prepare an 8-inch round cake tin as for a Christmas cake. Sift together the flours and cornflour. Cut the fruit into pieces about the size of half a cherry. Trim the angelica into matchsticks. Chop the nuts roughly. Mix the fruits and nuts together. Dust 2 tbsps. flour over all and coat the sticky fruit. Cream together the fat and sugar; slowly beat in the eggs one at a time, with a little flour. Lighly beat in the remaining flour, with the lemon juice and milk. Fold in the fruit and nuts. Turn the mixture into the prepared tin, hollow the centre and bake in the centre of the oven for 2–2½ hours. Leave in the tin for 15 minutes, then cool on a wire rack.

Devil's Food Cake

8 oz. plain flour
¼ level tsp. salt
½ level tsp. bicarbonate of soda
2 level tsps. baking powder
3 oz. plain or bitter chocolate, grated
8 fluid oz. milk (½ pint less 3–4 tbsps.)
5 oz. butter or margarine
10 oz. caster or soft brown sugar
3 eggs, beaten
1 tsp. vanilla essence
Chocolate butter cream (3 oz. butter, 6 oz. icing sugar) or
¼ pint double cream, whipped
Frosting *(see Lemon Gâteau, page 188, but omit yellow colouring)*
Chocolate flakes or vermicelli

Oven temperature: moderate (350°F., mark 4)

Line three 7-inch or two 9-inch sandwich cake tins.

Sift the flour, salt, bicarbonate of soda and baking powder together. Warm the chocolate in the milk until it has dissolved. Cream the butter, adding the sugar gradually until the mixture is pale and fluffy. Add the eggs and vanilla essence gradually, beating well after each addition. Stir in the dry ingredients alternately with the chocolate milk. Divide the mixture evenly between the tins and bake in the centre of the oven for 30–35 minutes.

When the cakes are cooked, cool on a wire tray, sandwich together with the chocolate butter cream or whipped cream and coat them with the frosting. Decorate with flaked chocolate or chocolate vermicelli.

Before the cakes are sandwiched together they can each be sprinkled with 1 tbsp. rum.

Note: It is not possible to get exactly the same result as with a packet mix, since the American type of cake flour used is not on sale, but this recipe gives a very similar effect.

Sachertorte (Chocolate Cake)

3½ oz. shelled hazel-nuts
3½ oz. butter
5 oz. caster sugar
5 large eggs, separated
1 tbsp. rum
3 oz. chocolate dots (cooking chocolate)
1½ oz. dried white breadcrumbs
¼ level tsp. powdered cloves
Chocolate glacé icing *(see below)*
Whipped cream

Oven temperature: fairly hot (400°F., mark 6)

This world-famous Viennese confection, moist-textured, nutty and chocolate-flavoured, is served with lightly whipped cream. It will keep for a day or two.

Grease and line with greaseproof paper the sides and base of a 9-inch straight-sided sandwich tin; the side band should come 1 inch above the edge. Lightly brown the hazel-nuts under the grill, then place in a paper bag and rub to remove the skins. Put them through a Baby Mouli or an electric blender to grind them. Cream together the butter and sugar until light and fluffy. Beat in the egg yolks one at a time. Place the rum and chocolate in a basin over hot water to melt. Fold the chocolate into the creamed mixture, with the nuts, crumbs and cloves. Lastly, fold in the stiffly whisked egg whites. When all is evenly mixed, turn the mixture into the tin. Bake in the centre of the oven for 30 minutes, or until well-risen and firm to the touch. Cool the cake on a wire rack. When it is completely cold (or the next day) coat with chocolate glacé icing and decorate with whipped cream.

Chocolate Glacé Icing: Melt 2 oz. cooking chocolate with 2 tbsps. water over a low heat and add 1 tsp. glycerine. Stir in enough sifted icing sugar (approx. 2½ oz.) to give a coating consistency.

Simnel Cake

Originally this cake was baked for Mothering Sunday, in the days when many girls went into service and Mothering Sunday was the one day in the year they were allowed home. It is now more usual to have Simnel Cake at Easter.

There is an amusing legend about the name – some people say that a sister Nell and her brother Simon

Battenburg Cake

were going to make a cake for their mother. They had an argument as to whether to bake the cake or boil it (which was then quite a usual method of cooking a cake). In the end they made a baked and a boiled cake and stuck the two together, giving the characteristic division through the centre. The name of the cake was accordingly formed from their two names!

1¼ lb. bought almond paste
12 oz. currants
4 oz. sultanas
3 oz. mixed candied peel, chopped
8 oz. plain flour
A pinch of salt
1 level tsp. ground cinnamon
1 level tsp. ground nutmeg
6 oz. butter or margarine
6 oz. caster sugar
3 eggs, beaten
Milk to mix
Apricot jam or beaten egg to use under almond paste
Glacé icing (optional)

Oven temperature: warm (325°F., mark 3)

Line a 7-inch cake tin.

Divide the almond paste into three; take one portion and roll it out to a round the size of the cake tin. Using the remaining ingredients and following the method for Rich Christmas Cake, make up the mixture. Put half of it into the prepared tin, smooth and cover with the round of almond paste. Put the remaining cake mixture on top. Bake in the centre of the oven for about 1 hour, lower the heat to cool (300°F., mark 2) and bake for 3 hours, until the cake is golden-brown, firm to the touch and no longer 'sings'. Allow to cool in the tin.

Take another third of the almond paste and roll out to a round the size of the tin; make small balls from the remaining third – eleven is the traditional number. Brush the top of the cake with apricot jam or beaten egg, cover with the round of paste and place the small balls round the edge. Brush the paste with any remaining egg or jam and brown under the grill.

The top of the cake can then be coated with glacé icing, made by mixing 3 tbsps. sifted icing sugar with a little cold water until it will coat the back of the spoon. Decorate the cake with a tiny model chicken or a few coloured sugar eggs.

Battenburg Cake

8 oz. butter or margarine
8 oz. sugar
4 eggs, beaten
8 oz. self-raising flour
Vanilla essence
Milk if necessary
½ oz. cocoa
Raspberry jam
½ lb. almond paste
Caster sugar

Oven temperature: fairly hot (375°F., mark 5)

Line a Swiss roll tin and divide lengthwise with a grease-proof paper "wall".

Combine the fat, sugar, eggs, flour and essence as for a Victoria sandwich *(see page 000)*; put half the mixture into one side of the tin. Add the cocoa to the other half, with a little more milk if necessary, and put into the second side. Bake for 45–50 minutes just above the centre of the oven, until well risen, firm to the touch and just coming away from the paper.

Cool the cakes, trim to equal size and cut each in half. Spread the sides of the strips with the warmed jam and stick them together, alternating the colours and pressing the pieces well together, then coat the whole outside of the cake with jam. Roll out the almond paste thinly in caster sugar, forming an oblong 8 by 10 inches. Wrap it round the cake, seal the join well and trim the edges. Crimp along the top outer edges to make a decorative border and score the top of the cake with a sharp knife to give a criss-cross pattern.

Ratatouille Niçoise, *page 133*

Carnival Macaroni Cheese, *page 143*

Biscuits and Cookies

Shrewsbury Biscuits

4 oz. butter or margarine
4 oz. caster sugar
1 egg, beaten
8 oz. plain flour
2 level tsps. grated lemon rind

Oven temperature: moderate (350°F., mark 4)
Yield: 20–24

Grease 2 baking trays.

Cream the butter and sugar until pale and fluffy. Add the egg a little at a time, beating after each addition. Stir in the flour and lemon rind and mix to a fairly firm dough. Knead lightly and roll out $\frac{1}{8}$–$\frac{1}{4}$ inch thick on a floured board. Cut into rounds with a 2$\frac{1}{2}$-inch fluted cutter and put on the trays. Bake towards the top of the oven for 15–20 minutes, until firm and very lightly browned.

If the dough is rather soft and difficult to handle, wrap it in waxed paper or polythene and leave in a cool place before rolling out.

Variations using Shrewsbury Biscuit Dough
(Yield as above, unless otherwise stated)

Spice Biscuits

Omit the lemon rind and add 1 level tsp. mixed spice and 1 level tsp. ground cinnamon, sifted with the flour.

Vanilla Biscuits

Omit the lemon rind and add a few drops of vanilla essence when beating in the egg.

Fruit Biscuits

Add 2 oz. chopped dried fruit to the mixture with the flour.

Orange Biscuits

Replace the lemon rind by the grated rind of 1 orange.

Cherry Rings

Omit the lemon rind and add 2 oz. chopped glacé cherries with the flour. Roll out the dough and cut into rounds with a 2$\frac{1}{2}$-inch fluted cutter, place the rounds on the baking trays and remove the centre of each biscuit neatly with a 1-inch fluted cutter.

Easter Biscuits

3 oz. butter or margarine
2$\frac{1}{2}$ oz. caster sugar
1 egg, separated
6 oz. self-raising flour
A pinch of salt
1$\frac{1}{2}$ oz. currants
$\frac{1}{2}$ oz. mixed peel, chopped
1–2 tbsps. milk or brandy
A little caster sugar

Oven temperature: fairly hot (400°F., mark 6)
Yield: 15–20

Grease 2 baking trays.

Cream the butter and sugar and beat in the egg yolk. Sift the flour with the salt and fold into the creamed mixture, with the currants and mixed peel. Add enough milk to give a fairly soft dough, cover and leave in a cool place to become firm. Knead lightly on a floured board and roll out $\frac{1}{4}$-inch thick. Cut into rounds, using a fluted cutter about 2$\frac{1}{2}$ inches in diameter. Put on the baking trays and bake for about 20 minutes, until lightly coloured: after 10 minutes baking brush the biscuits with the egg white, sprinkle with sugar and continue cooking.

Flapjacks

4 oz. butter
1 oz. sugar
2 tbsps. golden syrup, warmed
8 oz. rolled oats
$\frac{1}{4}$ level tsp. salt

Oven temperature: fairly hot (375 F., mark 5)

Crisp, delicous, home-baked biscuits are a traditional tea-time favourite.

Grease a tin measuring about 8 by 10 inches.

Beat the butter and sugar together until the mixture is creamy, then stir in the warmed syrup. Mix well and work in the rolled oats and salt. Put the mixture into the tin and bake for 30–45 minutes, until brown. When it is firm, cut into pieces, but leave in the tin until quite cold.

Brandy Snaps

2 oz. butter or margarine
2 oz. caster sugar
2 oz. golden syrup (1 rounded tbsp. approx.)
2 oz. plain flour
½ level tsp. ground ginger
1 tsp. brandy (optional)
Whipped cream

Oven temperature: moderate (350°F., mark 4)
Yield: 10

Grease the handles of several wooden spoons and several baking trays.

Place the butter, sugar and golden syrup in a saucepan and heat slowly until the butter is melted. Take off the heat and stir in the sifted flour and ginger and the brandy (if used). Place teaspoonfuls of the mixture on the baking trays, spacing them 6 inches apart to give plenty of room for spreading. Bake for 8–10 minutes, until golden-brown. Allow to cool for 1–2 minutes, then loosen with a palette knife and roll them round the spoon handles, with the upper surface of each brandy snap on

the outside. When the biscuits have hardened, slip them off gently. (If the biscuits cool too much while still on the tray and become too brittle to roll, return the tray to the oven for a moment to soften them.) Fill the brandy snaps with whipped cream just before serving.

Note: If you have not got enough baking trays, it is quite satisfactory to leave the surplus mixture and bake the brandy snaps in batches until all the mixture is cooked.

Ginger Nuts

4 oz. self-raising flour
½ level tsp. bicarbonate of soda
1–2 level tsps. ground ginger
1 level tsp. ground cinnamon
2 level tsps. caster sugar
2 oz. butter
3 oz. golden syrup

Oven temperature: fairly hot (375°F., mark 5)
Yield: 2 doz. approx.

Sift together the flour, bicarbonate of soda, ginger, cinnamon and sugar. Melt the butter, and stir in the syrup. Stir into the dry ingredients and mix well. Roll the dough into small balls. Place well apart on a greased baking sheet and flatten slightly. Bake just above the centre of the oven for 15–20 minutes. Cool for a few minutes before lifting carefully from the baking sheet. Finish cooling, and store in an airtight tin.

Shortbread

5 oz. plain flour
1 oz. rice flour
2 oz. caster sugar
4 oz. butter or margarine

Oven temperature: warm (325°F., mark 3)
Yield: 6–8

Grease a baking tray.

Sift the flours and add the sugar. Knead in the butter – keep it in one piece and gradually work in the dry ingredients. Knead well and pack into a well-floured shortbread mould or a 7-inch sandwich tin. Turn out on to the baking tray and prick well. Bake until firm and golden – about ¾ hour. Turn out and dredge with sugar. Serve cut into fingers.

Note: The rice flour is a traditional ingredient of shortbread, but it can be omitted, in which case use 6 oz. flour.

Macaroons

1 egg white
2 oz. ground almonds
3½ oz. caster sugar
½ level tsp. almond essence
A few split almonds
A little egg white to glaze

Oven temperature: moderate (350°F., mark 4)
Yield: 10

Line 1–2 baking trays with silicone (non-stick) paper or rice paper.

Whisk the egg white until stiff and fold in the ground almonds, caster sugar and almond essence. Place spoonfuls of the mixture on the baking trays, leaving plenty of room for spreading. (Alternatively, pipe the mixture on to the paper, using a piping bag and ½-inch plain pipe.) Top each biscuit with a split almond and brush with egg white. Bake for 20–25 minutes, until just beginning to colour.

Florentines

3¾ oz. butter or margarine
4 oz. caster sugar
4 oz. chopped nuts (walnuts and almonds mixed if possible)
1 oz. chopped sultanas
1 oz. glacé cherries
1 oz. candied peel, chopped
1 level tbsp. whipped cream
¾ oz. plain flour
4 oz. plain chocolate

Oven temperatue: moderate (350°F., mark 4)
Yield: 10

Line baking trays with silicone (non-stick) paper or rice paper.

Melt the butter, add the sugar and dissolve, then boil together for 1 minute. Add all the other ingredients except the chocolate and mix well. Drop the mixture in small, well-shaped heaps on to the baking trays 5 inches apart and bake for about 10 minutes, until golden-brown. Remove and cool; peel off any rice paper if used, then spread the backs of the biscuits with melted chocolate and mark lines across with a fork.

Bread, Rolls and Buns

INGREDIENTS FOR BREAD-MAKING

The Yeast

DRIED YEAST: This is available in tins and packets and can be stored for up to 6 months. It is in the form of small, hard granules, fawn in colour. Instructions for activating it are usually given by the manufacturer on the packet or tin, but we give directions in this chapter under 'Processes in Bread-making'. You should remember that it will take 10–15 minutes to activate, longer than for fresh yeast.

To measure $\frac{1}{4}$ oz. dried yeast, which is required in some recipes, you can take 2 level tsps. as the equivalent.

FRESH (BAKER'S) YEAST: Since this does not keep more than a few days, it must be bought in small quantities only. It looks rather like putty in colour and texture and should have a faint 'winey' smell. When stored in a polythene bag in a cool place, it will keep for 1–3 days, depending on its freshness when bought; in a refrigerator it will keep for up to a month – again, according to how fresh it was when bought. To freeze fresh yeast, weigh out into $\frac{1}{4}$-oz., $\frac{1}{2}$-oz. or 1-oz. cubes, whichever quantity you normally use; wrap individually in polythene and pack in a polythene bag or screw-top jar. Store for up to 1 year. To use, grate it from the frozen state, or thaw at room temperature for 30 minutes. (As soon as the outside of the yeast becomes dark and the yeast itself is dry and crumbly, it is no longer suitable for use and must be discarded.) Full instructions for using fresh yeast are given under 'Processes in Bread-making'.

When substituting fresh yeast for dried, remember you will need twice as much; thus 1 oz. fresh yeast is the equivalent of $\frac{1}{2}$ oz. dried yeast.

The Flour

The type to use depends of course on the bread being made, but it must always be a plain flour – self-raising flour should not be used, as it gives a close, cake-like texture. The best results are obtained by using a proper 'bread' or 'strong' flour, e.g. MacDougall's 'Country Life'. Although this is not sold very widely, most grocers will order if it asked, and sometimes a local baker will supply it.

These are other speciality flours:

WHOLEMEAL: 100 per cent wheat, e.g. Prewitt.

WHEATMEAL: 81–95 per cent wheat (i.e. some of the bran is removed), e.g. Allinson.

STONE-GROUND: More expensive, but of very good flavour, since the heat arising during the grinding 'toasts' the flour slightly. Available as wholemeal and wheatmeal.

RYE FLOUR: Gives the typical Continental rye bread.

PROCESSES IN BREAD-MAKING

The processes used in making the plainest of all yeast mixtures – household bread – from the basis of the method followed for nearly all yeast cookery. Richer mixtures have of course such additions as fat, sugar, spices and fruit, but they too are made by the same basic method.

MIXING THE DRY INGREDIENTS: Mix together the flour and salt in the proportions of 2 level tsps. salt to 1 lb. flour.

WARMING: For yeast mixtures the bowl, the flour and the liquid used for mixing should all be warmed. Liquids should be at about blood heat, 98°F., i.e. so that they feel just warm when tested with the little finger. Once the dough is mixed, it must be kept warm and away from draughts. On the other hand, too great a heat kills the yeast, so neither the mixing liquid nor the place where the dough is put to rise must be really hot.

ADDING FAT: Fat is not essential for plain mixtures, but the addition of a small amount helps to keep the bread moist. When used, it is generally rubbed into the warmed flour and salt, but in richer mixtures, when more fat is used, it can be melted and added with the liquid ingredients or flaked on to the basic dough, as for flaky pastry. Oil may be added instead of fat.

ACTIVATING THE YEAST: This varies according to the kind of yeast used.

DRIED YEAST: Take ½ cup (about ¼ pint) of the liquid given in the recipe, warm it to blood heat and dissolve 1 level tsp. sugar in it. Pour into a cup and sprinkle on the yeast, whisking with a fork. Leave to stand in a warm place for 10–15 minutes, or until the surface of the liquid is covered with bubbles and the yeast granules have dissolved. Stir the mixture lightly and use as stated in the individual recipe.

FRESH YEAST: Crumble the yeast into the basin. Warm about ½ cup (¼ pint) of the liquid and add it gradually to the yeast; stir until well blended and dissolved.

MIXING THE DOUGH: Add the liquid – whether water, milk, beaten eggs, melted fat or a combination of any of these ingredients – to the yeast all at once. Using a wooden spoon, mix with the dry ingredients until really well blended. Never let the dough get too stiff, or it will produce heavy, 'close' bread. The consistency of the dough will depend on the type of yeast mixture being made and is stated in each recipe.

KNEADING: This process strengthens and develops the gluten, making the dough elastic in texture, which enables it to rise more easily. It may be done in the bowl, but it is usually easier to knead on a floured board, which permits both hands to be used. Turn the dough round as you work and make sure it is all kneaded. Allow about 10 minutes' kneading for 3 lb. of flour. Continue kneading until the dough is firm and elastic and no longer sticky.

RISING: Place the prepared dough in a lightly oiled polythene bag or lidded container and leave to rise. It will take 24 hours in a refrigerator (and requires a further hour to return to room temperature); 12 hours in a cold room or larder; 2 hours at room temperature; 45 minutes in a warm place (e.g., above the cooker or in an airing cupboard, but take care, as too much heat at this stage will destroy the yeast).

PREPARING THE TINS: While the dough is rising, grease some bread tins or baking trays and flour them lightly.

SHAPING: Turn the risen dough on to a lightly floured board and knead it for 2–3 minutes to break down any large bubbles. Shape each piece by folding into three, or by rolling up like a Swiss roll, tucking in the ends so that the piece of dough fits the tin exactly, or by shaping into rolls, allowing approx. 2 oz. dough per roll. Place on a greased baking sheet.

PROVING: Put the filled tins or baking sheets inside a lightly oiled polythene bag, tie loosely and leave to rise until the dough is doubled in bulk and will spring back when lightly pressed with the finger.

BAKING: Bread is baked in a very hot oven (450°F., mark 8) for about 35 minutes. The cooked bread should be well risen and golden-brown and when

tapped underneath with the knuckles, it should sound hollow. Cool it on a wire tray.

Richer breads are often cooked at a slightly lower temperature between hot (425°F., mark 7) and fairly hot (375°F., mark 5), as they tend to burn more easily than plain bread.

GLAZING: Many of the richer breads, buns and cakes are brushed over with sugar glaze when they are taken from the oven – *see individual recipes*. Alternatively, an egg glaze may be used before baking; the addition of a little salt ensures a really professional finish. Plain salted water is used on wholemeal bread and rolls.

White Bread

1½ lb. bread flour
1 level tbsp. salt
½ oz. lard
½ oz. fresh yeast
¾ pint tepid water

Oven temperature: very hot (450°F., mark 8)

Prepare as described under 'Processes in Breadmaking'.

Shape into 1 large loaf and put into a 2-lb. tin, or into 2 small loaves and put into two 1-lb. tins. Prove, and bake for 35–40 minutes.

Quick White Loaf

¼ oz. dried yeast
¼ pint tepid water (approx.)
1 lb. plain flour
1–2 level tsps. salt

Oven temperature: very hot (450°F., mark 8)

Activate the yeast with about ¼ pint of the water. Mix the flour and salt, make a well in the centre and add the yeast and remaining water. Mix to an elastic dough, adding more water if necessary. Turn on to a floured board and knead for about 10 minutes, until really smooth. Divide the dough into 2 portions and put into 2 small prepared tins; allow to rise until the dough fills the tins and bake as already described.

The unrisen dough can also be divided in half, made into 2 round cakes, left to rise on a greased baking tray for 30–45 minutes and baked as for ordinary bread – allow 30–40 minutes.

If the dough is made into rolls, bake for 15–20 minutes.

QUICK CHEESE LOAF

Use the above recipe, but add 4 oz. finely grated Cheddar cheese, 1 level tsp. dry mustard and ½ level tsp. pepper to the flour and salt.

MILK BREAD

Use the same basic recipe and method as for White Bread (basic recipe), but rub 2 oz. lard or butter into the dry ingredients and mix the dough with milk or milk and water. This gives a close-textured loaf with a softer crust.

Wholemeal Bread

2 oz. fresh yeast
1½ pints water
3 lb. plain wholemeal flour
2 level tbsps. caster sugar
2 level tbsps. salt
1 oz. lard

Oven temperatue: very hot (450°F., mark 8)

Blend the yeast with ½ pint of the water. Mix the flour, sugar and salt; rub in the lard. Stir the yeast liquid into the dry ingredients, adding sufficient of the remaining water to make a firm dough that leaves the bowl clean. Turn it out on to a lightly floured surface and knead until it feels firm and elastic and no longer sticky. Shape it into a ball and leave to rise until doubled in size.

Turn the dough out on to a floured surface and knead again until firm. Divide into 2 or 4 pieces and flatten firmly with the knuckles to knock out any air bubbles. Shape to fit two 2-lb. or four 1-lb. tins. Brush tops with salted water and prove until the dough rises to the top of the tins – about 1 hour at room temperature.

Bake the loaves in the centre of the oven for 30–40 minutes. Cool on a wire rack.

Alternative Shapings
1. Divide each quarter-portion of dough into 4 smaller pieces, shape into rolls and fit side by side into the tin. Finish as above.
2. Shape each quarter-portion of dough into a round cob, dust with flour and put on a floured baking sheet. Fish as before.
3. Shape all the dough into a round cob and place on a large floured baking sheet. Partly cut into 4 wedges and scatter cracked wheat or flour over the top. Allow to rise, mark again and bake for 40–45 minutes.

Malt Bread

1 oz. fresh yeast
¼ pint water (approx.)
1 lb. plain household flour (*not* bread flour)
1 level tsp. salt
4 level tbsps. malt
1 level tbsp. black treacle
1 oz. butter or margarine
Sugar and water glaze (optional)

Oven temperature: fairly hot (400°F., mark 6)

Dissolve the yeast in the water in the usual way. Mix the flour and salt. Warm the malt, treacle and fat till just melted. Stir the yeast and malt mixtures into the dry ingredients and mix to a fairly soft, sticky dough, adding a little water if necessary. Turn on to a floured board, knead well and divide into two pieces. Shape both into an oblong, roll up like a Swiss roll and put into two prepared 1-lb..loaf tins. Leave to rise until the

dough fills the tins (this may take about 1½ hours, as malt bread dough usually takes quite a long time to rise). Bake in the centre of the oven for 30–40 minutes. When cooked the loaves can be brushed with a sugar glaze (1 level tbsp. sugar to 1 tbsp. water).

Bridge Rolls

1 level tsp. sugar
¼ pint milk (approx.)
¼ oz. dried yeast
8 oz. plain flour
1 level tsp. salt
2 oz. butter or margarine
1 egg, beaten

Oven temperature: hot (425 F., mark 7)

Dissolve the sugar in the milk and activate the yeast in the usual way. Mix the flour and salt and rub in the fat. Add the yeast and egg and mix to a fairly soft dough, adding a little extra milk if necessary. Beat and knead the dough lightly until smooth and allow to rise until doubled in size. Knead lightly on a floured board, then cut into 12–16 pieces. Make each into a finger or roll shape and place fairly close together in rows on a greased baking tray. Allow to prove for 15–20 minutes. Bake near the top of the oven for about 15 minutes. These rolls can be brushed with beaten egg before cooking, to give a glazed finish.

Milk Rolls

1 level tsp. sugar
¼ pint milk (approx.)
¼ oz. dried yeast
8 oz. plain flour
1 level tsp. salt
1 oz. margarine or lard

Oven temperature: hot (425°F., mark 7)

Dissolve the sugar in the milk and activate the yeast as usual. Mix the flour and salt and rub in the fat. Add the yeast and milk and mix to a fairly soft dough, adding a little more milk if necessary. Beat and knead the dough until smooth. Allow to rise until doubled in size, knead lightly on a floured board, divide into 8 pieces and shape in any of the following ways:

PLAIT: Divide the small piece of dough into three, shape each into a long roll and plait together, joining the ends securely.

TWIST: Divide a piece of dough into two, shape into long rolls, twist together and secure the ends.

COTTAGE LOAF: Cut two-thirds off a piece of dough and make into a bun shape; treat the remaining one-third in the same way; damp the smaller one, place on top of the larger one and secure by pushing your little finger right through the centre.

KNOTS: Shape each piece into a long roll and tie in a knot.

ROUND: Place the pieces on a very slightly floured board and roll each into a ball. To do this, hold the hand flat almost at table level and move it round in a circular motion, gradually lifting the palm to get a good round shape.

RINGS: Make a long roll with each piece of dough and bend it round to form a ring; damp the ends and mould them together.

Put the shaped rolls on a greased baking tray and allow to prove for 15–20 minutes. Bake near the top of the oven for about 15 minutes, until golden-brown and cooked. The rolls can if you wish be brushed with milk or beaten egg before cooking, to give a glazed finish.

Sally Lunn

2 oz. butter
¼ pint milk plus 4 tbsps.
1 level tsp. caster sugar
2 eggs
½ oz. fresh yeast or 2 level tsps. dried yeast
1 lb. strong plain flour
1 level tsp. salt
Sugar glaze (see below)

Oven temperature: very hot (450°F., mark 8)

Well grease two 5-inch round cake tins.
Melt the butter slowly in a pan, remove from the heat and add the milk and sugar. Beat the eggs and add with the warm milk mixture to the yeast. Blend well. Add to the flour and salt, mix well and lightly knead. Put into the cake tins and leave to rise in a warm place until the dough fills the tins – about ¾–1 hour. Bake just above the centre of the oven for 15–20 minutes. Turn the Sally Lunns out of the tins on to a wire rack, and glaze while still hot.

Glaze: Put 1 tbsp. water and 1 tbsp. sugar in a small pan, heat to boiling point and boil for a further 2 minutes; use at once.

Lardy Cake

1 level tsp. caster sugar for yeast
½ pint warm water
2 level tsps. dried yeast
1 lb. strong plain flour
2 level tsps. salt
Cooking oil
2 oz. butter
4 oz. caster sugar
1 level tsp. powdered mixed spice
3 oz. sultanas or currants
2 oz. lard

Oven temperature: hot (425°F., mark 7)

Grease a tin measuring 10 by 8 inches.

Dissolve the 1 tsp. sugar in the water, add the yeast and leave in a warm place until frothing – about 10 minutes. Sift the flour and salt into a basin and stir in the yeast mixture, with 1 tbsp. oil and enough water to give a soft dough. Beat until smooth. Leave in a warm place to rise until doubled in size.
Turn the dough out on to a lightly floured surface and knead for 5–10 minutes. Roll out to a strip ¼-inch thick. Cover two-thirds of the dough with small flakes of butter and 1½ oz. sugar, and sprinkle with half the spice and half the dried fruit. Fold and roll out as for flaky pastry. Repeat the process with the lard, 1½ oz. sugar and the remaining spice and fruit. Fold and roll once more. Place the dough in the prepared tin, pressing it down so that it fills the corners. Cover, and leave to rise in a warm place until doubled in size. Brush with oil, sprinkle with the remaining caster sugar and mark criss-cross fashion with a knife. Bake in the centre of the oven for about 30 minutes. Cool on a wire rack. Serve sliced, plain or with butter.

Hot Cross Buns

1 lb. strong plain flour
1 oz. fresh yeast or 1 level tbsp. dried yeast
1 level tsp. caster sugar for yeast
¼ pint milk
¼ pint water, less 4 tbsps.
1 level tsp. salt
½ level tsp. mixed spice
½ level tsp. powdered cinnamon
⅓ level tsp. grated nutmeg
2 oz. caster sugar
2 oz. butter, melted and cooled, but not firm
1 egg, beaten
4 oz. currants
1–2 oz. chopped mixed peel

For the Glaze
4 tbsps. milk and water
1½ oz. caster sugar

Oven temperature: fairly hot (375°F., mark 5)

Flour a baking sheet.
Place 4 oz. of the flour in a large mixing bowl and add the yeast and 1 level tsp. sugar. Warm the milk and water to about 110°F., add to the flour and mix well. Set aside in a warm place until frothy – 20 minutes for fresh yeast, 30 minutes for dried. Sift together the remaining 12 oz. flour, the salt, spices and 2 oz. sugar. Stir the butter and egg into the frothy yeast mixture, add the spiced flour and the fruit, and mix together. The dough should be fairly soft. Turn it out on to a lightly floured surface and knead until smooth. Leave to rise until doubled in size – about 1–1½ hours. Turn the risen dough out on to a floured surface and knock out the air bubbles, then knead.
Divide the dough into 12 pieces and shape into buns, using the palm of one hand. Press down hard at first on the table surface, then ease up as you turn and shape the buns. Arrange them well apart on the floured baking sheet, and prove for about 45 minutes (only 30

minutes if the dough has had an initial rising). Make quick slashes with a very sharp knife or razor, just cutting the surface of the dough, to make a cross. Bake just above the centre of the oven for 15–20 minutes. Brush the hot buns twice with glaze, then leave to cool.

Doughnuts

1 level tsp. sugar
4 tbsps. milk (approx.)
¼ oz. dried yeast
8 oz. plain flour
½ level tsp. salt
½ oz. butter or margarine
1 egg, beaten
Jam
Deep fat for frying
Sugar and ground cinnamon to coat

Dissolve the 1 tsp. sugar in the milk and activate the yeast in the usual way. Mix the flour and salt and rub in the fat. Add the yeast and egg and mix to a soft dough, adding a little more milk if necessary. Beat well until smooth and leave to rise until doubled in size. Knead lightly on a floured board and divide into 10–12 pieces. Shape each into a round, put 1 tsp. stiff jam in the centre and draw up the edges to form a ball, pressing firmly to seal them together. Heat the fat to 360°F. (it will brown a 1-inch cube of bread in 60 seconds). Fry the doughnuts fairly quickly until golden-brown (for 5–10 minutes, according to size). Drain on crumpled kitchen paper and toss in sugar mixed with a little cinnamon (if liked). Serve the same day they are made.

Devonshire Splits

1 level tsp. sugar
½ pint milk (approx.)
¼ oz. dried yeast
1 lb. plain flour
1 level tsp. salt
2 oz. butter
1 oz. sugar
Devonshire or whipped cream and jam

Oven temperature: hot (425°F., mark 7)

Dissolve the sugar in ¼ pint of the milk and activate the yeast in the usual way. Mix the flour and salt, dissolve the butter and sugar in the remaining milk and when at blood heat, stir into a well in the centre of the flour with the yeast. Beat to an elastic dough and knead until smooth. Allow to rise until doubled in size, then turn it on to a lightly floured board and divide into 14–16 pieces. Knead each lightly into a ball, place on a greased baking tray and flatten slightly with the hand. Prove for about 20 minutes and bake near the top of the oven for 15–20 minutes.

Before serving, split them and spread with jam and Devonshire or whipped cream, then sprinkle the tops with icing sugar.

Chelsea Buns

8 oz. strong plain flour
½ level tsp. sugar
½ oz. fresh yeast
4 fl. oz. warm milk
½ level tsp. salt
½ oz. butter or lard
1 egg, beaten
Melted butter
3 oz. dried fruit
1 oz. chopped mixed peel
2 oz. soft brown sugar
Clear honey to glaze

Oven temperature: fairly hot (375°F., mark 5)

Grease a 7-inch square cake tin.

Put 2 oz. of the flour in a large bowl and blend together with the sugar, yeast and milk until smooth. Set aside in a warm place until the batter froths – 20–30 minutes. Mix in the remaining flour and the salt; rub in the fat and add the egg to give a fairly soft dough that will leave the side of the bowl clean after beating. Turn the dough out on to a lightly floured surface and knead until it is smooth – about 5 minutes. Leave to rise for 1–1½ hours.

Knead the dough thoroughly and roll out to an oblong 12 by 9 inches. Brush with melted butter and cover with a mixture of dried fruit, peel and brown sugar. Roll up from the longest side like a Swiss roll, and seal the edge with water. Cut into 9 equal-sized slices and place these, cut side down, in the prepared cake tin. Prove until the dough feels springy – about 30 minutes. Bake the buns just above the centre of the oven for about 30 minutes.

While they are still warm, brush them with a wetted brush dipped in honey.

Bath Buns

1 lb. strong plain flour
1 oz. fresh yeast
1 level tsp. caster sugar
¼ pint milk
¼ pint water, less 4 tbsps.
1 level tsp. salt
2 oz. caster sugar
2 oz. butter, melted and cooled, but not firm
2 eggs, beaten
6 oz. sultanas
1–2 oz. chopped mixed peel
Beaten egg and crushed sugar lumps for topping

Oven temperature: fairly hot (375°F., mark 5)

Put 4 oz. of the flour in a large mixing bowl. Add the crumbled yeast and 1 level tsp. sugar. Warm the milk and water to about 110°F.; add to the 4 oz. flour and mix well. Set aside in a warm place until frothy – about 20 minutes. Sift together the remaining flour and salt and add the 2 oz. sugar. Stir the butter and eggs into the frothy mixture, add the flour, sultanas and peel and mix well – the dough is fairly soft. Turn it out on to a

Devonshire Splits

floured surface and knead until smooth. Leave it to rise in a covered bowl until doubled in size. When it is ready, beat well. Place in about 18 tbsps. on greased baking sheets, cover and leave to rise. Brush with egg and sprinkle with crushed sugar. Bake towards top of oven for about 15 minutes, until golden; cool on a rack. Serve buttered.

Rum Babas

1 oz. fresh baker's yeast
6 tbsps. warm milk
8 oz. strong plain flour
½ level tsp. salt
1 oz. caster sugar
4 eggs, beaten
4 oz. butter, soft but not melted
4 oz. currants
Whipped cream

For the Rum Syrup
4 tbsps. clear honey
4 tbsps. water
Rum to taste

Oven temperature: fairly hot (400°F., mark 6)

Lightly grease about 16 small ring tins with lard.

Put the yeast, milk and 2 oz. of the flour in a bowl and blend until smooth. Allow to stand in a warm place until frothy – about 20 minutes. Add the remaining flour, the salt, sugar, eggs, butter and currants, and beat well for 3–4 minutes. Half-fill the tins with the dough and allow to rise until the moulds are two-thirds full. Bake near the top of the oven for 15–20 minutes. Cool for a few minutes, then turn out on to a wire tray.

While the babas are still hot, spoon over each sufficient rum syrup to soak it well. Leave to cool. Served with whipped cream in the centre.

Rum Syrup: Warm together the honey and water and add rum (or rum essence) to taste.

Savarin

Oven temperature: fairly hot (400°F., mark 6)

Make up the same mixtures as for Rum Babas, but put into one large ring tin, with no currants at the bottom. Bake just above the centre of the oven for about 40 minutes, or until golden and shrinking away from the sides of the tin. Turn out straight away and allow to cool. Soak with rum syrup (*see Baba recipe*), brush with sieved apricot jam and serve on a dish surrounded by fruit salad and topped with whipped cream.

Quick Bread

1 oz. butter or margarine
1 lb. self-raising flour (or 1 lb. plain bread flour and 4 level tsps. baking powder)
1 level tsp. salt
1 egg, beaten
½ pint milk or milk and water (approx.)

Oven temperature: hot (425 F., mark 7)

Grease a baking tray.

Rub the fat into the flour and salt until the mixture resembles fine breadcrumbs. Make a well in the centre, pour in the egg and some of the milk or milk and water and gradually work in the dry ingredients, adding more liquid if necessary to give a soft dough. Knead very lightly on a floured board, shape into a round, plait or twist and brush with milk or egg. Place on the baking tray and bake towards the top of the oven for about 30–35 minutes.

Raisin Malt Loaf

8 oz. plain flour
¼ level tsp. salt
1 oz. soft brown sugar
1 level tsp. bicarbonate of soda
5 oz. seedless raisins
2 oz. golden syrup
2 tbsps. malt
¼ pint milk (approx.)

Oven temperature: warm (325°F., mark 3)

Grease and line an oblong loaf tin about 8½ by 4½ inches (top measurements). Sift the flour, salt, sugar and bicarbonate of soda; add the raisins. Melt the syrup and malt in half of the milk. Make a well in the centre of the dry ingredients and pour in the milk mixture; gradually work in the dry ingredients, adding more milk to give a sticky, stiff consistency. Put into the tin and bake in the middle of the oven for 1–1¼ hours. Keep for 24 hours before serving sliced and buttered.

Home Made Sweets

Equipment

SUGAR-BOILING THERMOMETER: Necessary for measuring temperature accurately – which often spells the difference between success and failure and makes a good result a matter of certainty rather than luck.

Choose a thermometer which is easy to read and well graduated from 60°F. to 360°F. or 450°F. These thermometers are usually mounted on brass, with a brass or wooden handle; it is useful to have a sliding clip that fits over the side of the pan.

To 'season' a new thermometer, place it in cold water, bring to the boil and leave in the water to cool.

To check a thermometer, try it in boiling water (212°F.) and note if it is at all inaccurate.

When using the thermometer, shake it well so that the mercury thread is unbroken and see that the bulb is completely immersed in the mixture. When the thermometer is not actually in the sweet mixture, stand it in hot water Clean it very thoroughly, as any sugar crystals left on might spoil the next boiling.

SAUCEPAN: This must be strong and thick-based, to prevent burning and sticking. Cast aluminium is a good choice; enamel is not suitable, as high temperatures may crack the lining.

SPATULA: A wooden spatula is useful for 'working' fondant mixtures and beating fudges.

FLEXIBLE-BLADED PALETTE KNIFE: One with a stainless steel blade is useful for lifting and shaping sweets.

MARBLE SLAB: Expensive to buy and not absolutely essential, since an enamelled surface can be used instead. Certain plastic surfaces will also withstand temperatures up to 280°F., but usually not beyond this.

Equipment for more Advanced Sweet-making

RUBBER FONDANT MAT: Consists of a sheet of rubber, 1-inch thick, with fancy-shaped impressions into which liquid fondant, jelly or chocolate is run and allowed to set. When the shapes are firm, they can easily be removed by bending back the rubber.

CREAM RINGS: These metal circles are useful for moulding peppermint creams and similar sweets.

DIPPING FORKS: Small forks with 2–3 wire prongs or a loop at the end; they are used for lifting sweets out or coating fondant or chocolate, the prongs or loops also serve to make a raised design on the top of the sweets.

Sugar Boiling

This process is the basis of all sweet-making. The sugar is first dissolved in the liquid, then brought to the boil (212°F.). The temperature continues to rise as the water is evaporated; the syrup thickens and then becomes darker in colour as the temperature rises – at 350°F. it is a very dark brown. The table below shows the most important stages.

To measure the temperature really accurately you need a sugar-boiling thermometer (see above), but for simple sweets you can use the homely tests described in the table.

SMOOTH (215°F.–220°F.): For crystallising purposes.

The mixture begins to look syrupy. To test, dip the fingers in water and then very quickly in the syrup; the thumb will slide smoothly over the fingers, but the sugar clings to the finger.

SOFT BALL (235°F.–245°F.): For fondants and fudges.

When a drop of the syrup is put into very cold water, it forms a soft ball; at 235°F. the soft ball flattens on being removed from the water, but the higher the temperature, the firmer the ball, till it reaches the next, Firm Ball, stage.

FIRM OR HARD BALL (245°F.–265°F.): For caramels, marshmallows and nougat.

When dropped into cold water, the syrup forms a ball which is hard enough to hold its shape, but is still plastic.

SOFT CRACK (270°F.–290°F.): For toffees.

When dropped into cold water, the syrup separates into threads which are hard but not brittle.

HARD CRACK (300°F.–310°F.): For hard toffees and rock.

When a drop of the syrup is put into cold water, it separates into threads which are hard and brittle.

CARAMEL (310°F.): For praline and caramels.

Shown by the syrup becoming golden-brown.

Crystallisation

Sugar must be dissolved and boiled with great care, as the syrup has a tendency to re-crystallise if incorrectly handled. These are the main causes of crystallisation:

(*a*) Agitation of the mixture by stirring or beating.

(*b*) The presence of solid particles, e.g. sugar crystals, during the boiling.

To obtain a clear syrup, note the following points:

(*a*) The pan must be clean.

(*b*) The sugar must be completely dissolved before boiling.

(*c*) If crystals do form, brush the sides of the pan with a brush dipped in cold water.

(*d*) Don't stir the mixture unless the recipe specifically calls for this. You can however use a wooden spatula to tap the grains of sugar on to the bottom of the pan to hasten the process.

(*e*) Once the sugar has dissolved and been brought to the boil, it can be heated rapidly to the required temperature. Remove it immediately from the heat, so that the temperature does not rise any higher.

(*f*) Glucose, honey or golden syrup ($\frac{1}{4}$ lb. to $1\frac{1}{2}$ lb. sugar) or a pinch of cream of tartar or a squeeze of lemon juice may be added; any of these will convert some of the sugar into 'invert' sugar, which does not crystallise so readily. Remember, however, that sweets made with glucose soften more quickly, so that while it is useful in making fondants, cream of tartar is of more use for other types of sweet.

FONDANTS

Fondant forms the basis of a large number of sweets and chocolate centres and is also used for icing cakes. To prepare it, dissolve 1 lb. sugar in $\frac{1}{4}$ pint water and boil the syrup to a temperature of 240°F.–245°F., following the general directions for sugar-boiling. Cool it on a marble slab or cool surface and 'work' it until it becomes opaque and firm. If necessary, thin it by adding more syrup; you can enrich the fondant by adding cream or milk.

Any fondant that is not required for immediate use may be stored in a covered jar or tin.

Boiled Fondant

$\frac{1}{4}$ pint water (good measure)
1 lb. granulated sugar
1 oz. glucose or a good pinch of cream of tartar

Put the water into a pan, add the sugar and let it dissolve slowly. Bring the syrup to the boil, add the

glucose or cream of tartar and boil to 240°F. Sprinkle a little water on a marble slab or other suitable surface, pour on the syrup and leave for a few minutes to cool. When a skin forms round the edges, take the spatula and collect the mixture together, then work it backwards and forwards, using a figure-of-eight movement. Continue to work the syrup, collecting it into as small a compass as possible, until it changes its character and 'grains', becoming opaque and firm. Scrape it off the slab and knead it in the hands until of an even texture throughout.

Use as required, or store as described above.

Note: If no slab is available, the fondant can be 'turned' in a bowl; leave it in the bowl for $\frac{1}{4}$ hour to cool, 'turn' it in the bowl until thick, then knead it on greaseproof paper.

Fondant Creams

Prepare some fondant and knead it well (particularly if it has been stored for some time). To improve the texture and flavour, add a little cream, evaporated milk or melted butter. (If you are using freshly made fondant, add the cream, milk or butter while the fondant is still melted.) Divide the mixture into portions and flavour and colour as required, e.g. with lemon, violet, coffee, etc. Roll the fondant out to the required thickness, using a little icing sugar on the board, and cut out with a small cutter or model it by hand.

To obtain fancy shapes, or to make chocolate centres, melt the fondant in a basin over a pan of hot water or in a double saucepan over a very gentle heat; use a little sugar syrup (or a few drops of water) to help to liquefy it. When it is liquid, pour it into moulds in a rubber fondant mat, using a funnel or a teaspoon.

FONDANT FRUITS: Cubes of crystallised ginger, glacé pineapple, bunches of raisins or grapes, Cape gooseberries and many other fruits may be dipped in liquid fondant (coloured if liked). Place them in paper cases when dry.

MOCHA NUTS: Flavour the liquid fondant with coffee and dip halved walnuts and whole Brazil nuts in it.

PEPPERMINT CREAMS: Knead a few drops of oil of peppermint into the fondant, roll it out $\frac{1}{4}$ inch thick and cut into rounds with a 1-inch cutter.

MARZIPAN

Boiled Marzipan

1 lb. loaf sugar
$\frac{1}{4}$ pint water
A pinch of cream of tartar
$\frac{3}{4}$ lb. ground almonds
2 egg whites
3 oz. icing sugar, sifted

Put the sugar and water into a pan and dissolve over

a low heat. When the syrup reaches boiling point, add the cream of tartar and boil to a temperature of 240°F. Remove the pan from the heat and stir rapidly until the syrup begins to 'grain'. Stir in the ground almonds and egg whites and cook for a few minutes over a low heat, stirring well.

Pour on to an oiled surface (marble or enamelled iron), add the icing sugar and work well with a palette knife, lifting the edges of the mixture and pressing them into the centre. As soon as the mixture is sufficiently cool, knead until smooth. Additional icing sugar may be kneaded in if required.

If necessary, the marzipan may be wrapped in greaseproof paper and stored in a cool place for 2–3 weeks.

MARZIPAN DATES: Choose best-quality dessert dates, remove the stones and fill the cavities with coloured marzipan. Roll them in caster sugar and place in paper cases.

MARZIPAN FRUITS: Mould the marzipan to resemble small fruits – for example, oranges, apples, bananas, pears. Paint them with edible colourings and use cloves for stalks.

MARZIPAN WALNUTS: Colour a small quantity of marzipan, roll it into little balls and press a halved walnut into the top of each.

NEAPOLITAN SLICES: Roll out lengths of marzipan in two contrasting colours and enclose them in a thin sheet of plain marzipan, shaping the whole to resemble a small Battenberg cake about 1 inch across. Brush with a little sugar syrup or gum arabic, then cut into $\frac{1}{4}$-inch slices; the pieces can if you wish be dipped into melted chocolate.

Turkish Delight

$\frac{1}{2}$ pint hot water
1 oz. powdered gelatine
1 lb. sugar
$\frac{1}{4}$ level tsp. citric acid
A few drops of vanilla essence
A few drops of almond essence
Cochineal
2 oz. icing sugar
1 oz. cornflour

Put the water in a pan. Sprinkle the gelatine over it, add the sugar and citric acid and heat slowly until the sugar has dissolved. Bring to the boil, boil for 20 minutes, remove from the heat and leave to stand for 10 minutes without stirring. Add the flavourings and divide the mixture, putting half in a tin measuring about 8 by 6 inches. Add a few drops of cochineal to the second half and pour it over the first layer. Leave in a cool place for 24 hours.

Sift the icing sugar and cornflour together and sprinkle evenly over a piece of paper. Turn the Turkish Delight out on to this paper and cut into squares with a sharp knife. Toss well in the sugar mixture, pack in greaseproof paper and store in an airtight tin. (*Makes 1$\frac{1}{4}$ lb. approx.*)

FUDGES

Vanilla Fudge

1 lb. granulated sugar
2 oz. butter
$\frac{1}{4}$ pint evaporated milk
$\frac{1}{4}$ pint milk
A few drops of vanilla essence

Grease a tin 8 by 6 inches.

Put the sugar, butter and milks into a 5-pint heavy-based saucepan and heat gently until the sugar has dissolved and the fat melted. Bring to the boil and boil steadily to 240°F. (soft ball stage), stirring occasionally. Remove the pan from the heat, place on a cool surface, add the essence and beat until the mixture becomes thick and creamy and 'grains' – i.e. until minute crystals form. Pour it immediately into the tin. Leave until nearly cold and mark into squares with a sharp knife, using a sawing motion. When it is firm, cut into squares.

Makes 1 lb. approx.

Chocolate Fudge

1 lb. granulated sugar
$\frac{1}{4}$ pint milk
5 oz. butter
4 oz. plain chocolate
2 oz. honey

Grease a tin 8 by 6 inches.

Place all the ingredients into a 5-pint heavy-based saucepan. Stir over a low heat until the sugar has dissolved. Bring to the boil and boil to 240°F. (soft ball stage). Remove from the heat, stand the pan on a cool surface for 5 minutes, then beat the mixture until thick, creamy and beginning to 'grain'. Pour into the tin, mark into squares and cut when cold.

Makes 1$\frac{1}{2}$ lb. approx.

MARSHMALLOW FUDGE. Add $\frac{1}{2}$ lb. chopped marshmallows to the mixture before beating; continue as above.

FRUIT AND NUT FUDGE: Add 2 oz. chopped nuts and 2 oz. seedless raisins; continue as above.

DATE FUDGE: Replace the $\frac{1}{4}$ pint ordinary milk by $\frac{1}{4}$ pint water and add 3 oz. dates, finely chopped.

TOFFEES

A toffee is basically a simple sugar mixture, requiring to be boiled to a high temperature – 280°F. to 310°F., according to type. These are important points to remember when making toffee:

1. You must use a large, heavy-based pan, as toffee tends to boil over.
2. Don't stir the mixture unless the recipe definitely states this should be done.
3. Move the thermometer from time to time, as the toffee may stick to the bulb and give an inaccurate reading.
4. Keep the heat very low after the mixture reaches 260°F.

Turkish Delight

5. Remove the pan from the heat when the mixture has reached a temperature about 5° below the figure required, because the pan holds the heat, so the mixture may be over-boiled. Make sure, however, that the toffee does actually come to the correct temperature.

6. Pour the mixture into the prepared tin as soon as the correct temperature is reached.

Nougat

Rice paper
3 oz. honey
3 egg whites
2 oz. glacé cherries, chopped
1 oz. angelica, chopped
5 oz. almonds, chopped
12 oz. sugar
¼ pint water
2 oz. glucose
Vanilla essence

Damp the inside of a tin 12 by 4 inches (or a 7-inch square in) and line it with rice paper.

Melt the honey in a basin over hot water, add the stiffly beaten egg whites and continue to beat until the mixture is pale and thick. Add the cherries and angelica to the almonds. Dissolve the sugar in the water in a small heavy-based saucepan. Add glucose and boil to 266°F. (soft crack stage). Pour this syrup on to the honey mixture, add the vanilla essence and continue beating over hot water until a little of the mixture forms a hard ball when tested in cold water. This may take 30–40 minutes, but is very important if the nougat is to set firmly. Add the fruit and nuts and put the mixture into the tin. Cover with rice paper, put some weights on top and leave until quite cold. Cut into pieces and wrap in waxed paper.

Makes 1¼ lb. approx.

Treacle Toffee

1 lb. demerara sugar
¼ pint water
3 oz. butter
¼ level tsp. cream of tartar
4 oz. black treacle
4 oz. golden syrup

Butter a tin 12 by 4 inches or a 7-inch square tin.

Dissolve the sugar and water in a 4-pint heavy-based pan over a low heat. Add the remaining ingredients and bring to the boil. Boil to 270°F. (soft crack stage). Pour into the tin, cool for 5 minutes, then mark into squares and leave to set.

Makes 1¼ lb. approx.

Entertaining

A GUIDE TO PARTY CATERING AND QUANTITIES

Cocktail Party
allow per person:
4–5 small savouries
3–4 drinks

Wedding Reception
allow per person:
4–5 savouries
1–2 sweet foods
3–4 drinks

Fork Buffet
allow per person:
1 starter
1 main savoury dish
1 sweet dish
3–4 drinks

Children's Party (under 10's)
allow per child:
4–6 savoury items *(include potato crisps and cheesy biscuits)*
1–2 sweet items *(ice cream is a favourite)*
2 cold drinks *(milk or squash)*

Teenage Party
allow per person:
1 main dish
Plenty of French bread, butter, cheeese
1 sweet dish
4–6 drinks *(coffee, cold drinks)*

Adult Tea Party
allow per person:
3–4 savoury items
2 small cakes or slices of cake
2 cups of tea

Serving of Wine, Spirits, etc., per bottle

Sherry	16
Wine	6–8
Champagne	6–8
Gin or Whisky *(with tonic, soda, etc.)*	20
Gin or Whisky *(as cocktails)* *(allow 8–10 splits of soda or tonic per bottle of spirit)*	32
Liqueur	30
Tomato juice *(1-pint can)*	4–6
Fruit cordials *(add 7 pints water to each bottle)*	20–25

DINNER PARTIES

The informal dinner party still remains a popular way of entertaining, but if it is to be fun for you as hostess as well as for the guests, you need to plan it intelligently. Allow yourself plenty of time for the preparation beforehand and make sure you are familiar with all the recipes.

Try out any new dish first – it's almost invariably a mistake to make a dinner party the occasion for launching some elaborate new idea.

Since most women have to double the rôles of cook and hostess – and that of parlourmaid thrown in – it's best to choose an easy menu, based on one really exciting and satisfying dish.

Three courses, followed by cheese and coffee, are usually quite enough. At least one course, if not two, can be made ready beforehand. Soups, hors d'oeuvre, casseroles and cold sweets all lend themselves to advance preparation. Avoid anything that demands last-minute attention, such as fried foods, hot soufflés, omelettes and so on, and if possible cook in attractive oven-to-table ware so that no hurried dishing up will be necessary. Cooking in foil also avoids washing up and constant attention. 'Convenience' foods save a lot of time and are easily transformed into party dishes with a little dressing up.

Having decided on the menu, see that everything is not only well cooked but also attractively served.

Garnishes give the finishing touch and make food look twice as appetising. The table arrangements set the mood for a meal and can give extra colour. Suiting the table setting to the occasion is an art that should be acquired by every woman who enjoys entertaining. There is no quicker way of creating a party atmosphere than by the use of candles and flowers. Supplement the candles, if necessary, with a standard or table lamp placed near enough to the diners for them to be able to see what they are eating without detracting from the romantic candlelight. Flower arrangements are better kept low, so that guests can see each other without stretching and peering; candles, flowers, cloths (or mats) and china should conform to one colour scheme to give a uniform appearance.

COOKED AT TABLE

One of the very best and gayest ideas, for a gathering of not more than eight friends, is the 'cook-it-yourself' party – perhaps inspired by the Japanese *sukiyaki*. Both Fondue Bourguignonne and Cheese Fondue (*see Meat and Cheese chapters*) are easy if you have a thermostatically controlled electric frying pan or skillet, and most guests thoroughly enjoy cooking their own meal from ingredients prepared in advance by their hostess.

A table cooker can also be the centre of an informal party, producing bacon and eggs, sausages, hamburgers or pancakes. A quick-cooking dish such as Chicken

Maryland or Boeuf Strogonoff (*see Poultry and Meat chapters*) can be partly made beforehand and then finished at table while guests are eating the first course. Serve it with tossed green salad, French bread and butter and follow it with a platter of fruit, or éclairs and meringues filled with fresh cream. A table cooker – electric frying pan or skillet – also ideal for sweets such as Crêpes Suzette (*see Hot Puddings chapter*) and the flickering blue flame of the lighted brandy gives a real cachet to the proceedings. What's more, the hostess who serves a flambé sweet can get away with the simplest possible first course.

ONE-DISH PARTY

For the times when you feel like having friends to a meal, but don't want to put on a full-scale effort – and for the bed-sitter girl who is pushed for time and space – the one-dish meal is the answer. The easiest thing is to have a generous, piping-hot spicy casserole, crammed with everything at once – meat, vegetables, herbs – so that there is no separate dishing up to do. A hotpot layered with onion, tomatoes and potatoes; a paella, deliciously spicy with saffron and stuffed with chicken,

mussels, prawns and peppers; rich beef stew; a savoury risotto, a fish chowder – these all lend themselves to such a meal and when accompanied by a green salad and followed by cheese and fruit, make a dinner fit for any guest. If you feel that crisp French bread and butter will not suffice as an accompaniment and that you must serve boiled rice with your casserole, choose one of the new quick-cooking types.

BRUNCH PARTY

Brunch, a combination of late breakfast and early lunch, makes a good weekend party meal. It is a wonderful opportunity to serve the good old favourite breakfast dishes which so few people have time to enjoy during the week. Sunday is of course the favourite day, and the most usual time for inviting the guests is about 11–11.30 a.m.

Start with fruit or fruit juices (bought in a large can) and follow with a choice of one or two main dishes. An egg dish – for instance, creamy scrambled eggs – is always a winner. Kedgeree, bacon and eggs, bacon and

kidneys, framed eggs or sausage scramble make equally suitable alternatives.

Give kedgeree a party look by adding a little chopped red pepper or a few cooked peas; the rice and fish can be cooked the previous evening and then it will take only a few minutes to heat all the ingredients up together. Bacon and eggs can be cooked in the oven and eggs can be scrambled in a basin over a pan of hot water. For sausage scramble add chopped cooked sausage to the eggs or make a 'fishy' scramble by adding some shrimps or prawns while the eggs are cooking.

Serve lots of butter, marmalade or black cherry jam, with hot rolls, crispbreads, home-baked scones or pancakes and of course plenty of coffee – though at this time of day, especially in warm weather, some of your guests may prefer beer.

COCKTAIL AND SHERRY PARTIES

These are a convenient way of entertaining a number of people, but do avoid over-crowding. It is better to have two smaller parties than to cram all your friends together into a small space.

It is quite usual to issue the invitations over the telephone, though written invitations have the advantage that they serve as a reminder and make quite clear the type and duration of the party.

Some of the furniture can be taken out of the room to make more space, but a few small tables are useful for guests to put down their glasses; some people will want to sit down before the end of the evening, so don't take away all the chairs. Have your 'bar' (a table or trolley) along one side of the room rather than tucked into a corner – there is less chance of causing congestion and preventing people from circulating. Pass some ready-mixed drinks round on a tray to prevent all the guests congregating in one place. (If you need extra glasses for a large party, by the way, you can hire them from your wine merchant.) Collect all the ash trays you can muster and distribute them round the room – you can't have too many.

Count on serving an average of three drinks per person. Unless it is a very large party and you have plenty of help, it is not necessary to provide a large variety – a choice of three or four is quite enough – say, dry Martinis, whisky and soda and sherry. If you want to branch out, offer Pink Gin, Bloody Mary, Manhattans or apéritifs such as Campari and Dubonnet (*see page*). Provide tomato or fruit juice for guests who prefer them and tonic water and bitter lemon for those who like a longer drink – such as gin and tonic or Dubonnet and bitter lemon. Be sure you have plenty of ice, thin slices of lemon and cocktail cherries.

For a sherry party provide medium dry and dry sherry. Not many people drink sweet sherry at this kind of party, but you may like to have one bottle handy, just to be on the safe side. Dry and medium sherries are best slightly chilled. Sweet sherry is served at room temperature or 'on the rocks'.

The food should be 'bite size'. You can include the usual small savoury things such as cocktail sausages or fried scampi on sticks, cocktail onions, cheese straws, olives, gherkins and salted nuts, savoury dips surrounded by plenty of small dry biscuits, breadsticks, potato crisps, cheese balls, celery or carrot sticks. For a more formal party, have hot cheese tartlets, sardine pyramids, savoury éclairs or fried meatballs with a tomato dip. Arrange the food attractively on trays or platters and distribute them around the room. If they are left on the same table as the drinks, people gather round the bar and the party tends to stagnate.

CHEESE AND WINE PARTIES

These parties are a popular way of entertaining and take surprisingly little trouble to organise.

If you feel a little hesitant about the choice of wines consult a wine merchant, who will be happy to advise you and will probably lend you extra glasses and so on; he will quite possibly not charge you for the hire, but of course breakages will have to be paid for.

Allow a bottle of wine for every two guests and have a selection of red and white. Most people prefer red wine with the stronger cheeses and white or rosé with the milder ones. If you get the wine on a 'sale or return' basis you will be able to relax knowing that you will have plenty – but remember not to open too many bottles at a time, or you may be left with a lot of half-bottles to dispose of. Many wines are sold in gallon or $\frac{1}{2}$-gallon jars and generally work out a little cheaper than wine in bottles.

Open some of the red wine in advance, about two hours before you need it. Chill white wine in the refrigerator for $1\frac{1}{2}$ hours or leave it in a really cold place. Serve the wine from a side table and the cheese from another table. Lay plates, knives and table napkins at each end of the table.

Allow 2 oz. cheese per person and provide a good selection of both English and Continental kinds. Try Wensleydale, Dunlop, Sage Derby, Double Gloucester, Brie, Gruyère, Roquefort, Bel Paese, smoked cheese and cream cheese. Some soft cheeses can be left whole, but cut the rest into fingers or cubes and arrange on large plates, clearly labelled with name and country or description and garnished with sprigs of watercress or parsley.

Have a good choice of bread; long French loaves can be left for guests to cut for themselves and you can have platters or baskets filled with slices of other kinds – Vienna, rye, pumpernickel, wholemeal – a selection of crispbread and some plain and digestive biscuits. Cut the butter into cubes or make it into pats if you have time. Allow 1 lb. for every 12–16 guests.

Crisp celery sticks are popular. If you provide other salad stuff, serve it in convenient portions, cutting tomatoes into wedges, using small leaves of lettuce and dividing watercress into sprigs – they are so much easier to handle. Small dishes of pickles, olives, nuts and radishes add colour to the table, and so do bowls of fruit.

Cheese Fondue

COFFEE PARTIES

Asking people in for morning coffee is an easy, informal way of meeting old friends or introducing a new neighbour. It's also a favourite way of collecting money for charity: a small charge is then made for the refreshments. Evening coffee parties are more social, but in either case nothing elaborate is required in the way of food.

Set everything ready on a trolley or large tray, so that all you have to do when the guests arrive is to make the coffee. Buns, scones, fancy biscuits, fruit cake and small cakes are ideal for a morning party. For an evening function, try a large gâteau or Continental pastries, with biscuits or a selection of small cakes. Chocolate and coffee cake go well with coffee.

Whatever the occasion, allow about 2 teacupfuls of coffee for each person and offer it both black and white. If the weather is hot, serve iced coffee, with whipped cream and powdered cinnamon. Small coffee cups are only used for after-dinner coffee.

TEA PARTIES

A tea party may be a purely social occasion or it may arise because a committee is meeting or some other activity is taking place in your home.

In any case, only a light tea is required. Make small sandwiches, filling them with salmon and cucumber, sardine and watercress, egg and tomato, ham and tongue and so on. Try also making some rolled sandwiches, which are easy and popular. Cut thin brown

215

bread and butter, remove the crusts, spread with a creamy filling (such as well-seasoned cream cheese) and roll up the bread. Alternatively, offer tiny bridge rolls, asparagus rolls or small scones. Add an assortment of small cakes and biscuits or fingers of fruit cake. In the winter, hot buttered scones or tea cakes would be welcome.

Provide both China and Indian tea, with milk and sugar and also thinly cut slices of lemon for those who prefer it.

WEDDING RECEPTIONS

If you are giving the reception at home, don't be tempted to invite more guests than you can comfortably accommodate. A morning wedding is often followed by a sit-down wedding breakfast, but if space is a problem it is better to serve a buffet meal.

If you are having a buffet indoors, arrange some chairs in odd corners so that guests may sit down if they wish; provide a few small tables so that wine glasses may be put down.

For a summer wedding, a garden setting can be delightful, but in our unpredictable climate it would be wise to have a marquee set up; there are many firms which will do this for you.

When you plan your menu, bear in mind the amount of help you will have available; even for a sit-down meal, a cold main course is a wise choice. Well-presented simple dishes make less work for the hostess and can be just as delicious as elaborate ones.

Choose savoury food which can be eaten easily with a fork and serve individual portions of moulded sweets and trifles – however splendid to look at when served in large dishes, these soon appear tired and unappetising when people have been helping themselves.

Suggested menus for a sit-down wedding breakfast

Winter

Soup

Hot Lobster Vol-a-Vents

Cold Turkey and Ham

Cranberry Sauce

Potato Salad

Apple Salad

Lemon Chiffon

Wedding Cake

Coffee

Champagne or Sparkling White Wine

Summer

Iced Melon or Grapefruit

Salmon Mousse

Chicken and Almond Salad

Peach Gâteau or
Raspberries or Strawberries and Cream

Wedding Cake

Coffee

Champagne or Sparkling White Wine

Suggestions for a Buffet Reception

Morning

Tomato Juice Cocktail
or Melon Balls in Orange Juice

Mixed Meat Platters
(a variety of English and Continental meats, such as Ham, Tongue, Pork, Salami, garnished with radish roses, celery curls and so on)

Ham Mould

Potato Salad   Tomato Salad

Lemon Soufflé   Caramel Nut Cream

Wedding Cake

Coffee

Champagne or Sparkling White Wine

Afternoon

Assorted Sandwiches   Asparagus Rolls

Chicken or Mushroom Patties

Cheese Dartois   Shrimp Horns

Chocolate Éclairs   Petits Fours
Meringues

Fruit Salad and Ice Cream

Wedding Cake

Tea or Coffee

Champagne or Sparkling White Wine

CHILDREN'S PARTIES

The highlight of any child's year is his or her own party – though the mother doesn't always think so! If possible, stick to suitable age groups (it's not wise to arrange a joint party for your two or three children of varying ages), and invite not more than a dozen guests at once. Five-to-eights generally play together quite well and so do eight-to-twelves; under-fives are almost impossibly difficult to organise – just two or three at a time to tea are enough to cope with.

Receiving an invitation through the post is half the enjoyment for small children, so buy pretty invitation cards and sent them out in plenty of time. Small hosts and hostesses love helping to fill in the names on the cards and send them out in plenty of time. The invitations should say very clearly what time the children are expected and no less clearly what time they are to go home. Don't be afraid to make the party time short – it is far more fun for children to have a couple of crowded hours than four loose-endish ones. It's a good idea to mention the fact if it is a birthday party, so that guests can bring a small present if they want to and not be embarrassed because they didn't know about it.

Children's parties don't run themselves, but must be most carefully organised. Clear some of the furniture and all precious breakables out of the party room and decorate it with balloons (to take away afterwards) and coloured streamers. Arrange for someone to play the piano or manage the record player for games like Musical Chairs. Make a really long list of games, alternating rowdy and quiet ones. Give small prizes but – like Alice – see that everybody gets one. If organising games seems too much to cope with for the entire time, provide a short programme of cartoon films or a conjuror to keep the children quiet for a little while after tea. When the party is over and parents come to collect their offspring, think twice before offering drinks or coffee – generally it is not necessary and the children will be tired by this time and will get either fractious or over-excited if they are kept waiting.

Serve the food in a separate room from the one where the games are played. Choose easy-to-eat food and keep it simple, as unspillable as possible and in small portions. Most children love savoury sandwiches of scrambled egg, cheese spread or tomato – flavours they meet every day; you can make the sandwiches exciting by cutting them into fancy shapes. Children in the eight-to-twelve year group have enormous appetites, so bridge rolls topped with savoury fillings are a better choice than sandwiches. Small sausages on sticks are always popular (use chipolata sausages, twisted or cut into 3 or 4, and served cold), so are sausage rolls, potato crisps and cheese pastries or scones. Little iced cakes are more appealing when decorated with small sweets, or better still with the initials of each guest. Meringues, éclairs and other rich cakes are best reserved for older children. Chocolate biscuits are a sure bet and so are iced home-made biscuits, in animal shapes or letters. Fruit jelly and ice cream (in waxed containers) vanish like snow in summer.

A BARBECUE PARTY

A barbecue party in the garden, on the terrace or at midnight by the sea can be the greatest fun – even the simplest food somehow tastes better out of doors. It does, however, pay to plan ahead and prepare in advance the barbecue sauces, dips and salads and perhaps something sweet.

A barbecue party can never be a hurried affair – the charcoal takes time to heat through and the food has to be individually cooked. If you can't get the fire started before the beginning of the party, keep your guests happy with drinks and appetisers.

The first course can be sausages, hamburgers, kebabs, gammon rashers, chops, steaks or joints of chicken. Served with French bread, crusty rolls or toasted buns, jacket potatoes and a salad, these are enough for most people, but you can add tomatoes and mushrooms if you wish, while bowls of potato crisps are always popular. A selection of cheeses and some fresh fruit will round off a satisfying meal.

Simple barbecue equipment can be bought for as little as £2, but there is a lot to be said for making your own. An old bucket or two, with holes punched round the sides, will serve the purpose for a small party. Stand the buckets on bricks and put a few stones in the bottom before filling up with charcoal. You will need about a 7-lb. bag of charcoal. (Available at coal merchants or hardware shops at about 55p. Have a second bag as reserve if possible.) Then cover the fire with chicken wire or use one of the slatted shelves from your oven.

For a large party, you could possibly persuade some of your guests to come in the day before and build a simple barbecue fireplace with bricks. Arrange 10 bricks in an oblong measuring about 33 inches by 23 inches, leaving a few gaps for air. Arrange 10 more bricks on top as a second course. Cover these with a doubled piece of $\frac{1}{2}$-inch chicken wire or some expended metal mesh, about 30 inches by 22 inches, to hold the charcoal. Use 10 more bricks to make a third course.

Put pieces of crumpled paper on the mesh and cover with half the bag of charcoal. Place a slatted metal rack (such as an oven shelf) on top as the cooking surface. An hour before starting to cook, light the paper under the charcoal. By the time you start, the fire will be burning evenly. During the cooking feed the fire regularly with *small* quantities of charcoal – large quantities are wasteful and reduce the heat.

If the charcoal should prove difficult to ignite, sprinkle it with a few drops of lighter fuel or wrap a few pieces of it in newspaper, put some unwrapped pieces on top and then set light to the paper. Newspaper screwed tightly into small balls and put amongst the charcoal is another way of speeding up the process.

Don't start to cook until the fire is really ready, which may take up to an hour. In the dark it will have a warm red glow, but if you are cooking in daylight, the charcoal will look ashen-grey as the flames die down.

Barbecue cooking is hot work, so provide long-handled forks or green sticks, a good pair of oven tongs and oven gloves. Provide a board to carve on, if necessary, and a really sharp knife, also a tray of seasonings – salt, pepper, bottled sauces, etc. – a bowl of oil or sauce to brush over the cooking food and a large brush.

Brush the food over with oil before starting to cook it. Meats can also be rubbed with garlic or with a savoury mixture of 1 level tbsp. flour, 1 level tbsp. prepared mustard, $\frac{1}{4}$ level tsp. salt and a pinch of pepper.

Such things as kebabs, sausages and other food on skewers must be turned frequently during the cooking; chops and steaks, which should be cut thick, only need to be turned once, but remember to trim off excess fat to prevent flaming.

Foreign Dishes

Pig's Trotters in Madeira *(Switzerland)*

4 pig's trotters
1 onion, skinned and sliced
1 carrot, peeled and sliced
½ a leek, sliced
1 clove of garlic
A pinch of dried thyme
A pinch of dried rosemary
A pinch of pepper
2 bay leaves
¾–1 pint white wine
2 tbsps. olive oil
3 tomatoes, skinned and chopped
2 tbsps. tomato paste
Madeira wine

Halve the trotters, wash them well and leave to soak for some hours in cold water. Drain and put in a casserole with the vegetables, herbs and pepper. Cover with white wine and marinade for 3 days. Drain the trotters, parboil them, drain and add the marinade, vegetables, olive oil, tomatoes and tomato paste; simmer gently for 4 hours. Strain the sauce and flavour with Madeira wine. Dish up the trotters and serve with the sauce, accompanied by noodles.

Basle 'Spinach Frogs' *(Switzerland)*

16 large spinach leaves
1½ oz. butter
1 shallot, minced
1 lb. minced cooked lean pork
Salt and pepper
Grated nutmeg
1 egg, beaten
Fat for frying

Wash the spinach and cook in boiling salted water for 2–3 minutes; drain well. Soften the butter and mix with the shallot and pork, then season well with salt, pepper and nutmeg and bind with the egg. Spread out the spinach leaves and place a little of the meat mixture in the centre of each. Fold the edges together and form into neat parcels. Heat a little fat in a frying pan and put in the spinach frogs. Fry gently, turning them once, until very hot.

Serve with Béchamel sauce.

Topfenknödel mit Apfelmus *(Austrian Crumb-crusted Dumplings with Apple Sauce)*

White bread
2 oz. butter
2 large eggs, separated
4 oz. cottage cheese
Double cream
2 oz. plain flour
A pinch of salt
Grated rind of ½ a lemon
Hot apple sauce

For the Buttered Crumbs
2 oz. butter
2 oz. stale white breadcrumbs
1 oz. caster sugar

Cut two thick slices off the loaf (about 4 oz.). Trim off the crusts and crumb the bread. Beat the butter until soft. Beat in the egg yolks one at a time. Stir in the cheese, 3 tbsps. cream and the breadcrumbs. Sift the flour with the salt and add the lemon rind; fold into the other ingredients and leave for ½ hour. Shape into about 8 small dumplings. Just before the dumplings are required, poach them very gently in simmering (not fast-boiling) salted water for about 20 minutes.

Meanwhile prepare the coating crumbs. Melt the butter and gently fry the breadcrumbs until golden; stir in the sugar. Drain the dumplings and toss them lightly in the fried crumbs. Serve at once, with apple sauce, or, when in season, with a thick purée of fresh plums.

Stewed Pike *(Switzerland)*

A pike weighing 2–3 lb.
Salt and pepper
3½ oz. fat bacon
1 carrot
¼ pint stock
¼ pint dry white wine
3–4 sage leaves
1 onion, spiked with 2 cloves
1 tsp. anchovy or lobster paste
2 oz. butter
1 tbsp. cream
Lemon juice

Oven temperature: moderate (350°F., mark 4)

Scale, clean and wash the fish; wipe it dry and put some salt inside, then pull off the skin on either side of the dorsal fin and insert tiny strips of bacon in the flesh. Wash and peel the carrot and put it in the abdominal slit. Butter an ovenproof dish, put in the fish, back uppermost, pour in the stock and wine, add the sage leaves, onion, fish paste, pepper and a little salt, cover the fish with knobs of butter and bake in the centre of the oven, covering the dish for the first 15 minutes, then uncovering it for the next 30 minutes, till the fish turns a light gold colour and is well cooked; baste it 2–3 times with the stock and wine. Dilute the cooking juices with a little water, strain, add the cream and a few drops of lemon juice and serve with the fish (which should be left whole). *(Serves 4–6.)*

Linzertorte *(Austrian Raspberry Flan)*

6 oz. plain flour
½ level tsp. powdered cinnamon
3 oz. butter
2 oz. caster sugar
2 oz. ground almonds
Grated rind of 1 lemon
2 egg yolks
1 tbsp. lemon juice
¾ lb. raspberry jam
¼ pint double cream, whipped

Oven temperature: fairly hot (375°F., mark 5)

Sift the flour and cinnamon into a bowl and rub in the butter. Add the sugar, ground almonds and the lemon rind. Beat the egg yolks and add with the lemon juice to the flour, to make a stiff dough. Knead lightly and leave in a cool place for 30 minutes. Roll out two-thirds of the pastry and use to line an 8½-inch loose-bottomed flan ring. Fill with raspberry jam. Roll out the remaining pastry and cut into ½-inch strips with a pastry wheel. Use to make a lattice design over the jam.
  Bake in the centre of the oven for 25–30 minutes. Allow to cool, remove from the flan ring, and serve with whipped cream.

Note: Fresh or frozen raspberries can be used in place of the jam: cook 1 lb. raspberries with 1 tbsp. water and ½ oz. butter, and add a little sugar to taste.

Paprika Chicken *(Austria)*

A 3-lb. chicken
1 lb. onions, skinned
6 oz. butter
1 level tsp. paprika
3 tsps. tomato paste
Salt
1 oz. flour
½ pint sour cream

Joint the chicken. Fry the onions in the butter until golden and add the chicken and paprika. Fry the chicken on all sides until nicely coloured. Add the tomato paste, thinned with a little water and salted to taste. Cover and simmer till the meat is tender – about 1–2 hours. Blend the flour and cream and pour over the chicken, boil up and simmer for 5 minutes. Serve with noodles.

Headless Birds *(Belgium)*

4 slices of beef
Salt and pepper
2 onions, skinned
Chopped parsley
4 rashers of bacon
4 hard-boiled eggs
Flour
Fat for frying
1 carrot, sliced
¼ pint stock

Beat the slices of beef flat and season each with salt and pepper. Slice 1 onion and chop the other. Sprinkle the beef slices with the chopped onion and parsley and cover each with a piece of bacon. Place a hard-boiled egg in the centre of each and roll up, tying securely with cotton. Dust the rolls with flour and brown them in a little hot fat in a frying pan. Add the sliced onion, the carrot and the stock, cover and simmer for 1½–2 hours. Remove the cottons, cut the rolls in half lengthwise and place on a bed of creamed potato; serve the gravy separately.

Chicory with Cheese and Ham *(Belgium)*

1 lb. chicory (about 8 small heads)
¼ pint milk
2 oz. butter
1 oz. plain flour
Salt and pepper
Ground nutmeg
2 oz. Gruyère cheese, grated
8 slices of cooked ham
Toasted breadcrumbs

Cook the chicory in boiling salted water until tender – about 15–25 minutes. Drain, keeping the stock. Make the milk up to ¾ pint with chicory liquor. Melt 1 oz. butter, add the flour and stir well. Cook gently for 2–3 minutes, stirring, until the roux begins to bubble. Remove from the heat and gradually add the milk and chicory liquor, stirring continually. Bring to the boil, stirring, and season with salt, pepper and nutmeg. Add most of the cheese. Wrap each head of chicory in a slice of ham and put in an ovenproof dish; pour the sauce over, top with breadcrumbs and the remaining cheese, top with a few pieces of butter and brown under a medium grill.

Crunchy-Topped Tea Bread *(Belgium)*

1 lb. plain flour
1 oz. fresh yeast
½ pint warm milk
A little salt
3 level tbsps. caster sugar
2 eggs, beaten
1–2 oz. butter, creamed

For the Topping
1 egg yolk
1 oz. butter
2 oz. caster sugar
2 oz. flour

Oven temperature: very hot (450°F., mark 8)

Grease a loaf tin measuring 9½ by 5½ inches.

Make a dough with 4 oz. flour, the yeast and half the warm milk and allow to rise slowly – about 45 minutes. Now add the salt, sugar, remaining milk and flour, eggs and lastly the creamed butter. Beat the dough until it forms bubbles and roll it out lightly on a board sprinkled with flour. Put into the prepared tin and allow to rise again. Make the topping by creaming the egg yolk, butter, sugar and flour together and sprinkle it evenly over the dough in the tin. Bake towards the top of the oven for 10 minutes, then turn down the heat to moderate (350°F., mark 4) and bake for a further 30 minutes.

Sole à la Normande *(France)*

1 oz. butter
2–3 shallots, skinned
1 quart mussels
2 oz. button mushrooms, washed
A little lemon juice
Salt and pepper
8 fillets of sole
½ pint white wine
4 oz. peeled shrimps

For the Sauce
½ pint milk
2 oz. butter
2 oz. flour
2 egg yolks
1 tbsp. cream

Oven temperature: moderate (350°F., mark 4)

Heat half the butter in a pan, add the shallots and cook gently. Wash the mussels thoroughly, put into another pan, cover and cook till the shells open; when they are ready, remove them from the shells, take off the beards and reserve the liquid. Place the mushrooms in a saucepan with a little water, the lemon juice, the remaining butter and the seasoning; cook until tender. Next make the sauce. Make the mussel and mushroom liquor up to 1 pint with milk. Make a roux with the butter and flour and add the liquid. Cook for 5 minutes, then add the egg yolks and cream blended together. Re-heat very gently without boiling.

Grease an ovenproof dish and put in the cooked shallots. Fold each fillet of sole in three, add to the dish and pour the white wine over. Cover and cook in the centre of the oven for 7 minutes. Garnish with the mussels, mushrooms and shrimps and return the dish to the oven for 5 minutes. Pour the hot sauce over.

Breton Roast Lamb *(France)*

1 leg of lamb, weighing 3–4 lb.
Salt and pepper
1 clove of garlic, sliced lengthwise into 2–3 pieces
Fat
½ lb. haricot beans, soaked overnight
1 onion, skinned
A bouquet garni

Oven temperature: hot (425°F., mark 7)

Rub the lamb with salt and pepper; cut several slits in the flesh close to the bone and insert the pieces of garlic. Place the joint in a roasting tin with the fat and cook in the centre of the oven, allowing 22 minutes per lb. and 22 minutes over. The meat should not be over-browned when cooked, but juicy and pink. Meanwhile cook the haricot beans by simmering them in salted water with the whole onion and the bouquet garni – about 45 minutes. Serve them round the joint, with some of the gravy from the roasting tin poured over.

Rillettes de Porc *(France)*

2 lb. belly or neck of pork, rinded and boned
Salt
1 lb. back pork, fat
1 clove garlic, skinned and bruised
A bouquet garni
Freshly ground black pepper

Oven temperature: cool (300°F., marks 1–2)

Rub the meat well with salt and leave it to stand for 4–6 hours. Cut it into thin strips along the grooves left when the bones were taken out. Put into an earthenware or other oven dish, with the pork fat, also cut into small strips. Bury the garlic clove and bouquet garni in the centre, season with a little pepper and add about 5 tbsps. water. Cover with a lid and cook in the centre of the oven for about 4 hours. Discard the bouquet garni and garlic. Season well. Strain the fat from the meat. Partly pound the well-drained meat, then pull it into fine shreds with two forks. Pile lightly into a glazed earthenware or china jar and pour the fat over the top. Cover with foil and keep in a cool place. Rillettes should be of a soft texture, so allow to come to room temperature before serving. (*Serves 4–6.*)

Tripe à la Mode de Caen *(France)*

2 lb. tripe
1–2 cow-heels
Salt and pepper
2 bay leaves
2 sprigs of thyme
2 sprigs of parsley
4 large onions, skinned; 4 cloves
4 leeks, sliced
2 carrots, peeled and sliced
1 pint cider or dry white wine
½ glass brandy (optional)

Oven temperature: warm (325°F., mark 3)

Wash the tripe very thoroughly and blanch it, then cut it into small pieces; divide up the cow-heels. Put both into an ovenproof casserole with the seasonings, herbs, onions (each stuck with a clove) and the leeks and carrots. Add the cider or wine and the brandy (if used), cover and cook in the centre of the oven for 6 hours. This dish may be left overnight; remove the fat from the surface and take out the cow-heel bones and the herbs before re-heating for serving.

Schweinefleisch Rippchen auf Kraut *(Pork baked on Sauerkraut) (Germany)*

A 3-lb. piece of loin pork, salted
A 25-oz. can of sauerkraut, drained
1 oz. dripping
1 large onion, skinned and sliced
1 bay leaf
A few juniper berries
A few caraway seeds
½ pint stock or water
A pinch of sugar

Oven temperature: warm (325°F., mark 3)

Remove the skin from the pork; trim down the fat and chine the joint. Place the sauerkraut in a dish large enough to take the meat. Melt the dripping, and sauté the onion for a few minutes. Add to the sauerkraut, with the bay leaf, berries, caraway seeds, stock and sugar. Put the meat on top, fat side uppermost, and pour the stock over. Cover and cook in the centre of the oven for about 1¾ hours. Serve with boiled potatoes or potato dumplings.

Note: Unsalted pork can be used if the butcher cannot salt it for you.

Roast Veal with Beer *(Germany)*

A loin of veal
Fat for larding
Salt and pepper
2–3 carrots, peeled and sliced
2–3 onions, skinned and sliced
Butter
½ pint German brown beer
1 bay leaf
2 cloves
1 level tbsp. flour

Oven temperature: hot (425°F., mark 7)

Lard the meat thickly with the fat and put it in a meat tin; season with salt and pepper. Add the carrots and onions, pour a little melted butter over and roast in the centre of the oven for 30 minutes. Pour the beer over the meat, add the bay leaf and cloves and return it to the centre of the oven. Turn down the heat to fairly hot (375°F., mark 5) and cook the meat until tender, basting frequently – allow 30 minutes per lb. When the meat is cooked place it on a serving dish. Blend the flour with the juices in the tin, heat until boiling, then strain over the meat.

Kalbsleber *(Liver in Cream Sauce) (Germany)*

1 lb. calves' liver
1 oz. seasoned flour
Paprika
1 oz. butter
3 tbsps. dry white wine
A small carton (2½ fl. oz.) of double cream
Chopped chives or parsley

Slice the liver, pour on boiling water to cover and leave for 5 minutes; drain off the water. Cut the liver into strips, removing any skin. Toss the flour and paprika together in a paper bag, add the liver and shake well to coat each piece. Melt the butter in a frying-pan and quickly brown the liver. Put on one side and keep warm. Put the wine into the pan and work in the meat residue, using a wooden spoon. Blend well and bring to the boil. Remove from the heat, add the cream and check the seasoning. Re-heat, but don't boil. Add the chives or parsley and the liver and again re-heat without boiling.

Kotelett mit Pflaumen *(Pork with plums) (Germany)*

4 pork chops
½ lb. fresh plums
1 oz. sugar
Powdered cinnamon
4 cloves
1 glass of dry red wine
Salt and pepper

Oven temperature: moderate (350°F., mark 4)

Trim any excess fat from the chops and heat the trimmings to extract some fat. Use this to fry the chops until lightly but evenly browned. Stew the plums with the sugar and just enough water to prevent the fruit from burning. Pass them through a sieve. Put the chops in a shallow heatproof dish in a single layer; add a pinch of cinnamon and the cloves to the plum purée and pour over the chops. Add the wine; season with salt and pepper, cover, and bake in the centre of the oven for 1 hour, adding a little water if necessary during the cooking.

Potato Dumplings *(Germany)*

3 lb. potatoes, peeled
1 level tsp. salt
½ level tsp. grated nutmeg
2 oz. semolina
3 oz. wheatmeal flour
2 eggs, beaten
2 slices of bread
Butter

Cook and sieve the potatoes and leave to become cold. Add the salt, nutmeg, semolina, flour and eggs and knead into a smooth dough. Cut the bread into small dice and fry light brown in the hot butter.

Flour the hands, make round dumplings about the size of a fist with the potato dough and press a few of the fried croûtons into each. Put the dumplings into boiling salted water and cook them thoroughly – about 12–15 minutes. Place them on a flat dish and pour melted butter (or margarine) over them; alternatively, chop and fry some bacon and pour over the dumplings. (Serves 6.)

These dumplings, which are very good, are much eaten in the south of Germany, where they are served with fat roast meat or accompanied by tomato, herb or onion sauce. They are also served with stewed fruit.

Melitzanes Salata *(Aubergine Appetiser)* *(Greece)*

3 large aubergines
½ pint olive oil
2 oz. onion, skinned and chopped
3 tbsps. lemon juice
1 clove of garlic, skinned and crushed
¼ level tsp. oregano
2 tomatoes, skinned and chopped
Salt and pepper

Slice the aubergines thickly and sauté in half the olive oil until barely coloured but soft. Remove the skins and pound the flesh in a bowl with the onion, lemon juice, garlic, oregano, tomatoes and seasoning until well mashed. Gradually beat in the remaining oil until all is smooth and thick.

Note: This is suitable alone as an appetiser, served in little pots, with a garnish of chopped parsley or thinly sliced green peppers and toast fingers, or as one of the items in a mixed hors d'oeuvre, called in Greece *mezethakia*.

Stuffed Vine Leaves *(Greece)*

1 pkt. of vine leaves
3 tbsps. lard or olive oil
1 lb. minced meat
1–2 onions, thinly sliced
2 heaped tbsps. cooked rice
A little chopped parsley
A little tomato sauce
Salt and pepper
Juice of 1 lemon

Dip the vine leaves in boiling water for 1–2 minutes, then leave them in a colander until you have made the stuffing. Put 2 tbsps. of the lard or oil in a frying pan with the meat, onions, rice, parsley, sauce and seasonings, mix well and fry. Add the lemon juice and stuff the vine leaves with the mixture, securing with skewers or fine string. Put in a saucepan with a little water, the remaining lard or oil and a little more sauce if desired, and cook over a low heat until the gravy has reduced considerably.

This stuffing can also be used for aubergines, peppers, tomatoes and so on.

Cabbage Stuffed with Meat *(Holland)*

1 cabbage
6 oz. minced pork
6 oz. minced veal
Salt and pepper
1 level tsp. ground nutmeg
2 oz. fresh white breadcrumbs
Stock
Butter

Remove the outer leaves from the cabbage, blanch them in boiling water for 10 minutes and drain well. Mix the pork and veal and season with salt, pepper and nutmeg. Add the breadcrumbs and moisten with a little stock. Arrange some of the cabbage leaves on a clean cloth, then cover with a layer of filling, put another layer of cabbage on this, and continue until all the minced meat has been used up. Gather the cloth together, tie up and boil in salted water for 1½ hours. Remove the stuffed cabbage leaves from the cloth, put into a fireproof dish, top generously with pats of butter and brown under a hot grill.

Dutch Braised Steak *(Holland)*

2 lb. braising steak, in one piece
Salt and pepper
2 oz. dripping
2 onions, skinned and sliced
2 bay leaves
Ground nutmeg

Paella, *page 148*

Wipe the meat and season well with salt and pepper. Melt the dripping and brown the steak on both sides. Add the onions, bay leaves, a little nutmeg and about 2 tbsps. water. Cover and cook over a very gentle heat for 1½ hours, adding a little more water as necessary. Serve with grilled tomatoes or a green salad.

Pea Soup *(Erwtensoep)* *(Holland)*

1 lb. dried or split peas
6 pints water
1 lb. meat (ham or boiling bacon for preference)
1 marrow bone
1 lb. potatoes, peled and sliced
About 1 pint milk
Salt and pepper
2 leeks, cut up small
2 sticks of celery, cut up small
Chopped parsley

Not just a soup, but a 'main-meal' dish, into which almost anything is flung, this *Erwtensoep* forms part of the staple Dutch diet in winter. Station restaurants and cafés always have it on the menu and it is served in huge bowls, with the meat on a smaller plate; a knife, fork and spoon are provided to eat it.

Wash the peas and soak them in 3 pints of the water overnight. The next day, simmer the meat and marrow bone in 3 pints boiling water; after 1 hour, add to the peas and the water in which they soaked and cook till soft – about 1 hour. Add the potatoes 40 minutes before serving. Take out the marrow bone and the meat, scrape out the marrow and put this back in the soup. Sieve or mash the soup thoroughly and add sufficient milk to thin. Season, add the leek and celery and cook for about 20 minutes, stirring occasionally. Stir in the parsley.

Vitello Tonnato *(Cold Veal)* *(Italy)*

Note: This requires to be prepared the day before it is served.

1½ lb. boned leg of veal
1 small carrot, peeled and sliced
1 onion, skinned and quartered
1 stick of celery, chopped
4 peppercorns
1 level tsp. salt
A 3-oz. can of tuna fish
4 anchovy fillets
¼ pint olive oil
2 egg yolks
Pepper
1 tbsp. lemon juice
Capers and lemon slices for garnish

Tie the meat into a neat roll and put into a saucepan with the bone, carrot, onion, celery, peppercorns, salt and some water. Bring to the boil, cover and simmer until tender – about 1 hour. Remove the meat and cool it. Meanwhile, mix together the tuna fish, anchovy fillets and 1 tbsp. olive oil. Break down the fish with a wooden

spoon, then stir in the egg yolks and pepper. Press all through a sieve into a small basin and add the lemon juice. Stir in the remaining oil a little at a time, beating well after each addition. Continue until the sauce resembles thin cream. Cut the meat into slices, arrange in a shallow dish and coat completely with the sauce. Cover and leave overnight. Serve cold, with a garnish of capers and lemon slices. *(Serves 6.)*

Calamares Fritos *(Fried Squid)* *(Italy)*

1 lb. squid (ink-fish)
6 oz. plain flour
2 large eggs
Salt and pepper
About 6 tbsps. cold water
Oil for frying
Sliced lemon and parsley for garnish

Wash the fish and discard the tentacles, ink sac and any bony parts. Slice the fleshy body into rings ¼–½ inch thick. Dry on absorbent paper. Make a batter by beating the flour, eggs and seasoning with enough water to give a coating consistency. Heat about 1-inch oil in a large saucepan and cook the pieces of squid, a few at a time, for 5–8 minutes; drain on kitchen paper as they are fried. Add more oil to the pan and re-heat. Dip the squid, a few pieces at a time, into the batter and deep-fry them, turning the pieces once, until golden and crisp. Drain well. Serve garnished with lemon slices and parsley.

Pollo Cacciatore *(Chicken in wine sauce)* *(Italy)*

A 3–3½-lb. oven-ready chicken
3 tbsps. oil
1 oz. butter
½ lb. onions, skinned and sliced
1 clove of garlic, skinned and crushed
A 14-oz. can of Italian skinned tomatoes
2 tbsps. chopped parsley
¼ level tsp. dried basil
½ level tsp. salt
Freshly ground pepper
¼ pint red wine
Chopped parsley to garnish

Remove and discard the skin from the chicken. Divide the chicken into 8 portions. Heat the oil and butter in a large saucepan. Fry the chicken a few pieces at a time until golden-brown all over; remove from the pan when brown, then fry the remaining pieces. Add the onion to the pan and fry until golden-brown. Add the garlic, tomatoes, parsley, basil, salt and pepper and bring to the boil. Return the chicken joints to the pan, add the wine, bring to the boil, cover, then reduce the heat and simmer for 40–45 minutes, until the chicken is tender. Serve sprinkled with chopped parsley.

Pastry Knots *(Malta)*

10 oz. plain flour
1 level tbsp. sugar
A knob of butter
2 egg yolks
1 small glass anisette
Oil for deep frying
Honey
Chopped chocolate and hundreds and thousands to decorate

Mix thoroughly together the flour, sugar and butter, add the egg yolks and anisette, mix into a dough and knead well. Roll out and leave to set for a few hours. Roll the pastry out very thinly, cut into long strips, curl each into a knot and fry in hot oil until golden-brown in colour. When done remove from the pan and drain on absorbent paper. Finally, whilst the knots are still hot, pour honey on each and decorate with chopped chocolate and Kosbor ('hundreds and thousands').

Polish Veal and Apple Stew

3 green apples, peeled and cored
1 oz. butter
1 oz. flour
¼ pint stock
12 oz. cooked veal, diced
Salt and sugar to taste

Quarter the apples and place them in a saucepan with ¼ pint water, bring to the boil and remove from the heat. Blend the butter and flour in a saucepan, cook for a minute or two without browning, then gradually stir in the stock. Bring to the boil and add the apples and water, meat and salt and sugar to taste. Cover and simmer for about 10 minutes.

Hungarian Layered Pancakes

½ pint pouring batter
Lard for frying

For the Fillings
4 oz. curd or cottage cheese
1 egg yolk
½ oz. sugar
Grated rind of ½ a lemon
Apricot jam
2 oz. nuts, finely grated
2 oz. plain chocolate, finely grated

For the Meringue
2 egg whites
4 oz. caster sugar

Oven temperature: fairly hot (375°F., mark 5)

Make the batter mixture in the usual way. Heat a little lard in a frying pan until really hot, running it round to coat the sides of the pan, and pour off any surplus. Pour or spoon in just enough batter to cover the base thinly and cook quickly until golden-brown underneath. Turn the pancake with a palette knife or by tossing it and cook

the second side until golden. Turn out and keep warm. Repeat with the remaining mixture until 8–12 pancakes have been made.

Make the first filling by mixing the cheese and egg yolk together and flavouring with the sugar and lemon rind. Warm the jam slightly. Mix the nuts with the chocolate to make the second filling.

Place one pancake on a buttered ovenproof plate and spread it with some of the cheese and lemon mixture. Cover with another pancake, spread with apricot jam, cover with a third pancake and spread this with the nut and chocolate mixture. Repeat this layering until all the pancakes and fillings have been used; keep warm while you make a meringue with the egg whites and sugar. Use to cover the pile of pancakes completely. Bake towards the top of the oven for 15–20 minutes or until the meringue is crisp and golden, and serve immediately, cutting it into slices like a cake. A rich chocolate sauce is often served with this sweet.

Baked Polish Ham with Rice and Raisins

8 thin slices of Polish ham
Mustard
2 oz. cooked rice
2 oz. chopped seedless raisins
2 sticks of celery, chopped
1 egg, beaten
¼ level tsp. paprika
¼ level tsp. salt
Milk

Oven temperature: fairly hot (375°F., mark 5)

Spread each side of the ham slices with a little mustard. Mix the rice with the raisins, celery, egg, paprika and salt. Place this filling on the slices of ham, roll them up and secure with cocktail sticks. Put them in an ovenproof dish, brush the tops of the rolls with a little milk and bake towards the top of the oven for 15–20 minutes. Serve with Cumberland sauce. (*See Sauces chapter.*)

Bacalhau a Gomes de Sa *(Codfish Pie)* *(Portugal)*

4 medium-sized potatoes
Salt and pepper
2 lb. fresh cod fillet
6 tbsps. olive oil
2 cloves of garlic, skinned and crushed
3 medium-sized onions, skinned and sliced
2 oz. stoned ripe olives, chopped
3 tbsps. dry white wine
2 eggs, hard-boiled
Chopped parsley

Oven temperature: moderate (350°F., mark 4)

Cook the potatoes in their skins in salted water until just tender; drain. Skin, cut into ¼-inch slices and cut each slice in half.

Cook the cod in a saucepan of lightly salted water

until tender. Drain, then flake the fish and discard any bones or skin. Heat the oil in a frying pan, add the garlic, onions and potatoes and brown well for about 10 minutes. Add the olives and some salt and pepper. Arrange half this mixture in the bottom of an oblong shallow baking dish. Lay the cod over and season to taste. Cover with the rest of the potato mixture and pour in the wine. Cook in the centre of the oven for 15–20 minutes. Garnish with finely chopped egg and chopped parsley. Serve hot, from the baking dish. (*Serves 4–5.*)

Note: Salt cod (which is available here in some shops) would be used in Portugal, but this version is adapted for more timid tastes.

Portuguese-Style Cutlets

1 oz. butter
1 onion, skinned and chopped
2 tomatoes, skinned and chopped
1 tbsp. tomato paste
1 level tsp. cornflour
¼ pint stock
Salt and pepper
1 level tsp. sugar
2 tsps. vinegar
8 lamb cutlets

Melt the butter, add the onion and cook for 2–3 minutes without browning. Add the tomatoes and the tomato paste, cover and cook slowly for 20–30 minutes; sieve. Blend the cornflour with a little stock and stir into the sieved mixture with the remaining stock. Bring to the boil and season to taste with salt and pepper. Stir in the sugar and vinegar and keep the sauce warm.

Grill the cutlets, arrange on a large dish and pour the hot sauce round them. A green vegetable may be piled in the centre.

Churros *(Fried Choux Pastries) (Spain)*

2 oz. butter
½ pint water
5 oz. plain flour
3 large eggs
Orange-flower water
Oil for deep frying
A mixture of caster sugar and icing sugar for dusting the churros

Warm the butter and water in a saucepan, bring to the boil, tip in all the flour at once and beat until smooth, off the heat. Add the eggs one at a time and beat until well incorporated. Add orange-flower water to taste – about 1 tbsp. Put the mixture into a forcing bag fitted with a plain vegetable nozzle – ¼–½-inch diameter. Heat a pan of deep fat to about 350–375°F. Carefully pipe lengths of the churros paste into the fat, in rings, spirals or horseshoes; cut the paste off to the required length with a knife. Fry until golden-brown, turning them once. (Don't fry more than about 3 at a time, as the paste swells during the cooking.) Drain thoroughly on kitchen

paper and keep warm. Before serving, dredge them heavily with the mixed sugars. Serve fresh as a dessert, or like doughnuts at tea-time. (*Serves about 6.*)

Arroz Doce *(Rice Dessert) (Portugal)*

3 oz. pudding rice
1½ pints milk
1½ oz. sugar
Thinly pared rind of 1 lemon
3 egg yolks
Powdered cinnamon
Caster sugar

Wash the rice in cold water and drain well. Put the rice, milk, sugar and lemon rind in a saucepan and mix well. Cook very slowly over a low heat until thick and creamy – about 45 minutes. Discard the lemon rind. Stir in the beaten egg yolks and re-heat but don't boil. Turn the mixture into a shallow dish. When it is cold but not chilled, lattice with stripes of cinnamon blended with a little sugar.

Lamb Cutlets Navarra *(Spain)*

4 lamb cutlets
Salt and pepper
1 oz. lard
A 1-lb. slice of gammon, diced
1 onion, skinned and chopped
1 lb. tomatoes, skinned and chopped
½ lb. chipolata sausages

Oven temperature: moderate (350°F., mark 4)

Season the cutlets with salt and pepper and fry them in the lard; when they are browned, transfer them to a casserole. Fry the gammon and onion in the same fat. When the onion is golden-brown, add the tomatoes, season and cook for a further 10 minutes. Pour this sauce over the cutlets, cover the casserole and cook in the centre of the oven for 20–30 minutes. Fry the sausages separately. Place the cutlets in a hot dish and garnish with the cutlets, or if preferred add the sausages to the casserole.

Tortilla *(Potato Omelette) (Spain)*

½ pint oil
1 lb. old potatoes, peeled and sliced
½ an onion, skinned and chopped
4 eggs
Salt and freshly ground pepper

Heat the oil and fry the potato slices until lightly browned, then drain well on absorbent paper. Pour off the oil from the pan, leaving only 1 tbsp. Sauté the onion until clear. Return the potatoes to the pan. Beat the eggs with salt and pepper and pour over the vegetables. Cook over a gentle heat and complete the cooking of the top under the grill. (*Serves 3–4.*)

Andalusian Flamenco Eggs *(Spain)*

2–3 slices of cooked ham
1 tbsp. finely chopped onion
Olive oil or butter
½ lb. tomatoes, skinned and sliced
½ lb. cooked peas
A few asparagus tips
½ lb. cooked potatoes, sliced
½ a green pepper, de-seeded and cut into strips
A little good stock
½ lb. Continental-type sausage
4–8 eggs

Oven temperature: very hot (450°F., mark 8)

Cut the ham into small pieces and fry with the onion in the oil or butter until it begins to colour. Add the other vegetables and sufficient stock to moisten, then sauté gently for a few minutes, stirring carefully. Add the sliced sausage and put the mixture into an ovenproof dish; break the eggs on top and cook towards the top of the oven for 2–3 minutes, until the eggs are just set.

Mackerel in Cream Sauce *(Norway)*

4 mackerel
A bunch of parsley
A little butter
2 level tbsps. flour
Fat for frying
Salt
¼ pint water
¼ pint soured cream

Wash the fish, fillet them and sprinkle the fillets with chopped parsley and a few flakes of butter. Roll up the fillets and tie them with fine string, toss them in flour and fry in a saucepan until brown. Add salt to taste, the water and the soured cream and let them simmer gently in the covered pan for 10 minutes. Remove the strings and serve the fillets with the liquor poured over.

Fish and Potato Casserole *(Finland)*

2 large salt herrings
1 lb. boiled potatoes, sliced
1 tbsp. chopped onion or spring onion
2 tbsps. melted butter
3 eggs
1 pint milk
½ level tsp. pepper
1 oz. dried breadcrumbs

Oven temperature: moderate (350°F., mark 4)

Soak the fish for 6 hours, skin and bone them and cut in long strips. Butter a baking dish and put in a layer of potato, then one of herring, with a little onion; repeat, finishing with a potato layer, and pour the melted butter over the top. Beat the eggs, add the milk and pepper, pour into the baking dish and sprinkle with breadcrumbs. Bake in the centre of the oven for 30–40

minutes, or until browned. (*These quantities make sufficient for 6 persons.*)

Canned salmon may be used instead of salt herring to make this dish.

Bodil's Pork Speciality *(Denmark)*

1½–2 lb. fillet of pork
2 oz. butter
2 onions, skinned and sliced
1½ oz. flour
¾ pint stock
4 tbsps. tomato paste
4 bay leaves
6 sage leaves
Seasoning
6 oz. button mushrooms
8 oz. shelled peas
12–18 asparagus tips

Oven temperature: moderate (350°F., mark 4)

Slice the meat, melt the butter in a pan and fry the meat until it is brown on both sides, then put it into a casserole. Fry the onions in the fat until tender and lightly coloured, then add to the meat, draining off as much fat as possible. Add the flour to the fat in the pan, heat gently until it has browned and gradually add the stock. Bring to the boil and add the tomato paste, bay leaves and sage. Season well, pour over the pork and bake in the centre of the oven for ¾ hour. Peel the mushrooms and pour boiling water on to them; leave for 3 minutes, drain well and add to the casserole. Cook the peas and asparagus tips separately and add them for a garnish. Serve with boiled rice. (*6–8 servings.*)

Rabbit Stew *(Sweden)*

2–3 lb. rabbit, jointed
2 level tsps. salt
1 level tsp. pepper
2 oz. butter or margarine
1 onion, skinned and sliced
½ pint chicken stock
¼ pint white wine
An 8-oz. can of tomato purée
1 level tsp. sugar
2 level tbsps. flour
2 tbsps. chopped parsley

Season the rabbit pieces with some of the salt and pepper and brown in the butter. Add the onion, stock, wine and remaining seasoning and simmer, covered, for ¾–1 hour. Remove the rabbit pieces and onion and keep hot. Stir the tomato purée and sugar into the liquid. Blend the flour with 2 tbsps. cold water, add to the mixture and cook till thickened. Replace the rabbit and onion and add the parsley, then simmer, covered, till heated through. Arrange on a large hot dish and sprinkle with more parsley, if desired. Serve with Browned Potatoes (*see recipe in this section*).

Puolukkaliemi *(Finnish Cranberry Cream)*

1 lb. cranberries (fresh or frozen)
8 oz. sugar (or according to taste)
2 oz. cornflour
Double cream for decoration

Stew the cranberries with $\frac{1}{2}$ pint water, with the lid on, until tender – about 10 minutes. Sieve or put in an electric blender. Add the sugar, using more or less according to taste; add sufficient water to make up to 1 pint with the juice. Mix the cornflour with 2 tbsps. water to a fairly thin paste, add to the cooked cranberries and boil for about 2 minutes, stirring all the time. Pour the mixture into a wetted china or glass mould and leave to set. Turn out, and decorate with whipped cream.

Alternatively, put the cranberry mixture (made with $1\frac{1}{2}$ oz. instead of 2 oz. cornflour) into individual dishes and serve hot, with whipped or single cream.

Note: In Finland, lingenberries would be used, but cranberries make a very good substitute. *(Serves 4–6.)*

Thousand Leaves Torte *(Sweden)*

8 oz. flour
8 oz. butter or margarine
Iced water
Apple pulp
Whipped double cream
White glacé icing
Browned chopped almonds, glacé cherries and angelica to decorate

Oven temperature: very hot (450°F., mark 8)

Sift the flour and cut in the fat, using a knife. Use iced water to mix the pastry and work it with a wooden spoon until it is smooth; cover and chill. Divide the pastry into 6–7 portions, roll out very thinly on waxed paper, cut into rounds and prick all over. Put the rounds on to baking trays, brush over with iced water and bake towards the top of the oven for 6–8 minutes. Leave them on the waxed paper until cold.

Spread alternate pastry rounds with apple pulp and cream, building them up like a layer cake; ice the top with the glacé icing and decorate with the almonds, cherries and angelica.

Beetroot Soup *(Bortsch) (Russia)*

4 large uncooked beetroots
1 oz. butter
3–4 pints very rich beef or pork stock
Salt and pepper
1 tsp. vinegar
Cooked sausages to garnish
Sour cream

Wash the beetroot and shred finely. Melt the butter in a

saucepan and sauté the shredded beetroot for about 10 minutes, then stir in a little hot stock and cook gently. When this stock is absorbed add the remainder of the stock; season, add the vinegar, simmer until the beetroot is quite tender and strain. Serve with a few thin slices of sausage as a garnish and to each plateful add 1 tbsp. very cold sour cream.

If the soup is pale in colour, put a raw beetroot into muslin and shake it in the soup to restore the scarlet colour. It should not be boiled, or it will turn a dull brown colour. *(Serves 8–10.)*

Note: With the Bortsch may be served hard-boiled eggs, small rusks or tartlets filled with cream cheese.

Fyrstekake *(Norwegian Almond Pie)*

6 oz. plain flour
3 oz. butter
3 oz. caster sugar
1 small egg

For the Filling
4 oz. ground almonds
4 oz. icing sugar, sifted
1 large egg, separated
Almond essence

Oven temperature: hot (425°F., mark 7)

Put the flour into a bowl, rub in the fat and stir in the sugar. Mix with beaten egg to form a stiff dough; add a little water if necessary. Chill. Grease a deep 8-inch, straight-sided sandwich tin or flan ring. Line with pastry, prick the base and knock up the edge. Knead together the pastry offcuts, roll out thinly and cut into narrow strips.

Blend the ground almonds, icing sugar, egg yolk and a few drops of essence together; whisk the egg white until stiff and fold into the mixture. Turn this filling into the lined tin. Lattice with the pastry strips. Bake in the centre of the oven for 15 minutes, then reduce the temperature to cool (300°F., mark 1–2) and cook for a further 30 minutes, approx. Serve cut in wedges, with whipped cream if you like. *(Serves 6.)*

Note: This rich pie – literally, 'Prince's Cake' – is traditionally served cold, but it is equally good hot.

Savoury Pancakes *(Russia)*

$\frac{3}{4}$ oz. yeast
$\frac{1}{2}$ pint milk, warmed
12 oz. plain flour, sifted
3 eggs, separated
2 tbsps. cream
A pinch of salt
Fat for frying
Butter, sour cream, caviare or smoked fish for filling

Dissolve the yeast in the milk, make into a dough with 6 oz. flour and leave to prove in a warm place for 2 hours. Add the remaining flour, egg yolks, cream and salt to the dough and mix well to make a thickish batter. Add the stiffly beaten egg whites and leave for $\frac{1}{2}$ hour. Make pancakes, using a small frying pan, spread the cooked pancakes with the chosen filling and pile up. Serve at once.

Easter Bread *(Russia)*

1 oz. yeast
$\frac{1}{2}$ pint milk
1 lb. plain flour
6 egg yolks
6 oz. sugar
2 oz. butter, melted
$4\frac{1}{2}$ oz. candied fruit, chopped

Oven temperature: very hot (450°F., mark 8)

Dissolve the yeast in the warm milk, mix with half the flour and leave to rise. Beat the egg yolks and sugar together and when the dough has risen, mix them in, with the melted butter. Add the remaining flour and the candied fruit. Beat the mixture well, leave to rise again and form it into plaited loaves. Place on a baking tray, prove for 20–30 minutes and bake until well-risen and browned – about 30–40 minutes.

Couscous *(Moroccan Rich Lamb Stew)*

2 tbsps. corn oil
6 shoulder lamb chops
2 onions, skinned and sliced
2 oz. chick peas, soaked overnight
$\frac{1}{2}$ lb. carrots, peeled and sliced
2 turnips, peeled and diced
Salt and pepper
1 pint water
2 oz. stoned raisins
2 oz. blanched almonds, halved
1 lb. courgettes, sliced
2 small green peppers, seeded and sliced
A 14-oz. can of tomatoes
1 level tsp. paprika pepper
$\frac{1}{2}$ lb. ready-bought couscous
1 pint boiling water
1 oz. butter
Chopped parsley

For the Hot Peppery Sauce
$\frac{1}{2}$ pint stock
1 level tsp. Harissa (concentrated pepper-paste sold in cans)
2 level tsps. condensed tomato paste

Heat the oil and brown the chops. Add the onions, peas, carrots, turnips, salt, pepper and water. Bring to the boil, cover and simmer for 1 hour. Add the raisins, almonds, courgettes, peppers, tomatoes, and paprika and simmer for a further $\frac{1}{2}$ hour, until the meat is tender.

Make up the couscous according to the directions on the packet, using the boiling water, butter and $\frac{1}{2}$ level tsp. salt. Blend $\frac{1}{2}$ pint stock from the stew with the Harissa and tomato paste; keep hot. To serve, spread the couscous on a large platter and pile the stew on top;

sprinkle with parsley. Serve the peppery sauce separately. *(Serves 6.)*

Ham Kariba *(E. Africa)*

2 avocados
Lemon juice
2 hard-boiled eggs
3 tomatoes
$\frac{1}{2}$ an onion, skinned
Lettuce
2 oz. peanuts, chopped
Mayonnaise
Salt, pepper and cayenne
12 oz. sliced cooked ham
Chopped parsley

Cut the avocados into thin strips and dip into lemon juice; chop the hard-boiled eggs; skin and slice the tomatoes; chop the onion and some of the lettuce. Mix all these and the peanuts and bind with mayonnaise, adding seasoning to taste. Pile the mixture on slices of ham, folding each slice into a cornet shape, lay them on lettuce leaves and sprinkle with parsley.

Guava Plate Pie *(E. Africa)*

6 oz. shortcrust pastry
$\frac{1}{2}$ lb. guavas
3 oz. sugar
3 eggs, beaten
1 pint milk (or canned evaporated milk)
1 lime

Oven temperature: moderate (350°F., mark 4)

Place a 7-inch flan ring on a baking tray. Line the ring with the pastry and decorate the edge. Stew the guavas with 1 oz. of the sugar and a little water. Make a custard with the eggs, milk and remaining sugar; when it is cool add the juice and grated rind of the lime. Sieve the guavas to remove the pips, put the pulp over the pastry and cover with the custard. Bake in the centre of the oven for 40–45 minutes.

Note: A 15-oz. can of guavas can be substituted for the fresh fruit; drain the contents and omit the stewing process. Lemon can replace the lime if necessary.

Turkish Grilled Lamb

2 lb. leg of lamb
1 tbsp. olive oil
Juice of $\frac{1}{2}$ a lemon
Salt and pepper
1 onion, skinned and sliced
3 tomatoes, sliced
Bay leaves
1 green pepper, seeded and sliced
2 aubergines, sliced

Cut the meat into 1-inch cubes. Mix the oil and lemon

juice and rub into the meat; place it in a dish, sprinkle with salt and pepper and cover with slices of onion and tomato and a few bay leaves. Cover and chill it for 4–5 hours. Arrange the meat on skewers alternately with the pieces of tomato, onion, pepper, aubergine and an occasional bay leaf. Cook under a hot grill, turning the skewers occasionally, until the meat and vegetables are cooked and tender. Broiling over charcoal is of course the best way of cooking the meat, and it may also be cooked over an open wood fire. (Serves 6–8.)

Savoury Meatballs with Rice (Lebanon)

1 lb. lean meat
3 level tbsps. pine kernels
Salt and pepper
Butter for frying
8 onions, skinned
8 tomatoes, skinned and chopped

Mince the meat several times or pound it in a mortar until it is almost like a paste. Add the pine kernels and some salt and mix well. Roll into balls the size of a large marble and fry in hot butter until brown; remove from the pan. Slice the onions lengthwise and fry in the same pan until golden. Combine the meat and onions in a thick saucepan, just cover with cold water, put the tomatoes over them, season to taste and simmer for 1½ hours. Serve with boiled rice.

Turkish Baclava (Baklawa)

4 oz. sugar
7 tbsps. water
6 oz. unsalted butter
8 oz. walnuts, chopped
½ level tsp. ground cinnamon
1 lb. fillo pastry

For the Syrup (best made a day or two before it is required)
4 oz. sugar
7 tbsps. water
8 level tbsps. clear honey
Juice of ½ a lemon

Oven temperature: moderate (350°F., mark 4)

Dissolve the sugar in the water, bring to the boil, draw aside and add 2 oz. of the butter. Allow to melt, then cool, and add the walnuts and cinnamon. Melt the remaining butter, brush a little over a Swiss roll tin and line with layers of fillo pastry, brushing each layer with butter. When half the fillo is used, cover with the walnut filling. Fold the untrimmed edges over and continue covering with layers of buttered fillo. Cut off the overhanging edges of the top layer. Score into squares or diamonds. Brush with butter and bake towards the top of the oven for about 45 minutes, until crisp and golden-brown.

To make the syrup, dissolve the sugar in the water and add the honey and lemon juice. Bring to the boil and while still hot, pour over the baclavas. Cool before cutting into pieces for serving. (Makes about 24 pieces.)

Note: Fillo pastry may be bought from Greek delicatessen shops.

These Turkish (and Greek) sweetmeats are traditionally served with little cups of thick black coffee and a glass of iced water.

Scalloped Aubergines with Meat (Israel)

8 slices of aubergine, ½ inch thick
Salt
1 lb. lamb, mutton or beef, chopped
1 onion, skinned and chopped
4 tbsps. chopped parsley
Pepper or paprika to taste
4 tbsps. tomato paste
2 tbsps. water

Oven temperature: warm (325°F., mark 3)

Salt the aubergine slices and drain them dry as soon as they are softened. Mix the meat with the onion and parsley and season to taste. Spread some of this mixture on each slice of aubergine and arrange them in a well-greased ovenproof dish. Mix the tomato paste and water and pour over the aubergine slices; bake in the centre of the oven for 1 hour. If desired, put under a hot grill to brown the top a few minutes before serving. Garnish with parsley or serve on toast or on a bed of mashed potato or boiled rice.

Persian Chicken Pilau

2 chickens, cooked
1 orange
1 lemon
A few pistachio nuts
2 oz. seedless raisins
8 oz. long-grain rice
Salt
2 oz. butter

Carve good thick slices of breast from the chickens (keeping the rest for some other dish). Put them in a covered dish in the oven to keep hot. Peel the orange and boil the peel with the lemon for about 10 minutes, or until the pith is soft. Cut the lemon and scrape out the pulp and pith with a spoon, so as not to pierce the skin. Scrape the pith from the orange skin. Shred both into very fine threadlike slivers about 1 inch long. Peel and shred the pistachios. Wash and dry the raisins. Boil the rice with plenty of salt until the grains are only just done, take if off the heat and drain at once, drying it in a cloth if necessary – the grains must be clean and separate. Toss it with a good piece of butter while it is still hot. Mix the rice well with the nuts, raisins and shredded peel and then bank some up on a large dish. Arrange the hot chicken breasts over it and cover the chicken completely with the remainder of the rice, so that only a mound of rice shows. Keep it hot by steaming until required for serving.

Spicy Halva (*Turkey*)

6 oz. sugar
¼ pint water
4 oz. butter
4 oz. semolina
2 oz. raisins, seeded
Grated rind of 1 orange
2 oz. ground almonds
4–5 cardomom seeds
Powdered cinnamon

Put the sugar and water into a pan and when the sugar has dissolved, bring to the boil; boil until the syrup thickens, then remove it from the heat. Melt the butter, put in the semolina and brown it, then add the raisins, orange rind, ground almonds and cardomom seeds. Finally add the syrup and cook the mixture over a low heat, stirring all the time, until it is thick. Pour into wetted moulds and when cool, turn out and serve sprinkled with powdered cinnamon.

Prawn Sambol (*India and Pakistan*)

Fat for frying
2 large onions, skinned and chopped
½ level tsp. curry powder
2 bulbs of garlic, chopped
A few slices of ginger, chopped
A little chilli powder
6 oz. peeled prawns
A few cardamoms
A few cloves
A small piece of cinnamon stick
2 ripe tomatoes
½ cup milk
A little tamarind
1 level tsp. sugar
Salt

Heat 1 tbsp. fat and lightly fry a little of the chopped onion with the curry powder. Mix the remaining onion, the garlic, ginger, chilli powder, prawns, cardamoms, cloves and cinnamon, and fry all together for about 5 minutes, stirring all the time. Now add the tomatoes and cook for a few minutes longer; add the milk and cook for about ½ hour over a low heat. Dissolve the tamarind in a little water and add; lastly, add the sugar and season to taste with salt.

Lentil Purée (*Dhal*) (*India and Pakistan*)

4 oz. red lentils
½ pint cold water
Pepper and salt
1 medium-sized onion, skinned
Fat for frying
1 oz. butter or dripping

There is no need to soak the lentils. Wash them, put them into the cold water, add pepper and salt and let them cook steadily for about 1–1½ hours, adding more water if they get too dry. Meanwhile, chop the onion finely and fry it. When the lentils are tender, remove them from the heat and stir vigorously. Add the butter or dripping and the fried onion and stir over the heat to blend well. Serve with curry.

Madras Curry (*India*)

2 oz. almonds, chopped
2 oz. butter or fat
2 onions, skinned and chopped
1 clove of garlic
1 level tsp. coriander powder
1 level tsp. black pepper
½ level tsp. chilli powder
½ level tsp. cardamom powder
½ level tsp. cumin powder
A small piece of cinnamon stick
½ level tsp. ground cloves
2 level tsps. flour
1 pint stock or water
1 lb. meat, cut small
2 level tsps. turmeric powder
1 level tsp. sugar
Salt
Juice of 1 lemon

Cover the almonds with ¼ pint boiling water and leave for 15 minutes, then strain the infusion. Melt the fat and lightly fry the onion and garlic. Add the spices and flavourings (except the turmeric) and the flour and cook for 5 minutes. Add the stock and meat and simmer till tender – 1½–2 hours. Add the almond infusion, turmeric, sugar and salt to taste and simmer for ¼ hour; finally, add the lemon juice.

Pakistan Carrot Sweet

1 lb. carrots
3 pints milk
2 level tbsps. rice
Sugar to taste
½–1 oz. almonds, blanched and chopped

Peel and wash the carrots and grate them, leaving out the hard core. Put the milk on a very slow heat for 2 hours. Boil the rice separately and add the carrots and boiled rice to the milk. Cook until the carrots are well done and the mixture is thickened. Add the sugar and sprinkle with the nuts.

Avocado Soup (*South East Asia*)

2 tsps. butter
1 level tsp. flour
½ pint milk
2 pints chicken stock
1 avocado
Salt and pepper

Cream the butter and flour together until quite smooth, then stir in the milk slowly and cook until thickened, stirring all the time. Add the stock and keep hot. Mash the avocado smoothly and add to mixture, but don't allow it to boil. Adjust the seasoning and strain before serving.

Egg Flower Soup *(China)*

2 pints chicken stock
6 eggs
2 tbsps. soy sauce
1 tsp. vinegar
½ level tsp. salt
2 spring onions, finely chopped

Heat the stock in a saucepan. Meanwhile beat the eggs well, then pour in a thin stream into the stock, stirring. Add the soy sauce, vinegar and salt and simmer for 1 minute. Garnish with the chopped spring onion.

Sweet-Sour Chicken *(South East Asia)*

1 oz. fat
2 cloves of garlic, crushed
1 chicken breast, sliced
4 chicken livers, quartered
2 carrots, peeled
1 cucumber, peeled
2 tomatoes, skinned
1 onion, skinned
¼ pint (approx. a 10-oz. can) of condensed chicken soup
1 level tbsp. flour
2 level tbsps. sugar
3 tbsps. soy sauce
3 tbsps. vinegar

Heat the fat and sauté the garlic until browned. Add the chicken breast and livers. Slice the carrot into ½-inch slices. Split the cucumber lengthwise and cut into pieces ⅛-inch thick. Cut the tomatoes into eighths and the onion in ¼-inch wedges. Add to the meat mixture, with the soup, cover and simmer until tender – about 20–30 minutes. Blend the remaining ingredients and pour over the chicken mixture, then cook for 2–3 minutes. Serve in a bowl, with rice and noodles.

Fried Crispy Noodles *(China)*

½ lb. cabbage, onions or bean sprouts, or a mixture
½ lb. pork
1 lb. noodles
Oil for deep frying
1 tbsp. soy sauce

Shred the vegetables and meat. Put the noodles into boiling water and boil for 5 minutes, then drain; run cold water through them and drain well. Fry in deep oil for 5 minutes, until golden-brown and crisp. Meanwhile fry the vegetables and meat together in 1 tbsp. oil for 5–10 minutes, adding the soy sauce halfway through. Serve the noodles on the vegetables.

Prawns with Bean Sprouts *(China)*

6 oz. shelled prawns
2½ tbsps. sherry
3 tbsps. oil
½ level tsp. salt
6 oz. bean sprouts
1½ tbsps. light soy sauce
½ level tsp. sugar

Soak the prawns in the sherry for 1½ hours. Heat the oil, add the drained prawns and the salt and fry for 2 minutes. Add the bean sprouts and fry for 1 minute. Add the soy sauce and sugar, mixing well. Serve with plain boiled rice. *(Serves 2.)*

Chicken with Almonds *(China)*

¾ lb. raw chicken meat
4 tbsps. cooking oil
4 oz. almonds, blanched
2 oz. mushrooms
1 green pepper
1 carrot
1 bamboo shoot
1 onion, skinned
Salt
2 level tsps. cornflour
2 level tsps. sugar
1 tbsp. soy sauce
2 tsps. sherry
½ pint water
6 oz. boiled rice

Cut the chicken into cubes. Heat a little oil and fry the almonds until golden-brown. Cut up the vegetables. Cook the onion in 2 tbsps. of oil until it is transparent; fry the chicken until it begins to brown; add the rest of the oil and some salt and cook, stirring occasionally, for 5–6 minutes. Blend the cornflour, a little salt, the sugar, soy sauce, sherry and water, bring to the boil, stirring all the time, and pour over the chicken. Add the almonds and make very hot. Serve at once, with the boiled rice.

Sweet-Sour Ribs of Pork *(China)*

2½ lb. belly of pork *(see note)*
½ pint soy sauce
½ pint pineapple juice
¼ pint sherry
1½ level tbsps. brown sugar
1 clove of garlic, crushed

Cut the pork between the bones. Combine all the other ingredients and marinade the pork in this mixture for 6 hours. Cook about 1 inch away from a medium-hot grill for about 7 minutes; turn the meat over and grill for about 5 minutes on the other side.

Note: Ask for the belly of pork to be cut including the rib-ends, that is, as the Americans call spare-ribs – this dish originated among the Chinese in the U.S.A.

Fried Prawns in Batter *(China)*

2 egg whites
6–8 tbsps. flour
Oil for deep frying
1 lb. peeled prawns

Make a batter of the egg whites and flour. Heat the oil; when it is ready dip the prawns into the batter and then drop them one by one into the oil. When they are brown and float to the top, they are done. Serve hot.

Crispy Noodles with Pork and Water Chestnuts *(China)*

1 lb. fresh egg noodles
Oil for deep frying
4 oz. diced pork
Salt and pepper
2 oz. water chestnuts, shredded
2 oz. mushrooms, diced
2 oz. onion, chopped
6 oz. bean sprouts
1 level tsp. cornflour
2 tsps. soy sauce
A few drops of sesame oil (optional)

Boil the noodles for 5 minutes, rinse under cold water and drain. Heat the oil, arrange the noodles in a frying basket in the shape of a nest and deep-fry for 5 minutes, until crisp and golden.

Cook the pork in a hot oiled pan for 1 minute; season to taste. Add the vegetables and cook for 1 minute. Add the cornflour, blended with the soy sauce and enough water to make a thin paste, and cook for 1 minute. Sprinkle with sesame oil (if used) and serve in the noodles.

Sukiyaki *(Japan)*

1 aubergine
6 leeks
2 large onions, skinned
3 medium-sized carrots, peeled
4 large mushrooms
A few sticks of celery
¼ of a cabbage
2 oz. bean curd, if available
A small can of bamboo shoots, drained
1 bunch of watercress
2 oz. Japanese vermicelli, if available
1½ lb. topside or entrecôte steak
2 level tsps. monosodium glutamate
2 level tsps. sugar
2 tsps. soy sauce
¼ pint fish stock
4 tbsps. saké (or other white wine)
6–8 eggs

Sukiyaki means literally 'roasted on a plough-share', and Japanese farmers say that from time immemorial meat has been cooked on the blades of a plough. The modern interpretation of this is a heavy iron casserole or an electric hotplate, which may be put on the table, so that the dish is cooked in front of your guests as they help themselves from it. This is a fine dish for a cool evening.

Each person has chopsticks and a bowl into which a raw egg has been broken; this is beaten up with the chopsticks and each piece of cooked food is then dipped in egg – the hot food cooks the egg and the egg cools the boiling food. The casserole may be refilled as the food is eaten out of it. Add extra sugar, soy sauce, etc., as desired; if the gravy becomes too salty, add broth or water to thin it down. The vegetables used can be varied according to the season, your taste and the number of people eating. (*Serves 6–8.*)

This is the method of cooking. Prepare the vegetables, slicing the aubergines, leeks, onions, carrots, mushrooms and celery. Leave the cabbage in one piece and cook in boiling salted water until nearly tender, then slice thinly. Cut the bean curd in small squares, slice the bamboo shoots, wash the watercress and soak the vermicelli in hot water for 1–2 minutes. Slice the meat as thinly as possible and beat it flat, then cut into small pieces.

Heat a heavy casserole, put in the fat trimmed from the meat and heat until smoking hot, then add the vegetables, bean sprouts and vermicelli and stir them round. Lay the meat on top, covering the vegetables completely, then sprinkle with monosodium glutamate and sugar and add the soy sauce, stock and saké. Leave to cook for 20 minutes over quite a good heat, or until the meat is done to your taste; turn the slices over at half-time. Serve as already described.

Maple Salad *(Japan)*

¼ lb. cucumber, cut into strips without peeling
Salt
1 carrot, peeled and cut into thin strips
½ lb. radishes, cut into thin strips
A few dried mushrooms, soaked and cut into thin strips
Vinegar
3 eggs
½ level tbsp. sugar
1 oz. butter
½ lb. peeled prawns, cut in half lengthwise
Monosodium glutamate

Cover the cucumber strips with salt and allow to stand until they become soft, then press out the liquid. Mix the cucumber, carrot, radishes and mushrooms with 1½ tbsps. vinegar.

Beat the eggs, add 1 level tsp. salt, the sugar and the butter and scramble them, stirring all the time. Force this egg mixture through a sieve while it is hot and allow to cool; mix in 2 tbsps. vinegar.

Combine the vegetables, prawns and a pinch of monosodium glutamate with the egg mixture, stirring gently. Arrange the salad on individual plates, preferably in the form of a maple leaf. (The colours of these foods are chosen to suggest the autumn colouring of the Japanese maple.)

Fish and Vegetable Tempura *(Japan)*

About 1½–2 lb. mixed fish, vegetables, etc. *(see recipe)*
Oil for deep frying

For the Batter
½ level tsp. sugar
1 egg, beaten
4 oz. plain flour
¼ pint milk

Any kind of white fish, prawns or shrimps, carrots, onions, sweet potatoes, French beans, radishes and so on can be used in this dish.

Cut the fish into strips about ¼–¾-inch thick and of even length; leave prawns and shrimps whole. Wash and prepare the vegetables and cut into strips of about the same size as the fish.

Make the batter by adding the sugar and egg to the flour and beating in the milk; add a little water if the batter is too stiff. Dip the fish pieces and the vegetable strips into the batter and fry in the hot oil.

Boston Clam Chowder *(U.S.A.)*

3 oz. raw soft-shell clams, peeled
The clam liquor, strained
¾ pint cold water
4 oz. diced salt pork or 2 level tbsps. butter or margarine
2 medium-sized onions, sliced
2 level tbsps. plain flour
¼ level tsp. celery salt
Salt and pepper
1¼ lb. potatoes, peeled and diced
1¼ pints milk
1 level tbsp. butter or margarine

Snip off the necks of the clams and cut them up finely with scissors; leave the soft parts whole. Place the clams in a saucepan with the strained liquid, add the water and bring to the boil. Lift out the clams with a perforated spoon, retaining the liquid. Sauté the salt pork in a large saucepan until golden; add the onions and cook until tender. Stir in the flour, celery salt, pepper, the retained clam liquor and the potatoes. Cover and cook for 20 minutes, or until the potatoes are tender. Add the milk, clams and butter and correct the seasoning. Re-heat and ladle into large soup bowls, or into mugs if it is to be served out-of-doors. (*8 servings.*)

Peach-Braised Ham *(U.S.A.)*

1 gammon hock
1 onion, skinned
1 carrot, peeled
1 bay leaf
6 peppercorns
2 oz. brown sugar
Peaches in syrup
2 cloves
½ oz. cornflour
Parsley and celery hearts to garnish

Soak the ham for 12–24 hours. Simmer it gently in water with the vegetables and herbs, allowing 20 minutes to the lb. Let it cool slightly in the liquid. Remove the brown skin carefully from the ham and press brown sugar over the fat. Strain the juice from some canned or stewed peaches and add a little of the ham stock and 2 cloves, heat gently in a pan and thicken with a little cornflour; some cider may also be added. Braise the ham in the oven, basting with this liquid for ½ hour before serving. The peach halves may be placed round the ham 10 minutes before it is taken from the oven. Strain the basting liquid and serve with the ham, accompanied with the parsley, peaches and braised celery hearts.

Pilgrim Pumpkin or Squash Pie *(U.S.A.)*

8 oz. granulated sugar
½ level tsp. salt
1½ level tsps. ground cinnamon
½ level tsp. ground ginger
½ level tsp. grated nutmeg
½ level tsp. allspice
½ level tsp. ground cloves
1½ cooked pumpkins
¾ pint evaporated milk
2 eggs, well beaten
An unbaked 9-inch pie shell
Decoration as desired

Oven temperature: hot (425°F., mark 7)

Combine the sugar, salt and spices, add the pumpkin, milk and eggs and beat until smooth. Pour into the pie shell and bake in the centre of the oven for 35 minutes, or until the filling is set. Cool.

To serve, top each wedge with a whirl of whipped cream; in the centre of this place some honey, chocolate curls or well-drained canned crushed pineapple. Alternatively, top with spoonfuls of ice cream or with whipped cream cheese and chopped nuts.

Texas Barbecued Chicken *(U.S.A.)*

4 oz. butter or margarine
2 oz. granulated sugar
¼ level tsp. cayenne pepper
½ tsp. prepared mustard
⅓ pint salad oil
A 14-oz. bottle of ketchup
3 tbsps. Worcestershire sauce
2 cloves of garlic, skinned and minced
2 oz. onion, minced
2 tbsps. lemon juice
¼ tsp. Tabasco sauce
2 ready-to-cook chickens, about 3 lb. each
Salt and pepper

Early in the day, make the barbecue sauce. Melt the butter in a small saucepan, stir in the sugar, then the rest of the ingredients, except the chickens, salt and pepper. Simmer, uncovered, stirring occasionally, for 20 minutes.

About 2½ hours before the meal, start the barbecue fire. When the coals are glowing, rub the whole chickens with salt and pepper; then mount them on the spit and cook for about 1 hour, or until tender, basting them frequently with the sauce and turning them now and then (if the spit is not of the revolving type). Serve half a chicken per person, and hand the rest of the hot sauce separately.

Tortière *(Canadian Double-crust Pork Pie)*

1 onion, skinned and chopped
½ oz. lard
½ lb. pork shoulder, minced
1 clove of garlic, skinned and crushed
¼ pint water
Salt and pepper
A dash of grated nutmeg or powdered mace
A little summer savory, if available
8 oz. shortcrust pastry

Oven temperature: very hot (450°F., mark 8)

Fry the onion in the melted lard until soft but not coloured. Add the meat and garlic and continue frying to seal the meat. Add the water and cook without the lid until the meat mixture is almost tender and the texture thick; if necessary, add more water during the cooking to prevent sticking. Add seasonings and flavourings to taste and leave to cool.

Make up the pastry and use to line an 8¾-inch pie plate or a deep sandwich tin; reserve some pastry for the lid. Spoon the pork mixture into the pastry case and top with a pastry lid. Seal the edges and make a slit to let steam escape. Bake just above the centre of the oven for 10 minutes. Reduce the heat to moderate (350°F., mark 4) and bake for a further 40 minutes. Serve hot, with chilli sauce or other relishes.

Note: French-Canadian families traditionally serve this pie at Christmas and New Year.

Cabbage Slaw *(Canada)*

1 small cabbage, finely shredded
1 level tsp. salt
1 medium-sized red apple (diced and cored but not peeled)
2 sticks of celery, chopped
½ a green pepper, de-seeded and diced
½ level tsp. caraway seeds
Salad dressing to moisten
Lettuce

Combine all the ingredients except the lettuce and toss lightly. Serve immediately in lettuce 'cups'.

Guacamole *(Mexican Appetiser)*

1 small firm tomato, skinned and finely chopped
1 tiny onion, skinned and chopped
6 avocados
2 level tsps. salt
2 tsps. lemon juice
2 tbsps. mayonnaise
1 tsp. salad oil
4 drops of Tabasco sauce
Shredded lettuce

Just before serving, place the tomato and onion in a bowl. Cut the avocados in half and remove the stones; scoop out the flesh, cut into small pieces and add to the tomato. Add all the other ingredients except the lettuce. Toss lightly until blended, then arrange on the shredded lettuce. *(Serves 8.)*

Crisp Sweet Pancakes *(Mexico)*

12 oz. plain flour
1 level tsp. baking powder
1 level tsp. salt
1 level tsp. sugar
4 eggs
2 oz. butter, melted
About ½ pint milk
Oil for deep frying
Sugar and ground cinnamon

Sift the flour, baking powder and salt together and add the sugar and eggs. Beat well and add the butter and as much milk as is necessary to make an easily handled dough. Knead the dough well and form into small balls. Cover the balls with a cloth and leave for 20 minutes; then sprinkle some flour on a board and roll out each ball into a very thin round pancake. Leave them to stand for 5 minutes, then fry them in deep hot oil until they are golden-brown, crisp and flaky. Drain on absorbent paper and dip into a mixture of sugar and cinnamon or serve covered with thin honey. Mexicans often break the pancakes into a soup bowl and add a syrup made with brown sugar and cinnamon.

Coffee Custard *(Argentine)*

1 pint milk
¼ pint single cream
8 level tbsps. instant coffee powder
Grated rind of ½ an orange
4 eggs, beaten
1 egg, separated
3 oz. caster sugar
1 tsp. vanilla essence
1 tsp. almond essence
½ level tsp. salt
Grated nutmeg
3 oz. Brazil nuts, chopped
3 tbsps. guava jelly

Oven temperature: warm (325°F., mark 3)

Heat the milk until boiling, cool slightly, then add the cream, coffee powder and orange rind: leave the mixture to cool. Beat the eggs, egg yolk and caster sugar together until fluffy, then slowly beat in the coffee mixture and the essences and salt. Strain the mixture into 6–8 buttered custard cups and sprinkle each with grated nutmeg. Place in a baking tin and fill the tin with cold water up to $\frac{3}{4}$ inch from the top of the cups. Place the tin in the centre of the oven and cook for 1 hour, or until the mixture is set. Cool and chill.

Just before serving turn the custards out and arrange upside-down on the serving dish. Sprinkle with chopped nuts. Beat the egg white stiffly, fold in the guava jelly and swirl this over the custards.

Montego Pepperpot *(Caribbean)*

1 medium-sized onion, finely chopped
$\frac{1}{2}$ lb. spinach, washed and chopped
$\frac{1}{4}$ of a firm cabbage, shredded
6 oz. frozen or 1 pint fresh prawns or shrimps
1 beef or chicken stock cube
Salt
$\frac{3}{4}$ level tsp. cayenne pepper
2 oz. block creamed coconut *(see note)*
$\frac{1}{4}$ pint hot water

Put the onion, spinach and cabbage into a saucepan and add the prawns (reserving a few for garnish). If you are using fresh prawns, the shells can be added to give extra flavour. Make up the stock cube to 1 pint with hot water and add to the ingredients in the pan. Season, bring to the boil, cover and simmer for 30 minutes. Sieve into another pan, add the creamed coconut dissolved in the hot water and bring slowly to the boil. Serve very hot, garnished with the remaining prawns and accompanied by croûtons or unsalted crackers. This is a smooth, creamy soup with a subtle flavour of coconut. There are many variations in the West Indies, some rather more solid and meaty than this Jamaican version.

Note: Creamed coconut in a solid block may be bought at large food stores and Oriental grocers.

Jug-Jug *(Caribbean)*

4 oz. lean pork, cut in small pieces
4 oz. fresh or salt beef, cut in small pieces
8 oz. pigeon peas
1 small onion, chopped
2–3 blades of chives
$\frac{1}{4}$ level tsp. dried thyme
A sprig of parsley
2 pints water
1 oz. cornflour
1 tbsp. chopped parsley
Salt and cayenne pepper

A hot meat mould served in Barbados at Christmas time, when pigeon peas are in season. It accompanies other meat dishes and fresh salads.

Place the pork, beef, peas, onion, chives and herbs in a saucepan with the water, bring to the boil and reduce the heat. Cover and simmer for 2 hours. Strain off the liquor, reserving $\frac{1}{2}$ pint. Mince the meat and pea mixture. Blend the cornflour and liquor and cook over a low heat for 15 minutes, stirring all the time, then add the minced mixture. Stir in the chopped parsley and season well with salt and cayenne pepper. Press the mixture into a buttered basin, then turn it out, keeping the shape, and serve hot.

Corroboree Curry Hot-Pot *(Australia)*

$\frac{1}{2}$ oz. dripping
1 lb. braising steak, cut into 1-inch cubes
2 onions, skinned and sliced
2 cooking apples, peeled, cored and sliced
2 tomatoes, skinned and sliced
2 level tsps. curry powder
2 oz. sultanas
1 oz. seedless raisins
$\frac{1}{2}$ pint stock
1 level tbsp. flour
Salt
Brown sugar
1 tbsp. chopped parsley
3 hard-boiled eggs, sliced
2 pkts. of potato crisps

Oven temperature: moderate (350°F., mark 4)

Heat the dripping in a pan, add the meat, onion and apple and fry until golden-brown. Add the tomatoes and curry powder and cook for a few minutes longer. Place the mixture in a casserole, add the dried fruit and the stock, cover and cook in the centre of the oven for $1\frac{1}{2}$ hours. Blend the flour with a little extra water and stir into the casserole. Season to taste with a little salt and brown sugar and garnish with the chopped parsley and sliced egg. Surround the casserole with the potato crisps and serve at once.

Colonial Goose *(Australia)*

4-5 lb. leg of lamb, boned
$\frac{3}{4}$ lb. pork, minced
1 onion, finely chopped or grated
Salt and pepper
1 clove of garlic, crushed
1 tbsp. chopped parsley
1 egg, lightly beaten
1 tbsp. dry white wine

Oven temperature: moderate (350°F., mark 4)

Wipe the leg of lamb. Mix together the pork, onion, seasoning, flavourings, egg and wine. Fill the cavity left by the bone and truss firmly. Place in a baking dish with 1 pint water and cook, allowing 25–30 minutes per lb. *(Serves 6–8)*

(See colour picture facing page 257)

Cootamundra Cream *(Australia)*

3 eggs, separated
2 level tsps. sugar
2 level tsps. gelatine
¼ pint hot water
Juice of 1 lemon
¼ pint milk
A 15-oz. can of passion fruit, drained
Halved grapes or glacé cherries to decorate
Whipped cream

Place the egg yolks and sugar in a basin and beat lightly. Dissolve the gelatine in the water and add to the mixture, with the lemon juice and milk; stir in the passion-fruit pulp. Leave to stand until on the point of setting, then whisk well. Lastly fold in the stiffly beaten egg whites, pour the mixture into a glass dish or individual glasses and chill well. Decorate with halved grapes or glacé cherries and serve with whipped cream.

Passion Fruit Cream *(New Zealand)*

2 level tbsps. gelatine
1 tbsp. sherry
½ pint milk
4 oz. sugar (less if canned fruit is used)
¼ pint double cream
6 passion fruit (pulped) or an 8-oz. can of passion fruit (drained)

Soak the gelatine in the sherry. Bring the milk to blood heat and add the sugar, pour on to the gelatine and stir; allow to cool until the mixture is beginning to set. Whip the cream until it is stiff, fold the fruit and gelatine mixture into the cream, pour into a mould and leave in a cool place to set.

Note: The pips of the passion fruit need not be removed – they can safely be eaten.

Toheroa Soup *(New Zealand)*

1 can of toheroa
2 oz. butter
2 oz. flour
Court-bouillon
1 pint milk
1 level tsp. curry powder
Salt and pepper

This is a speciality of New Zealand, particularly of the North Island. Toheroas are large shellfish rather like clams, native to the part of the world, but it is possible to buy them canned in this country.

Drain the liquor from the can and mince the fish. Make a roux with the butter and flour and add the liquor, made up to 1 pint with court-bouillon. Stir in the milk, bring to the boil, then add the minced fish and curry powder and season with salt and pepper to taste. Re-heat before serving.

The Home Freezer

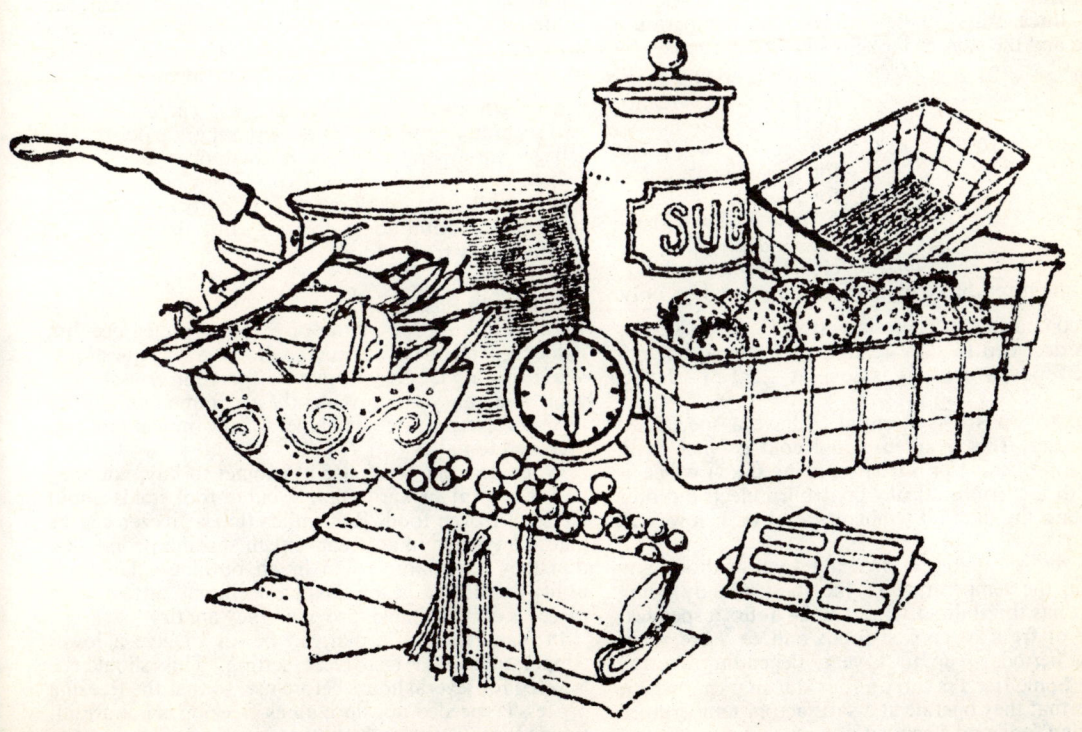

More and more households find it worth while to preserve food in this way – either to make good use of an abundant supply of fruit, vegetables or other food, or to enjoy the luxury of out-of-season delicacies. Some people find it a great convenience to be able to do a large batch of cooking at a time most suitable for themselves and put some of it by for future use, or else to spread the catering for a party over the preceding week or two.

Nearly all refrigerators available in this country have a frozen food storage compartment marked with one, two or three stars; these indicate the temperature achieved and the storage life of ready-frozen foods.

One star*   21°F. (−6°C.)   Frozen food will keep
                                  for *1 week*; ice cream
                                  for 1 day
Two stars**   10°F. (−12°C.) Frozen food will keep
                                  for *1 month*; ice cream
                                  for 2 weeks
Three stars*** 0°F. (−18°C.)   Frozen food will keep
                                  for *3 months*; ice
                                  cream for 1 month
No star marking – Store frozen foods for 2–3 days only.

Any compartment operating at 0°F. (−18°C.) or above is designed to store ready-frozen items, but not to freeze foods, as freezing is done at −5°F. (−21°C.) or below.

To freeze foods it is essential to have a specialised home freezer. This is an insulated cold cabinet (with either a top-opening or a front-opening door) which is fitted with a thermostatically controlled electric motor to maintain the internal temperature at or below 0°F. (−18°C.).

A freezer is capable of freezing food without any change in the temperature of the food already being stored. It has the ability to freeze in 24 hours a specified quantity of fresh or cooked foods and to store them for long periods – up to 1 year, depending on the product. Some freezers carry a four star marking which indicates that they operate at a satisfactory temperature for freezing food and storing it.

Types of Freezer

UPRIGHT MODELS: These resemble a refrigerator and are fitted with shelves. The coldest parts are generally on the shelves. When the door is opened, cold air tends to 'fall out', so if you open the door several times a day, the running costs can be affected. They are however easy to load and unload.

CHEST TYPE: These have a top-opening lid and there is almost no loss of cold air when the lid is opened. The coldest places are at the sides and the base. Most models are supplied with plastic-covered wire baskets to hold the most-often used items and so make them easier to find.

COMBINATION REFRIGERATOR-FREEZERS: These consist of two separately insulated units, with separate doors. The refrigerator operates like a normal one; the freezer (which may be as small as 1 cubic foot or as large as 7 or 8 cubic feet) operating at 0°F, or below, which is suitable for both home freezing and the storing of commercially frozen food.

To Choose a Freezer

Choice is naturally a matter of personal preference, but it does depend on the answers to the following questions: What size model do you require for your household – what size can you conveniently accommodate – what types of freezer are available – how much are you prepared to pay?

When deciding what size of cabinet to buy, you may find it helpful to know that 1 cubic foot holds about 20 lb. of frozen food. Remember that a freezer can be placed anywhere that is convenient – some people find that they have more room in an outhouse, larder or utility room than in the kitchen itself, and any of these places is quite suitable, provided they are dry.

In many freezers a dial can be set to give a lower temperature or a fast-freeze setting. This should be lowered for several hours before use, so that the freezing process is speeded up, since quick freezing is important. Foods contain water which is progressively converted to

240

Useful standbys that keep well in the freezer. Breadcrumbs, egg yolks and whites (separated), lemon and orange peel (grated or slivers), herbs and white sauce—all packed in suitable-sized containers and labelled

ice as the temperature falls. If the process is slow, then large ice crystals are formed, causing deterioration of the texture, flavour and general appearance. If the process is rapid, the food will when thawed be close to the original fresh product.

Once the foods have been frozen, the setting can be returned to 'normal' from 'low', maintaining a temperature of 0°F. (−18°C.). (Using lower temperatures for storage will do no harm whatever to the food but the running costs of the freezer will be unnecessarily high.)

It is an advantage if the freezer has a warning device (a light is the most usual arrangement) which comes on when the temperature starts to rise above 0°F. Alternatively, the electrician who installs the freezer may be able to fit a warning buzzer or light to the plug, which will come on when the current is cut off.

Looking after a Freezer

Most freezers are supplied with full instructions for defrosting. If you don't receive this information, we strongly recommend you to contact the maker, as the procedure for different models varies considerably. However, as a general guide, defrosting should be carried out once every 9 months, or when the ice coating is about

$\frac{1}{4}$ inch thick on the sides of the cabinet. Choose a time when the freezer contains as little as possible; 2–3 hours before switching off, put some old sheets or newspaper in the freezer. Turn off the current at the wall switch, remove any packages, wrap them in several layers of the chilled sheeting or newspaper and put them in a refrigerator or somewhere cold. Put a bowl of boiling water in the freezer and close the lid or door. When the ice has started to melt, you can help the defrosting by scraping the sides with a *plastic* scraper; pick off any loose pieces of frost – it's much easier than dealing with water. Mop up as necessary, drying the sides and base of the freezer well. Turn on the current and leave for about 1 hour for the temperature to drop before you replace the packages.

POWER FAILURE: If the power fails for any reason, don't open the freezer unless you really must. If it is not a general power failure, but the trouble is confined to your particular home, contact your electrician as soon as possible. Meanwhile, the contents of the freezer will keep cold for at least 12–24 hours. When you do open the cabinet, inspect the packages – provided there are still ice crystals present in them, it is safe to keep them in the freezer. If however the food is quite thawed out, it should be used up as soon as possible – that is, within 3 days – and not re-frozen. Remember that once thawed, the food deteriorates rapidly and it must therefore be stored in a refrigerator if possible.

Food for Freezing

It is possible to freeze almost any food. Most varieties of vegetables and fruit freeze well, except for bananas, whole melons, lettuce and some other salad vegetables. Some fruits however tend to lose their colour.

All raw meat, poultry, game and fish may be frozen, also soups, stocks, stews and baked foods, e.g. pies, cakes, biscuits, bread and sandwiches. Some milk and milk dishes may curdle when frozen and are therefore not generally so satisfactory.

The food should be in first-class condition; vegetables and fruits should be nearly ripe, firm and freshly picked; meat and poultry should be of high quality and hung for the necessary time before freezing. Fish should be freshly caught. The preparation process should be carried out rapidly, for foods left lying around soon deteriorate.

Packaging

Pack the foods carefully, for faulty packaging results in loss of quality. Special moisture-proof and vapour-proof packaging materials should be used. Some of the most useful are:

TUBS: Firm, round waxed tubs with airtight lids. They stack well and are very suitable for liquids and for soft, squashable foods, e.g. soups, sauces, fruit in syrup, purées. Let the food cool before putting it in the tubs.

CARTONS: Box-shaped containers of a waxed material slightly thinner than that used for tubs; they are used for foods which might squash – fruit, vegetables, cooked carved meats. The edge of the lid should be sealed with special freezer tape *(see later)*.

RIGID PLASTIC BOXES: Transparent boxes, of the kind often found in refrigerators or sold for carrying sandwiches, can be used for freezing most foods. Seal the lids with freezer tape *(see later)*.

POLYTHENE BOXES: Storage boxes with airtight lids can be used for freezing most foods. Choose the size carefully, so that there is not too much air space round the food. If necessary, seal the lid with Politape.

POLYTHENE BAGS: These bags, which are available in assorted sizes, are very useful. They should be of a fairly heavy guage and must be sealed by special covered metal strips or by heat-sealing with an iron. (When using the latter method, shield the polythene with a piece of paper before applying the iron.)

Use small bags for small, firm, prepared vegetables (e.g. peas, beans), pastry, sandwiches and leftovers.

Medium and large bags are better for poultry, meat, vegetables in 2-lb. lots, etc.

POLYTHENE SHEETING: Very useful for covering joints of irregular shape and for individually wrapped chops, fish fillets, pies, tarts, cakes, etc. Seal with freezer tape.

POLITAPE: Special adhesive sealing tape used for closing packs before freezing.

FREEZER PAPER: Paper with a special coating inside and an uncoated surface outside. It is specially treated so that it doesn't become brittle at low temperatures. It must be sealed with freezer tape. Use as for polythene sheeting.

FOIL DISHES AND BASINS: Good cooking containers for pies, tarts and puddings which are to be frozen.

SHEET FOIL: Tends to puncture, so use carefully.

GLASS BOTTLING JARS WITH SCREW-LIDS. Ordinary bottling jars are very useful for holding soft fruits such as currants, raspberries, strawberries, for liquids and for wet foods such as soups, sauces and stews.

A little soda water in the polythene bag, shaken well, will prevent ice cubes sticking together in the freezer

Labelling

Label all packages carefully with the date of freezing, contents, weight, number of servings, any special processing, etc. Keep account in a notebook of what is in the freezer, and cross off each item as it is used. Use items in rotation. Special freezer adhesive labels can be obtained, but ordinary labels fixed on with freezer tape are equally satisfactory. Tie-on luggage labels can also be used. Waxed containers and foil dishes can be marked with a wax pencil or a felt-tipped pen. (These markings cannot be removed, so avoid them if you wish to re-use the containers.)

General Points about Packing

1. Cleanliness is vital, to avoid contamination.
2. Pack in the most appropriate container for the type of food (*see overleaf*); seal well.
3. Make the packs of a practical size, suitable for your family's needs, since once opened, they should be used up straight away.
4. Allow $\frac{1}{2}$ inch head space for expansion with liquids and with any foods packed in liquid.
5. Exclude as much air as possible before sealing.
6. Label each pack carefully with contents and date, sticking the label on with freezer tape or using a wax pencil to write on the container itself.
7. Make an inventory of the contents of the freezer and use the food in the correct order – storing for too long leads to deterioration. (*For recommended storage times see chart on right.*)

Storing Frozen Foods

Once it is frozen, food should be stored at a minimum temperature of 0°F. (−18°C.), to prevent any increase in the micro-organisms present. Fluctuating temperatures, or storing at a higher temperature, will cause gradual deterioration, with conditions conducive to growth of spoilage agents.

Maximum Storage Period in the Home Freezer

Vegetables, Fruit	Any kind	10–12 months; use up before new season's supply arrives
Meat, uncooked	Beef	8 months
	Lamb, Pork, Veal	6 months
	Mince, Tripe, Offal	3 months
	Sausages	3 months
	Vacuum-packed cured bacon	1–2 months
	Vacuum-packed smoked bacon	1 month
Poultry, uncooked	Chicken	12 months
	Turkey	6 months
	Duck	6 months
	Giblets	3 months
Game (after hanging)	Any kind	6–8 months
Fish (freeze with 24 hrs. of catching)	White fish	6 months
	Oily (salmon, trout, etc.)	4 months
Dairy Produce	Eggs, separated	10 months
	Butter, unsalted	6 months
	Butter, salted	3 months
	Cream (40% butterfat & over)	12 months
	Soft cheese	8 months
	Hard cheese	3 months

LEFTOVER FROZEN FOODS: As a general rule, don't re-freeze leftover foods, especially preparing meat and fish, as they may have deteriorated during thawing.

Technique of Freezing – *General Notes*

Check the temperature of the freezer: it must be capable of freezing fresh food while maintaining the temperature of the foods already frozen at or below 0°F. (−18°C.). Several hours beforehand set the dial or switch to the lowest temperature (−13°F. (−25°C.), check the manufacturer's instructions).

The amount of food to be frozen should not exceed one-tenth of the total capacity of the freezer in any 24 hours.

Pack the food in as shallow a container as practicable, to allow for rapid freezing, and place in direct contact with the coldest part of the freezer, allowing a little space between packages. Don't place in direct contact with any food already frozen, as this will cause some degree of thawing. Once food has been frozen it can be transferred to the storage compartments; the dial or switch is then re-set.

FREEZING FRUIT

Preparation

Rinse all but soft fruits (such as raspberries) in ice-cold water, doing only a few at a time to prevent undue handling. Drain very thoroughly, as wet fruit dilutes the sugar syrup. Avoid using chipped enamel or iron utensils, which may give the fruit a metallic taste. To prevent fruits such as apricots, peaches, pears and yellow plums from discolouring, keep them covered with water and lemon juice (the juice of 1 large lemon to 1 quart water) during the preparation.

Packing

Fruit may be frozen in one of three ways:
1. As a dry pack.   2. In sugar.   3. In syrup.

DRY PACK: Suitable for fruit that is to be used for pies or preserves and for small whole fruits (so long as the skins are undamaged) and for those not likely to discolour, e.g. currants, blackberries, strawberries, gooseberries. Pick over, wash, dry on paper towels and use a rigid container to prevent damage during handling and storage.

FREE-FLOW DRY PACK: This method is suitable for small fruit (or pieces of fruit), e.g. raspberries, strawberries, cherries, grapefruit segments. Pick the fruit over, prepare as necessary, spread out on a baking sheet and freeze until firm, then pack for storage in the cabinet.

IN SUGAR: Particularly suitable for soft fruits. Pick over the fruit but don't wash it unless really necessary. The sugar and fruit can be put into the cartons in layers or

Removal of air—a very important step in the freezing of all food. Extract air by either placing the polythene bag in water to displace the air, or by sucking the air out with a straw

To remove an obstinate frozen 'parcel' from a rigid container or bag, dip it in warm water for just a few minutes to loosen; this is a good way to extract apple purée which is to be reheated straight from the frozen state

they can be well mixed together before being put in. The fruit is more likely to retain its shape if layered, for when it is mixed with the sugar, the juice is drawn out, leaving the fruit almost in purée form when thawed. Use caster sugar.

IN SYRUP: Best for non-juicy fruits or for those which discolour during preparation and storage.

The strength of the syrup varies with the fruit being treated. The usual strength for most fruit is 30%, although soft fruits need a heavier syrup of 40–50% and mild-flavoured ones (such as apples) need only a light syrup of 20%.

20% syrup consists of 4 oz. sugar dissolved in 1 pt. water
30% syrup consists of 8 oz. sugar dissolved in 1 pt. water
40% syrup consists of 10 oz. sugar dissolved in 1 pt. water
50% syrup consists of 1 lb. sugar dissolved in 1 pt. water

To make the syrup, dissolve the sugar in the water by heating gently and bringing to the boil; cover and allow to become quite cold before using.

Use approximately $\frac{1}{2}$ pint syrup to each 1 lb. fruit – this is normally enough to cover the fruit. Leave $\frac{1}{2}$–$\frac{3}{4}$ inch space for expansion during the freezing. If the fruit tends to float above the level of the syrup in the carton, hold it down with a piece of crumpled waxed paper.

Thawing and Cooking Fruit

If the fruit is to be served raw, thaw it slowly in the unopened container and eat while still slightly chilled; turn it into a dish just before serving. Fruits which tend to discolour, e.g. peaches, benefit by being thawed more rapidly. Stone fruits which tend to discolour should be kept submerged in the syrup while thawing. The times to allow (per 1 lb. fruit) are as follows (remember that dry sugar packs thaw rather more quickly than fruit in syrup):

In a refrigerator   allow 6–8 hours
At room temperature   allow 2–4 hours

For quick thawing, place the container in slightly warm water for $\frac{1}{2}$–1 hour.

If the fruit is to be cooked, thaw it until the pieces are just loosened. Cook as for fresh fruit, but don't forget when adding sugar that it will be fairly sweet if it has been packed in dry sugar or in syrup.

FRUIT FREEZING CHART

FRUIT	METHOD OF PREPARATION	PACK
Cooking Apples *Raw*	Peel, core and slice, keeping in water containing lemon juice during preparation. Blanch for 2 minutes in boiling water. Cool in ice-cold water and drain.	1. **Sugar:** mix the blanched fruit with 4 oz. sugar to each 1 lb. fruit. 2. **Syrup:** mix with a 20% syrup.
Cooked	Peel, core and simmer with the juice of a lemon and a minimum of water. Sweeten with 4 oz. sugar to each 1 lb. of fruit.	Pack in rigid containers – cartons or bottling jars.
	Peel, core and simmer with the juice of a lemon and the minimum of water. Sieve or blend.	Pack in small rigid containers.
Apricots	Plunge them in boiling water for 30 secs to loosen skins, then peel. Halve and stone, or leave whole.	Mix with 30% syrup.
Blackberries	Use only large, juicy fruits. Pick over and wash only if really necessary, in ice-cold water; drain.	**Sugar:** mix with 4 oz. sugar to each 1 lb. fruit.
Black-currants	Use only large, juicy fruits and prepare as for blackberries.	**Sugar:** mix with 4 oz. sugar to each 1 lb. fruit.
Cherries *(only dark varieties)*	Pick over, remove stems; stone for packing in sugar or syrup, leave whole for dry pack.	1. **Dry Pack:** add no sweetening. 2. **Sugar:** mix with 3–4 oz. sugar to 1 lb. fruit. 3. **Syrup:** mix with a 30% syrup.
Gooseberries	Top and tail. Wash in ice-cold water, drain.	1. **Dry Pack:** add no sweetening. 2. **Syrup:** mix with 45% syrup. 3. **As purée.**
Nectarines	Treat like apricots.	
Pears *(ripe)*	Peel, core and slice, keeping in water containing lemon juice. Drain and pack at once.	**Syrup:** cover with a 30% syrup.
Peaches	Dip in boiling water and then in ice-cold water. Peel, stone and slice. Keep in water containing lemon juice during preparation. Drain well and pack at once. Alternatively, leave whole, dip in boiling water, then in cold, and peel. Immerse in syrup.	**Syrup:** mix with 30% syrup. Pack individually in polythene bags, each peach completely immersed in syrup.
Plums – Victorias, dark types *(including Damsons)*	Wash, cut in half and stone, but leave the skin on.	**Syrup:** mix with 45% syrup.
Raspberries **Loganberries**	Use firm, dry fruit. Pick over and don't wash unless really necessary; drain.	1. **Dry Pack:** add no sweetening. 2. **Sugar:** 4 oz. sugar to each 1 lb. fruit (layer the fruit and sugar rather than mixing together, or the fruit will pulp).
Strawberries	Use firm, ripe fruit. Hull and wash only if necessary, in ice-cold water; drain.	1. **Dry Pack:** add no sweetening. 2. **Sugar:** mix 4 oz. to each 1 lb. fruit.
Rhubarb	Use young, tender rhubarb; trim, wash and cut in 1-inch lengths.	1. **Dry Pack:** add no sweetening. 2. **Sugar:** 6–8 oz. sugar to each 1 lb. fruit. 3. **Syrup:** mix with 40% syrup.

FREEZING VEGETABLES

Speed is important when dealing with vegetables and they should be frozen only if really fresh, i.e. not more than 12 hours after harvesting.

It is necessary to blanch vegetables (*see next paragraph*) in order to inactivate the enzymes present, so that the colour, flavour and nutritive value of the vegetables can be preserved during storage.

VEGETABLE FREEZING CHART

VEGETABLE	METHOD OF PREPARATION	SCALDING TIME
Asparagus	Grade into thick and thin stems. Wash; discard tough parts of stalks. Leave spears in lengths to fit the package or cut into 2-inch lengths.	Thick stems: 4 mins. Thin stems: 2 mins.
Beans:		
Broad *(young and tender)*	Remove from pods.	3 mins.
French *(small and tender)*	Wash, top and tail; leave whole.	2–3 mins.
Runner *(small and tender)*	Wash, top, tail and string, then slice.	2–3 mins.
Beetroots *(use baby beets)*	Wash, cook and drain; cool, then remove skin. Slice or dice, or if very small, leave whole. Pack.	5–20 mins.
Broccoli, purple sprouting	Trim off large leaves and tough parts of stems; wash thoroughly and cut into even lengths.	3 mins.
Brussels Sprouts *(small and even)*	Trim, wash carefully, drain.	3–4 mins.
Carrots *(young, even-sized)*	Remove tops, wash well and scrape off skins; leave whole, slice, dice or cut lengthwise.	Whole, small: 5 mins. Diced or sliced: 2 mins. Lengthwise strips: 2 mins.
Cauliflower	Wash, then break up the sprigs into small pieces; don't use the leaves.	3 mins.
Courgettes *(use young ones)*	Wash, slice and blanch: drain, cool and pack. (To cook, sauté in butter with seasonings.)	1 min.
Mushrooms	Wash and drain if necessary. Leave whole, or slice if large. Sauté in butter for about 3 mins., drain and pack.	—
Peas *(short, firm pods; sweet, tender peas)*	Remove pods; discard any hard peas.	1½ mins.
Peppers, Green or Red	Wash, halve and remove seeds. Slice and blanch; drain and pack.	3 mins.
Potatoes: these are not very satisfactory in the whole form, but creamed and Duchesse potatoes freeze quite well	Cook and mash in usual way.	—
Spinach	Wash very thoroughly in several changes of water, drain. Remove tough stems. Divide into batches of about 3 oz. each for blanching.	2 mins.
Sweet Corn *On the cob* *Whole-grain*	Husk, remove silk, wash and sort cobs according to size. After scalding the cobs *(see 3rd column)*, cut off grains with a sharp knife.	Small: 4 mins. Medium: 6 mins. Large: 9 mins.
Tomatoes, Whole	Blanch, skin, cool, then pack into cartons.	—
Tomato Juice	Wash and trim tomatoes, cut in quarters, simmer for 5–10 mins. and sieve. Add 1 level tsp. salt to 1 quart of juice; cool and pour into containers.	—
Vegetable Purées *(Asparagus, Beetroot, Carrot, Parsnip, Turnip)*	Cook until tender in boiling water, or steam; mash or sieve.	—

Note: The following vegetables do not freeze well: Celery, Cucumber, Lettuce, Marrow, Onions, Radishes, Watercress and other green vegetables that are eaten raw.

Blanching

Use a pan large enough to hold a colander or wire basket. Place the vegetables in the basket and immerse this in boiling water (approx. 3 quarts to 1 lb. of vegetables). When the water re-boils, cook the vegetables for the recommended length of time (*see table*), then plunge them into ice-cold water; drain and pack immediately. Don't add salt until the frozen vegetables are cooked for serving. Don't scald more than 1–2 lb. vegetables at a time; the same water may be used for scalding successive batches of the same kind.

Packing

Cool and drain thoroughly. Pack into rigid containers, leaving little space for expansion for those vegetables that pack tightly, e.g., peas, whole-grain corn. If free-flow packs are required (peas, beans), then freeze on a tray until just firm before packing.

Thawing and Cooking

Place the frozen vegetables in a minimum amount of boiling salted water (about $\frac{1}{2}$ pint water and $\frac{1}{2}$ level tsp. salt to a 1-lb. package), cover the pan and simmer until tender.

FREEZING MEAT

If good quality meat is available direct from a farm or at a wholesale price, then freezing is a practical proposition.

Very lean meats tend to dry out during freezing, but a layer of fat and good 'marbling' help to prevent this. Too much fat, on the other hand, tends to become rancid. It is important to select the meat carefully. Buying meat that is already frozen is another possibility, particularly if you are inexperienced at butchering. Ready-frozen meat is available in bulk packs, sold as whole carcasses, halves or quarters. If required, specified joints can be bought, but at increased cost.

Preparation of Raw Meat

JOINTS: Trim off excess fat. Pad any sharp bones to avoid puncturing the wrapping. Don't freeze unnecessarily large amounts of bone.

STEAKS AND CHOPS: Trim as usual. Separate the portions by placing freezeproof paper between them, to prevent their freezing together; alternatively, wrap them individually in polythene sheeting.

OFFAL: Trim as required. If necessary, divide into convenient-sized pieces.

Packing and Freezing

This is very important, for incorrect or inadequate packaging will result in rancidity and/or drying out of the meat, with possible freezer burn. Pack in quantities suitable for use. Use a polythene bag or wrap in polythene sheeting. Large joints may be given an outer wrapping of strong paper or stockinette. Seal carefully. Freeze rapidly until solid.

Thawing and Cooking

There is some discussion as to whether or not it is better to thaw meat before cooking. In general, joints cooked from frozen have a better flavour than those that have been thawed first, although when thawed they are on the whole more tender. The only snag about cooking straight from frozen is the difficulty of ensuring that the inside is done without overcooking the outside. (This is no problem, of course, with steaks, chops and other cuts that are 1 inch or less in thickness.) *See the more detailed instructions under the heading 'To Cook Joints from Frozen'.*

Obviously, for very large or solid joints, thawing before cooking is the safer bet. As a rough guide, allow 6 hours per lb. in the refrigerator, or 3 hours per lb. at average room temperature; slow thawing results in less dripping, incidentally. Mince and stewing or braising meats are also best thawed, though in an emergency partial thawing will suffice. Once thawed, the meat should be cooked at once; if for some reason it has to wait a short time, be sure to keep it in the refrigerator.

Completely thawed frozen meats are cooked in exactly the same way as their fresh meat counterparts. It is perfectly in order to use frozen meat in making up a dish, and then to freeze this dish in the usual way.

To cook Joints from Frozen

Place in a cold oven, set to the required temperature, and time from the moment when that temperature is reached (approx. 30 minutes). Always use a meat thermometer, inserting it as soon as the joint has thawed enough to pierce the flesh.

BEEF: fairly hot (375°F., mark 5); allow 30 mins. per lb. and 30 mins. over.

LAMB: moderate (350°F., mark 4); allow 25 mins. per lb. and 20 mins. over.

PORK: hot (425°F., mark 7); allow 25 mins. per lb. and 25 mins. over.

To cook Chops, Steaks, etc., from Frozen

Grill or fry from frozen, using a gentle heat until the meat is thawed, then increase the heat.

FREEZING POULTRY AND GAME

POULTRY: Choose a young, tender bird and starve it for 24 hours before killing. After plucking it carefully, leave it to hang in a cool larder for a day.

GAME: All game must be hung prior to freezing, for the same length of time as for immediate use and according to individual taste.

Preparation

Remove the head and the feet (*see Poultry chapter*). Draw the bird, clean it well by washing it in cold running water, then drain it. Discard the gall bladder and clean and wash the giblets.

If required, divide the bird into joints, which will take up less room in the freezer; wash and drain the pieces as above.

Containers which are only part-filled or whose contents rise above the surface of the liquid, such as fruit salad, should be given an inner cover of crumpled greaseproof or waxed paper before being wrapped

Packaging

Truss the bird as for the table (but don't stuff it, in the case of poultry). Pad any protruding bones with grease-proof paper. Put the bird in a polythene bag, squeeze out as much air as possible, then seal the bag. Wrap the giblets separately and freeze them with the bird.

Joints of poultry should be wrapped separately in polythene sheeting, then put all together in a polythene bag and sealed.

Thawing

Thaw the bird completely, leaving it in its wrapping; the time required depends both on the size of the bird and on the method of thawing. A 4-lb. bird will take 7–8 hours at room temperature or 12 hours in a refrigerator. Alternatively, put the bird in cold running water, allowing $\frac{1}{2}$ hour per lb. Don't open the packaging.

Correct thawing, and subsequent sterilising temperatures in the cooking, are a safeguard against any bacterial contamination. If the bird is not thawed completely, take the added precaution of prolonging the cooking time. At the end of the cooking the juices should be clear.

Note: Once thawed, the bird should be used as soon as possible.

FREEZING FISH

Only **very** fresh fish must be used.

Preparation

Clean as usual – that is, scale, remove the fins and gut the fish. Leave small fish whole, but remove the heads and tails of larger fish. Skin and fillet flat fish.

Salmon to be frozen whole requires special care. Wash it and remove the scales, gut and wash thoroughly under running water; drain and dry. Place the whole fish (unwrapped and firmly supported) in the freezer, and freeze until solid. Remove, and dip in cold water; this forms a thin ice over the fish; return it to the freezer. Repeat the process until the ice glaze is approx. $\frac{1}{8}$ inch thick.

Packaging
Wrap the fish individually in polythene sheeting. Pack in flat cartons.

Wrap ice-glazed salmon in heavy-duty polythene and support with a thin board.

Thawing
Thaw slowly in the unopened package in a cool place, continuing just long enough to separate the pieces – 45 minutes at room temperature, 3–4 hours in a refrigerator. Small fish may be cooked in the frozen state, in which case the cooking time must be a few minutes longer than usual.

Whole salmon: allow to thaw before cooking (24 hours in a refrigerator). Once thawed, use promptly.

Steaks may be cooked from frozen.

FREEZING SHELLFISH

Freeze the same day as they are taken from the water.

OYSTERS AND SCALLOPS: Wash the outside of the shell thoroughly, removing all dirt and sand. Open carefully and drain, retaining the liquor. Wash the fish in a brine solution (1 level tbsp. salt to 1 pint water). Drain, pack in small containers with the reserved liquor and freeze.

PRAWNS AND SHRIMPS: Freeze raw. Remove the heads but not the shells. Wash in a brine solution ($\frac{1}{2}$ level tbsp. salt to 1 pint water); drain, pack and freeze.

CRAB AND LOBSTER: Cook before freezing. Remove the meat from the shells and pack in small containers. The brown and white meat of the crab should be packed separately.

FREEZING EGGS

Preparation
Eggs cannot be frozen whole because they crack, so they must be broken and the yolks and whites frozen separately. Yolks congeal and are not very satisfactory, but are better if mixed with either a little salt or a little sugar, depending on how they are to be used; for 6 yolks add 1 level tsp. salt or 2 level tbsps. sugar.

Packaging
Used waxed cartons or polythene bags.

Thawing
Thaw completely in the unopened package for $\frac{1}{2}$ hour.

FREEZING COOKED FOODS

See chart on pages   –   for choice of foods for freezing.

Preparation
In general, prepare and cook the foods as if they were to be served immediately, but reduce seasonings or omit them altogether (adding them during the re-heating). Take care not to overcook the foods, particularly if they are to be re-heated for serving.

Chill the foods promptly after cooking and package them as carefully as when freezing fresh foods.

Remember that liquids such as soups and sauces expand, so leave space for this.

Use aluminium foil dishes for foods which will be re-heated for serving.

Freeze immediately, at 0°F.

Notes:
1. Pies, Flans, Tartlets: Fillings thickened with cornflour or gelatine freeze well. Cooked custards may curdle. Jam, fruit and mince pie fillings all freeze satisfactorily in a pastry case.
2. All Pastries are improved by re-heating, but must then be used at once, for they fairly quickly become stale.
3. Packing Cakes and Pastries: If you use waxed cardboard boxes and wish to store the foods for the maximum period, enclose the boxes in polythene bags.
4. Take particular care with the sealing of all meat dishes.
5. Unless otherwise directed, thaw foods in the refrigerator.

See the chart which follows for details of preparation, packing, etc., for various individual cooked foods.

Headspace—allow about $\frac{1}{2}$ in. space for solids in thickened liquids, about 1 in. for 1 pt. liquid, and a little more for larger amounts. Don't forget that when a lid is to be fitted onto, say, a rigid foil container, the contents should be below the line where the lid is to be put in position

HOME FREEZING REFERENCE CHART

FOOD & STORAGE TIME	PREPARATION	FREEZING	THAWING AND SERVING
Meat, Raw (*leave unstuffed*) Beef: 8 months Lamb: 6 months Veal: 6 months Pork: 6 months Freshly minced meat: 3 months Offal: 3 months Cured and smoked meats: 1–2 months Sausages: 3 months	Use good quality, well-hung fresh meat. Removing bones will save space. Butcher in suitable quantities. Place polythene sheets between individual chops or steaks.	Package carefully in heavy-quality polythene bags. Group in similar types, and overwrap with mutton cloth, stockinette, thin polythene or newspaper, to protect against puncturing and loss of quality.	All meats may be cooked from frozen (*see p. 410*) but with large joints avoid over-cooking meat on outside and leaving it raw at centre. Thaw in the refrigerator, keeping wrappings on; allow about 6 hrs. per lb. Small items like chops, steaks, can be cooked frozen, but use gentle heat. Partial thawing is necessary before egg-and-crumb-coating, etc.
Meat, Cooked Dishes Casseroles, stews, curries, etc.: 2 months	Prepare as desired. See that the meat is cooked but not over-cooked to allow for re-heating. Do not season too heavily – check this at point of serving. Have enough liquid or sauce to immerse solid meat completely. Don't add potato, rice or spaghetti, as they acquire a warmed-up flavour best added at point of serving; unless otherwise stated same applies to garlic and celery.	When mixture is quite cold, transfer to waxed cartons; for dishes with a strong smell or colour, inner-line cartons with polythene bags. Or use foil dishes, or freeze in foil-lined cook-ware.	Re-heat food from cartons or polythene bags in a saucepan or casserole dish. Pre-shaped foil-wrapped mixtures can be re-heated in the original dish. When re-heating in a casserole, allow at least 1 hr. for heating through in a fairly hot oven (400°F., mark 6) then if necessary reduce heat to moderate (350°F., mark 4) until really hot. Alternatively, heat gently in a pan, simmering till hot through.
Meat, Roast 2–4 weeks	Joints can be roasted and frozen for serving cold – don't over-cook. Re-heated whole joints are not very satisfactory. Sliced frozen cooked meat tends to be dry when re-heated.	Best results are achieved by freezing whole joint, thawing, then slicing prior to serving. But small pieces can be sliced and packed in polythene if required to serve cold, or put in foil containers and covered with gravy, if to be served hot.	Allow plenty of time for thawing-out – about 4 hrs. per lb. at room temperatures, or double that time in the refrigerator, in the wrapping. Sliced meat requires less time.
Meat Loaves, Pâté 1 month	Follow regular recipe. Package in the usual way, after cooling rapidly. Keep for minimum time.	When quite cold, remove from tin, wrap and freeze.	Thaw, preferably, overnight or for at least 6–8 hrs. in the refrigerator.

251

HOME FREEZING CHART *continued*

FOOD & STORAGE TIME	PREPARATION	FREEZING	THAWING AND SERVING
Poultry and Game Chicken: 12 months Duck: 6 months Goose: 6 months Turkey: 6 months Giblets: 3 months Game birds: 6–8 months Venison: 12 months	Use fresh birds only: prepare and draw in the usual way. Do not stuff before freezing. Cover protruding bones with greaseproof paper or foil. Hang game desired time before freezing.	Pack trussed bird inside polythene bag and exclude as much air as possible before sealing. Freeze giblets separately. If wished, freeze in joints, wrap individually, and then overwrap.	Thaw in wrapping, preferably in refrigerator. Thaw a small bird overnight; birds up to 4 lb. up to 12 hrs.; 4–12 lb. up to 24 hrs.; over 12 lb., 48–72 hrs. Joints, 6 hrs.
Fish, uncooked Salmon: 4 months White fish: 6 months Whole (salmon and freshwater fish)	Must be really fresh – within 12 hrs. of the catch. Wash and remove scales by scraping tail-to-head with back of knife. Gut. Wash thoroughly under running water. Drain and dry on a clean cloth.	For best results, put whole fish unwrapped in freezer till solid. Remove, dip in cold water. This forms ice over fish. Repeat process until ice glaze is $\frac{1}{4}$-inch thick. Wrap in heavy-duty polythene; support with a thin board.	Allow to thaw for 24 hrs. in a cool place before cooking. Once thawed use promptly.
Fish steaks	Prepare in usual way.	Separate steaks with double layer of Saran; wrap in heavy polythene.	May be cooked from the frozen state.
Shellfish	It is not advisable to home-freeze this.		
Fish, cooked Pies, fish cakes, croquettes, kedgeree, mousse, paella: 2 months	Prepare according to recipe, but be sure fish is absolutely fresh. Hard-boiled eggs should be added to kedgeree before reheating.	Freeze in foil-lined containers, remove when hard, then pack in sealed bags.	Either slow-thaw in refrigerator or put straight into moderate oven (350°F., mark 4) to heat, depending on type of recipe.
Sauces, Soups, Stocks 2–3 months: if highly spiced, 1–2 weeks	All are very useful as stand-bys in the freezer.	When cold, pour into rigid containers, seal well and freeze.	Either thaw for 1–2 hrs. at room temperature or heat immediately until boiling point is reached.
Pizza, unbaked Up to 3 months	Prepare traditional yeast mixture to baking stage. Wrap in foil or polythene.	Freeze flat until solid, then overwrap in ones, twos, threes or fours.	Remove packaging and place frozen in cold oven set at 450°F. (mark 8) and bake for 30–35 min.

Pizza, baked Up to 2 months	Bake traditional yeast mixture in usual way.	Package in foil or polythene and freeze as for unbaked pizza.	Remove packaging and place frozen in a pre-heated fairly hot oven (400°F., mark 6) for about 20 mins., or leave in packaging at room temperature for 2 hrs. before baking as above for 10–15 mins.
Pancakes, unfilled 2 months	Add 1 tbsp. corn oil to a basic 4 oz. flour recipe. Make pancakes, and cool quickly on a wire rack. Interleave them with lightly oiled greaseproof paper or polythene film. Seal in polythene bags or foil.	Freeze quickly.	To thaw: leave in packaging at room temperature for 2–3 hrs., or overnight in the refrigerator. For quick thawing, un-wrap, spread out separately and leave at room temperature for about 20 mins. To re-heat, place stack of pancakes wrapped in foil in the oven at 375°F. (mark 5) for 20–30 mins. To re-heat individual pan-cakes, place in a lightly greased heated frying pan, allowing ½ min. for each side.
Pancakes – Filled 1–2 months	Only choose fillings suitable for freezing. Don't over-season.	Place filled pancakes in a foil dish, seal and overwrap.	Place frozen in packaging in oven at 400°F. (mark 6) for about 30 mins.
Pastry, uncooked Shortcrust: 3 months Flaky and puff: 3–4 months	Roll out to size required (or shape into vol-au-vent cases). Freeze pie shells un-wrapped until hard to avoid damage. Use foil plates or take frozen shell out of dish after freezing but before wrapping. Discs of pastry can be stacked with waxed paper between for pie bases or tops. *Note:* There is little advantage in bulk-freezing unshaped pastry, as it takes about 3 hrs. to thaw before it can be rolled out.	Stack pastry shapes with 2 pieces of Saran or waxed paper between layers, so that, if needed, one piece can be removed with-out thawing the whole batch. Place the stack on a piece of cardboard, wrap and seal.	Thaw discs at room temperature, fit into pie plate and proceed. Return unbaked pie shells or flan cases to their original con-tainer before cooking; they can go into oven from the freezer (ovenproof glass should first stand for 10 mins. at room temperature); add about 5 mins. to normal baking time.
Pastry Pies, uncooked Double-crust: 3 months	Prepare pastry and filling as required. Make large pies in a foil dish or plates, or line an ordinary dish or plate with foil and use as a pre-former. Make small pies in patty tins or foil cases.	Freeze uncovered. When frozen, remove small or pre-formed pies from containers and pack all pies in foil or polythene bags.	Unwrap unbaked fruit pies and place still frozen in a hot oven 425°F. (mark 7) for 40–60 mins., according to type and size. Slit tops of double crusts when beginning to thaw.
Top Crust; 3 months	Prepare pie in usual way; cut fruit into fairly small pieces, blanch if necessary, and toss with sugar. Alternatively, use cold cooked savoury filling. Cover with pastry. Do not slit crust.	Use ovenproof glass or foil dishes. Wrap in foil or plastic film, protecting as for cooked pies.	Unwrap and place in pre-heated oven. (Ovenproof glass should first stand for 10 mins. at room temperature.) Cut a vent in pastry when it begins to thaw. Add a little to usual cooking time.

HOME FREEZING CHART *continued*

FOOD & STORAGE TIME	PREPARATION	FREEZING	THAWING AND SERVING
Pastry, cooked Pastry cases: 6 months Meat pies: 3–4 months Fruit pies: 6 months	Prepare as usual. Empty cases freeze satisfactorily, but with some change in texture. Prepare pies as directed (using an aluminium foil dish). Brush pastry cases with egg white before filling. Cool completely before freezing.	Wrap carefully – very fragile. Protect the tops of pies with an inverted paper or aluminium pie plate, then wrap and seal.	Leave pies at room temperature for 2–4 hrs., depending on size. If required hot, re-heat in the oven. Flan cases should be thawed at room temperature for about 1 hr. 'Refresh' them if you wish.
Biscuit Pie Crust 2 months	Not easy to handle unfilled unless the crust is pre-baked. Shape in a sandwich tin or pie plate, lined with foil or waxed paper. Add filling if suitable.	Freeze until firm, then remove from tin in the foil wrapping and pack in a rigid container.	Filled, to serve cold, thaw at room temperature for 6 hrs.
Sweets Mousse, creams, etc.: 2–3 months	Make as usual; these can be frozen in new toughened tableware glasses by Duralex.	Freeze, unwrapped, in foil-lined container until firm, then remove container, place in polythene bag, seal and return to freezer.	Unwrap and thaw in refrigerator for about 6 hrs. or at room temperature for about 2 hrs.
Ice cream 3 months Commercially made: 1 month	Either home-made or bought ice creams and sorbets can be stored in the freezer.	Bought ice creams should be re-wrapped in moisture-proof bags before storing. Home-made ones should be frozen in moulds or waxed containers and over-wrapped.	Put in freezing compartment of the refrigerator for 6–8 hrs., to soften a little. Some 'soft' bought ice cream can be used from freezer – keep away from elements, or sides of chest model.
Cream Up to 12 months: ideally about 4 months	Use pasteurized only, with a 40% butter-fat content, or more (i.e. double cream). Whipped cream may be piped into rosettes on waxed paper.	Transfer cream to suitable container, e.g. waxed carton, leaving space for expansion. Freeze rosettes unwrapped; when firm, pack in a single layer in foil.	Thaw in refrigerator, allowing 8 hrs. or 1–2 hrs. at room temperature. Put rosettes in position as decoration before thawing, for they cannot be handled.
Cakes, cooked Including sponge flans, Swiss rolls and layer cakes: 6 months (Frosted cakes lose quality after 2 months; since aging improves fruit cakes, they may be kept longer)	Bake in usual way. Leave until cold on a wire rack. Swiss rolls are best rolled up in cornflour, not sugar, if to be frozen without a filling. Do not spread or layer with jam before freezing. Use minimum amount of essences, and go lightly with spices.	Wrap plain cake layers separately, or together with Saran or waxed paper between layers. Freeze frosted cakes (whole or cut) unwrapped until frosting has set, then wrap, seal, and pack in boxes to protect icing.	Iced cakes: unwrap before thawing, then the wrapping will not stick to the frosting when thawing. Cream cakes: may be sliced while frozen, for a better shape and quick thawing. Plain cakes: leave in package and thaw at room temperature. Un-iced layer cakes and small cakes thaw in 1–2 hrs. at room temperature; frosted layer cakes take up to 4 hrs.

Food	Preparation	Packing/Freezing	Thawing and Serving
Scones and Teabreads 6 months	Bake in usual way.	Freeze in polythene bag in convenient numbers for serving.	Thaw teabreads in wrapping at room temperature for 2–3 hrs. Tea scones: cook from frozen, wrapped in foil, in fairly hot oven (400°F., mark 6) for 10 mins. Girdle scones: thaw for 1 hr. Drop scones: thaw for 30 mins.
Croissants and Danish Pastries Unbaked in bulk: 6 weeks	Prepare to the stage when all the fat has been absorbed, but don't give the final rolling.	Wrap in airtight polythene bags and freeze at once.	Leave in polythene bag, but unseal and re-tie loosely, allowing space for dough to rise. Preferably thaw overnight in a refrigerator, or leave for 5 hrs. at room temperature. Complete final rolling and shaping and bake.
Baked: 4 weeks	Bake in usual way. (Don't ice Danish Pastries.)	Cool, wrap and freeze.	Thaw wrapped at room temperature, 1–2 hrs. 'Refresh', wrapped in foil, in hot oven for 5 mins.
Biscuits, Baked and Unbaked 6 months	Prepare in the usual way. Rich mixtures – i.e. with more than ¼ lb. fat to 1 lb. flour – are the most satisfactory.	Freeze these either baked or non-baked. Pack carefully. Wrap rolls of uncooked dough or pipe soft mixtures into shapes, freeze and pack when firm. Allow cooked biscuits to cool before packing.	Thaw uncooked rolls of dough slightly; slice off required number of biscuits and bake. Shaped biscuits can be cooked direct from frozen state: allow 7–10 mins. extra time. Cooked biscuits may need crisping.
Bread and Rolls 4 weeks	Freshly-baked bread, both bought and home-made, can be frozen. Crisp, crusty bread stores well up to 1 week, then the crust begins to 'shell off'.	Bought bread may be frozen in original wrapper for up to 1 week; for longer periods, seal in foil or polythene. Home-made bread: freeze in foil or polythene bags.	Leave to thaw in the sealed polythene bag or wrapper at room temperature, for 3–6 hrs. or overnight in the refrigerator, or leave foil-wrapped and crisp it in a fairly hot oven (400°F., mark 6) for about ¾ hr.
Sandwiches 1–2 months	Most types may be frozen, but those filled with hard-boiled eggs or bananas tend to go tasteless and soggy.	Wrap in foil, then in polythene bag.	Thaw unwrapped at room temperature or in refrigerator. Time varies according to size of pack. Cut pinwheels, sandwich loaves, etc., in portions when half thawed.
Marmalade 6 months: useful if it's not convenient to make marmalade when Seville oranges are in season	Wash, dry and freeze Seville oranges whole or prepare marmalade to cooked pulp stage – i.e. before addition of sugar.	Pack whole oranges in polythene bags, pulp in suitable containers.	Thaw, still wrapped, in fridge, allowing 6–8 hrs. per lb. for whole fruit and 9–12 hrs. per lb. for pulped, then finish cooking.

HOME FREEZING CHART *continued*

FOOD & STORAGE TIME	PREPARATION	FREEZING	THAWING AND SERVING
Herbs Thyme, sage, rosemary, parsley, mint: 2–3 months	Wash and dry herbs. These can be chopped before freezing, or crumbled when frozen. Prepare bouquet garni, if required.	Wrap in small bundles and place in moisture-proof bags. Make individual foil-wrapped packs of chopped herbs.	If kept accessible, frozen herbs are as useful as dried, for they can be popped into stews, etc., while still frozen.
Butter Salted: 3 months Unsalted: 6 months	Always buy fresh stock (farmhouse butter must be made from pasteurised cream).	Overwrap in foil in quantities of $\frac{1}{2}$–1 lb.	Allow to thaw in refrigerator.
Commercially Frozen Foods Up to 3 months as a rule *Note:* The times quoted by the manufacturers are often less than those given for home-frozen foods, because of the handling in distribution, before the foods can reach your own freezer.	No further preparation, etc., needed, except for ice cream, which should be overwrapped if it is to be kept for longer than 3 weeks.		Follow directions on packet.

Lemon Gâteau, *page 188*

Colonial Goose, *page 237*

Wines

The Nature of Wine

Wine, as most people know, is the juice from freshly gathered grapes, extracted by crushing the fruit and then fermented. This process turns the grape sugar into alcohol (which acts as a preservative) and the juice becomes wine. In table wines the actual amount of alcohol is rarely less than 9% or more than 15%. When additional alcohol is added, you have a 'fortified' wine – *see later*.

There are many different kinds of grape, grown in various parts of the world, and also different methods of vine-growing and wine-making. The soil, climate and aspect of the vineyards all influence the character of the wine, and the quality of the grape juice also varies from year to year according to the weather, just as other crops do. So the same wine varies from vintage to vintage.

How to Buy Wine

The reliable wine merchant with a reputation to lose is the best adviser you can have, if you are not conversant with the different styles and brands of wine on the market. True, increased travel abroad has been largely responsible for an increase in wine consumption at home. But sometimes the wine you liked on a foreign holiday seems disappointing in the home environment and in a different climate. That is why professional wine buyers taste a wine both in its country of origin *and* in Britain before they draw conclusions. It can't be emphasised too often that the best wine for you is the one that most pleases your taste at the price you want to pay – and by means of experimental tastings the wine merchant worth his salt can aid you in finding it.

The Price

You can buy palatable table wine from around 60p a bottle. But if you pay an extra 10–15p or so for the same kind of wine, it will usually be more than that much better, since the costs of bottling and shipping are the same for each bottle. For instance, pay 50p for a bottle of wine and you get say 12p of sheer wine value. Pay 75p for the same kind of wine and you get 35p wine value. You can do your own arithmetic after that – bearing in mind the provisos that follow. Unless you are a connoisseur it isn't likely you'll want to spend, say, £8 a bottle, which one *can* pay for the finest, rarest wines from small, perfectly sited vineyards.

Expect to pay more for Château- or Domaine-bottled wine, simply because it's dearer to ship bottles than to ship in bulk.

Wines that don't state the vintage may be blends of different years or of a year that doesn't have a reputation for quality.

For general interest the following are the good vintages to look for, though some of them in one or other category may by now have achieved a scarcity value which will make the best of their kind more expensive:

RED BURGUNDY: 1952, '53, '55, '57, '59, '61.

WHITE BURGUNDY: 1952, '55, '59, 61.

RED BORDEAUX (CLARET): 1945, '48 (sometimes), '52, '53, '55, '57 (sometimes), '59, '61, '62.

WHITE BORDEAUX: 1959, '61, '62.

RHENISH (Hocks, Moselles, Alsatians, Stein Wines): 1957, '59, '61, '62.

There are, for several reasons, exceptions to the rule. Sometimes, in an otherwise bad year, wines from certain vineyards may be quite splendid; in a good year, wines from other vineyards can be quite ordinary.

How to Serve Wine

1. All white wines should be served chilled, but not iced. Don't put ice into them.
2. Red wines are best served at room temperature, but since room temperatures vary, let them stand for a couple of hours in a 'comfort zone' of around 60–65°F. Don't

however subject them to fierce, direct heat. Uncork red wines an hour or so before serving.

3. Decant as necessary. The object of this is to separate the wine from its lees and, with a red wine, to let it take the air. However, it is not always necessary to decant red wine. So long as the bottle has stood still for an hour or so before serving and you take the glasses to the bottle and pour carefully, thus giving it the minimum disturbance, it should be perfectly clear in the glass. With some of the cheaper red wines we have over the years followed the advice of Raymond Postgate, which is to decant the wine into a carafe that has been thoroughly heated with hot water. Decanted thus and left at room temperature for a couple of hours, the wine noticeably matures. If red wine has a very heavy sediment, then it is obviously better to decant it, but this condition is more often found in older and more expensive wines, in which case your merchant should advise you how to treat the wine before serving.

4. Glasses for wine should be clear, colourless and thin, preferably with a bowl that narrows towards the rim so as to hold the wine's perfume. Stemmed glasses are much more pleasant than tumblers for wine. And some of those 'public-house' stemmed glasses which are obtainable at the bigger Woolworth's are jolly good for everyday serving of any style of wine. The purist will have a short-stemmed glass for red wines (holding the glass by the bowl the further to warm the wine) and a long-stemmed one for delicate white wines that are served chilled (the glass being held by the stem only). Generally speaking, the 'bigger' the wine, the larger the glass – it is pleasant to stick one's nose into a glass of Burgundy that isn't much more than half-full.

5. Don't overfill wine glasses – there should be room enough left in the glass to be able to rotate it and so get the aroma of the wine without spilling.

How to Store Wine

Place the bottles horizontally, so that the wine keeps the cork moist. They can be stored in anything from a 12-bottle carton to specially made 'bins' or 'racks'. Keep them in a cool, dark place, but never in either the refrigerator or the airing cupboard.

Never 'bin' a bottle if the wine is beginning to ooze out through the cork. Watch your stored wines and use quickly any bottle that shows signs of 'weeping'.

The Wine for the Food

The classic and formal order is:

WITH OYSTERS: Chablis or Dry Champagne.

WITH SOUP: Pale Sherry or Dry Madeira.

WITH FISH: Dry White Wines or Champagne.

WITH ENTRÉES: Claret.

WITH ROASTS OR GAME: Red Burgundy.

WITH SWEETS: Sauternes.

WITH CHEESE: Port, Brown Sherry or Madeira.

However, the order and number of wines to be served is naturally a matter of personal taste and of the food chosen for the meal. When one wine only is served throughout, then it should be the one most appropriate to the main course. An everyday guide is given below.

LIGHT, DRY WHITE WINES which act as a stimulant to the palate are good as an apéritif or with hors d'oeuvre or shellfish. (Chablis, Champagne, sparkling Hock, Portuguese Vinho Verde.)

FULLER DRY OR MEDIUM DRY WHITE WINES suit veal, poultry and fish and drink well throughout the meal. (White Burgundy such as Montrachet or Pouilly Fuissé, a mellow Hock or Moselle.)

ROSÉ WINES, DRY OR MEDIUM DRY, are also pleasant throughout the meal. (Tavel, Couhins, Bouquet de Provence.)

LIGHT RED WINE is good with chops, veal, poultry. (Light Clarets, young Beaujolais, Portuguese or Spanish claret types.)

FULLER RED WINE does justice to meat roasts, game dishes and the stronger-flavoured entrées. (Burgundy, Rhône, Chianti, Rioja.)

SWEET WHITE WINES belong to sweets, desserts. (Sauternes, Barsac, Tokay.)

MOST DRY OR MEDIUM-DRY TABLE WINES, WHITE OR RED, are acceptable with a cheese course.

Warning

The purist says that most good, sensitive wines are lost on a salad that has vinegar in the dressing, but don't let that deter you. A salad tossed in a French dressing made with a wine or herb vinegar, with oil to smooth it and the addition of a little sugar, is quite friendly to a robust red wine or a full, Burgundy-style white one.

A BRIEF GUIDE TO THE WORLD'S WINES

FRANCE

A. Bordeaux

CLARET (RED BORDEAUX) – the great red wine of the Bordeaux region, the most prodigious vineyard in the world. The Châteaux or properties that make it up run into many hundreds and the character of the wine varies from district to district, but it should *always* be bright ruby-red in colour.

Four principal districts are:

THE MÉDOC, where the notable parishes or communes are Margaux, Saint Julien, Pauillac and Saint Estèphe. These are names worth asking about when you want a claret of delicacy and finesse for a special dinner party.

SAINT-ÉMILION, where the wines are full and fragrant.

POMEROL adjoins SAINT-ÉMILION; the wines are noted for their distinctive bouquet.

GRAVES south of the Médoc, best known in Britain for its white wines, though it produces some memorable red ones. The first claret known in this country, seven centuries ago, is likely to have come from CHÂTEAU HAUT-BRION – one of the big four among the lordly clarets.

WHITE BORDEAUX: There are two main styles of this wine – Graves and Sauternes.

GRAVES is a wine that comes in many tastes, from the quite dry to the very sweet. A good choice for beginners, if taken chilled with poultry or fish.

SAUTERNES: Naturally sweet wines of great quality. Among them, CHÂTEAU D'YQUEM is the great one, the finest dessert wine. BARSAC and MONBAZILLAC are good-natured sweet wines that cost much less.

From ENTRE-DEUX-MERS come medium-sweet white wines of that name (and also inexpensive red wines).

B. Burgundy

This region produces an abundance of red wines and the greatest white wines of all France.

RED BURGUNDIES: Most of the great wines are grown in the area known as the Côte de Nuits, from Dijon in the north down to Nuits-Saint-Georges. These wines are full-bodied, with a superb bouquet, and at their best when they are really well matured. The commune of Vosne-Romanée produces some of the superlative ones. Most of the villages and towns in this area have annexed the names of their most famous vineyards. Among them are the wines of GEVREY-CHAMBERTIN, CHAMBOLLE MUSIGNY, VOUGEOT, NUITS-SAINT-GEORGES and VOSNE-ROMANÉE.

From ALOXE-CORTON, just south of the Côte de Nuits,

comes the delicate and beautiful wine of that name. In the area between Beaune and Chagny – known as the Côte de Beaune – the red wines are elegant and round, though less full-bodied than those from the more northerly vineyards. Names synonymous with good Burgundy and worth remembering are POMMARD, VOLNAY and of course BEAUNE itself.

BEAUJOLAIS: This most popular of red wines comes from the hilly district between Mâcon and Lyons and is more often than not classified as a Burgundy, except by the purists. These wines are fruity and light, usually best drunk when they're young – after 1 or 2 years in the bottle. Remember the names of JULIENAS, FLEURIE, CHENAS, MOULIN-À-VENT, for instance, when you want a 'better' Beaujolais, for these are village names and the wine has indeed come from there. It may cost five or ten pence more, but it is well worth it.

WHITE BURGUNDIES: The best ones come from the Côte d'Or, but only a small amount is produced there. CHABLIS is the best-known white Burgundy, and when indeed it comes from the place by which it is named, north-west of Dijon, it can be superb – bone-dry, very clear and light and perfect to drink with shellfish.

The other white Burgundies, which notably come from south-west of Beaune, are full, fruity, pale golden and dry. The vineyard of Montrachet produces the finest of all white Burgundies. PULIGNY-MONTRACHET and CHASSAGNE-MONTRACHET are well-favoured wines that come from the area. POUILLY-FUISSÉ, MEURSAULT and white MÂCON can be wonderful wines – or just pleasant table wines that come in the more reasonable price ranges.

C. Loire

A wide variety of red, white and rosé wines are grown down the length of this great river.

MUSCADET is very dry and fresh, a white wine that is pleasant with shellfish.

POUILLY BLANC FUMÉ is a white wine of elegance and subtle bouquet, not as dry as Muscadet.

SANCERRE wines are light and fruity (both red and white); the white ones, well chilled, are delightful for summer drinking.

ANJOU is a rather sweet rosé wine: VOUVRAY a sparkling wine that is medium-dry and drinks pleasantly.

D. Rhône

From this part of France – below Lyons and extending down almost to Avignon – come the very robust and full-bodied red wines of HERMITAGE and CHÂTEAUNEUF-DU-PAPE. Also the young, medium-dry rosé wines of TAVEL and LIRAC.

E. Champagne

This is the region of France where the grapes are grown for true Champagne.

Unlike most of the other great wines of France, Champagne is not known by the names of the vineyards, but by the names of the numerous houses which make the wine. Vintage Champagne is of a year selected as of outstanding quality, non-vintage a blend from different years.

Note: Other sparkling French white wines, made by the Champagne method (*la méthode champénoise*) come from Burgundy, the Rhône and the Loire, and are certainly worth trying. They usually cost much less than Champagne but are excellent celebration drinks.

F. Alsace

The delicate white wines from this beautiful part of France are sold under the name of the grapes from which they are made: these are:

SYLVANER: Agreeable, light, dryish.
RIESLING: Distinguished, delicate and sometimes full-bodied.

TRAMINER and GEWÜRTZTRAMINER: Much more full-bodied and fruity, the latter being especially spicy.

MUSCAT D'ALSACE: A dry, spicy table wine, not to be confused with the rather cloying dessert wine usually associated with the Muscat grape.

All of these wines drink very well with fish and light poultry dishes.

GERMANY

A. Hock

This is the name generally used in English-speaking countries for the white wines of the Rhineland: it is a corruption of the name of the village of Hochheim. The wine is made notably from the *Riesling* grape, from the *Sylvaner* grape or from a blending of the two, which is usually what is meant by the word *Scheurebe* on the label.

Names on labels are very important when you're buying hocks – if you don't study them you can be very disappointed or surprised, for the wines can range from a light and dryish type to the full sweetness of a dessert wine. LIEBFRAUMILCH, for instance, is one of the most popular hocks in this country. It derives its name from the Church of Our Lady, at Worms, but none of the wine comes from there nowadays. It is in fact an invented name for any blend of German table wine, and that is why it is important to enquire of your reputable wine merchant about the best kind of Liebfraumilch. As with Beaujolais, the extra 5 pence or so can make all the difference to your enjoyment.

The important wine districts of the Rhineland are:

THE PALATINATE: The sunny, southernmost part, where the wines mature early and are round, mellow and sweet; good with spicy foods. Famous centre is *Bad Dürkheim*.

RHEINGAU: Where the aristocratic hocks come from— slower in maturing, achieving delicate elegance and bouquet. The finest – and most expensive – are bottled on the estates where they are grown, e.g., SCHLOSS VOLLRADS, SCHLOSS HOCHHEIM, SCHLOSS JOHANNISBERG.

RHEINHESSE: The hocks from this area – which falls geographically between the Palatinate and Rheingau – are never quite as sweet as the former, but have some of the maturing quality of the latter. NIERSTEINER wines from this area are specially worth looking for; so are those with a METTENHEIMER label.

NAHE: The wines from this area, which are comparatively little known in Britain, are often said to be reminiscent of both the Rhine and the Moselle. KREUZNACHER and SCHLOSS BOCKELHEIM are distinguished examples.

B. Moselle

The white wines of the Moselle, which is a tributary of the Rhine, are less grand than the hocks, but their fragrance is ineffable. They have a green delicacy and are best drunk when they're young. At table, they are at their best with simple fish dishes or with plain grilled veal or lamb. Some of the Moselle wines make leisurely apéritifs for a sunny evening. Among the finest – and names to look out for – are those from *Wehlen* and *Berncastel*.

Glossary. Both Hocks and Moselles are the better en-joyed for knowing even more about the terms of reference that appear on the bottle.

Important words are:

SPÄTLESE: Wine made from late-gathered grapes.

AUSLESE: From the specially selected late-gathered, ripest grapes.

BEERENAUSLESE: Wine made from grapes which have been left on the vine until they have shrivelled to wrinkled berries, full of sugar.

TROCKENBEERENAUSLESE: From the choicest grapes left on the vine longest of all, until they're like raisins.

Following the order in which they are listed above, each of the wines bearing such labels will be richer, mellower, sweeter than the last; the last two indeed are natural liqueurs and are usually very highly-priced. Hocks with these appellations can be very perfumed and even heavy; Moselles keep more sweetness of taste and smell.

C. Franconian

These white wines – which come in flat, oval green flasks, unlike the classic hock and Moselle bottles – are produced on the banks of the Main. They are very robust, less fragrant than the Rhine wines. The most famous is STEINWEIN, from Würzburg.

ITALY

A. Red Wines

CHIANTI the most famous Italian wine, is made near Florence, in the heart of Tuscany. Wine from a now-extended area is entitled to be called *Chianti Classico,* and being bottled there, carries a black cock on its label. This wine is of a vivid crimson colour, sunny aroma and robust flavour. There are also pleasant white Chiantis.

VALPOLICELLA is called the claret of the Veronese; at its best it is ruby-red, dry and fresh. It is pleasant when young, but is also worth keeping to mature.

BAROLO is a full-bodied but not heavy wine from villages near Alba; it is rather reminiscent of red Burgundy.

BARBERA is a pleasant wine of Piedmont, of a rich garnet colour and with an almost smoky bouquet.

B. White Wines

SOAVE DI VERONA is one of Italy's best dry white wines – drunk in Venice with scampi.

FRASCATI wines are full bodied, honey-coloured, medium-sweet.

ORVIETO is golden in colour, has a rather aromatic bouquet, is fairly sweet.

LACRYMA CHRISTI, made on the slopes of Vesuvius, is rather sweet, golden in colour, nice after dinner in sunny Italy.

SPAIN

Spain means *Jerez,* that is Sherry – see later, under Fortified Wines.

However, good-value table wines, both red and white, also come from the adjoining districts of *Rioja Bajo* and *Rioja Alto* in the old kingdom of Aragon. Labelled as Spanish Burgundy, Claret, Sauternes or Chablis, they are sound, drinkable wines, costing very little.

PORTUGAL

From the homeland of Port wine (*see Fortified Wines, later in this chapter*) come honest wines in the lower price ranges.

VILA REAL table wines (from the Douro), red and white, are both very dry.

DAO wines, red and white, have more fullness and smoothness. They are gaining deserved popularity here, for they're pleasantly refreshing and very good value for their price.

SANTOS white wine is made in the Lisbon district, where the sweeter wines come from.

VINHO VERDE is a slightly effervescent 'green' wine which comes from the extreme north-west; pleasant taken well-chilled as a before-dinner apéritif or drunk with fish.

MATEUS ROSÉ and SANTOS ROSÉ, which also need to be well chilled, are medium-dry pink wines with a little natural sparkle.

YUGOSLAVIA

LUTOMER hock-style wines, from the district of that name in the north-east corner of the country, near the Hungarian border, are excellent value. They carry the Riesling label – this type of grape has been growing in that part of the world for about a thousand years.

ŽILAVKA is a white Burgundy-style wine, from inland of Dubrovnik.

CABERNET BRDA, a soft red wine, comes from the Trieste region.

HUNGARY

Tokays, which are all estate-bottled, include the following kinds:

TOKAY ASZU, the most renowned wine, delicate, sweet and golden – a dessert wine.

TOKAY SZAMARODNI, which can be very dry or medium-sweet; this also is pale golden.

Cheaper wines from Hungary are BALATONI RIESLING and BIKAVER, the latter a very dry red wine, otherwise known as Bull's Blood.

OTHER EUROPEAN WINES

From the Wachau district of AUSTRIA come:

SCHLUCK, a fresh, dry white wine, and TRIFALTER, rather more fragrant and sweet; both are good value, lower-priced table wines.

SWITZERLAND produces reasonable white wines, made from the Riesling grape, in the VALAIS region; the best-known of the red wines, DÔLE, also comes from there.

GREECE: Largely for holiday reasons, more people have acquired a taste for the national resin-wine, RETSINA. This, and one or two red table wines, are available in Britain at reasonable prices.

THE COMMONWEALTH

AUSTRALIAN table wines are grown around Adelaide in South Australia and the Hunter River in New South Wales. Among those exported to Britain are dependable 'Burgundies', 'Sauternes' and 'Hocks'. A splendid list of

Australian wines is available from the Australian Wine Centre in London; it is always up-to-date and the people there really know about the wines of their country.

OTHER WINES

SOUTH AFRICA supplies us with about a hundred bottles of sherry to every one of table wine. The popularity of the 'Hock' type wines is increasing, however, for those who like a drier wine than those from Europe.

SOUTH AMERICA produces much red and white wine – in the Argentine in particular – but as yet not much is exported. However, Chile is sending more and more of her wines and reasonably priced ones, too, to Britain: notably a Cabernet red and a German-style white, fairly full, called Steinwein.

CALIFORNIAN wines, of the cheaper red and white table kind, compare quite favourably with those of the same price from other countries.

BRITAIN doesn't produce wine from the grape on a really commercial scale. But there is, outside this definition, an increasing market for wines made from other fruits. Particularly worth trying as a table wine is the gooseberry wine – white and medium-dry – in the Merrydown range.

SPARKLING WINES

True Champagne is of its own quality and price, but there are other kinds of sparkling wines which as a whole are much in demand for festive occasions – and often as pick-me-ups.

GERMAN sparkling wine is usually made by the blending of good Hocks and Moselles and is called 'Sekt', often with a trade name attached.

ITALY'S sparkling wines are the famous sweet, white ASTI SPUMANTE and a red wine of VALPOLICELLA.

FRANCE produces, in addition to the white sparkling wines already mentioned in the French section, some pink and red SPARKLING BURGUNDY and MUSCATEL.

BRITAIN'S sparkling wine is Moussec, which is fermented and matured in England from French grape juice.

FORTIFIED WINES

Wine is 'fortified' by the addition of spirit, usually brandy, which gives it a greater alcoholic strength.

PORT is made from grapes grown in the upper valley of the Douro river in Portugal and is shipped from Oporto. The brandy is added when the grapes are being pressed. There are many types of port – red, white and tawny in colour, and differing in style, strength, age and sweetness. Vintage port, which is red, is the great dessert wine; it is shipped from Oporto about two years after the vintage, bottled in England and may then be left to mature for ten or even twenty years.

Wood ports are blends of wines of different years and ages which are matured in cask; they may be ruby, tawny, crusted or vintage character. Ruby is generally a blend of young wines, tawny a blend of older ones. White port, which can be sweet or dry, is now increasingly popular and dry white port makes a pleasant apéritif if chilled.

SHERRY the glory of Spain, is made from white grapes grown in the Jerez district. It is usually, but not always, fortified with brandy. Sherry is a blend of wines, matured by what is called the SOLERA system, to ensure a continuing supply of wines of the same style and quality. There are four main types of sherry: lightest in colour and dryest to the taste are the FINOS; next come the MANZANILLAS, pale and slightly sharp, a favoured apéritif; the AMONTILLADOS are more full-bodied, rather nutty and of a medium dryness; then come the OLOROSOS, rich, dark-golden sherries, used principally as sweet dessert wines.

We get, too, some good sherries from South Africa, made by the *solera* system, and only an expert could tell the difference between some of these and the less expensive Spanish ones.

MADEIRA made and matured on the Island of Madeira, is fortified by the addition of cane spirit. The wines are then blended and left for some years to mature. There are four basic types of Madeira, named after the grapes from which they are made. They are: SERCIAL, dry and pale; VERDELHO, medium dry, darker in colour; BUAL, which is medium-sweet; and MALMSEY, a rich, dark-brown dessert wine that is slightly nutty.

MARSALA the famous wine of Sicily, is made from a blend of local wines, brandy and unfermented grape juice. Marsalas can be dry or sweet, This wine's particular distinction is in its use for two classic Italian dishes – *scallopine alla marsala* and the luscious sweet, *zabaglione*.

APÉRITIFS

The patent or branded appetisers are either wine-based or spirit-based. Wine-based ones include Vermouths, which come from both France and Italy.

Vermouths

FRENCH VERMOUTHS: NOILLY PRAT: Bone-dry, very pale in colour. Mix it with gin and it becomes a dry Martini.

CHAMBÉRY: A subtle regional vermouth from Haute Savoie. Nice to drink 'straight', slightly chilled.

CHAMBÉRYZETTE: A variant that is pink and perfumed with wild strawberries.

ITALIAN VERMOUTHS: These are sweet and there are two kinds, *rosso* and *bianco*. The red is used for the classic Manhattan cocktail, when it is mixed with American whiskey. The white (called *bianco* to distinguish it from the French dry vermouth) is nicest taken straight or

diluted just with soda water. Names of Italian vermouths are CINZANO, MARTINI and GANCIA.

OTHER WINE-BASED APÉRITIFS: These are descended, like the vermouths, from concoctions of medicinal herbs, spices and wine, but they also have quinine as an ingredient.

From France we get the following, all of them best served iced, with a twist of lemon peel:

DUBONNET: White or red.

ST. RAPHAEL: White or red.

LILLET: White.

BYRRH: Red.

From ITALY comes PUNT È MES, red and bitter-sweet.

SPIRIT-BASED APÉRITIFS include the following:

CAMPARI: An Italian bitters, rosy-pink when served with ice and soda – and a twist of lemon.

AMER PICON: The French equivalent of Campari, very bitter and black to look at, too. English people like it with a measure of Grenadine, ice and a dash of soda.

SUZE: Very bitter, bright yellow, no stronger than the wine-based apéritifs, it is made basically from the root of the gentian and is rather a good restorative, drunk straight with a little ice.

FERNET BRANCA; UNDERBERG: Two ferocious-looking and tasting medicinal bitters, recommended for hangovers.

ANIS drinks – PERNOD, PASTIS, RICARD and OUSO – should be taken well diluted with water, for they are very potent, though they taste sweetly harmless.

LIQUEURS

These are ideally after-dinner drinks and are most usually made of grape spirit, with the addition of sugar syrup and a variety of flavourings – herbs, spices or fruit. The list that follows shows the liqueurs that are more familiar in this country, but most regions have their own local ones, which are not necessarily exported.

ADVOCAAT: A Dutch liqueur, yellow in colour, with a predominant flavour of eggs and brandy.

ANISETTE: Colourless, with aniseed flavour; comes from France.

BÉNÉDICTINE: One of the most popular French liqueurs, with a subtle herby flavour and aroma.

BRANDY: A spirit distilled from wine, of which COGNAC is the king. ARMAGNAC, from South of Bordeaux, is a brandy with a rather herby flavour and aroma, well worth tasting as a change from Cognac.
   Other brandies, which are essentially liqueurs, are flavoured with *apricot, cherry* and *peach,* and they come from many countries.

CASSIS: A black-currant-flavoured liqueur from Provence.

CHARTREUSE: One of the most famous herb-flavoured French liqueurs; the yellow type is sweeter, the green stronger.

COINTREAU: Colourless, orange-flavoured; comes from France.

CRÈME DE CACAO: A very sweet chocolate-coloured and cocoa-flavoured liqueur from the West Indies.

CRÈME DE MENTHE: Green in colour, with a pronounced peppermint flavour.

CURAÇAO: Golden-coloured, orange-flavoured.

DRAMBUIE: From Scotland, with the flavour of whisky and heather honey; golden in colour.

GOLDWASSER: Aniseed-flavoured liqueur from Germany; colourless, with gold particles in it.

GRAND MARNIER: Golden, orange-flavoured French liqueur.

KIRSCH: An Alsatian spirit distilled from cherries; colourless, with a strong bitter-almond flavour.

KÜMMEL: A colourless liqueur with a caraway flavour that originated in Holland.

MANDARINE: French, red in colour, with the flavour of tangerines.

MARASCHINO: From Dalmatia; colourless, with a distinctive bitter-cherry flavour.

PRUNELLE: A French liqueur, pale green, with a plum flavour.

SLIVOVITZ: A dry, plum-flavoured, colourless liqueur that originated in Yugoslavia.

SLOE GIN: Ruby in colour and one of the most popular of all English-made liqueurs and cordials.

STREGA: Aromatic, pale yellow liqueur from Italy.

TIA MARIA: Coffee-flavoured and dark brown; from Jamaica and increasingly popular in England.

TRIPLE SEC: The name given to a white Curaçao.

VAN DER HUM: South Africa's best liqueur, russet-brown and tasting of the *naartje,* the South African tangerine.

LA VIEILLE CURÉ: A French liqueur, with a distinct flavour of aromatic herbs; golden in colour, very potent.

Cocktails, Cups and Soft Drinks

Manhattan Cocktail

Broken ice
1–2 dashes of Angostura Bitters
2–3 dashes of Curaçao
3 tbsps. rye whiskey
3 tbsps. Italian vermouth
Cherry and lemon peel

Fill a cocktail glass half-full of ice. Mix the liquid ingredients, stir up well, strain into the glass, add a cherry and squeeze a piece of lemon peel on top.

This is comparatively speaking a very old cocktail, named after the district in New York, but it is still one of the best-known.

If a dry Manhattan is required, use French vermouth instead of Italian. For a medium cocktail use half each of French and Italian.

Dry Martini Cocktail

2 parts French vermouth
1 part dry gin
Cracked ice
Stuffed olives or lemon rind curls

Shake the vermouth and gin together with some cracked ice in a shaker. Pour into glasses and float a stuffed olive or a curl of lemon rind on top of each.

The proportions of a Martini are a matter of personal taste: some people prefer 2 parts of gin to 1 of vermouth, others equal parts of gin and vermouth.

Sweet Martini

2 parts Italian vermouth
1 part dry gin
A few drops of orange bitters per cocktail (optional)
Cracked ice
Maraschino cherries

Shake all the ingredients thoroughly together in a shaker and strain into glasses. Serve with a cherry in each glass.

Whisky Sour

Juice of ½ a lemon
1 level tsp. sugar
1 measure of whisky
Cracked ice

Mix together the lemon juice, sugar and whisky and shake well with the cracked ice.

Bloody Mary

1 part vodka
2 parts tomato juice
A dash of Worcestershire sauce
A squeeze of lemon juice
Cracked ice

Shake all the ingredients with the cracked ice.

Cups and Punches

When making these drinks, especially the cold cups, it is often convenient to add the sugar in the form of a syrup (*see next recipe*), which dissolves more readily.

In addition to the wine cups given here, a popular and useful standby is the proprietary long drink sold as Pimms' No. 1. It is diluted with lemonade (instructions are on the bottle), and served with ice and a garnish of a sprig of borage or mint.

Stock (sugar) Syrup for Drinks

1 lb. sugar
½ pint water

Put the sugar in a saucepan with the water and dissolve slowly. Bring to the boil and boil to 220°F. Cool and bottle. Use as required.

Claret Cup

¼ pint stock syrup
Juice and thinly peeled rind of 1 lemon and 2 oranges
2 bottles of claret
4 'splits' of tonic water
A few thin slices of cucumber
Sprigs of borage, if available

Put the stock syrup and the lemon and orange rind in a saucepan and simmer together for about 10 minutes. Cool and add the strained juice of the lemon and oranges, together with the claret; chill. Just before serving, add the tonic water, cucumber and borage (if used).
   Makes approx. 4 pints.

White Wine Cup

Crushed ice
3 bottles of white wine
¾ bottle of dry sherry
4 tbsps. Curaçao (or any other orange liqueur)
4 'splits' of tonic water
3 slices of cucumber, a slice of apple and a sprig of borage per jug

This is an excellent summer drink.
   Mix all the ingredients together in one or more jugs and chill before serving. Makes approx. 6½ pints.

Vin Blanc Cassis *(Kir)*

4 parts dry white wine (Chablis or similar)
1 part Crème de Cassis

Thoroughly chill the wine before combining it with the Cassis; serve in a claret glass.
   This French refresher makes a good mid-morning drink or apéritif.

Glühwein

1 pint red wine
3 oz. brown sugar
2 sticks of cinnamon about 2 inches long
1 lemon stuck with cloves
1 wineglass of brandy

Put all the ingredients except the brandy in a pan, bring to simmering point and simmer gently with the lid on for 2–4 minutes. Remove from the heat, add the brandy, strain and serve at once.
   Makes approx. 1¼ pints.

The Bishop

2 lemons
12 cloves
1 quart port
1 pint water
1 level tsp. mixed spice
2 oz. lump sugar

Stick 1 lemon with the cloves and roast it in a moderate oven (350°F., mark 4) for 30 minutes. Put the port into a saucepan and bring to simmering point. In another saucepan boil the water with the spice; add to the hot wine, with the roasted lemon. Rub the sugar on the rind of the remaining lemon. Put the sugar into a bowl, adding the juice of ½ the lemon, and pour on the hot wine. Serve as hot as possible.
   Makes approx. 3½ pints.

Dr. Johnson's Choice

1 bottle of red wine
12 lumps of sugar
6 cloves
1 pint of boiling water
1 wineglass of orange Curaçao
1 wineglass of brandy (optional)
Nutmeg

This is the classic mull of the Eighteenth century.
   Pour the wine into a saucepan, add the sugar and cloves and bring to near boiling point; add 1 pint boiling water. Pour in the Curaçao and the brandy (if used). Pour into glasses and grate nutmeg on top.
   Makes approx. 3 pints.

Mulled Ale

1 lemon
1 pint ale
4 tbsps. brandy
2 tbsps. rum
2 tbsps. gin
1 oz. Demerara sugar
½ pint water
⅛ level tsp. ground nutmeg
⅛ level tsp. ground cinnamon

Peel the lemon thinly and squeeze out the juice. Place the peel and all the other ingredients in a large pan and heat, but do not boil. Strain and serve at once in punch glasses.
   Makes approx. 2 pints.

Note: Brown ale gives a pleasant, fairly bland drink, but for a change of flavour try using a pale ale.

Mulled Wine

½ pint water
4 oz. sugar
4 cloves
A 2-inch stick of cinnamon
2 lemons, thinly sliced
1 bottle of Burgundy or claret
1 orange or lemon, thinly sliced, to decorate

Boil the water, sugar and spices together. Add the lemons, stir and leave to stand for 10 minutes. Pour back into the saucepan and add the red wine. Heat but don't boil. Strain the wine into a bowl and serve hot, decorated with the orange or lemon slices.
   Makes approx. 1½ pints.

SOFT DRINKS

Lemon Barley Water

2 oz. pearl barley
1 pint water
Juice of 2 lemons
2 oz. sugar

Put the barley into a saucepan, just cover with cold water and bring to the boil; strain off the water and rinse the barley under cold running water. Return it to the saucepan, add 1 pint water, bring to the boil again, cover and simmer for 1 hour. Strain the liquid into a jug or basin, add the sugar and cool. When the mixture is cold, add the strained lemon juice. Use as required; it will keep indefinitely in the refrigerator.

Note: A quicker way of making barley water is to use 'patent' barley (*see Diets chapter*).

Grapefruit Barley Water
Make this as for Lemon Barley Water, above, but substitute the strained juice of 1 large grapefruit for the lemon juice. Sweeten to taste.

Spicy Fruit Punch

1 pint orange juice
½ pint canned pineapple juice
Juice and rind of 1 lemon
½ level tsp. ground nutmeg
½ level tsp. ground mixed spice
6 cloves
1 pint water
6 oz. sugar
2 pints ginger ale (chilled in the bottle)

Mix the fruit juices, lemon rind and spices in a large jug. Put the water and sugar into a saucepan and heat gently to dissolve the sugar; cool slightly and add to the other ingredients in the jug. Chill. Strain the liquid and add the ginger ale and some crushed ice before serving. Makes approx. 5 pints.

Home-made Ginger Beer

To Start the Ginger Beer 'Plant'
2 oz. fresh baker's yeast
2 level tbsps. caster sugar
2 level tbsps. ground ginger
½ pint water

Blend the yeast and sugar until they cream and form a liquid. Add the ground ginger and the water, stir well and place the mixture in a covered jar with a loose-fitting lid.

Each Day
Add 1 level tsp. ground ginger and 1 level tsp. caster sugar to the 'plant' and stir well.

After 10 Days
Dissolve 18 oz. caster sugar in 1½ pints water, bring to the boil and cool slightly. Add the strained juice of 2 lemons.

Strain the prepared ginger beer plant through fine muslin and add the strained liquid to the sugar and lemon juice, together with 6 pints water. Stir well and bottle at once in strong, screw-topped bottles (as used for cider or beer). Store in a cool place (this is essential) and use as required.

To Make More Ginger Beer
Halve the 'plant' (the sediment left on the muslin) and place in 2 separate jars. Add ½ pint water, 2 level tsps. ground ginger and 2 level tsps. caster sugar to each jar; stir and continue to feed daily as above for 10 days; proceed as before.

Index